SUNDAY OBSERVANCE AND THE SUNDAY LETTER

IN ANGLO-SAXON ENGLAND

Few issues have had such far-reaching consequences as the development of the Christian holy day, Sunday. Every seven days, from the early Middle Ages on, the Christian world has engaged in some kind of change in behaviour, ranging from participation in a simple worship service to the cessation of every activity which could conceivably be construed as work. An important text associated with this process is the so-called *Sunday Letter*, fabricated as a letter from Christ which dropped out of heaven. In spite of its obviously spurious nature, it was widely read and copied, and translated into nearly every vernacular language. In particular, several, apparently independent, translations were made into Old English.

Here, the six surviving Old English copies of the *Sunday Letter* are edited together for the first time. The Old English texts are accompanied by facing translations, with commentary and glossary, while the introduction examines the development of Sunday observance in the early Middle Ages and sets the texts in their historical, legal and theological contexts. The many Latin versions of the *Sunday Letter* are also delineated, including a newly discovered and edited source for two of the Old English texts.

Dorothy Haines gained her Ph.D. from the University of Toronto, where she currently teaches Old English.

Anglo-Saxon Texts

ISSN 1463–6948

Anglo-Saxon Texts is a series of scholarly editions (with parallel translations) of important texts from Anglo-Saxon England, whether written in Latin or in Old English. The series aims to offer critical texts with suitable apparatus and accurate modern English translations, together with informative general introductions and full historical and literary commentaries.

1. *Wulfstan's Canon Law Collection*
edited by J. E. Cross (†) and Andrew Hamer

2. *The Old English Poem* Judgement Day II: *a Critical Edition with Editions of* De die iudicii *and the Hatton 113 Homily* Be domes dæge
edited by Graham D. Caie

3. Historia de Sancto Cuthberto: *A History of Saint Cuthbert and a Record of his Patrimony*
edited by Ted Johnson South

4. Excerptiones de Prisciano: *The Source for Ælfric's Latin-Old English* Grammar
edited by David W. Porter

5. *Ælfric's* Life of Saint Basil the Great: *Background and Context*
edited by Gabriella Corona

6. *Ælfric's* De Temporibus Anni
edited by Martin Blake

7. *The Old English Dialogues of Solomon and Saturn*
edited by Daniel Anlezark

SUNDAY OBSERVANCE
AND THE SUNDAY LETTER
IN ANGLO-SAXON ENGLAND

Edited with a translation by

DOROTHY HAINES

D. S. BREWER

First published 2010
D. S. Brewer, Cambridge

ISBN 978 1 84384 222 4

D. S. Brewer is an imprint of Boydell & Brewer Ltd
PO Box 9, Woodbridge, Suffolk IP12 3DF, UK
and of Boydell & Brewer Inc,
668 Mt Hope Avenue, Rochester, NY 14620, USA
website: www.boydellandbrewer.com

A CIP catalogue record for this book is available
from the British Library

This publication is printed on acid-free paper

The publisher has no responsibility for the continued existence or accuracy
of URLs for external or third-party internet websites referred to in this book,
and does not guarantee that any content on such websites is, or will remain,
accurate or appropriate.

Typeset by Word and Page, Chester

Printed in the United States of America

Contents

Preface

Few issues are likely to have had as far-reaching consequences as the development of the Christian holy day, Sunday. Every seven days since the early Middle Ages the Christian world has engaged in some kind of change in behaviour, ranging from participation in a simple worship service to the cessation of every activity which could conceivably be construed as work. The restrictions which arose in the medieval world are by no means trivial: they called for bringing to a complete halt all physical labour, all commerce, all legislative activity, and, in some cases, even such private activities as bathing and sexual intercourse. How did these beliefs arise? They certainly find little support in the pages of the New Testament, nor do the early Church fathers seem to promote the creation of a kind of taboo day to replace the Jewish sabbath.

A close examination of the surviving testimony reveals that Sunday observance involving rest did not and, in truth, could not have been an important dogma until the Church was able to gain some influence in the secular affairs of the state, placing its inception in the time of Constantine. From that time on, the Church sought to free Sunday from the pursuits of everyday life so that Christians might devote the day to the practice of religion: attendance at church services, private devotion and prayer and the performance of good deeds. This could not have been an easy matter. The economic rewards for Sunday work and the temptation to make the day when everyone was already gathered for church the favourite market day were strong incentives to ignore the Church's edicts. And as if such pressures were not enough to make enforcing Sunday rest difficult, the Church was also faced with the uncomfortable fact that, as noted above, there were no early and universally accepted authorities which had spoken unambiguously in favour of a work-free Sunday.

At a time when some were encouraging an increase in Sunday restrictions, but when no firm Church tradition had yet been established, one enterprising churchman decided to take matters into his own hands and wrote a document that would clearly solve this predicament. This is the so-called Sunday Letter, a message which claims to have been written by Christ himself and sent to Rome (or Jerusalem). It urges a strict observance of Sunday and imitates the Old Testament in promising blessings for those who comply and a variety of afflictions for those who dare to disobey. Almost immediately it was condemned as spurious, but it appears to have proven quite valuable to certain priests desperate for some strong words with which to exhort their congregations. Not only did it survive, but it was translated into every medieval vernacular, spreading to the East and as far north as Scandinavia. So we also hear of its presence in ninth-century England, and there are no fewer than six extant copies of the Sunday Letter in Old English, all dating from the eleventh century.

Once one has read the Sunday Letter, one cannot help but wonder about its audience and reception. It stands out, even among the rhetorical excesses of Old English sermons, as an extreme diatribe which could not possibly have been taken seriously. Or could it? The multiple versions and the respectable manuscripts in which they are found argue that it was not some fringe group which fostered the Sunday Letter, but rather mainstream churchmen who found it worthy of being copied, collected and, perhaps, read to their congregations.

In order to resolve this apparent contradiction, the following chapters will attempt to reconstruct, as thoroughly as possible, the cultural environment which made acceptance of the Sunday Letter conceivable in eleventh-century England. I have drawn on several types of evidence. First, I have examined the development of Sunday observance on the Continent and in Ireland, including its mention in secular and ecclesiastical legislation, narrative sources, and homiletic texts. This provides the foundation for a similar study of the same kinds of materials during the Anglo-Saxon period. As in so many matters, the Anglo-Saxons were greatly influenced by their continental counterparts while also resisting a wholesale embrace of their norms.

The picture that emerges clarifies the place of the Sunday Letter in the practice of Sunday observance during the early Middle Ages. It does not stand alone in prohibiting a large number of activities; such restrictions were increasingly a part of the legislative standard. If it caused offence after the eighth century, this was probably due more to the preposterous claim of divine authorship and the extravagant language it uses to support that claim rather than to the kind of Sunday observance that it encourages. The historical background reconstructed for this edition of the Old English Sunday Letters situates this sermon in a cultural environment that found some measure of usefulness and perhaps even appreciation for it, despite its shortcomings. It is my hope that the Sunday Letter will no longer elicit simply curiosity or dismissal as a misguided theological tract, but that it will be read with a new appreciation for its contribution to our understanding of Anglo-Saxon culture.

Acknowledgements

Whenever I have had the opportunity to share the subject of this research with other scholars, I have, without exception, been pleasantly surprised by the interest shown and encouragement offered. Many have also been generous with their time and knowledge. To David McDougall must go the dubious honour of drawing my attention to the Old English Sunday Letter. I am enormously grateful for his continuing help throughout the project's development. I am also grateful to Michael Lapidge, Roberta Frank, Toni Healey and especially George Rigg and Ian McDougall for their inspiration and aid.

Several sources of funding were crucial in the completion of this edition. The National Endowment for the Humanities supported me with a summer research stipend; the American Association of University Women Educational Foundation provided a pre-publication grant, and the International Society for Anglo-Saxonists helped with a travel grant to visit European libraries. Apart from the monetary value of these funds, I was honoured by the support of these institutions and greatly encouraged by their endorsement of my project.

Several libraries gave permission for my study of the manuscripts housed there. I would especially like to thank librarians and assistants at the Parker Library at Corpus Christi College, Cambridge (in particular, Gill Cannell), the Lambeth Palace Library, the British Library in London and the University Library in Basel for access to the manuscripts used in this edition. In addition the Murhardsche Bibliothek and Landesbibliothek of Kassel and the Dominikanerkloster in Vienna kindly supplied me with images for the texts edited in Appendix III. Thanks are also due to two interlibrary-loan librarians at Shorter College, Karen Simpkins and Julie Harwell, who went to incredible lengths to procure the obscure materials needed for this study and did so with unfailing patience and perseverence.

A good portion of this book was written during evenings and weekends (yes, on Sundays) while working as a drafting editor (without research leave) at the Dictionary of Old English. The person most to be thanked for maintaining my sanity and good spirits is my husband John, who provided endless support in every way imaginable, and it is to him that I would like to dedicate this book.

Abbreviations

(For full bibliographical references, see the Bibliography)

A–F	The Old English Sunday Letters A–F, as edited in the present volume, followed by line numbers
Assmann	Assmann, *Angelsächsische Homilien und Heiligenleben*
Belfour	Belfour, *Twelfth-Century Homilies in MS Bodley 343*
Bethurum	Bethurum, *The Homilies of Wulfstan*
BL	British Library, London
Blickling	Morris, *The Blickling Homilies*
BN	Bibliothèque nationale de France, Paris
Bodl.	Bodleian Library, Oxford
BTS	Bosworth and Toller, *An Anglo-Saxon Dictionary*, with supplement
CCCC	Cambridge, Corpus Christi College
CCSL	Corpus Christianorum, Series Latina
CH I	P. A. M. Clemoes, ed., *Ælfric's Catholic Homilies: The First Series: Text*
CH II	M. R. Godden, ed., *Ælfric's Catholic Homilies: The Second Series: Text*
Cmpb.	Campbell, *Old English Grammar*
CSEL	Corpus Scriptorum Ecclesiasticorum Latinorum
DANW	F. Robinson, 'The Devil's Account of the Next World'
DOE	A. diPaolo Healey *et al.*, *Dictionary of Old English*
EETS	Early English Text Society (ES: Extra Series; OS: Original Series; SS: Supplementary Series)
EWS	Early West Saxon
Gmc	Germanic
Hogg	R. M. Hogg, *A Grammar of Old English*
Kalbhen	U. Kalbhen, *Glossen und kentischer Dialekt im Altenglischen*
Ker	N. R. Ker, *Catalogue of Manuscripts Containing Anglo-Saxon*
LS	W. W. Skeat, ed., *Ælfric's Lives of Saints*
LWS	Late West Saxon
Mansi	P. Mansi, ed., *Sacrorum conciliorum nova, et amplissima collectio*
MGH	Monumenta Germaniae Historica

Napier	A. S. Napier, ed., *Wulfstan: Sammlung der ihm zugeschriebenen Homilien*
nWS	non-West Saxon
OE	Old English
PGmc	Primitive Germanic
PL	Patrologia Latina
Pope	J. C. Pope, ed., *Homilies of Ælfric: A Supplementary Collection*
S–B	E. Sievers and K. Brunner, *Altenglische Grammatik*
Schaefer	'An Edition of Five Old English Homilies'
Vercelli	D. G. Scragg, ed., *Vercelli Homilies and Related Texts*
WGmc	West Germanic
WS	West Saxon

Introduction

1

The Development of Sunday Observance in the Early Middle Ages

In order to understand the Sunday Letter and its roots in the culture of the early Middle Ages, it will be helpful to examine the history of Sunday observance, insofar as this is possible from the limited witnesses of legislative, homiletic and narrative records.[1] At first glance the language and the beliefs found in the Sunday Letter seem to be excessive; however, a careful study of the historical context will show that they would not necessarily have appeared so to a medieval audience. As the sanctity of the Lord's day grew in significance, so did the need to employ unconventional theology and forceful rhetoric in order to undergird the practice of complete Sunday rest from labour and attendance at the required church services. In the following, the issue of rest, rather than Sunday worship, will be the focus of the discussion, since that is the subject of the Sunday Letter.[2]

The question would never have caused much concern had it not been a part of the one element of Old Testament law that was adopted wholesale into Christianity: the Ten Commandments. The two biblical listings of the decalogue formulate the commandment in quite different ways. They are reproduced in full here because of the recurrence of many of the following elements in medieval conceptions of Sunday observance:

> Memento ut diem sabbati sanctifices; sex diebus operaberis et facies omnia opera tua; septimo autem die sabbati Domini Dei tui non facies omne opus, tu et filius tuus, et filia tua, servus tuus et ancilla tua, iumentum tuum et advena qui est intra portas tuas. Sex enim diebus fecit Dominus caelum et terram et mare et omnia quae in eis sunt et requievit in die septimo; idcirco benedixit Dominus diei sabbati et sanctificavit eum. (Exodus XX.8–11)[3]

---

[1] The history of Sunday observance has been the subject of many scholarly treatments. Those that cover the medieval period are H. Dumaine, 'Dimanche', *Dictionnaire d'archéologie chrétienne et de liturgie*, ed. F. Cabrol and H. Leclercq, 15 vols. (Paris, 1907–53), IV, cols. 859–994; W. Rordorf, *Der Sonntag; Geschichte des Ruhe- und Gottesdiensttages im ältesten Christentum*, Abhandlungen zur Theologie des Alten und Neuen Testaments 43 (Zürich, 1962); W. Thomas, *Der Sonntag im frühen Mittelalter*, Studia Theologiae Moralis et Pastoralis 4 (Göttingen, 1929); H. Huber, *Geist und Buchstabe der Sonntagsruhe* (Salzburg, 1958); and L. L. McReavy, '"Servile Work" I. The Evolution of the Present Sunday Law', *The Clergy Review* 9 (1935), 269–84.

[2] Scholars are not all agreed that Sunday was the Christian day of worship from the outset. Some have argued that it remained the sabbath; see, for example, S. Bacchiocchi, *From Sabbath to Sunday: A Historical Investigation of the Rise of Sunday Observance in Early Christianity* (Rome, 1977).

[3] 'Remember that thou keep holy the sabbath day. Six days shalt thou labour, and shalt do all thy works.

1

Observa diem sabbati ut sanctifices eum sicut praecepit tibi Dominus Deus tuus. Sex diebus operaberis et facies omnia tua; septimus dies sabbati est id est requies Domini Dei tui; non facies in eo quicquam operis tu et filius tuus et filia, servus et ancilla, et bos et asinus, omne iumentum tuum et peregrinus qui est intra portas tuas, ut requiescat servus et ancilla tua sicut et tu. Memento quod et ipse servieris in Aegypto et eduxerit te inde Dominus Deus tuus in manu forti et brachio extento idcirco praecepit tibi ut observares diem sabbati. (Deuteronomy V.12–15)[4]

Whereas the passage from Exodus traces the origin of the sabbath back to the Creation,[5] the second passage mentions God's deliverance of the Israelites from slavery in Egypt as a rationale, but both make clear that the entire household was to cease from all work in acknowledgement of God's rest after creation. Infraction of this commandment was a serious matter and could result in death, as can be seen from an incident recorded in Numbers XV.32–6, in which a man is stoned to death for gathering wood on the sabbath.[6]

Interpretations of the Mosaic Sabbath Law

To the early Church, it was not immediately clear how or whether this commandment of rest should be transferred to Sunday, the day on which the early Christians worshipped in celebration of Christ's Resurrection, and thus the observance of Sunday as a day of rest developed only gradually in the following centuries. The New Testament has little to say on the subject; the Gospels, after all, record

But on the seventh day is the sabbath of the Lord thy God: thou shalt do no work on it, thou nor thy son, nor thy daughter, nor thy manservant, nor thy maidservant, nor thy beast, nor the stranger that is within thy gates. For in six days the Lord made heaven and earth, and the sea, and all things that are in them, and rested on the seventh day; therefore the Lord blessed the sabbath day, and sanctified it.' All biblical quotations are taken from the Latin Vulgate, *Biblia sacra iuxta vulgatam versionem*, ed. R. Weber, 3rd ed. (Stuttgart, 1975); English translations are from the Douai-Rheims version (rev. R. Challoner; London, 1914).

4   'Observe the day of the sabbath, to sanctify it, as the Lord thy God hath commanded thee. Six days shalt thou labour, and shalt do all thy works. The seventh is the day of the sabbath, that is, the rest of the Lord thy God. Thou shalt not do any work therein, thou nor thy son nor thy daughter, nor thy manservant nor thy maidservant, nor thy ox, nor thy ass, nor any of thy beasts, nor the stranger that is within thy gates: that thy manservant and thy maidservant may rest, even as thyself. Remember that thou didst serve in Egypt, and the Lord thy God brought thee out from thence with a strong hand, and a stretched out arm. Therefore hath he commanded thee that thou shouldst observe the sabbath day.'

5   See Genesis II.2–3: 'And on the seventh day God ended his work which he had made: and he rested on the seventh day from all his work which he had done. And he blessed the seventh day, and sanctified it: because in it he had rested from all the work which God created and made.'

6   Death was the required punishment, as stated in Exodus XXXI.14–15: 'Keep you my sabbath: for it is holy unto you: he that shall profane it, shall be put to death: he that shall do any work on it, his soul shall perish out of the midst of his people. Six days you shall work: in the seventh day is the sabbath, the rest holy to the Lord. Every one that shall do any work on this day, shall die' (cf. Exodus XXXV.2–3).

unsettling encounters between Christ and the religious leaders of his time, who were incensed by his breaking of the Jewish sabbath as they conceived it.[7] One would expect the writings of the Apostle Paul to resolve the difficulty as they do in the case of other Jewish practices such as circumcision and dietary restrictions, but he provides only the barest hint that any controversies concerning the day of worship or rest even existed: 'For one judgeth between day and day: and another judgeth every day: let every man abound in his own sense.'[8] This remark, though it names neither sabbath nor Sunday, may be seen as emblematic of the early Church's struggle between Christian freedom and Jewish custom: what was pious observance to one was reprehensible 'Judaizing' to another.

Thus, the writings of the earliest fathers indicate that Sunday was observed primarily as a day of worship rather than rest.[9] This was based on the belief that it was the day when Christ had risen from the dead, hence the designation 'Lord's day' (*dies dominica*). On this day of joyful celebration it was forbidden to kneel and fast, the very first Sunday prohibitions.[10] During this early period it would have been impractical, if not impossible, for Christians to keep Sunday free from work, particularly for those who were servants or slaves. Furthermore, there is evidence that in certain places, the Jewish sabbath continued to be kept among Jewish Christians.[11]

The third commandment was accordingly interpreted in various ways, offering anagogical, typological and moral interpretations.[12] The first sees the Old Testament sabbath rest from work as a prefiguration of the eternal rest of the believer. Origen

---

7   These usually concern Christ's performance of miracles on the sabbath, most often acts of healing, presumably in order to expose the extreme legalism of his contemporaries; see Matthew VIII.14–17, XII.1–14; Mark I.29–34, II.23–8, III.1–6; Luke IV.38–9, VI.1–11, XIII.10–17; and John V.1–18, IX.1–41.

8   Romans XIV.5: *Nam alius iudicat diem plus inter diem alius iudicat omnem diem unusquisque in suo sensu abundet*. See also Colossians II.16: *nemo ergo vos iudicet in cibo aut in potu aut in parte diei festi aut neomeniae aut sabbatorum* ('Let no man therefore judge you in meat or in drink or in respect of a festival day or of the new moon or of the sabbaths').

9   Rordorf, *Der Sonntag*, pp. 154–6. In this view, early mentions of cessation from work, such as that by Tertullian (*c.* 160–220) in his *De Oratione* (*Quinti Septimi Florentis Tertulliani opera. Pars I*, ed. A. Reifferscheid and G. Wissowa, CSEL 20 (Vienna, 1890), pp. 196–7), are interpreted as a reservation of a space of time for the purposes of worship, presumably in the early morning or late evening, rather than a setting aside of the entire day for rest; Rordorf, *Der Sonntag*, pp. 158–62. For the view that both worship and rest from labour were a part of Sunday observance from the second century on, see Bacchiocchi, *From Sabbath to Sunday*.

10   Huber, *Geist und Buchstabe*, pp. 71–2; Rordorf, *Der Sonntag*, pp. 267–8; Tertullian, for example, states this as already well established in *De Corona* 3 (*Quinti Septimi Florentis Tertulliani opera. Pars II.2*, ed. E. Kroymann, CSEL 70 (Vienna, 1942), 158: *Die dominico ieiunium nefas ducimus vel de geniculis adorare*).

11   See McReavy, 'Servile Work', p. 271; Ignatius (*c.* 50–117), 'Letter to the Magnesians' (section 9), edited by K. Bihlmeyer in *Die apostolischen Väter, Neubearbeitung der Funkschen Ausgabe* (Tübingen, 1924), pp. 88–92 (no. 15). Later, the Council of Laodicea (*c.* 360) forbids Christians to rest on the sabbath, and suggests that they do so on Sunday instead, if possible; canon 29, *Die Kanones der wichtigsten altkirchlichen Concilien nebst den apostolischen Kanones*, ed. F. Lauchert (Frankfurt am Main, 1961), p. 75.

12   See Huber, *Geist und Buchstabe*, pp. 49–61.

and Eusebius, and later Jerome, Augustine and perhaps Gregory the Great all make use of this interpretation.[13] The typological exegesis similarly equates Christ's rest in the tomb with the final rest of Christians after their work on earth.[14] Most common and persistent, however, is perhaps the moral or tropological interpretation, in which, eventually, the *opera servilia* cited in Mosaic law become the 'works of the world', i.e. sins, from which Christians are to rest daily.[15] So, for instance, Augustine states that this commandment alone is to be observed figuratively:

> Spiritualiter observat sabbatum christianus, abstinens se ab opere servili. Quid est enim ab opere servili? A peccato. Et unde probamus? Dominum interroga: 'Omnis qui facit peccatum, servus est peccati'. Ergo et nobis praecipitur spiritualiter observatio sabbati.[16]

Such interpretation was not necessarily abandoned once a transference of the sabbath rest to Sunday became commonplace, but rather continued to be used as a supplemental explanation of the third commandment or to bolster the case for the sanctity of Sunday.[17] However, most of the early Church fathers do not mention a Christian obligation of ceasing all physical labour, though some may appear to encourage it.[18]

Sunday Observance in Roman Law

How is it then, that even during the lifetimes of Augustine and Jerome, in the late fourth and early fifth centuries, the prohibition of various kinds of Sunday work emerged among Christian peoples? This question has elicited several answers. A shift in attitude can be traced back to Emperor Constantine's promulgation of the first official Sunday legislation in 321. The 'day of the sun' (*dies solis*) is to be set aside for rest; singled out were the activities of judges and those living and working in cities.[19] The new edict was not a blanket demand for a work-free day, however:

---

13 See, for example, Augustine, *Epistola* 55 (*Aureli Augustini Hipponiensis episcopi epistulae*, ed. A. Goldbacher, CSEL 34 (Prague, 1895–1923), pp. 194–5); further references in Dumaine, 'Dimanche', cols. 920–4; cf. also Hebrews IV.9–10.

14 Dumaine, 'Dimanche', cols. 924–5; Huber, *Geist und Buchstabe*, p. 53.

15 Dumaine, 'Dimanche', cols. 925–6; Huber, *Geist und Buchstabe*, pp. 54–61. The term *opus servile* occurs in Leviticus XXIII.8.

16 'The Christian observes the Sabbath spiritually, abstaining from servile work. What is it to abstain from servile work? From sin. And how do we prove it? Ask the Lord: Everyone who commits sin, is the servant of sin. Therefore the observance of the Sabbath spiritually is commanded to us', *In Iohannis Evangelium tractatus cxxiv*, 3.19 (PL 35, col. 1404); the biblical quotation is from John VIII.34.

17 See, for example, statements by Ælfric discussed on pp. 33–4, or of Alcuin, *Commentaria in sancti Iohannis Evangelium* 3.9 (PL 100, col. 806).

18 See Eusebius of Caesarea's (*c*. 260–340) commentary on Psalm 91, *Commentaria in Psalmos* (PG 23, cols. 1168–72).

19 *Omnes iudices urbanaeque plebes et artium officia cunctarum venerabili die solis quiescant. Ruri tamen positi agrorum culturae libere licenterque inserviant, quoniam frequenter evenit, ut non alio aptius die frumenta sulcis aut vinea scrobibus commendentur, ne occasione momenti pereat*

4

field-work was allowed on the grounds that farmers need to take advantage of favourable weather without regard to the day of the week. Whatever Constantine's motives may have been, this official recognition at the very least introduced the concept of Sunday as a day of rest rather than solely as a day of worship.[20]

Subsequent emperors continued to restrict Sunday and feast day activities, particularly in the areas of judicial operations and certain public entertainments; these laws were not as novel as they seem, however, since Roman law had already prohibited such things on pagan feast days (*feriae*), even going beyond them to include rural labour and any kind of work for personal profit.[21] The Theodosian Code, a collection of imperial decrees published in 438, mentions prohibitions against activities of the courts (except for emancipations and manumissions) and of tax collectors, the exaction of the payment of debts and also of games in the circus and theatre performances.[22] Judges were to make special inquiry into the welfare of prisoners to ensure that they received food, water and a bath on Sunday (section 9.3.7). The rationale for these laws concerning Sunday – in the earlier decrees again often called the 'day of the sun' – is that they interfered with worship services. They reveal a gradual strengthening and elaboration of Constantine's pronouncement, which is also cited (without the exclusion for rural labour), and thus they may be seen as a part of a general 'reordering [of] public religion into a Christian framework'.[23] In some respects they correspond to what remains of the medieval Sunday in most Western societies today: the closure of banks and public offices.

Parts of the Theodosian Code were incorporated into the body of law often referred to as the Germanic or barbarian codes, since these were, in fact, regional collections modelled on Roman precedent, particularly in the southern regions of the Continent.[24] The dating of this legislation presents some difficulties. Although the original formulation of these laws may have occurred as early as the beginning of the sixth century, the earliest manuscripts date from the early eighth century, many being part of a Carolingian effort to collect and record these local codes. Thus certain accretions, particularly those which pertain to a distinctly Christian practice such as Sunday observance, could have been added at any time between these two dates.

commoditas caelesti provisione concessa, *Codex Iustinianus* III.12.2 (*Corpus juris civilis*, ed. P. Krüger, vol. 2 (Berlin, 1888), p. 127).

[20] Constantine's intent in the formation of this edict has been disputed. There is some indication that it was designed to placate members of the cult of Mithras, who were sun-worshippers, rather than the Christians in the empire. It may also have been an attempt to accommodate both groups, though there is little evidence that Sunday rest was a requirement of the Church at this time. Cf. Huber, *Geist und Buchstabe*, pp. 78–80. For Mithraic influence on the development of the Christian Sunday, see Bacchiocchi, *From Sabbath to Sunday*.

[21] Huber, *Geist und Buchstabe*, pp. 43–5.

[22] The relevant laws are 2.8.1,18–20; 8.8.1,3; 11.7.10, 13; 15.5.2, 5; *Theodosiani libri XVI cum constitutionibus Sirmondianis et leges novellae ad Theodosianum pertinentes*, ed. T. Mommsen and P. M. Meyer, vol. I, 2nd ed. (Berlin, 1954).

[23] D. Hunt, 'Christianising the Roman Empire: The Evidence of the Code', p. 145.

[24] P. Wormald, *The Making of English Law*, p. 44.

For example, the code compiled in Rhaetia in eastern Switzerland known as the *Lex Romana Raetica curiensis* or simply *Lex Romana curiensis*, copies the Theodosian Code when it forbids court proceedings and exaction of debts (8.3), and enjoins special care of prisoners on Sundays (9.2.3).[25] Similarly, the influence of Roman law can be seen in this statute (II.I.12, c. X) from the Visigothic *Liber iudiciorum* (654):

> Die dominico neminem liceat executione constringi, quia omnes causas religio debet excludere; in quo nullus ad causam dicendam nec propter aliquod debitum fortasse solvendum quemquam inquietare presumat.[26]

This decree by King Chintasvintus (r. 642–53), which also applied to other festivals, goes on to explain the precise circumstances under which court cases may proceed, allowing, for instance, that some accused of crimes punishable by execution should be kept in custody until after the holy day, whereas others accused of lesser crimes could be required to return to court.[27]

Another group of the Germanic codes exhibits a basic similarity in that they emphasize the payment of penalties for the breaking of the Sunday rest. The most straightforward edict is that of the *Lex Frisionum*, probably compiled in 802, but drawing on earlier sources:[28]

> Qui opus servile die dominico fecerit, ultra Laubachi solid(os) XII, in caeteris locis Fresiae IIII solidos culpabilis iudicetur. Si servus hoc fecerit, vapuletur, aut dominus eius IIII solid(os) pro illo componat.[29]

[25] *Lex Romana Raetica curiensis*, ed. K. Zeumer, MGH, LL, 5 (Hanover, 1889), 360. Appended to one manuscript (St Gall 72, *c.* 800) are the *Capitula Remedii*, attributed to Bishop Remedius of Chur (d. 820); in its first capitulary, this text goes well beyond the Theodosian Code, proscribing a list of rural activities similar to Charlemagne's *Admonitio generalis* (789) and requiring that anything produced on a Sunday should be confiscated by the local judge and distributed to the poor by a priest; Zeumer, p. 442. See E. Meyer-Marthaler, *Lex Romana curiensis*, lviii–lix; and idem, 'Die Gesetze des Bischofs Remedius von Chur', *Zeitschrift für schweizerische Kirchengeschichte* 44 (1950), 81–110, 161–87, at 93–6.

[26] 'No litigation shall be commenced on Sunday, for religion should take precedence of all legal matters, and upon that day no one shall presume to subject another to annoyances either for the trial of a case, or for the payment of a debt', S. P. Scott, trans., *The Visigothic Code (Forum Judicum)* (Boston, 1910) p. 21; *Lex Visigothorum*, ed. Zeumer, pp. 59–60. Cf. *Leges Burgundionum* (XI, 5), which draws on the Theodosian Code (XII, 8.19, interpretation); *Leges Burgundionum*, ed. L. R. de Salis, MGH, LL nat. Germ., 2/1 (Hanover, 1892), 136.

[27] Book II.1.12 (*Lex Visigothorum*, ed. Zeumer, pp. 59–60). More details about Sunday observance in Visigothic Spain may be gleaned from the section which concerns the Jews, added to the Visigothic Code by King Ervig in 681. Here we find both the celebration of the sabbath (along with other Jewish festivals) and work on Sunday – including such household chores as spinning and weaving – strictly prohibited. Even masters of Jewish slaves could be fined 100 solidi for permitting them to engage in any labour (Book XII.3.6, *Lex Visigothorum*, ed. Zeumer, pp. 434–5); see R. Collins, *Visigothic Spain 409–711* (Malden, MA, 2004), pp. 235–6.

[28] N. E. Algra, 'Grundzüge des friesischen Rechts im Mittelalter', in *Handbuch des Friesischen*, ed. H. Munske (Tübingen, 2001), pp. 555–70.

[29] 'He who does servile work on the Lord's day, should be judged guilty of [a payment of] twelve solidi beyond the Lauwers, and four solidi in the other areas of Frisia. If a slave does this, he shall be flogged, or his lord shall pay four solidi for him' (Tit. XVIII), *Lex Frisionum*, ed. K. A. Eckhardt

So also *Pactus legis Salicae*,[30] in an addition composed under Childebert II, king of Austrasia (r. 575–95) states:

> De die dominico similiter placuit obseruari, ut si quis<cumque> ingenuus, excepto quod ad coquendum uel ad manducandum pertinet, alia opera <seruilia> in die dominico facere praesumpserit, si Salicus fuerit, .xv. solidos culpabilis iudicetur. Romanus .vii. semis solidos conponat. Seruus uero aut .iii. solidos reddat aut de dorsum suum conponat.[31]

One might compare this relatively straightforward capitulary with the following, from the eighth-century Bavarian code, *Lex Baiuvariorum*:[32]

> Si quis die dominico operam servilem fecerit, liber homo, si bovem iunxerit et cum carro ambulaverit, dextrum bovem perdat; si autem secaverit fenum vel collegerit aut messem secaverit aut collegerit vel aliquod opus servile fecerit die dominico, corripiatur semel vel bis; et si non emendaverit, rumpatur dorso eius .l. percussionibus et si iterum praesumpsit operare de dominico, auferatur de rebus eius tertiam partem; et si nec cessaverit, tunc perdat libertatem suam et sit servus, qui noluit in die sancto esse liber. Si servus autem, pro tale crimine vapuletur; et si non emendaverit, manum dextram perdat. Quia talis causa vetanda est, quae deum ad iracundiam provocat et exinde flagellamur in frugibus et penuria patimur. Et hoc vetandum est in die dominico. Et siquis in itinere positus cum carra vel cum nave, pauset die dominico usque in secunda feria. Et si noluerit custodire praeceptum domini, quia dominus dixit: 'Nullum opus facias in die sancto neque tu neque servus tuus neque ancilla tua neque bos tuus neque asinus tuus neque ulla subiectorum tuorum', et qui hoc in itinere vel ubicumque observare neglexerit, cum .xii. solidis condamnetur; et si frequens hoc fecerit, superiora sententia subiaceat.[33]

---

and A. Eckhardt, MGH, Font. iur. Germ. ant. 12 (Hanover, 1982), 62.

[30] The *Pactus legis Salicae* was originally issued by Clovis I between 507 and 511; see K. F. Drew, *The Law of the Salian Franks* (Philadelphia, 1991), p. 52. This portion was drawn up by the chief legal officer, Asclepiodatus, who had worked for Childebert's uncle, Guntram, issuer of an edict in 585 which also prohibits all physical work (*ab omni corporali opere*) on Sunday except that pertaining to food preparation, but including lawsuits; *Capitularia regum Francorum I*, ed. Boretius, p. 11; see also I. Wood, 'Roman Law in the Barbarian Kingdoms', in *Rome and the North*, ed. A. Ellegård and G. Åkerström-Hougen (Jonsered, Sweden, 1996), pp. 5–14 at 11.

[31] 'It is pleasing that this be observed with regard to the Lord's day. If any freeman presumes to do any servile work on the Lord's day, except for that pertaining to cooking and eating, if he is a Salic Frank, he shall be liable to pay fifteen solidi. If he is a Roman, he shall pay seven and one-half solidi as compensation. If he is a slave he shall pay three solidi or pay composition by his back [i.e., be flogged]' (III.7), Drew, trans., *The Law of the Salian Franks*, p. 159; *Pactus legis Salicae*; ed. K. A. Eckhardt, MGH, LL nat. Germ., Legum, Sectio I, t. 4, pt. 1 (Hanover, 1962), p. 269.

[32] Cf. Wormald, *The Making of English Law*, p. 43.

[33] 'If anyone does servile work on Sunday, for a freeman, if he yokes oxen and drives about in a cart, let him lose the right-hand ox. If, however, he cuts or collects hay, or cuts and collects a harvest, or does any servile work on Sunday, let him be warned once or twice. And if he does not correct himself, let him be beaten upon his back with fifty blows, and if he presumes to work on Sunday again, let a third of his property be carried off. And if he still does not cease, then let him lose his freedom and be a slave, because he does not wish to be free on a holy day. If he is a slave, however, let him be flogged for such a crime. And if he does not correct himself, let him lose his right hand, since

7

Although the basic outlines of monetary penalities, flogging and even loss of freedom are similar to the *Pactus legis Salicae*, this is clearly a much more elaborate production. It not only provides more detail concerning illicit work – riding in a cart, yoking an ox and harvesting – but it also features a paraphrase of Deuteronomy V.14 as a rationale for the prohibitions (conflating the sabbath and Sunday by shrewdly substituting *die sancto* for *dies sabbati*), and suggests that one consequence of non-compliance may be widespread disaster in the form of crop failure, a threat similar to those found in the Sunday Letter. Yet the basic building blocks of various penalties assigned for the breaking of this law are still clear in this code. Though presumably carried out by secular authorities, they seem severe; one possible explanation for this that has been put forward is that the absence of Sunday observance was one way of identifying any recalcitrant pagans who were seen as resisting efforts towards a unified Christian society.[34]

Sunday Observance in Early Church Councils

At the same time, various Church councils provide parallel evidence for a grow-ing sabbatarianism. More clearly than the secular legislation, these show the ten-sion which accompanied the transitional nature of this time period, particularly evident in the testimony from Merovingian Gaul. A striking early record is the Council of Orleans (538), which notes that 'the people are persuaded that one may not ride out with horses or with a cart and oxen, may not prepare anything to eat, may not exert oneself in the beautification of house or person' on Sunday.[35] The

such acts are prohibited that incite God to anger, and, furthermore, we will be punished regarding our crops and afflicted with want. Thus, this [work] is forbidden on Sunday. And if one is taking a journey with a cart or boat, let him pause from Sunday until Monday. And if he does not wish to observe the Lord's command, because the Lord has said, "No work shall you do on the holy day, neither you nor your servant nor your maidservant nor your ox nor your ass nor any which is subject to you", and if he neglects to observe this either on a journey or anywhere, let him be fined twelve solidi. And if he does this frequently, let him be fined the punishment described above'; T. J. Rivers, trans., *Laws of the Alamans and Bavarians* (Philadelphia, 1977), p. 137; K. A. Eckhardt, ed., *Die Gesetze des Karolingerreiches, 714–911* (Weimar, 1934), II, 114–16. A similar but shorter version also appears in the Laws of the Alamans, c. 38; cf. *Lex Alamannorum*, c. 38; *Leges Alamannorum*, ed. K. Lehmann, MGH, LL nat. Germ. 5/1 (Hanover, 1888), 98. The ultimate source is Theodore of Canterbury's penitential; see C. Schott, 'Pactus, Lex und Recht', in *Die Alemannen in der Frühzeit*, p. 147.

34 Schott, 'Pactus, Lex und Recht', p. 147.
35 *Quia persuasum est populis die Domineco [for Dominico] agi cum caballis aut bubus et veiculis [for vehiculis] itinera non debere neque ullam rem ad victum praeparari vel ad netorem [for nitorem] domus vel hominis pertenentem ullatenus exerciri [for exerceri], quae res ad Iudaicam magis quam ad Christeanam [for Christianam] observantiam pertenere [for pertinere] probatur, id statuimus, ut die Dominico, quod ante fieri licuit, liceat. De opere tamen rurali, id est arata vel vinea vel sectione, messione, excussione, exarto vel saepe, consuimus abstenendum [for abstinendum], quo facilius ad ecclesiam venientes orationis gratiae vacent. Quod si inventus fuerit quis in operibus supra scriptis, quae interdicta sunt, exercere qualiter emundari debeat, non in laici districtione, sed in sacerdotis castigatione consistat*; Council of Orleans, c. 31, *Concilia aevi Merovingici*, ed.

council finds such taboos more Jewish than Christian and notes, rather vaguely, that whatever was permitted before is still permitted, showing an awareness of the shift in belief and practice. However, in an illustration of the ambiguities of the times, the canon then oddly goes on to forbid rural labour and provides a detailed list of forbidden work, ostensibly making a distinction between spurious populist taboos and the prohibition of labour that might interfere with Sunday church attendance.

Later Church councils, however, follow the direction of the new trend. Even as early as the late sixth century, only fifty years after the Council of Orleans, the Council of Mâcon (585) castigates the people for their neglect of the Lord's day rather than for improper sabbatarianism, and, in addition to prohibiting 'servile work' (*opus servile*), oxen are not to be used,[36] and no court proceedings are to take place; severe punishments, including some that reflect the secular legislation mentioned above, are threatened: automatic loss of the court case, flogging for farmers and slaves and six months' isolation from the brethren for a monk.[37] As in the *Lex Baiuvariorum*, the notion that pestilence and infertility may be avoided through proper observance of the Lord's day echoes the kind of collective punishment used to compel obedience in the Sunday Letter.[38] By the mid-seventh century, the authors of a statute decided at the Council of Châlon (639–54) can state, citing from the Council of Orleans (538), that the prohibition of farm labour is nothing new, but rather a restoration of what has already been decreed, while silently omitting concern expressed in that earlier council about 'Judaizing' sabbatarianism.[39]

At the beginning of that century, no less a figure than Gregory the Great weighs in on sabbath and Sunday observance in a letter to the citizens of Rome, which has often been interpreted as a last hold-out of the Augustinian view. Curiously, he begins by condemning those who observe the Jewish sabbath, calling them 'preachers of the Anti-Christ' (*praedicatores Antichristi*) and states that when the Anti-Christ comes, he will want to see both sabbath and Sunday free from work,

---

Maassen, p. 82.

[36] All labour and specifically the use of oxen is also prohibited in canon 16 of the Diocesan Council of Auxerre (between 573 and 603): *Non licet die Dominico boves iungere vel alia opera exercere*; *Concilia aevi Merovingici*, ed. Maassen, p. 181.

[37] Council of Mâcon, c. 1f.; *Concilia aevi Merovingici*, ed. Maassen, pp. 165–6. Similarly, the Council at Narbonne in 589 threatens fines of 6 solidi for freemen and 100 lashes for slaves: *Quod si quisque presumpserit facere, si ingenuus est, det comiti ciuitatis solidos sex; si seruus, centum flagella suspiciat* (c. 4, Mansi IX, col. 1015). Cf. the decree of Childebert II in the *Pactus legis Salicae*, where the penalties are 15 solidi for the Salic Frank, 7½ solidi for the Roman and 3 solidi or a flogging for the slave (cited above, p. 7).

[38] *Haec namque omnia et placabilem erga nunc Dei animum reddunt et plagas morborum vel sterilitatum amovent atque repellunt*; *Concilia aevi Merovingici*, ed. Maassen, pp. 165–6.

[39] *Non aliquid novi condentes, sed vetera renovantes instituemus*, Council of Châlon, c. 18; *Concilia aevi Merovingici*, ed. Maassen, 212. It is the Council of Rouen (650) which seems to be the first use of the phrase *a vespero usque ad vesperam* (used in Leviticus XXIII.32 in reference to the day of atonement): *ut dies festi a vespera usque ad vesperam absque opere servili cum debito honore celebrentur* (c. 15, Mansi X, col. 1203).

9

a comment that has been seen as frowning on Sunday rest. Gregory does insist that the sabbath is to be observed spiritually, rather than literally,[40] but, especially in light of the trend towards a work-free Sunday, it seems peculiar that he would then single out the prohibition of bathing on Sundays as excessive, a prohibition which is not found in most civil or ecclesiastical laws, rather than condemning Sunday rest in general.[41] Furthermore, he clarifies what may be seen as his notion of appropriate Sunday observance: the practice of prayer and the cessation of 'earthly work', for which, however, the term *labor terrenus* and not the more common *opera servilia* is employed.[42] The letter does not, in the end, represent an unequivocal censure of Sunday rest, but only of sabbath observance and certain immoderate restrictions in regard to the Lord's day.

Homiletic and Narrative Sources

Gregory's letter draws attention to another side of Sunday observance during this period: the possibility that what one might call 'popular' conceptions of it perhaps differed from the official statements examined thus far. We have seen that a tendency towards extreme sabbatarianism was condemned in the Council of Orleans, which notes that some people believed it was forbidden to travel by horse or cart, prepare food or, as in Gregory's letter, clean house and person. Additional glimpses of sixth-century popular thought and practice may be found in sermons and hagiographical writing such as the works of Caesarius of Arles (d. 542), Martin of Braga (d. 580) and Gregory of Tours (d. 593/4). For instance, Caesarius, the influential bishop of Arles, notes in his homilies that his parishioners still engage in the pagan practice of refraining from work on Thursday (Jove's/Donar's day). He blames them for transferring to Thursday what ought to be done on Sunday,[43] and instead for working on Sunday without fear or shame.[44] He particularly singles out women who will not spin or weave on Thursday in honour of Jove.[45] These interesting references to a pagan Germanic taboo-day have led

---

40 *Epistola* XIII,3, *Gregorii I papae registrum epistolarum. Libri VIII–XIV*, ed. P. Ewald and L. M. Hartmann, MGH, Epp. (Berlin, 1891), 367.

41 *Aliud quoque ad me perlatum est, vobis a perversis hominibus esse praedicatum, ut dominicorum die nullus debeat lavare*; ibid. 368. The source of this restriction may have been penitential literature; see below, pp. 29–31.

42 *Dominicorum vero die a labore terreno cessandum est atque omni modo orationibus insistendum*; ibid. p. 368. For the view that Gregory's letter represents a protest against sabbatarianism applied to Sunday, see, for example, L. L. McReavy ('The Sunday Repose from Labor', 317) who notes that *labor terrenus* is 'a more general term applicable to any earthly occupation calculated to distract a man's attention from God and fix it to the things of this world'; cf. Huber, *Geist und Buchstabe*, pp. 124–6.

43 *Sermo* XIX.4, ed. Morin, CCSL 103, p. 90: *qui, quod obervari die dominico debet, in die Iovis hoc sacrilege transferunt.*

44 *Sermo* XIII.5, ibid. p. 68: *Isti enim infelices et miseri, qui in honore Iovis quinta feria opera non faciunt, non dubito quod ipsa opera die dominico facere nec erubescant nec metuant.*

45 *Sermo* LII.2, ibid. pp. 230–1. *Sermo* XIII.5; ibid. p. 68. Various forms of Thursday rest have also

some scholars to speculate that a 'transference' of practice was a contributing factor in the influx of Sunday prohibitions during the fifth and sixth centuries.[46] However, evidence of another possible origin is also mentioned in Caesarius' sermons: Jewish sabbath observance. In two of his sermons, he holds Jews up as examples of piety in their honouring of the sabbath, urging Christians similarly to devote themselves solely to God on Sundays.[47] Caesarius does not himself provide a list of any prohibited activities – he only states that proper observance of Sunday for the Christian involves church attendance, reading and prayer[48] – but his comments concerning Jewish practice would appear to invite sabbatarianism even if he did not intend to do so.[49]

Caesarius' reference to Jewish observance of the sabbath does raise the question of how much influence it might have had on the development of the Christian Sunday. Certainly the earliest conception of Sunday resembled that of the sabbath in certain respects: a day of celebration on which it was forbidden to fast. And even though, beyond the scriptural sources,[50] our knowledge of precise Jewish practice in the early-medieval period is at best sketchy, at least one list of restrictions contains many of the same activities which appear in the various documents under

been observed among Germanic peoples; cf. Hoffmann-Krayer and Bächtold-Stäubli, 'Donnerstag', *Handwörterbuch des deutschen Aberglaubens* (Berlin, 1927–42), cols. 331–45. Thursday observance is also condemned by a contemporary of Caesarius, Martin of Braga (*c.* 515–579), in his *De Correctione Rusticorum*, and not long thereafter at the Synod of Narbonne in 589 (Mansi IX, col. 1014). For additional examples and discussion, see D. Harmening, *Superstitio: Überlieferungs- und theoriegeschichtliche Untersuchung zur kirchlich-theologischen Aberglaubensliteratur des Mittelalters* (Berlin, 1979), pp. 155–64.

46 Thomas, *Der Sonntag im frühen Mittelalter*, pp. 17–23.

47 *Sermo* XIII.3 (ed. Morin, CCSL 103, 66): *Si enim infelices Iudaei tanta devotione celebrant sabbatum, ut in eo nulla opera terrena exerceant, quanto magis christiani in die dominico soli deo vacare, et pro animae suae salute debent ad ecclesiam convenire?*; cf. *Sermo* LXXIII.3 (ibid. p. 308).

48 *Sermo* XIII.3; ibid. p. 66. *Sermo* LXXIII.4 (ibid. pp. 308–9). However, Caesarius probably influenced the 538 Council of Orleans which prohibits farm work; see O. Pontal, *Die Synoden im Merowingerreich* (Paderborn, 1986), p. 79; and E. F. Bruck, 'Cæsarius of Arles and the Lex Romana Visigothorum', in *Studi in onore di V. Arangio-Ruiz nel XLV anno del suo insegnamento*, vol. I (Naples, 1953), 201–17 at 211.

49 One restriction which has received some attention in connection with Caesarius is that forbidding sex on both feast days and Sundays. While the prohibition itself is not unusual, the threatened divine discipline seems extreme: in one passage, children conceived on Sundays or feast days may be born either *leprosi aut epileptici aut forte etiam daemoniosi* ('lepers, or epileptics or perhaps demoniacs'); *Sermo* XLIV.7; ed. Morin, CCSL 103, 199. Cf. *Sermo* XVI.2; ibid. p. 78. See discussion in Klingshirn, *Caesarius of Arles: The Making of a Christian Community*, pp. 155–6. This cruel punishment is reminiscent of the fate of children conceived on Sunday in the Sunday Letter, who it is said will be born blind, deaf, weak, leprous and lame (see D89–90 and its Latin source; see also A73–5 and B123–5 in which the children are similarly punished). For the prohibition of sex on Sunday and other holy days, see R. Kottje, *Studien zum Einfluss des Alten Testaments auf Recht und Liturgie des frühen Mittelalters (6.–8. Jahrhundert)*, Bonner historische Forschungen 23 (Bonn, 1970), 69–83.

50 Exodus XVI.23–5 (gathering manna); XX.8 (work, generally); XXIII.12 (work); XXXIV.21 (work); XXXI.15 (work); XXXV.2–3 (work, kindling of fire); Leviticus XXIII.3 (work); Deuteronomy V.12 (work); Nehemiah X.31 (buying), XIII.15–22 (buying and selling); Jeremiah XVII.21–2 (carrying burdens, work); Amos VIII.5 (buying and selling).

discussion here as well as in the Sunday Letter. Robert Goldenberg discusses a list in the third-century Mishnah which includes farm work, the baking of bread, spinning, weaving, hunting, writing, kindling a fire and the carrying of burdens.[51] Goldenberg notes, however, that this list is artificial and partial, leaving out such obvious choices as buying and selling. The frequent labelling in Christian sources of excessive restrictions as 'Judaizing' as well as the implied knowledge of what those practices were lend further support to the notion that they were perceived as resulting from undue Jewish influence.[52] Thus it seems reasonable to see the influence of the Jewish sabbath as at least partially responsible for the development of the character of the Christian Sunday during the early Middle Ages.

Southern Gaul and Spain would appear to have been likely areas for this to occur. In his sermon *De correctione rusticorum*, which condemns a variety of pagan practices, Martin of Braga sets a quite specific standard for the honouring of the Lord's day. He is clear that no servile work – defined here as work in field, meadow or vineyard – and no lengthy journeys must be undertaken on Sunday.[53] Martin, like Caesarius, castigates Christians for showing less zeal in honouring their holy day than pagans do for Thursday (Jove's day) or that of other demons. It is indeed remarkable that already in the sixth century such a clear statement regarding the Christian obligation to rest on Sunday could be made.

An even better idea of how these new Sunday rules were presented to the public and how the fear of immediate divine retribution was used to enforce them may be seen from a phenomenon that is particularly in evidence in hagiographical writing but is also found elsewhere:[54] the anecdotes which involve *Strafwunder* (miracles of punishment), such as tales of farmers and craftsmen whose limbs

---

[51] 'The Jewish Sabbath in the Roman World up to the Time of Constantine the Great', in *Aufstieg und Niedergang der römischen Welt: Geschichte und Kultur Roms im Spiegel der neueren Forschung*, ed. H. Temporini and W. Haase, II.19.1 (Berlin, 1972), pp. 414–47 at 423–4. Goldenberg also provides citations from Josephus that mention travel and appearances at court (pp. 416–18).

[52] Cf. the Council of Laodicea and the Council of Orleans (538), discussed above. The possibility is entertained by Robert Priebsch (*Letter from Heaven*, pp. 26–7). Some scholars suggest a widespread Christian fascination in Jewish festivals during late antiquity and the Merovingian period, as evidenced by the repeated legal injunctions against Christian participation; see Geisel, *Die Juden im Frankenreich*, pp. 146–8, and Goldenberg, 'The Jewish Sabbath', pp. 441–4. As late as the end of the eighth century, the Council of Friaul (c. 13) suggests that in some rural areas the sabbath was still being observed by non-Jews; see Schreckenberg, *Die Christlichen Adversus-Judaeos-Texte*, p. 479.

[53] *Martini episcopii Bracarensis opera omnia*, ed. C. W. Barlow, p. 202: *Opus servile, id est agrum, pratum, vineam, vel si qua gravia sunt, non faciatis in die dominico, praeter tantum quod ad necessitatem reficiendi corpusculi pro exquoquendo pertinet cibo et necessitate longinqui itineris. Et in locis proximis licet viam die dominico facere, non tamen pro occasionibus malis, sed magis pro bonis.*

[54] See the summary by R. Van Dam in *Leadership and Community in Late Antique Gaul* (Berkeley, 1985), pp. 285–7. Van Dam provides an intriguing, though perhaps too fanciful, rationale for the development of these beliefs, arguing that the forbidden activities all have to do with a 'civilized way of life' which was to be eschewed on Sundays and feast days in favour of living 'in conformity with nature' (pp. 285–8).

are immobilized as they attempt to engage in forbidden activities on Sunday.[55] Gregory of Tours and other writers of the period offer many examples of such stories. One of these illustrates the taboo-like restrictions which take the idea of Sunday rest to its extreme:

> Puella quaedam die dominico dum caput suum componeret, pectine adprehenso, credo ob iniuriam diei sancti, in manibus eius adhæsit, ita ut adfixi dentes tam in digitis quam in palmis magnum ei dolorem inferrent.[56]

The girl is delivered from her agony when she prays at the tomb of St Gregory, but the notion that even the combing of hair was forbidden indicates the discrepancy between what was popularly thought to be required and official prohibitions against Sunday labour seen above. A more typical recipient of such punishment is the common labourer who was in the process of completing some kind of farm work:[57] ploughing,[58] the mending of a fence or hedge,[59] yoking of oxen,[60] making a key,[61] running a mill,[62] or a woman of the same status engaged in household duties such as baking bread.[63] One narrative tells of a poor man called Sisulf who wakes to find his hand painfully disfigured. He is told by St Martin to travel throughout the countryside to preach against perjury, usury and Sunday work to avert God's wrath; once he does so, his hand is healed.[64]

Into this category of *Strafwunder* falls also the mention of a deformed child that is said to have been conceived on Sunday, reminding us of Caesarius' (and

---

55 See the discussion and examples cited by Huber, *Geist und Buchstabe*, pp. 110–14; F. Graus in *Volk, Herrscher und Heiliger im Reich der Merowinger. Studien zur Hagiographie der Merowingerzeit* (Prague, 1965), pp. 481–4; and by G. Scheibelreiter, 'Sonntagsarbeit und Strafwunder: Beobachtungen zu hagiographischen Quellen der Merowingerzeit', in *Der Tag des Herrn: Kulturgeschichte des Sonntags*, ed. R. Weiler (Vienna, 1998), 175–86. See also I. Wood, 'How Popular was Early Medieval Devotion?', online.

56 'A certain girl was fixing her hair on a Sunday. I believe because of the injury done to the holy day that when she took hold of the comb, it stuck to her hand so that the teeth pressed as much into her fingers as into her palm and caused great pain', *Liber vitae patrum* VII.5, *Gregorii Turonensis opera*, ed. B. Krusch, MGH, SSRM I/2 (Hanover, 1885), 690.

57 These agree generally with those mentioned in the Council of Orleans (538) in c. 31, which prohibits ploughing, pruning of vines, harvesting, winnowing, tilling and mending fences (*Concilia aevi Merovingici*, ed. Maassen, p. 82).

58 Gregory of Tours, *Liber de virtutibus S. Iuliani* 11, *Gregorii Turonensis opera*, ed. Krusch, MGH, SSRM I, pt. 2, p. 119.

59 Gregory of Tours, *Libri I–IV de virtutibus sancti Martini episcopi* III.29, 45; *Gregorii Turonensis miracula*, ed. Krusch, pp. 189, 193. *Liber vitae patrum* XV.3; *Gregorii Turonensis miracula*, ed. Krusch, p. 690. Venantius Fortunatus, *Vita sancti Germani* L.138; *Venanti Honori Clementiani Fortunati presbyteri Italici opera pedestria*, ed. B. Krusch, MGH, Auct. Ant. 4/2 (Berlin, 1885), 22.

60 Gregory of Tours, *De virtutibus sancti Martini* IV.45 (pp. 210–11).

61 Gregory of Tours, *De virtutibus sancti Martini* III.7 (pp. 183–4).

62 *Vita Audoini episcopi Rotmagnensis*, ed. B. Krusch and W. Levison, MGH, SSRM 5 (Hanover, 1920), p. 559. Gregory of Tours, *De virtutibus sancti Martini* III.3 (p. 183).

63 Gregory of Tours, *Liber in gloria martyrum* 15; ed. Krusch, *Gregorii Turonensis miracula*, p. 48. Gregory of Tours, *De virtutibus sancti Martini* III.31, 56 (pp. 190, 195–6).

64 Gregory of Tours, *De virtutibus sancti Martini* II.40 (pp. 173–4).

the Sunday Letter's) threat of just such an outcome.[65] As will be seen, many of the prohibitions listed in the Sunday Letter coincide with the broad range of obligations implied in these narratives. Curiously, however, the promised punishments are not as individual as they are in the latter; the Sunday Letter's threats are more collective in nature including disasters such as famine, disease or foreign invasion which will affect an entire community or nation. In a few instances the narrative sources also approach this kind of communal discipline: in one story many are struck by heavenly fire for working on the Lord's day and in another, land worked on a Sunday becomes sterile.[66]

A more immediate source of correction for wrongdoing may also have been taken into account by would-be offenders. The earliest penitential texts include prohibitions against a variety of activities including many which do not appear with any frequency in the legislation such as bathing or sexual relations. These will be discussed in the next chapter, but it is worth noting here that another layer of restriction is reflected in these texts.

Whatever one might deduce about its origins from the sum of the evidence collected above, it is fair to say that by the sixth century there was a powerful movement towards a sabbath-like Sunday of rest and worship. What was lacking was a solid theological basis for the shift.[67] While Sunday was always seen as exceptional since it was the day of the Resurrection, that was an insufficient argument for making it also a day of complete physical rest; the notion of a 'transference' of the sabbath to Sunday was only beginning to take on that role. The realization of this lacuna goes a long way towards explaining the existence of the Sunday Letter which was composed at some point before the end of the sixth century. It reflects the desire for a more authoritative, indeed, a divine, statement on the subject. Nevertheless, while the device of a letter sent from heaven is clearly an extravagant piece of apocryphal invention, the other main ingredients are not unique to the Sunday Letter. Already we have encountered most of the prohibitions listed in the letter, whether in official pronouncements or circulating in popular belief. And the notion that God may send terrible disasters on a people for non-compliance also had some currency during this time period. No wonder that the Sunday Letter appears to have been in great demand as soon as it was penned, especially as Sunday rest continued to be the subject of legislation in the following centuries.

---

[65] *De virtutibus sancti Martini* II.24 (p. 167). The wording is similar: *Quia, cum evenerit, exinde aut contracti aut ephilentici aut leprosi nascuntur.*

[66] Gregory of Tours, *Gregorii Episcopi Turonensis libri historiarum X*, X.30; ed. B. Krusch and W. Levison, MGH, SSRM I/1 (Hanover, 1951), p. 525. *Vita et miracula Leutfredi abbatis Madriacensis* 22. B, ed. B. Krusch and W. Levison, MGH, SSRM 7 (Hanover, 1920), p. 8.

[67] As R. J. Baukham notes: 'The laws for Sunday rest . . . existed for several centuries as rules in search of a theological context and justified by a divine authority curiously difficult to locate'; 'Sabbath and Sunday in the Medieval Church in the West', in *From Sabbath to Lord's Day: A Biblical, Historical, and Theological Investigation*, ed. D. A. Carson (Grand Rapids, 1982), p. 303.

14

1. The Development of Sunday Observance

Carolingian Legislation

The Carolingian evidence is of interest here mainly because of its ties to the late Anglo-Saxon period when the extant Old English Sunday Letters were produced. On the whole, we see a repetition and strengthening of earlier legislation[68] along with additional efforts to develop a rationale for Sunday rest. In any case, there can be no doubt that sabbatarianism had gained a significant foothold by this time. The best-known illustration of how detailed the Sunday prohibitions had become is found in the *Admonitio generalis* issued by Charlemagne in 789 which stipulates that work in field and vineyard – ploughing, harvesting, mowing, erecting of fences, felling of trees – as well as building of houses and garden work are all prohibited.[69] The use of a cart is allowed only in certain specified circumstances. Women's work – such as sewing, weaving and the washing of clothes – is also forbidden. The opening assumes scriptural support for what follows (*secundum quod et in lege Dominus praecipit*), and Charlemagne denies that restriction of these activities is in any way innovative; he refers to *bonae memoriae genitor meus* ('my father of good memory') who issued similar edicts.[70] The Sunday Letter, however, is condemned in the same document, not, it would appear, because of its overly stringent views on Sunday observance, but as part of a list of heterodox writings where it is denounced as *epistola pessima et falsissima* ('a most wicked and false letter'), which should not be believed or read but burnt.[71]

The purpose of embracing a work-free Sunday is made clear in the *Admonitio* and in other legislation from the same period. The establishment of a well-regulated Christian society, particularly among the newly converted, required a day devoted to attendance at mass and instruction in Christian mores.[72] The Council

---

[68] The pronouncement on Sunday made at the Synod of Dingolfing (*c.* 755), for example, is content to refer to previously decided canons (*sicut in lege scriptum est et in decretis canonum*); *Concilia aevi Karolini*, ed. Werminghoff, Conc. 2/1, 94.

[69] Cap. 81. *Capitularia regum Francorum I*, ed. Boretius, p. 61: *Omnibus. Statuimus quoque secundum quod et in lege Dominus praecipit, ut opera servilia diebus dominicis non agantur, sicut et bonae memoriae genitor meus in suis synodalibus edictis mandavit, id est quod nec viri ruralia opera exerceant nec in vinea colenda nec in campis arando, metendo vel foenum secando vel sepem ponendo nec in silvis stirpare vel arbores caedere vel in petris laborare nec domos construere nec in orto laborare; nec ad placita conveniant nec venationes exerceant. Et tria carraria opera licet fieri in die dominico, id est ostilia carra vel victualia vel si forte necessse erit corpus cuiuslibet ducere ad sepulcrum. Item feminae opera textilia non faciant nec capulent vestitos nec consuent vel acupictile faciant; nec lanam carpere nec linum battere nec in publico vestimenta lavare nec berbices tundere habeant licitum, ut omnimodis honor et requies diei dominicae servetur. Sed ad missarum sollempnia ad aeclesiam undique conveniant et laudent Deum in omnibus bonis quae nobis in illa die fecit.*

[70] He may be referring to his father Pepin's promulgation of the statutes decided at the Council of Verneuil (755), which simply repeats (in c. 14) the statement on Sunday from the Council of Orleans in 538.

[71] C. 78; *Capitularia regum Francorum I*, ed. Boretius, p. 60.

[72] An edict issued for the newly subdued Saxons only forbids judicial proceedings, but enjoins church attendance; c. 18, *Capitulatio de partibus Saxoniae* in *Capitularia regum Francorum I*, ed. Boretius, p. 69. Cf. *Admonitio generalis* (c. 81): 'But they should assemble from everywhere at church for

15

of Frankfurt in 794 specified that an entire day, from Saturday evening to Sunday evening, is to be set aside.[73] Another council which took place around the same time in Italy stated that the Lord's day begins with Saturday evening (with the tolling of the church bell), and urges all to devote themselves to prayer and church attendance.[74] In addition, the statute offers a rationale for the dignity of Sunday, which would also be inserted into the later versions of the Sunday Letter: a rudimentary form of the 'Sunday list', a catalogue of important events said to have happened on that day and here including the Resurrection, Pentecost, the feeding of the five thousand and the first manna in the desert.[75] Subsequent councils also address Sunday observance, but not always in quite the same detail. The local councils of 813 all appear to agree that court cases, 'servile work' and trade (not mentioned in the *Admonitio*) are forbidden.[76]

Two additional witnesses to the development of Sunday observance merit our attention. The records of a council held at Rome in 826 include an extended homiletic argument which quotes the Old Testament sabbath law as though it referred to Sunday and, like Caesarius, holds up Jewish sabbath-keeping as a shaming example.[77] A similar and even more lengthy canon in the records of the Council of Paris (829) claims that the obligation of Sunday rest is backed by the holy fathers and the authority of the Church and bemoans the fact that compliance has all but disappeared.[78] Drawing on elements we have already seen elsewhere, the canon provides a short 'Sunday list' and reports of *Strafwunder* in which those engaging in farm work were struck by lightning, disabled or burned to ashes in an instant. The Jews, who obey their sabbath laws without any earthly compulsion, are again brought up as a positive example. Here we see the full arsenal of current thinking applied to the defiant breaker of Sunday laws. The honour of the day derives from the authority of the Church and its historical significance as a day of miracles. Jewish sabbath-keeping is meant to shame Christians and the threat of horrific punishments is designed to instil fear of divine retribution. In such a context, the Sunday Letter, by this time spreading prolifically throughout the West, must have seemed a plausible aid, and in at least one region, it seems to have had an exceptionally central role to play.

---

the solemnities of the mass and praise God for all the good things which He did for us on that day' (the Latin is cited above, n. 69).

73 C. 21: *Ut dies dominica a vespera usque ad vesperam servetur*; *Concilia aevi Karolini*, ed. Werminghoff, Conc. 2/1, 168. The council was important, attracting papal legates, bishops from Italy, Spain and England, and many of its edicts were apparently intended to supplement those in the *Admonitio generalis*; see W. Hartmann, *Die Synoden der Karolingerzeit im Frankenreich und in Italien* (Paderborn, 1989), pp. 106–13.

74 *Concilium Foroiuliense* (Friuli), c. 13; *Concilia aevi Karolini*, ed. Werminghoff, Conc. 2/1, 194–5. Both of these councils were attended (and the latter presided over) by Paulinus of Aquileia; Hartmann, *Die Synoden der Karolingerzeit*, pp. 106, 117.

75 See discussion of the Sunday List in Chapter 3, pp. 59–60.

76 *Concilium Arelatense*, c. 16; *Concilium Remense*, c. 35; *Concilium Moguntinense*, c. 37; *Concilium Turonense*, c. 40; *Concilia aevi Karolini*, ed. Werminghoff, Conc. 2/1, 252, 256, 269, 292.

77 *Concilium Romanum*, c. 9; *Concilia aevi Karolini*, ed. Werminghoff, Conc. 2/2, 557–8.

78 C. 50; *Concilia aevi Karolini*, ed. Werminghoff, Conc. 2/2, 643–4.

1. The Development of Sunday Observance

Sunday Observance in Ireland

As these developments were taking place on the Continent, a particularly intense sabbatarianism seems to have found adherents in Ireland. It is difficult to date precisely when this began or how widespread it was, but there can be no doubt that the Sunday Letter played a significant part in the movement. The textual evidence includes three related documents which often appear in the manuscripts together:[79] an adaptation of the Sunday Letter into Old Irish, the *Epistil Ísu*,[80] the *Cáin Domnaig* ('Law of Sunday')[81] and three short *Strafwunder* narratives concerning Sunday observance.[82] Remarkably, the first two of these texts are, in fact, based on the Sunday Letter, a copy of which probably arrived in Ireland at least as early as the beginning of the ninth century.[83] It was translated and its proscriptions incorporated into elaborate legal tracts which offer specific fines for violating Sunday and describe the manner in which offenders are to be identified and prosecuted as well as the exceptional circumstances under which the prohibitions (particularly those concerning travel) may be suspended. There is even reference to 'Sunday guarantors and bailiffs' who apparently were responsible for enforcing the code.[84] In character, these legal portions resemble Irish secular codes of the period though they were most likely compiled by clerics.[85]

The origin of these texts is uncertain, and the legal codes may never have been widely enforced.[86] D. A. Binchy suggests that the *Cáin Domnaig* was a local

---

[79] The manuscript distribution is summarised by L. Breatnach in *A Companion to the Corpus iuris Hibernici*, Early Irish Law Series 5 (Dublin, 2005), p. 209. See also J. F. Kenney, *The Sources for the Early History of Ireland: Ecclesiastical: An Introduction and Guide* (New York, 1966), pp. 476–7.

[80] As the Irish Sunday Letter is a close analogue to the Old English Letters E and F, it will be discussed in more detail in the chapters on the transmission of the Latin Sunday Letter and the Old English Sunday Letter.

[81] Edited by V. Hull in 'Cáin Domnaig', *Ériu* 20 (1966), 151–77. The letter is edited and translated into English by J. G. O'Keeffe, 'Cáin Domnaig', *Ériu* 2 (1905), 189–214. See McNamara, *The Apocrypha in the Irish Church*, pp. 60–3.

[82] For the *Strafwunder* see K. Meyer, 'Göttliche Bestrafung der Sonntagsübertretung', *Zeitschrift für celtische Philologie* 3 (1900), 228. The three punishments are as follows: a boy is immolated for gathering firewood on Sunday, a sage no longer receives food brought by an angel when he knocks a chip of wood from his path on Sunday, a tribe's herd of cattle is destroyed by the sea when they ask a pilgrim to put it in an enclosure on Sunday. (I am grateful to Connell Monette for providing me with a translation of the Irish). A verse adaptation of a Sunday List has been edited by J. G. O'Keeffe, 'Poem on the Observance of Sunday', *Ériu* 3 (1907), 143–7.

[83] Their relationship is discussed in Chapter 3, pp. 40–2.

[84] 'Five seds [is the fine] for assaulting the Sunday guarantors or bailiffs, as they are claiming the Law of Sunday'; O'Keeffe, 'Cáin Domnaig', p. 209.

[85] Binchy, *Corpus iuris Hibernici*, I, x and F. Kelly, *A Guide to Early Irish Law* (Dublin, 1988), p. 234. Kelly makes note however that the 'Cáin Domnaig's treatment of the offence of working on Sunday relies on principles which I have been unable to discern in other law-texts'. In particular, the discrepancies he notes are the severity of the punishments, the inordinate inducements to report violations and the lack of agreement as to whether or not the grinding of corn is permitted (p. 235).

[86] Hull, 'Cáin Domnaig', p. 152, and Binchy, *Corpus iuris Hibernici*, I, x. Westley Follett, however, thinks that at least at the monastery of Tallaght, founded by a *céli dé*, 'the strict Sunday ideals of the

17

production, perhaps intended to produce revenue for a monastic federation.[87] However, it is worth noting that interest in the subject matter appears to coincide with the emergence of a strict sabbatarianismm associated with the appearance in the late eighth century of the *céli dé* ('clients of God') in Ireland, an ascetic reform movement.[88] In keeping with their high regard for Mosaic law,[89] they advocated strict Sunday observance, which included prohibitions against washing, splitting wood, eating food prepared on Sunday or, for married lay members, sexual relations.[90]

However, such sabbatarian attitudes may not have been entirely new to the Irish. There is evidence for it as early as the end of the seventh century in Muirchú's *Vita sancti Patricii*. In one chapter, the saint forbids 'heathen folk' who are making a rath to work on the Lord's day. When they ignore his warning, a storm destroys their work.[91] In another chapter, we are told that Patrick would not go out from Saturday evening to the Monday morning.[92] Several other lives of saints who lived in the seventh and eighth centuries, though composed much later, also hint at a similar tradition of strict Sunday observance featuring restrictions such as the washing of the head and the cutting of wood.[93]

In any case, there is no doubt that an exceptional sabbatarian focus resulted in the adoption of the Sunday texts. Liam Breatnach, in a recent re-examination

---

day were put into practice' (*Céli Dé in Ireland*, p. 209). The *Annals of Inisfallen* record an interesting strengthening of Sunday laws for the year 1040: 'A law and ordinance, such as was not enacted in Ireland from Patrick's time, was made by Brian's son, to the effect that none should dare to steal, or do feats of arms on Sunday, or go out on Sunday carrying any load; and furthermore, that none should dare to fetch cattle within doors'; *The Annals of Inisfallen*, ed. Mac Airt, pp. 204–5.

[87] Binchy, *Corpus iuris Hibernici* I, x. Follett suggests Armagh (*Céli Dé in Ireland*, p. 154).

[88] Hughes, *The Church in Early Irish Society*, pp. 174–9. See also Kenney, *The Sources for the Early History of Ireland*, p. 477. While some have sought the author of the *Cáin Domnaig* and the *Epistil Ísu* within this group, Follett thinks it more likely that, 'so influenced by these texts, or at least by the *zeitgeist* they fostered, were *céli dé* that they acquired a reputation for stringent Sunday observance in their own right and became associated with the origin myth of the Letter from Heaven' (*Céli Dé in Ireland*, p. 155); see the discussion of Irish annals which seem to associate the two in Chapter 3, pp. 42–3.

[89] For the observance of the sabbath at an earlier date, see Herren and Brown, *Christ in Celtic Christianity*, pp. 37, 109–13.

[90] See Hughes, *The Church in Early Irish Society*, pp. 178–9 and Follett, *Céli Dé in Ireland*, pp. 207–9. A text recording adherents' practices at the monastery of Tallaght (founded by Máel Ruain in 774) has been edited under the name 'The Monastery of Tallaght' by E. J. Gwynn and W. J. Purton in *Proceedings of the Royal Irish Academy*, 29, section C, no. 5 (Dublin, 1911); the sections which mention Sunday restrictions are §§13, 49 (gathering or preparing food on Sunday), §§14, 50 (for lay members: sexual abstinence on Saturday, and, if possible, Sunday nights), §45 (bathing), §55 (tonsure, washing, splitting wood, working), §69 (working), §71 (travel) (pp. 132, 144–6, 148, 156–7). Cf. O'Dwyer, *Céli Dé*, pp. 116–17.

[91] *Muirchú Moccu Macthéni's 'Vita sancti Patricii': Life of St Patrick*, ed. D. Howlett (Dublin, 2006), p. 104.

[92] Ibid. p. 116.

[93] The details are provided in Kottje, *Studien zum Einfluß des Alten Testaments* (pp. 48–51), and in Maclean, *The Law of the Lord's Day in the Celtic Church* (pp. 37–43). The washing of the head is mentioned in the *Vita sancti Aed* (*Vitae sanctorum Hiberniae partim hactenus ineditae: ad fidem codicum manuscriptorum recognovit prolegomenis notis indicibus instruxit*, ed. C. Plummer (Oxford, 1910), I, 43) and the cutting of wood in *Vita sancti Colmani* (ibid. p. 263).

of the linguistic evidence for dating all three, concludes that they belong to the ninth century.[94] Their transformation of the Sunday Letter into an elaborate legal code, however marginal, is unique. Perhaps the support of its prohibitions by an influential religious group facilitated the quiet acceptance of these Sunday laws and the Sunday Letter, even while the latter was being violently denounced elsewhere.[95]

Insofar as can be ascertained from the extant evidence, it appears that Sunday rest evolved from its moderate beginnings as a mere *desideratum* to an obligation accompanied by threats of severe punishment for non-compliance as a result of two factors. One was perhaps a tendency – whether based on Germanic custom or in imitation of Jewish practice – among some elements of the wider public to produce a taboo-day with ever-increasing restrictions. The other impetus clearly lay in what McReavy terms 'liturgical necessity', the need for a designated time for Christian worship and instruction.[96] The latter clearly made the Church's reluctant embrace of the former almost inevitable, and theology eventually followed practice. It should come as no surprise that the uncertainty caused by the transition to a stricter regulation of Sunday proved fertile ground for extra-canonical support such as the Sunday Letter to spring up.

2

Sunday Observance in Anglo-Saxon England

The regulation of Sunday observance in Anglo-Saxon England offers a good example of how the legislative body of a particular people gradually developed a definition of what should be considered 'illicit work' on that day. The Anglo-Saxons initially drew on the so-called 'Germanic' law codes and later on Carolingian precedent, but there are also significant differences, which indicate that they were reluctant to adopt the detailed proscriptions sometimes seen in continental legislation. Even so, a trend of increasing prohibitions is evident throughout the period.

The Early Law Codes

The ordinances concerning Sunday activities in Anglo-Saxon England go back at least as far as the late seventh century. The West Saxon King Ine (d. 726) and Kentish King Wihtræd (d. 725) both included edicts forbidding Sunday work in

---

94   *A Companion to the Corpus iuris Hibernici*, pp. 210–11. Hull dates the *Cáin Domnaig* to the first half of the eighth century ('Cáin Domnaig', p. 156). See also the comments by D. Binchy cited by D. Whitelock in 'Bishop Ecgred', p. 66.

95   As will be seen in Chapter 3, such approval was not necessarily available at about the same time in England.

96   McReavy, 'Servile Work', p. 270.

their codes.[1] They are very similar to each other and are most closely related to the Germanic law codes on the Continent, particularly to the *Pactus legis Salicae* (in this case identical to the *Lex Salica*) and the *Lex Frisionum*, which also list the penalties to be exacted for Sunday work according to the status of the offender. In the Anglo-Saxon laws there are only two categories, slave and freeman, whereas the continental codes differentiate by ethnic or regional grouping.[2] The following is the relevant section in Ine's code:

> Gif ðeowmon wyrce on Sunnandæg be his hlafordes hæse, sie he frioh, and se hlaford geselle XXX scill. to wite. Gif þonne se ðeowa butan his gewitnesse wyrce, þolie his hyde. Gif ðonne se frigea ðy dæge wyrce butan his hlafordes hæse, ðolie his freotes.[3]

Of interest is the acknowledgment, also in Wihtræd's code, that a lord must be held responsible when he has ordered his slave to work on Sunday.[4] Both texts impose a severe penalty for the freeman, either the loss of freedom or *healsfang*, a fine equivalent to a man's *wergeld*. Wihtræd's code also offers some interesting differences. The penalties are not the same: whereas Ine's penalty for forcing a slave to work is the slave's freedom and a 30-shilling fine, Wihtræd only stipulates an 80-shilling fine, and a slave who works without his lord's knowledge may pay a fine of 6 shillings instead of receiving a flogging. A time span for the restriction is specified: from sundown on Saturday to sundown on Sunday. A greater innovation (unique in the Anglo-Saxon period) is the addition of an incentive to report illicit Sunday labour consisting of half the fine as a reward and the opportunity to complete the job, presumably not on a Sunday, for the would-be informants.

These early statutes leave the issue of what constitutes illicit Sunday work rather vague, perhaps intentionally so, but they may have been in effect throughout the rest of the Anglo-Saxon period since they are repeated as late as Cnut's code of 1020/1.[5] It is important to notice that even in this early period, the Church was able to exert its influence on an issue which must have had a significant eco-

---

[1] Ine's laws are preserved only in an appendix to Alfred's code, but they are generally accepted to be genuine; see Wormald, 'Inter cetera bona . . . genti suae', p. 191, and *The Making of English Law*, pp. 103 and 278–80.

[2] See Chapter 1, pp. 5–8. *Pactus legis Salicae* specifies that only work related to food preparation was to be allowed, and there are differing penalties for the Salic Frank, the Roman and the slave; the slave's punishment could be a flogging. Similar distinctions are found in the *Lex Frisionum*, this time between those living in eastern and western parts of Frisia.

[3] Sections 3–3.2: 'If a slave should work on Sunday by his lord's command, he should be set free, and let the lord give thirty shillings in payment. If the slave should work without [the lord's] knowledge, let him suffer his hide. If a free man should work on that day without his lord's command, let him lose his freedom' (manuscript E); *Gesetze*, ed. Liebermann, I, 90.

[4] Sections 9–11: *Gif esne ofer dryhtnes hæse þeowweorc wyrce an sunnan æfen efter hire setlgange oþ monan æfenes setlgang, LXXX scll' se dryhtne gebete. Gif esne deþ his rade þæs dæges, VI se wið dryhten gebete oþþe sine hyd; gif friman þonne an ðane forbodenan timan, sio he healsfange scyldig; and se man se þæt arasie, he age healf þæt wite and ðæt weorc*; ibid., I, 13. The Kentish laws are preserved only in a twelfth-century manuscript, the *Textus Roffensis*.

[5] C. 45.1–46; ibid., I, 342–4. Here English and Dane, as well as free man and slave, are distinguished.

nomic impact.[6] Perhaps this is less surprising if one considers that high-ranking Church officials, bishops and archbishops, were instrumental in the formation of both of these codes.[7] Their commitment in this period is further exemplified by a canon of the Council of Clofesho (747), which requires that all secular pursuits cease to make time for the mass and instruction of the people.[8]

The laws of King Alfred add no new Sunday provisions to those of Ine, except to decree that a theft occurring on a Sunday or other holy day must be repaid two-fold.[9] During the reign of King Æthelstan (d. 939), it seems that a new ordinance, the prohibition of Sunday trade, was a matter of some controversy. IV Æthel-stan, a summary of previous codes, mentions the repeal of an earlier enactment at Grately forbidding Sunday markets.[10] The law in question threatens forfeiture of the goods and a 30-shilling fine for offenders, and, though its implementation apparently failed on this occasion, the restriction of trade and markets was to return during the time of Æthelred.[11] The following article in this code suggests how such prohibitions were to be enforced: the responsibility presumably fell to the local reeve.[12] Again, the close cooperation between ecclesiastical and secular leadership is seen in the involvement in the drafting of these codes by Archbishop Wulfhelm,[13] who perhaps knew about the prohibition of Sunday trade in Carolingian capitularies.[14]

---

6   Patrick Wormald remarks that Ine's and Wihtræd's law codes reveal 'the Church's tightening grip on Anglo-Saxon society' as well as a new determination on the part of the king to enforce (and perhaps profit from) a distinctly Christian ordering of society; *The Making of English Law*, p. 103; cf. Wormald, 'Inter Cetera Bona . . . Genti Suae', pp. 193–4.

7   Wormald speculates that Wihtræd's code is possibly a translation of a Latin synodical decree; *The Making of English Law*, p. 102, n. 355. Cf. Lendinara, 'The Kentish Laws', pp. 212–13, 218.

8   C. 14, *Councils and Ecclesiastical Documents*, ed. Haddan and Stubbs, III, 367. The council's main concern appears to have been the unity and uniformity of liturgical practice, in particular in the observance of feast days and other events in the Church calendar; see C. Cubitt, *Anglo-Saxon Church Councils, c. 650–850* (London, 1995), pp. 142–52.

9   Laws of Alfred 5.5; *Gesetze*, ed. Liebermann, I, 52–3. Translation taken from *Councils and Synods*, ed. Whitelock *et al.*, p. 25. Translations of the following laws, unless otherwise noted, are taken from this edition.

10 C. 2; *Gesetze*, ed. Liebermann, I, 171. Cf. VI Æthelstan 10; *Gesetze*, ed. Liebermann, I, 182. See Wormald, *The Making of English Law*, p. 291 and n. 130.

11 II Æthelstan 24.1 (dated by Whitelock to between 926 and 930): *And ðæt nan cyping ne sy Sunnondagum; gif hit ðonne hwa do, þolige ðæs ceapes and gesylle XXX scll.* (manuscript H); *Gesetze*, ed. Liebermann, I, 164–5. See *Councils and Synods*, ed. Whitelock *et al.*, p. 52. Apparently, Sunday markets were difficult to suppress; they were common in the twelfth century; P. Sawyer, 'Early Fairs and Markets in England and Scandinavia' in *Anglo-Saxon History: Basic Readings*, ed. D. A. E. Pelteret (New York, 2000), pp. 323–42 at 330–1.

12 II Æthelstan 25: *Gif minra gerefena hwylc (þonne) þis don nylle and læs ymbe beo þonne we gecweden habbað, þonne gylde he mine oferhryrnesse; and ic finde oþerne ðe wile* (manuscript H); *Gesetze*, ed. Liebermann, I, 164–5.

13 Wormald, *The Making of English Law*, pp. 298–300.

14 One possible source would be the collection made by Ansegisus in 825. Ansegisus I, 139 (also II, 7) reproduces Aachen 809, c. 8: *De mercato: Ut mercatus die dominico in nullo loco habeatur*; *Die Kapitulariensammlung des Ansegis*, ed. Schmitz, pp. 509 and 527–8. Around this same time Archbishop Oda issued a set of canons which include one that encourages observance of various fasts *et super omnia dominicum diem et sanctorum festivitates, sicuti canon et exempla præcedentium*

Later in the tenth century, the ecclesiastical portion of Edgar's enactments at Andover (960/2) refers to previous punishments for the neglect of Sunday observance as recorded in the *domboc*, most likely the laws of Ine as preserved by Alfred. While this seems to emphasize continuity, there also appears to be innovation: this is the first code to define the duration of Sunday observance as the period from Saturday mid-afternoon (*none*) to Monday at dawn:

> And healde man ælces Sunnandæges freols fram nontide þæs Sæternesdæges oð ðæs Monandæges lihtinge, be þam wite, þe domboc tæcð, and ælcne oðerne mæssedæg, swa he beboden beo.[15]

The earlier span of Saturday evening to Sunday evening, modelled on Leviticus XXIII.32, as seen in Wihtræd and also in Frankish sources, has been replaced, though there seems to be no precedent for this extension, whether Insular or continental.[16] Perhaps some caution is advisable, given the eleventh-century dates of the surviving manuscripts, but this is the length of time mentioned in all Old English texts thereafter, including the Sunday Letter.[17] For example, Wulfstan, bishop of Worcester and archbishop of York in the early eleventh century, clearly found it to be the usual time-span, as may be seen by his addition of the word *Sæternesdæges* in his own hand in one of the manuscripts containing the code.[18] Even the cautious Ælfric, Wulfstan's contemporary and a learned author, seems to assume that this is the correct time span in his pastoral letter written for Wulfsige, bishop of Sherborne.[19]

Wulfstan and the Eleventh-Century Law Codes

Most of the surviving Sunday legislation was written in the early part of the eleventh century by or under the direct influence of Wulfstan as he carried out his duties on behalf of two kings, Æthelred and Cnut. Judging by the frequency with

patrum affirmant, ab omni sęculari opere cautissime custodire procuretis; *Councils and Synods*, ed. Whitelock *et al.*, pp. 73–4.

[15] *Gesetze*, ed. Liebermann, I, 198–9 (manuscript G); *Councils and Synods*, ed. Whitelock *et al.*, p. 101, section 5: 'And every Sunday shall be observed as a festival from Saturday noon until dawn on Monday, under pain of the punishment which the lawbook prescribes, and every other festival as it is enjoined'. Although Whitelock here translates *nontide* as 'noon' rather than 'mid-afternoon', this seems to have been a later definition, possibly due to the desire to move the meal-hour to earlier in the day; cf. *Oxford English Dictionary*, s.v. *noon*. See also Jungmann, 'Die Heiligung des Sonntags', p. 68.

[16] Later instances may be found in 'Ælfrics Brief an Bischof Wulfsige'; *Die Hirtenbriefe Ælfrics*, ed. Fehr, p. 32; 'Letter from Cnut to the People of England' 18; *Councils and Synods*, ed. Whitelock *et al.*, pp. 440–1. I Cnut 14.2; ibid., p. 478.

[17] The manuscripts are BL Cotton Nero A.i (s. xi^med), BL Harley 55 (s. xi^1), and CCCC 201 (s. xi^med).

[18] BL Harley 55. See *Councils and Synods*, ed. Whitelock *et al.*, p. 101.

[19] C. 151, 'Ælfric's Pastoral Letter for Wulfsige III', *Councils and Synods*, ed. Whitelock *et al.*, p. 225. Whitelock, however, warns that this may be material inserted by Wulfsige, since cc. 150–8 have no counterpart in Ælfric's other letters (pp. 194–5).

which it appears in his legal writings, it was clearly one of the archbishop's key concerns. In order to ensure the proper observance of Sunday (and feast days), he repeats earlier legislation, but also draws on Carolingian enactments on the matter. One of his earliest productions is a code, probably compiled for his northern subjects after he became archbishop of York in 1002, the so-called 'Laws of Edward and Guthrum'. Whitelock has suggested that the preface attributing this code to a treaty between Edward and Guthrum was meant to convince the recalcitrant northern diocese of its antiquity, and she speculates that Wulfstan himself thought that 'the practices it mentions had been established from the time when Alfred reached an agreement with Guthrum'.[20] Echoing II Æthelstan, this code prohibits trading on pain of loss of the goods[21] and a fine, and continues the formulation in Ine/Wihtræd, in which specific penalties are set for work in general:

> Sunnandæges cypinge gif hwa agynne, þolie þæs ceapes and XII orena mid Denum and XXX scill' mid Englum. Gyf friman freolsdæge wyrce, ðolie his freotes oððe gylde wite, lahslite. Ðeowman ðolige his hyde oþþe hydgyldes. Gyf hlaford his ðeowan freolsdæge nyde to weorce, gylde lahslitte se hlaford inne on Dæne lage and wite mid Englum. Gyf friman rihtfæsten abrece, gylde wite *uel* lahslite. Gyf hit ðeowman gedo, ðolie his hyde oððe hydgyldes. Ordel and aðas syndan tocwedene freolsdagum and rihtfæstendagum; and se ðe þæt abrece, gylde lahslit mid Denum and wite mid Englum. Gif man wealdan mage, ne dyde man næfre on Sunnandæges freolse ænigne forwyrhtne, ac wylde and healde, þæt se freolsdæg agan sy.[22]

Though the amount is not specified, work, or compelling a slave to work on any feast day (*freolsdæg*), is punishable by a fine (or the Danish *lahslit*) as in Ine's code. New in this legislation is the prohibition of ordeals, oaths and executions,[23] which seems to be linked to the restriction of any legal proceedings which was

---

20 *Councils and Synods*, ed. Whitelock *et al.*, p. 302. See also Whitelock, 'Wulfstan and the So-Called Laws of Edward and Guthrum', p. 391.

21 This clause (*þolie þæs ceapes*) is omitted in c. 19 of the 'Canons of Edgar' (see below); *Councils and Synods*, ed. Whitelock *et al.*, p. 321.

22 *Gesetze*, ed. Liebermann, I, 132–3 (manuscript B); *Councils and Synods*, ed. Whitelock *et al.*, p. 310, sections 7–9.1: 'If anyone engages in trading on a Sunday, he is to forfeit the goods and 12 ores among the Danes and 30 shillings among the English. If a freeman work on a feast-day, he is to forfeit his freedom or to pay *lahslit* or a fine. A slave is to suffer a flogging or redeem himself from one. If a master compels his slave to work on a feast-day, he – the master – is to pay *lahslit* within the Danelaw and a fine among the English. If a freeman break a legally ordained fast, he is to pay a fine or *lahslit*. If a slave does so, he is to suffer a flogging or redeem himself from one. Ordeals and oaths are forbidden on feast-days and legally ordained fast-days; and he who breaks that is to pay *lahslit* among the Danes, a fine among the English. If it can be arranged, no condemned man should ever be put to death during Sunday festival, but he is to be seized and kept until the feast-day is over'.

23 Executions were prohibited at the Synod of Mainz in 813 (c. 37): *Omnes dies dominicos cum omni veneratione observare decrevimus et a servili opere abstinere, et ut mercatus in eis minime sit nec placitum, ubi aliquis ad mortem vel ad poenam iudicetur; Concilia aevi Karolini*, ed. Werminghoff, Conc. 2/1, 270. This rule is repeated by Regino of Prüm (d. 915) in *De Synodalibus causis et disciplinis ecclesiasticis* I, 386 (ed. F. G. A. Wasserschleben (Leipzig, 1840)), and by Burchard of Worms (d. 1025) in his *Decretorum Libri XX*, II.85 (PL 140, col. 641).

in evidence as early as Constantine and the Theodosian Code and later included capital punishment.[24] To Wulfstan, the equivalents appear to be the ordeal, oath-taking and the public assemblies (*folcgemota*) at which these processes took place.[25] Into the general category of legal transactions one might also place the ban on disputes (*geflit*) and the exaction of debts, both prohibited in Wulfstan's later statements.[26]

At about the same time, Wulfstan was also working on the so-called 'Canons of Edgar', also a collection of directives for the priests of his northern diocese, which again superimposes the name of a revered king in order to lend authority to its contents.[27] In a reflection of its ecclesiastical rather than secular nature, it commands sexual abstinence on feast days, an item more commonly found in penitential texts.[28] Yet it also mentions markets and public meetings, as do the secular laws. In truth, attempts to distinguish secular and ecclesiastically oriented codes in this period are bound to be misleading, since there is clearly a great overlap between the two, and the same person, Wulfstan, was composing both.

Over time, Wulfstan built on these earlier formulations. In the laws he compiled for King Æthelred (between 1008 and 1014), earlier restrictions are reiterated – markets and public meetings (now punishable by a fine), ordeals, oaths, lawsuits and sexual relations[29] – and two new additions appear, collection of debts and hunting,[30] perhaps reflecting Wulfstan's reading in Frankish legislation.[31] This

---

24 See Chapter 1, pp. 4–6.
25 For the prohibition of assemblies see V Æthelred 12.3, VI Æthelred 44, Letter of Cnut 18, I & II Cnut 15, Northumbrian Priest's Law 55, all discussed below.
26 V Æthelred 19, 20; I Cnut 17.2–17.3; *Gesetze*, ed. Liebermann, I, 242–3, 298–9. Disputes are mentioned in the *Theodulfi capitula*, c. 45; *Theodulfi capitula in England*, ed. Sauer, pp. 336–7. The term *geflit* is probably best translated '(legal) dispute(s)' in such contexts; cf. *DOE* s.v. *geflit* sense 3.a.iii 'legal dispute, lawsuit'.
27 Cc. 19, 23–5; 'The So-Called Canons of Edgar', *Councils and Synods*, ed. Whitelock *et al.*, pp. 313–38: [19] *And riht is þæt man geswice Sunnandæges cypincge* [CCCC 201 adds *and folcgemota*]; [23–5] *And riht is þæt freolsdagum and rihtfæstendagum ænig geflit ne beo betweox mannum; and riht is þæt man freolsdagum and rihtfæstendagum forga aþas and ordela; and riht is þæt ælc wer forga his wif freolstidum and rihtfæstentidum.* Whitelock suggests that c. 19 is perhaps a later addition (*Councils and Synods*, p. 303 and p. 321, n. 3).
28 See below, pp. 29–32.
29 This is apparently what is meant by the term *wifunga* here, and not, as Liebermann suggests *Hochzeiten* ('weddings'). For a full discussion of the word *wifung* and its appearance in the Old English Sunday Letter E, see the commentary, note 28.
30 VI Æthelred, c. 22.1; *Gesetze*, ed. Liebermann, I, 252–3. Hunting is also subsequently forbidden in 'An Early Draft' and in Cnut I, 15.1; see Kennedy, 'Cnut's Law Code of 1018', 76. Ælfric also alludes to this restriction in his *Colloquy* (see below). Cf. Charlemagne's *Admontio generalis*, cited on p. 15 n. 69. An interesting, albeit twelfth-century, narrative which illustrates the conflict between church attendance and private amusement may be found in the life of St Dunstan written by Eadmer (d. 1130). This records St Dunstan having to wait for King Edgar to return from hunting so that mass could begin, and subsequently exhorting the king not to hunt on Sundays; *The Memorials of St. Dunstan*, ed. W. Stubbs, Rolls Series 63 (London, 1874), p. 207.
31 The relevant clauses are V Æthelred 12.3, 13, 13.1, 18–20 (*Gesetze*, ed. Liebermann, I, 240–3); VI Æthelred 22–22.1, 25–25.2, 43.1, 44, VI Æthelred (Latin) 22.1 (*Gesetze*, ed. Liebermann, I, 252–5, 258–9 and 253); VIII Æthelred 16–17 (*Gesetze*, ed. Liebermann, I, 265). The VI Æthelred

is the last time that Wulfstan includes sexual relations in the law codes – it has been left out of his later compilation for Cnut – which suggests that he eventually considered it a subject more properly dealt with through Church discipline.[32]

There is no doubt Wulfstan's additions to his list of prohibitions were based on his continued study of legislative precedents. We have first-hand evidence of this activity in two manuscripts which were owned and annotated by him. Hatton 42 in the Bodleian Library, a ninth-century manuscript produced in northern France and brought to England, contains a copy of Ansegisus' collection of Frankish capitularies and exhibits many corrections in Wulfstan's hand.[33] Schmitz has identified many of these alterations as being the result of the archbishop's comparison between this text and a copy of Charlemagne's *Admonitio generalis*, the source for most of Ansegisus' first book. Of special interest here is one capitulary which was heavily worked over by Wulfstan but seems to have been rejected by him as inappropriate for his purposes. This is the very detailed capitulary (81) concerning Sunday observance found in the *Admonitio generalis* which forbids a long list of activities having to do with rural labour and women's household work.[34] Wulfstan apparently considered such precision in delineating Sunday work unsuitable for the Anglo-Saxon environment.[35] Another indicator of Wulfstan's interests may be seen in his 'Canon Law Collection', one copy of which – BL Cotton Nero A.i – was personally revised by him.[36] Several of the excerpts found here concern Sunday. One canon from the Frankish collection known as the *Quadripartitus* merely states that nothing other than religious duties is to be carried out on Sundays and during Easter week.[37] There is one passage concerning sexual

provisions are repeated in what Whitelock labels 'An Early Draft of Cnut's Laws' (*Councils and Synods*, pp. 431–4); this code is printed in its entirety with an introduction by A. G. Kennedy, 'Cnut's Law Code of 1018', pp. 17–81.

[32] He included it in the *Institutes of Polity*, however; see below, p. 32 n. 74. The prohibition of sexual relations on Sundays is found in only one of the manuscript versions of VI Æthelred – BL Cotton Claudius A.iii – which Wormald deems to be a kind of draft for later legislation (*The Making of English Law*, p. 334–5), and Whitelock describes as intended to provide 'guidance and clarification for a parish priest' (*Councils and Synods*, 342). Cf. K. Jost, *Wulfstanstudien*, pp. 22–30. It is worth noting that a selection from this law code was incorporated into one of Wulfstan's sermons and from there found its way into one of the Old English Sunday Letters in CCCC 419 (E56–81). Furthermore, it was copied again in another place in the same manuscript.

[33] *Die Kapitulariensammlung des Ansegis*, ed. Schmitz, pp. 110–13; see Wormald, 'Æthelred the Lawmaker', p. 73. Cf. Ker, 'The Handwriting of Archbishop Wulfstan', pp. 328–30. For Wulfstan's use of Frankish capitularies, see also Wormald, 'Archbishop Wulfstan: Eleventh-Century State-Builder', p. 18.

[34] See Chapter 1, p. 15, n. 69.

[35] As Wormald has pointed out, in reading Ansegisus' collection, Wulfstan seems to prefer the simpler statement which mentions only trade and court proceedings (Ansegisus 2.7: *Ut etiam dies dominicus sicut decet, honoretur et colatur, omnes studeant, et ut liberius fieri possit, mercata et placita a comitibus, sicut saepe ammonitum fuit, illo die prohibeantur*; *Die Kapitulariensammlung des Ansegis*, ed. Schmitz, p. 528). Bodl. Hatton 42 does not contain this book of the collection, but Wulfstan may have had access to additional copies which did (Wormald, 'Æthelred the Lawmaker', pp. 72–3).

[36] The collection has been edited by J. E. Cross and A. Hamer in *Wulfstan's Canon Law Collection*.

[37] *Quadripartitus* IV.295; *Wulfstan's Canon Law Collection*, ed. Cross and Hamer, p. 143; the inclusion

abstinence on Sunday.[38] Finally, two statutes concern what *should* take place on Sunday: priests are to preach the Gospel, and prisoners are to be looked after on that day.[39] Also informative is the inclusion of a short sermon-like piece, probably written by Ælfric, which offers a figurative interpretation of the sabbath.[40] These insights into Wulfstan's reading material, incomplete as they must necessarily be, show that he quite deliberately selected, from a variety of approaches towards Sunday legislation, what would be the most appropriate formula for English law.

It is in I and II Cnut (1020/1) that one sees the most comprehensive expression of Wulfstan's views on Sunday observance. This is a collection of previous laws, divided into ecclesiastical (I Cnut) and secular (II Cnut).[41] Of particular note is how Wulfstan divides up the various statutes which concern Sunday between these two. The former includes the following statements:

> And freolsa and fæstena healde mon rihtlice. And healde man ælces Sun-nandæges freolsunge fram Sæternesdæges none oð Monandæges lihtingce and ælcne oðerne mæssedæg swa he beboden beo. And Sunnandaga cypingce we forbeodað eac eornostlice and ælc folcgemot, butan hit for micelre neodþearfe sig. And huntaðfara and ealra woruldlicra weorca on þam halgan dæge geswicæ man georne. . . . And we forbeodað ordal and aðas freolsdagum and ymbrend-agum and lengctendagum and rihtfæstendagum and fram Aduentum Domini oð se eahtaþa dæg agan sig ofer Twelftan mæssedæge and fram Septuagessima oð XV nihton ofer Eastron. . . . And beo þam halgum tidum, ealswa hit riht is, eallum Cristenum mannum sib and som gemæne and ælc sacu totwæmed. And gyf hwa oðrum sceole borh oððe bote æt woruldlicum þingum, gelæste hit him georne ær oððe æfter.[42] (14.1–15.1, 17–17.3)

Here we have a restatement of II Edgar's general admonition to keep the feast and fast days, including Sunday from Saturday *none* until dawn Monday, though

---

of Easter week is an addition in this manuscript. For a discussion of the *Quadripartitus* as a source for this collection, see Cross and Hamer, pp. 32–3.

[38] *Wulfstan's Canon Law Collection*, ed. Cross and Hamer, p. 143 (no. 117); the sources for these are the Pseudo-Theodore II.ii (17).6, 7 and 3; *Die Bussordnungen der abendländischen Kirche*, ed. F. W. H. Wasserschleben (Halle, 1851), p. 577.

[39] *Wulfstan's Canon Law Collection*, ed. Cross and Hamer, pp. 95 (no. 67) and 115 (no. 4); the former is based on the Council of Orleans in 549 (c. 20) and the latter on Gerbald of Liège's *Statuta* (I.3).

[40] *Wulfstan's Canon Law Collection*, ed. Cross and Hamer, pp. 127–8. See the discussion of Ælfric below.

[41] I Cnut: cc. 14.1–15.1, 17–17.3; II Cnut: cc. 45–45.3; *Gesetze*, ed. Liebermann, I, 294–9 and 342–5.

[42] 'And festivals and fasts are to be properly observed. And every Sunday shall be observed as a festival from Saturday noon until dawn on Monday, and every other festival as it is enjoined. And also we earnestly forbid trading on Sundays and every public meeting, unless it be for great necessity. And one is to abstain from hunting expeditions and all secular work on that holy day. . . . And we forbid ordeals and oaths on feast-days and Ember days and days in Lent and legally ordained fast-days and from Advent until the eighth day after Twelfth Night is over and from Septuagesima until fifteen days after Easter. And at these holy seasons, as it is right, there is to be peace and unity among all Christian men, and every suit is to be laid aside. . . . And if anyone owes another a debt or compensation concerning secular matters, he is to pay it to him readily before or after'; *Councils and Synods*, ed. Whitelock *et al.*, pp. 478–81.

2. Sunday Observance in Anglo-Saxon England

no penalties are mentioned. Like VI Æthelred it forbids trading, public meetings, all secular work (*woruldlicra weorca*), ordeals and oaths, and hunting, law suits, disputes and the payment of debts.[43] One would have thought that most of these, being public activities, would more properly belong in the secular portion of Cnut's code. It is possible that the penalty was the organizing principle here. Listed under the secular provisions in II Cnut are the edicts which specify the fines for feast-day work also found in the so-called 'Laws of Edward and Guthrum'. The specific fines have, however, been changed to *healsfang* for a free man and a flogging or *hydgyld* ('a fine to escape a flogging') for a slave, which also draws on the Laws of Wihtræd in that a lord compelling a slave to work must give the slave his freedom and pay *lahslit* among the Danes and *wite* among the English. What is new is that none of these fines are assigned a specific monetary amount. As in 'Edward and Guthrum', executions are prohibited, but a provision is added to permit the sentence to be carried out if the prisoner is struggling and may try to flee.

This summary of Sunday observance laws in I and II Cnut poses no surprises; most of the previous restrictions are included and it must therefore be seen as a far-reaching authorization of rigorous Sunday observance. Royal confirmation comes in the 'Letter from Cnut to the People of England', written during this same period and at least influenced, if not revised, by Wulfstan.[44] It mentions the prohibitions against trade and assemblies and, in its homiletic ending, urges everyone to attend church, observe the fasts and honour the saints.[45]

One final Anglo-Saxon law code, this time apparently not composed by Wulfstan though certainly influenced by his writings, must be mentioned.[46] The Northumbrian 'Priests' Law', composed some time after 1023, also deals with Sunday observance in some detail.[47] Wormald has proposed that one of Wulfstan's successors wrote this text in order 'to combine and update the "Canons of Edgar" and "Peace of Edward and Guthrum"'.[48] It is divided into two parts, one aimed at priests and the other at the laity. The latter portion is to be upheld by the secular authorities, and it is this which contains the Sunday injunctions:[49]

Sunnandæges cypingc we forbeodað æghwar and ælc folgemot and ælc weorc and ælce lade ægðer ge on wæne ge on horse ge on byrdene. Se þe ænig þissa do, gilde wite: friman XII or, ðeowman ða hyde; buton wegferende, þa moton

---

43 All high feast days and other feast days were included for the prohibition of oaths, ordeals, and sexual relations in VI Æthelred, but these are applied only to Sunday in I Cnut.
44 Wormald, *The Making of English Law*, pp. 347–8.
45 *Councils and Synods*, ed. Whitelock *et al.*, pp. 440–1. The letter here draws on II Edgar and VI Æthelred, mentioned above.
46 Wormald, *The Making of English Law*, pp. 396–7.
47 Cc. 55–7; *Gesetze*, ed. Liebermann, I, 383–4 and *Councils and Synods*, ed. Whitelock *et al.*, pp. 463–4. Cf. *Das nordhumbrische Priestergesetz: Ein nachwulfstanisches Pönitential des 11. Jahrhunderts*, ed. H. P. Tenhaken (Düsseldorf, 1979), pp. 11–21. Wormald suggests it may post-date 1023 (*The Making of English Law*, p. 396).
48 *The Making of English Law*, p. 396.
49 *Councils and Synods*, ed. Whitelock *et al.*, p. 450.

27

for neode meteneade ferian; and for unfriðe man mot freolsæfenan nide fulfaran betweonan Eferwic and six mila gemete. Se þe freols oððe riht fæsten brece, gilde wite XII or.[50]

These provisions are similar to those in I Cnut, but the added details which forbid the carrying of goods by wagon, horse or on one's back are not found in other Anglo-Saxon legislation. The code also appears to forbid travel, though it does so indirectly by mentioning the exception to the rule: permission in the case of hostilities. On the other hand, it permits travellers the carrying of food, so the intent of this code remains somewhat unclear. In these two items – the carrying of goods and travel – the Northumbrian 'Priests' Law' may be drawing on another witness of additional Sunday restrictions, the penitentials, which will be examined below.[51]

The legislative record concerning Sunday observance in Anglo-Saxon England is characterized by continuity, as seen in the repetition of Ine's and Wihtræd's basic prohibition of work, though fines were adjusted to current standards. However, one can also observe a continued attempt to refine and modify this foundation: Æthelstan's codes temporarily attempt to introduce trade restrictions, and Edgar's appears to lengthen the time period to include Saturday afternoon and Monday morning. Yet the most comprehensive legislation in this area is linked to one man, Wulfstan of York, in work compiled during the first quarter of the eleventh century. His interest in this issue – and in the process of writing law itself – can be seen as parallel to that of the administrations of Charlemagne and his immediate successors.[52] Both hoped to establish an ordered Christian society, a goal which required that the populace regularly participate in the rites of the Church and receive at least a rudimentary education in their Christian duties during the Sunday meeting.[53] In order to ensure that this participation took place, the importance and sanctity of Sunday had to be underscored by both secular and ecclesiastical authorities.

We will never know, of course, to what extent the English people were aware

[50] *Councils and Synods*, ed. Whitelock *et al.*, pp. 463–4, sections 55–7: 'Sunday market we forbid everywhere, and every public assembly and all work and all carrying (of goods), whether by wagon or by horse or on one's back. He who does any of these things is to pay the penalty: a freeman twelve ores, a slave with a flogging; except for travellers, who are permitted to carry sustenance for their needs; and in case of hostility one may travel because of necessity between York and a distance of six miles on the eve of festivals. He who then violates a festival or a legal fast is to pay twelve ores' fine.'

[51] However, a statute (c. 81) in Charlemagne's *Admonitio generalis* specifies the circumstances under which the use of a cart may be allowed, in the case of hostilities, the need for provisions or to carry a corpse to the grave: *et tria carraria opera licet fieri in die dominico, id est ostilia carra vel victualia vel si forte necesse erit corpus cuiuslibet ducere ad sepulcrum*; *Capitularia regum Francorum I*, ed. Boretius, p. 61. Cf. *Lex Baiuvariorum*, cited above, p. 7. See also Jeremiah XVII.27, which forbids carrying a load on the sabbath.

[52] See Wormald, 'Æthelred the Lawmaker', pp. 73–5.

[53] For the close connection between ecclesiastical concerns and the secular law codes see M. P. Richards, 'Anglo-Saxonism in the Old English Laws', pp. 40–59. The similarities to Carolingian objectives have been most recently discussed by Joyce Hill, 'Archbishop Wulfstan: Reformer?', p. 318.

of the existence of these laws, let alone how widespread compliance to them was. Some additional evidence from ecclesiastical sources can bear further witness to an interest in the subject, but at the same time underscores our lack of evidence concerning actual practice. Nevertheless, it is clear that the Church sought to apply additional pressures in order to enforce Sunday observance.

The Penitential Texts

The penitential texts produced and translated during the Anglo-Saxon period offer another perspective, which corroborates but also complicates the picture.[54] An early example in Latin is the penitential associated with Archbishop Theodore (d. 690), which records that the Greeks and Romans permit rowing and riding on Sunday, but that the baking of bread, riding in a cart to go anywhere other than church, bathing and – for the Greeks alone – writing in public are forbidden.[55] Washing of head and feet was, however, permitted; an interesting distinction.[56] Discipline for Sunday work was – and here the reference is again to Greek practice – first a reprimand, then confiscation of part of the goods produced and finally a whipping or penance of fasting.[57] The tariff for sexual relations on Sunday is

---

54 Thomas P. Oakley sees the assignment of penance for various offences as supplemental to the secular codes; 'The Cooperation of Mediaeval Penance and Secular Law', *Speculum* 7 (1932), 515–24 and idem, *English Penitential Discipline and Anglo-Saxon Law in their Joint Influence* (New York, 1923), pp. 136–49. A more recent study by Carole Hough, however, maintains that 'the evidence indicates rather that the penitential system derived support from secular law' and not vice versa; 'Penitential Literature and Secular Law in Anglo-Saxon England' *Anglo-Saxon Studies in Archaeology and History* 11 (2000), 133–41 at 139.

55 *Pœnitentiale Theodori*, Book 2, VII.1–2: *In Dominico Greci et Romani navigant et æquitant, panem non faciunt, neque in curru pergunt nisi ad æcclesiam tantum, nec balneant se. Greci in Dominica non scribunt publice; tunc pro necessitate seorsum in domu scribunt; Councils and Ecclesiastical Documents*, ed. Haddan and Stubbs, III.196. Allen Frantzen notes that, unlike much of Theodore's penitential, the section on Sunday observance was not based on Irish sources; 'Tradition', pp. 28–9. For authorship, see T. Charles-Edwards, 'The Penitential of Theodore and the *Iudicia Theodori*', pp. 141–74. Egbert of York (d. 766), in his own compilation which draws heavily on Theodore's, leaves out the subject of Sunday observance. The penitential attributed to Bede, though it was most probably compiled on the Continent, makes only brief mention of Sunday (7.7: *Qui operatur die Dominico, VII. dies peniteat*); *Councils and Ecclesiastical Documents*, ed. Haddan and Stubbs, III, 332. See Frantzen, 'Tradition', pp. 30–5.

56 See also the *Judicium Clementis* (c. 7), of disputed authorship (perhaps Willibrord), which forbids shaving and the washing of the head and proposes the severe tariffs of a seven-day penance for the first offence, forty days for the second, and even excommunication for the recalcitrant; *Councils and Ecclesiastical Documents*, ed. Haddan and Stubbs, III, 226. The Council of Orleans (538) condemns the belief that nothing pertaining to the beautification of house or person should be done, and Gregory I, as noted above (pp. 9–10), also mentions the prohibition against bathing as reprehensible 'Judaizing'. The *Penitential of Silos* (XI [107], *c*. 800) implies that the washing of the head on Sundays was forbidden by permitting it in the case of necessity; J. T. McNeill and H. M. Gamer, *Medieval Handbooks of Penance* (New York, 1990), p. 289.

57 Book 1, XI.1: *Qui operantur die Dominico, eos Greci prima vice arguunt, secunda tollunt aliquid ab eis, tertia vice partem tertiam de rebus eorum, aut vapulent, vel VII. diebus peniteant; Councils*

comparatively mild: one to three days of penance.[58] The references to differing Greek and Roman practices in Theodore's penitential suggest an awareness of varying customs, but unfortunately do not offer much insight into which of these would have been considered obligatory at the time the penitential was in use.

It is clear that this penitential text points to a somewhat different sphere of Sunday regulation from what we have seen in the law codes, though occasionally there are points of overlap. The requirement of sexual abstinence on Sundays (which includes Saturday nights) is a persistent one which appears frequently in the penitentials but is also, as we have seen, occasionally found in other contexts.[59] Its origin may lie in the notion that some time should elapse between sexual relations and reception of the eucharist.[60] Bathing was also seen as forbidden, as was travel (at least by wagon).[61] The latter, though a more public act, is rarely mentioned in the laws. In general, though there is some overlap, one can observe two more or less distinct sets of restrictions, one enforced by a fine or other civil penalty and the other by Church discipline through an act of penance.

---

and Ecclesiastical Documents, ed. Haddan and Stubbs, III, 186. See a similar loss of a third of one's property in the *Lex Alamannorum* (c. 38): *Si autem post tertiam correptionem in hoc vitio inventus fuerit et Deo vacare die Dominico neglexerit et opera servile fecerit, tunc tertiam partem de hereditatem suam perdat*; *Leges Alamannorum*, ed. K. Lehmann, MGH, LL nat. Germ. 5/1 (Hanover, 1888), 98.

[58] Book 1, XIV.20: *Qui nubit die Dominico, petat a Deo indulgentiam, et I. vel IIbus vel IIIbus. diebus peniteat*; Haddan and Stubbs, III, 189. Cf. Book 2, XII.1 (*Councils and Ecclesiastical Documents*, ed. Haddan and Stubbs, III, 199). See also *Wulfstan's Canon Law Collection*, Recension B, 117 (ed. Cross and Hamer, p. 143). The source is Pseudo-Theodore (II.ii [17]), and the tariff is seven days' penance for sexual relations on Sunday, three days for Wednesdays and Fridays, and a year for the same during Lent. An Old English penitential containing extracts from those of Cummean, Halitgar and Theodore, also forbids sexual relations during certain periods, including the eve of Sunday: *and ælcon gesynhiwen gebyreð, þæt hy heora clænnesse healdon XL daga and nihta ær þam halgan eastron and ealle þa easterwican and æfre sunnannihte and wodnesnihte and frigenihte*; *Die Altenglische Version des Halitgar'schen Bussbuches*, ed. Raith, p. 29.

[59] Apart from the law codes mentioned above, Wulfstan mentions it in his *Institutes of Polity* (see below, n. 74), and, as noted above (pp. 11 n. 49, 13), Caesarius of Arles and Gregory of Tours speak of the horrible fate of children conceived on Sunday. Cf. *Concilium Foroiuliense* (Friuli), c. 13; *Concilia aevi Karolini*, ed. Werminghoff, Conc. 2/1, 194: *mandamus Christianis, abstinere primum ab omni peccato et ab omni opere carnali, etiam a propriis coniugibus*.

[60] See P. Payer, 'Early Medieval Regulations concerning Marital Sexual Relations', *Journal of Medieval History* 6 (1980), pp. 353–76 at 367; H. Lutterbach, *Sexualität im Mittelalter: eine Kulturstudie anhand von Bußbüchern des 6. bis 12. Jahrhunderts* (Cologne, 1999), pp. 76–80; and Kottje, *Studien zum Einfluss des alten Testaments*, pp. 69–83. See also a chart provided by Thomas in *Der Sonntag im frühen Mittelalter*, pp. 109–10. Caesarius of Arles mentions the need for abstinence a few days prior to sacred feasts; *Sermo XVI.2*, ed. Morin, CCSL 103, 78. Theodulf of Orléans requires sexual abstinence before reception of the eucharist in his *Capitula* (c. 44); *Theodulfi capitula*, ed. Sauer, pp. 398–9. The issue also seems to be implied in the question of how soon after sexual relations a man may enter the church which is addressed in Bede's *Historia ecclesiastica* in the responses given by Pope Gregory; B. Colgrave and R. A. B. Mynors, ed. and trans., *Bede's Ecclesiastical History of the English People* (Oxford, 1969), pp. 94–9.

[61] See above, pp. 7–8. The Council of Orleans (538) notes that the people are convinced that travel by means of horse, oxen or wagon as well as cleaning house or person and cooking are all forbidden but does not condone such 'Jewish' restrictions (see above, p. 8).

Theodore's penitential was also used on the Continent and, in the tenth century, returned to England and was translated into Old English.[62] Three manuscripts containing penitential material excerpt the above passages in the vernacular: Brussels, Bibliothèque royale, 8558–63 (s. x¹); Bodl. Laud Misc. 482 (s. xi^med); and Bodl. Junius 121 (s. xi³ᐟ⁴).[63] All of these include the references to Greek practice concerning a first warning and the confiscation of goods, but one (Laud) adapts the punishment for a third offence to what looks like something closer to the secular legal codes: slaves are to be flogged and freemen to do seven days of penance.[64] They omit the permission to wash head and feet,[65] and the latest manuscript, Junius 121, omits entirely the section on riding, rowing, baking and bathing.

Another witness to the penitential tradition is a confessional prayer which survives in two manuscripts dated more than a century apart.[66] The neglect of Sunday features as part of a detailed list of sins, and *sunandæges 7 nihtes gylta* ('sins of Sunday and of [Saturday] night'), presumably of a sexual nature, are confessed, as are the neglect of spiritual works and church attendance in favour of improper behaviour such as unnecessary wandering about, idle speech and laughter, and indulgence in food and drink.[67]

In its introduction – unusual for this date – of what later becomes a central complaint,[68] people's habit of spending the day in debauchery, rather than in prayer and the performance of good deeds, this prayer resembles a section of another Old English text, the *Theodulfi capitula*.[69] Originally written at the

---

[62] Frantzen, 'Tradition', pp. 30 and 49–56.

[63] These manuscripts are discussed by Frantzen in 'Tradition', pp. 40–9.

[64] *Gyf hit synt þeowe men, and hig hit hyra willes doð, syn hy beswungene, and gif hit syn freo men, fæsten hy VII niht flæsce and ealað*; *Quellen*, ed. Mone, pp. 515–16.

[65] Brussels 8558–63 and Laud 482; see *Quellen*, ed. Mone, pp. 482–548 (sections 90–1, 108). Mone edits the collection from the Brussels and Laud manuscripts. The relevant sections of the Junius manuscript are printed in *Das altenglische Bussbuch*, ed. Spindler, pp. 185 and 188 (sections 19p, 21g). See Frantzen, *The Literature of Penance*, pp. 132–3.

[66] The first is in BL Cotton Vespasian D.xx (s. x^med); the second, shortened version is in BL Cotton Tiberius C.i (s. xi²). Both are edited by H. Logeman, in 'Anglo-Saxonica minora', *Anglia* 11 (1889), 97–120 at 97–110 and 100–3, respectively. They are compared by Max Förster, 'Zur Liturgik der Angelsächsischen Kirche', *Anglia* 66 (1942), 1–51 at 30–6. See also Frantzen, 'Tradition', pp. 45–7. Frantzen notes that although the context in the Vespasian version seems to be devotional, such prayers seem to have their origin in public confession taking place in a reconciliation ceremony before a bishop, as in the Tiberius version.

[67] *Ic eom ondetta goda & ðe menniscum men minum gastlicum læce sunandæges & nihtes gylta & oðerra haligra tida þonne ice sceolde gastlicu weorc wyrccan & on ðæm ic yfelade ðæs ðe ic ðonne don ne sceolde onnyttum luste ge on manifealdum recceleasnyssum gedyde & on oferæte & on oferdruncne & me is & me wæs min unnyt willa micles leof ge on dæg ge on niht, Ic ondette þæt ic wæs to læt mine ciricean to seccanne in ealle tid*; Logemann, 'Anglo-Saxonica minora', p. 99.

[68] See G. R. Owst, 'The People's Sunday Amusements in the Preaching of Mediæval England', *Holborn Review*, n.s. 17 (1926), 32–45.

[69] C. 45 (manuscript A): *Forþon hit is se wyresta gewuna þæt monige men ægðer ge Sunnandagum ge eac oðrum mæssedagum begað, þæt is þætte hig sona on ærnemergen willað mæssan gehyran, ond sona æfter þære mæssan, from ærnemergenne ofer ealne dæg, on druncennysse ond on wiste hiora wombe þeowiað, nas God*; *Theodulfi capitula*, ed. Sauer, p. 401.

beginning of the ninth century by Theodulf of Orléans and translated into Old English in the second half of the tenth century, the *Capitula* were important to the tenth-century Benedictine reform.[70] Perhaps drawing on the penitential tradition, it forbids worldly work (*weoruldweorc*), but significantly permits food preparation and travel in the case of necessity.[71] In support of the sanctity of the day, it uses a short Sunday List which includes creation, the sending of manna, the Resurrection and Pentecost. Not surprisingly the penitentials, prayers and Theodulf's collection do not present a consistent picture, and their selection of restricted activities seems arbitrary to the modern mind, but that does not mean that they were never applied or enforced. Though Frantzen comments on the conservative nature of the penitential literature which complicates its use as a guide to current practice, such evidence can at the very least supplement other sources.[72]

Sunday Observance in the Anglo-Saxon Sermons

In light of this caution, it may be telling that the two major writers of this time period, Wulfstan and Ælfric, abbot of Eynsham, though they knew and used the penitentials and Theodulf's *Capitula*, did not, when it came to other matters, draw on them for their own statements on the subject of Sunday.[73] In the educational material which they and others produced, there is a surprising lack of specificity, given that one might have expected it to provide support for the evidence examined thus far. Wulfstan himself curiously only mentions the honouring of Sunday briefly in his homiletic work.[74] The obligation to honour Sunday is conspicuously absent in the homiletic literature predating Ælfric, i.e. in the Blickling and Vercelli collections; the observance of Sunday as a day of rest seems to be taken for granted. In a homily preserved in three eleventh-century manuscripts,[75] the first

---

[70] Ibid., pp. 7 and 74.

[71] C. 24, ibid., p. 337.

[72] 'Tradition', p. 27.

[73] Ælfric's use of Theodulf's *Capitula* is less certain; *Theodulfi capitula*, ed. Sauer, pp. 281–3.

[74] Bethurum Xc.107: *Sunnandæges weorðunge nænig man forgyme* ('No one should neglect the honouring of Sunday'). Also, the *Sermo Lupi ad Anglos* mentions *freolsbryca* in a list of sinners (Bethurum XX[c] 139). In addition, two pieces by him, Napier XXIII and L, which were probably unfinished drafts of homilies also mention Sunday, though they simply cite the law codes forbidding trade, meetings, oaths and ordeals (XXIII only). Another composition, Napier LVIII, includes a passage drawn from Wulfstan's *Institutes of Polity*, which forbids marital sex on many days including on the eve of every Sunday: *þeah læwedum mannum wif si alyfed, swaðeah hi agan micele þearfe, þæt hi understandan, hu hit is alyfed. ... Nagan læwede men þurh hæmedþingc, gif hi godes milste habban willað, wifes gemanan sunnannihtum ne mæssenihtum ne wodnesnihtum ne frigenihtum ne næfre on lenctentide ne næfre, þonne fæsten aboden sy, þe ma, þe man mot on lenctene oððe frigedagum flæsces brucan* (17–26); The *Institutes of Polity* has a shorter version of this: *Nagan læwede men freolstidum ne fæstentidum þurh hæmedþingc wifes gemanan* (II.92, *Die 'Institutes of Polity Civil and Ecclesiastical'*, ed. K. Jost (Bern, 1959), pp. 134–5); cf. 'The So-Called Canons of Edgar' c. 25, cited in note 27.

[75] CCCC 162 and 198 and Bodl. Bodley 340. CCCC 162 contains three texts which deal with Sunday: Old English Letter D and two homilies, for Holy Saturday and Easter Sunday, Schaefer III and V.

sabbath is called *se æresta restedæg* ('the first rest-day') and is then equated with *se halga drihtenlica dæg þe we nu Sunnandæg nemniað* ('that holy Lord's day which we now call Sunday').[76] The homilist explains that under the New Law we are commanded to rest on this day because of Christ's Resurrection, but then goes on to bolster his argument with a reference to its being the first day of creation and the day on which all the most holy spiritual events (*þa gastlican gewyrde*) took place.[77] A statement that those who do not observe Sunday with honour, rest and worship are breaking God's law closes this very brief explanation of Sunday observance.

Other anonymous homilists content themselves with simple exhortations to cease all work and attend church, but they sometimes also attempt to provide some rationale for the sanctity of Sunday.[78] So a homily preserved in two manuscripts written around the turn of the millennium simply exhorts the congregation, *forlæten we ælc oðer wurc, and ælce woruldlice bysga, and cumen we to godes ciercean* ('let us forsake all other work and every worldly business and come to the church of God').[79] An Easter day sermon, following a list of negative events that happened on a Friday, offers a version of the Sunday List, a catalogue of positive events meant to underscore the importance of Sunday.[80] It begins with creation and includes Christ's baptism, St John's vision on Patmos, and, of course, the Resurrection.[81] Similarly, in another sermon, the subject of the six days of creation leads to the typological interpretation which sees these as Christ's labour on earth, after which he rested on the seventh day in the tomb; believers will receive their reward on the seventh day, and on the eighth day, those who kept Sunday will rejoice.[82] These varying statements on the subject of Sunday observance show little concern with specific restrictions and instead assume that congregations would know from other sources what was required.

Characteristically, Ælfric reaches back to a patristic explanation of the sabbath commandment, but also finds reasons to honour Sunday with worship and rest. His view, as laid out in a pastoral letter he wrote for Wulfstan as well as in two homilies,[83] is that the Jews honoured the sabbath as a day of rest (*restendæg*),

[76] Schaefer III.122–4. Though the source of this homily, Haymo of Auxerre, makes clear that Sunday is the first day after the sabbath (*primum diem post sabbatum*), this homily does not appear to draw a distinction between the two (*Hwæt is se æresta restedæg þe he on ðam wordum mænde, buton þæt hit wæs se halga drihtenlica dæg þe we nu Sunnandæg nemniað*).

[77] Schaefer III.127.

[78] The early prohibition against fasting on Sundays is also repeated, for example in Assmann XI.52.

[79] R. Brotanek, ed., *Texte und Untersuchungen zur altenglischen Literatur und Kirchengeschichte* (Halle, 1913), p. 23.

[80] The Sunday List is discussed in more detail below, pp. 59–60, 93–8; the Old English versions of the Sunday Letter make extensive use of it.

[81] Schaefer V.31–69.

[82] Napier XLVII, 244.10–21.

[83] 'Ælfrics zweiter altenglischer Brief an Erzbischof Wulfstan (Chrismabrief)' (sections 126–7); *Die Hirtenbriefe Ælfrics*, ed. Fehr, pp. 194–6. The homilies are *CH* II, XII.273–311 and Irvine III.272–311 (commentary at pp. 52–6); S. Irvine, ed., *Old English Homilies from MS Bodley 343*, EETS os 302 (Oxford, 1993). In addition, a short piece entitled *Incipit de sabbato* and attributed to Ælfric is

which typologically prefigured Christ's body resting in the tomb after his life and work on earth,[84] but for Christians the prohibition against servile work (*þeowetlicum weorce*) on the sabbath has the spiritual (tropological) meaning of cessation from sin during life, since the one who sins is the servant of sin.[85] One mention is also made of the anagogical interpretation of the sabbath, its prefiguration of eternal rest.[86]

Ælfric is also interested in the interactions between Christ and the Jews concerning the sabbath which he finds in the Gospels. In two different sermons the above typological interpretation of the Jewish sabbath is prompted by a narration of Christ's healing and the ensuing controversy. Even though Ælfric in one instance feels compelled to explain how a sinless Christ could have broken the sabbath, his answer is far from satisfying: *He heold þonne restandæg þeah ðe he ihælde þonne blindan, forðan ðe he leofede his lif buton synnum* ('He kept the sabbath day, though he healed the blind man, because he lived his life without sin').[87] On the whole Ælfric appears to be more concerned that the members of his audience understand that the Jewish rest-day is no longer a requirement for Christians.

Having thus dispensed with the sabbath commandment, Ælfric simply states as fact that Sunday, the rest-day of Christians (*cristenra manna restendæg*), is to be held in honour instead, because it is the day on which Christ rose from the dead.[88] In some places, Ælfric adds other events, which suggests he may have known of the Sunday List tradition,[89] and in his homily for the tenth Sunday after Pentecost he adds that Christ *manega wundra geworhte on ðam dæge* ('performed many miracles on that day [Sunday]').[90] Proper Sunday observance is simply stated in Ælfric's writings: church attendance is required,[91] and worldly labour (*woroldlicum weorcum*),[92] fasting or kneeling, excessive feasting and drunkenness are all

printed in *Wulfstan's Canon Law Collection* (ed. Cross and Hamer, pp. 127). See a discussion of the latter in M. R. Godden, 'Anglo-Saxons on the Mind', *Learning and Literature in Anglo-Saxon England: Studies Presented to Peter Clemoes on the Occasion of his Sixty-Fifth Birthday*, ed. M. Lapidge and H. Gneuss (Cambridge, 1985), pp. 271–98 at 282–5; and idem, *Ælfric's Catholic Homilies: Introduction, Commentary and Glossary*, EETS ss 18 (Oxford, 2000), pp. 456–9; in the latter, Godden provides sources for Ælfric's thought including passages from Augustine and Bede.

84   *CH* II, XII.300–7 and *De sabbato*. Cf. Pope II.216–19.
85   'Brief III', section 127; Irvine III.278–92; and *De sabbato*.
86   *CH* II, XII.308–11: *Oðer restendæg is us eac toweard. þæt is þæt ece lif. on ðam bið an dæg buton ælcere niht. on þam we us gerestað ecelice. gif we nu ðeowtlicera weorca. þæt sind synna geswicað.*
87   Irvine III.293–4. The other homily in which a discussion of the Jewish sabbath follows the Gospel narrative is Pope II.211 ff.
88   Irvine III.295–7; *CH* II, XII.302–8; 'Brief III', *Die Hirtenbriefe Ælfrics*, ed. Fehr, section 127.
89   In the letter to Wulfstan, he lists the Resurrection and the first day of creation and in *De sabbato* adds Pentecost.
90   Pope XVI.81. Cf. D10–11: *and þæt ge gehealdan sunnandæg fram eallum woruldlicum weorcum, forðanðe God geworhte manega wundra on ðam sunnandæge*; also C29–30. Both of these homilies follow this statement with a Sunday List. Cf. *CH* I, VI.169: *Se sunnandæg is fyrmest on gesceapenysse and on endebyrdnysse, and on wurþmynte.*
91   Pope XVI.83.
92   Pope XVIII.341.

2. Sunday Observance in Anglo-Saxon England

forbidden.[93] Such lack of detail in defining illicit work suggests that Ælfric, like the other Anglo-Saxon homilists, assumes his audience already knows how to keep the Lord's day holy.[94]

In this regard we do have one interesting clue that Ælfric supported the Sunday legislation of his time. In his *Colloquy*, an educational text for schoolboys learning Latin, the hunter is asked whether he hunted that day and answers: *'Non fui, quia dominicus dies est, sed heri fui in uenatione'* ('I did not, because it is the Lord's day, but yesterday I hunted').[95] It may be said that Ælfric represents the attitude towards Sunday observance which we might expect from a learned scholar of the time. He combines his knowledge of the patristic interpretations of the sabbath law with the by now well-established custom of Sunday rest and worship, based on the sanctity of the day originating in its association with the Resurrection. Nothing suggests that Ælfric saw the legislative activities of his contemporary, Wulfstan, as in any way excessively sabbatarian.

Nevertheless, apart from the Sunday Letter itself, Anglo-Saxon homilists show little interest in detailed descriptions of Sunday prohibitions. One can only surmise that the clergy were content to allow the secular arm to regulate the various Sunday restrictions regarding work, trade and legal proceedings. The evidence of the penitentials provides us with the possibility for the enforcement of additional restrictions which are not mentioned in the law codes, but their application is far from certain. However, for present purposes, it is significant that nearly every restriction mentioned in the Sunday Letter can be found in either the law codes or in the penitential literature, and, at the very least, this helps the modern reader to gain some perspective on what may otherwise be seen as reflecting excessive sabbatarianism in that text. Since all of the extant copies of the Old English Sunday Letter date from the eleventh century, and the scarcity and nature of the references to Sunday in other homiletic texts hardly echo the urgency of the letter, we should exercise caution when it comes to determining the actual scope of the letter's influence, especially before that time. On the other hand, the disparity between the stated requirements and the paucity of texts which might be used to communicate them may point to a need for just the kind of strong reinforcing statement that the Sunday Letter provided and may have contributed to its surprisingly warm reception at the end of the Anglo-Saxon period.

---

93 *LS* XII.7–9.
94 In his homily *De falsis diis*, Pope XXI.174–5, Ælfric shows that he knows of a Danish habit of celebrating Thursday in honour of Jove: *þone fiftan dæg hi freolsodan mærlice, Ioue to wyrðmynte, þam mærestan gode* ('the fifth day [of the week] they celebrate greatly, in honour of Jove, the most famous god'). However, what practices this may have involved is not stated, so we cannot be sure that it refers to the kinds of taboos mentioned by Caesarius of Arles centuries earlier (see above, p. 10).
95 *Ælfric's Colloquy*, ed. Garmonsway, p. 24.

3

The Latin Sunday Letter

As seen from the preceding brief look at Sunday observance in the early Middle Ages, the sixth century was fertile ground for the creation of a piece such as the Sunday Letter.[1] It was a time when there was a great need to convince the newly converted of the importance of setting aside time once a week for the rituals of the Church and basic instruction in its tenets. Although one might assume that compliance with this injunction was at best intermittent, it seems that a popular belief in taboo-like restrictions developed independently and was perhaps encouraged to ensure that the day was set aside for worship and, ideally, good deeds. Whoever wrote the Sunday Letter – and we should bear in mind that we can only guess at its original form – he must have felt either that the obligation of Sunday rest was not sufficiently recognized or that it was inadequately observed. In the absence of convincing theological justification from the Church, our writer saw himself as providing divine confirmation of practices which, though not required by the fathers, were in the process of becoming obligatory. He clearly had no reservations about the new dogma, nor, apparently, about composing a piece which claims to speak in the voice of Christ. As we shall see, it is this latter offence that caused the most consternation among the letter's medieval readers.

In this chapter, I will outline the recensions of the known Latin versions of the Sunday Letter. It may, however, be useful to begin with a brief synopsis of its contents.[2] The way in which the Sunday Letter accounts for its divine origin is by devising an elaborate narrative of its arrival in Christendom. Written by Christ, it falls from heaven to Jerusalem (Recensions I and III) and travels to Rome or is received there by a Bishop Peter (Recension II). In the earliest version, a story of its being transmitted from priest to priest is related, after which a three-day period of fasting and prayer is held in which divine guidance on its import is sought. In the letter proper Christ speaks in the first person and warns believers of impending doom if Sunday is not honoured more zealously. While the initial version featured lists which enumerate specific prohibitions, the bulk of the letter, particularly in the later recensions, concerns the dire consequences of disobedience, which are drawn predominantly from biblical sources: for example, many resemble the plagues visited on the Egyptians prior to the Exodus of the Israelites, while others promise a devouring fire or other national calamities, or introduce novel horrors such as venomous flying serpents. Similarly, the blessings of obedience (fewer in number) also derive from those promised to the ancient Israelites for obeying the laws laid out in Leviticus. The letter closes with a return to the external framework of its arrival. In some versions the receiving bishop swears to its origin and

---

[1] The Sunday Letter is also referred to as the 'Heavenly Letter', 'Letter from Heaven' or the 'Letter of Christ' in the literature; its designation in the manuscripts is most often some variation of *Epistola Christi*. The term *Carta Dominica* has no basis in the Latin versions and should be retired. The Sunday Letter also bears no relationship to the so-called 'Letter of Abgar'.

[2] More details may be found below, pp. 57–62.

authenticity, and in others a date for the coming destruction is suggested. The conclusion may also contain exhortations which urge the dissemination of the letter. These, very broadly, are the elements which appear with great regularity in the letter as it was rewritten and adapted over its long history.

That history spans the entire Middle Ages and extends even into the modern period.[3] The letter was translated into numerous vernaculars including Old Norse, Old French, Old Irish, Middle High German, Welsh, and, of course, Old English.[4] In the East we find Greek, Armenian, Syriac, Garshuni, Arabic, and Ethiopian versions.[5] It is astonishing, and perhaps somewhat disturbing, to see the phenomenal success of such doubtful material.

Fortunately, though the popularity and survival of the Sunday Letter may confirm our worst suspicions about the gullibility and lack of discernment of medieval clergy, we can also derive some comfort from the fact that it was regularly recognized as a fraud. As it happens, we would have no knowledge of its earliest manifestations were it not for several authoritative condemnations which are still extant, and it is particularly instructive to observe what most worried its earliest readers.

The first of these denunciations dates from the end of the sixth century and appears in a letter written by Licinianus, bishop of Cartagena, to Vincentius, bishop of Ibiza, concerning his possession of the Sunday Letter. Licinianus is clearly offended by the letter's claim to be Christ's words and condemns its inferior style and unsound doctrine (*nec sermo elegans, nec doctrina sana*).[6] He believes that the practices advocated in the letter go well beyond honouring the day for the sake of Christ's Resurrection and accuses its author of trying to 'Judaize' by forbidding travel and the preparation of food.[7] Licinianus would prefer that a man garden and travel or a woman engage in spinning wool on Sunday than dance and sing worthless songs which only stir up the passions. In addition to this, he cannot believe that Christ would add to scripture (the prophets and the apostles), which, with the exception of Moses' stone tablets, did not drop from heaven but

---

3   The early history of the letter has been laid out in numerous places; the most detailed are the following: Priebsch, *Letter from Heaven*, pp. 1–9; Delehaye, 'Note sur la légende de la lettre du Christ tombée du ciel', pp. 174–7 and 207–13; Renoir, 'Christ (lettre du) tombée du ciel', cols. 1534–77; Jones, 'The Heavenly Letter in Medieval England', pp. 163–78; Deletant, 'The Sunday Legend', pp. 431–51.

4   For references, see below.

5   See Bittner, *Der vom Himmel gefallene Brief Christi*, pp. 1–240. These have more recently been examined by M. Van Esbroeck, 'La lettre sur le dimanche, descendue du ciel', *Analecta Bollandiana* 107 (1989), 267–84. Cf. A. Otero, 'Der apokryphe sogenannte Sonntagsbrief', *Studia Patristica* 3 (Berlin, 1961), 290–6 (includes references to Slavic and Romanian versions); and F. Praetorius, *Mazhafa Tomâr, das äthiopische Briefbuch* (Leipzig, 1869). Additional, mostly post-medieval, versions (in Hungarian, Polish, Czech, Russian) are discussed by Deletant (see n. 3, above). See also F. Stegmüller, *Repertorium biblicum medii aevi* (Barcelona, 1940), I, 121–3 (no. 148).

6   *Liciniani, Carthaginensis episcopi, Epistola III, ad Vincentium episcopum, Ebositanae insulae*, PL 72, cols. 699–700.

7   *Sed, quantum sentio, ideo novus iste praedicator hoc dicit, ut nos judaizare compellat, ut nullus sibi in eodem die [necessarium victum] praeparet, aut viam ambulet* (col. 699).

was given by the Holy Spirit. Clearly, Licinianus' theology of Sunday is based on the view that requires no rest and indeed considers such abstention from work a temptation to engage in frivolous amusements. Just as importantly, we learn from his correspondence of the claim that this early form of the letter had fallen from heaven onto the altar of Christ at the shrine of St Peter the Apostle,[8] elements which will help to identify it with Recension I, as will be shown below.

The next witness to the letter provides further evidence of its spread and a first glimpse of its contents.[9] A certain Aldebert, an itinerant preacher active in Gaul, was condemned at the Council of Soissons in 744 and again came under scrutiny at a Lateran synod the following year.[10] On the latter occasion, Archbishop Boniface sent Pope Zacharias all the evidence, including a Sunday Letter, he had accumulated against both Aldebert and an Irishman named Clemens. After a review of this material, the two are unanimously denounced. The letter does not occasion much debate but is left to speak for itself in the meeting, eliciting only the following remark from the pope:

> Pro certo, karissimi fratres, et predictus in insaniam conversus Aldebertus et omnis, qui hanc utitur scelere commentatam epistolam, parvulorum more absque memoria mentium esse possunt et quibusdam mulieris insaniunt sensibus. Sed ut ne leviores adhuc amplius decipiant, indiscussam et absque sententia causam hanc in eum relinquere minime possumus.[11]

There is no question that Pope Zacharias considers the contents of the letter to be beyond the need for extensive deliberation and the entire assembly agrees with this verdict. He identifies the letter as 'fabricated' (*commentatam*) and also notes that it was 'used' (*utitur*), in other words, he suspects some manipulative intent which takes advantage of the letter's apocalyptic tone and subject matter. No doubt this impression was prompted by the other stratagems of Aldebert,[12] but it was not to be the last time that a marginal figure would avail himself of the letter's evident ability to stir up religious emotion and produce a following.

The assembly of 745 decided, perhaps unwisely, not to burn the heretical writings used by Aldebert, but rather to preserve them as evidence.[13] Any effort to stop reproduction of the Sunday Letter was doomed to fail, however, since it would

---

8   *Ipsa epistola ... de coelo descendit super altare Christi in memoria sancti Petri apostoli* (col. 700).

9   The records preserve a short excerpt of the letter's introduction, revealing it to be an example of the Recension I-type letter, which details its being passed from priest to priest before its arrival in Rome; *Die Briefe des heiligen Bonifatius und Lullus*, ed. Tangl, p. 115.

10 A full account is given by J. B. Russell in 'Saint Boniface and the Eccentrics', *Church History* 33 (1964), 235–47; see also A. Hauck, *Kirchengeschichte Deutschlands* (Berlin, 1952), I, 515–17.

11 *Die Briefe des heiligen Bonifatius und Lullus*, ed. Tangl, pp. 115–16. 'Certainly, beloved brothers, this aforementioned Aldebert is insane, and all who make use of this wickedly fabricated letter are able to lose their senses altogether in the manner of children and they rave with certain womanish notions. But in order that he may no longer deceive the simple, we certainly cannot leave the case without discussion and a judgment against him.'

12 Among other things, Aldebert was alleged to have distributed his own fingernails and hair as relics and to have granted absolution without hearing confession (ibid. p. 112).

13 Ibid. pp. 117–18.

seem that it was already being widely disseminated. Some fifty years later, a document which we should probably identify as our text appears in Charlemagne's *Admonitio generalis* (789) as part of a warning against heterodox writings, where it is denounced as 'a most wicked and false letter' which should not be believed or read but burnt.[14]

Outrage accompanied the letter even to places where some form of Sunday rest had become customary. Thus yet another condemnation provides evidence that the letter had reached Ireland and England no later than the early ninth century. This is the letter by Ecgred, bishop of Lindisfarne, to Wulfsige, archbishop of York, written in the 830s.[15] Its immediate concern is a certain Pehtred who had collected heterodox writings, among them the Sunday Letter. Ecgred, like Licinianus, sees in the letter a tendency towards dangerous Judaizing: *honoremque Dominici diei ob gloriam resurrectionis Ejusdem Filii Dei, non sabbatum cum Judæis, omnimodis servare justum credimus et vere scimus.*[16] He doubts the story of Niall, an Irish hermit who, Pehtred's version claims, died and came back to life seven weeks later to testify to the letter's authenticity, living without food for the rest of his life. Ecgred has researched the names found in this version because he says that he cannot find a Pope Florentius in his list of popes. Moreover, he reasons that such an important event as a divine letter arriving on St Peter's tomb would surely have occasioned a general announcement from Rome. Ecgred advises that Pehtred, the owner of the offending book containing the letter, be severely admonished, and should he persist in error, be anathematized. We do not know what actions were taken on receipt of Ecgred's letter, but the news of the existence of this version at such an early date is valuable evidence for its transmission to England.

We should note that those who disapprove of the letter associate its strict prohibitions with Jewish rather than pagan influences.[17] The second cause of outrage seems to have been the claim that Christ himself wrote the letter. Even so, such scruples did not occur to those who continued to disseminate it, or, if they did, were set aside in the face of more pressing needs. As noted in Chapter 1, such approval and use of the the Sunday Letter is particularly evident in Ireland around

---

[14] Canon 78: *Item et pseudografia et dubiae narrationes, vel quae omnino contra fidem catholicam sunt et epistola pessima et falsissima, quam transacto anno dicebant aliqui errantes et in errorem alios mittentes quod de celo cecidisset, nec credantur nec legantur sed conburentur, ne in errorem per talia scripta populus mittatur*; *Capitularia regum Francorum I*, ed. Boretius, p. 60.

[15] The correspondence is discussed by Whitelock in 'Bishop Ecgred', pp. 47–68. The unique version mentioned in Ecgred's letter was later translated into Old English (Letters E and F); see below, pp. 82–8.

[16] 'And we believe it right, and know it as true, to observe in every way the honour of the Lord's day on account of the glory of the Resurrection of the same Son of God, and not the sabbath with the Jews' (*Councils and Ecclesiastical Documents*, ed. Haddan and Stubbs, III, 615); translated by D. Whitelock in *English Historical Documents I: c. 500–1042*, 2nd ed. (London, 1979), pp. 875–6 (no. 214).

[17] This does not necessarily invalidate the possibility of pagan influence on the kinds of practices prohibited in the Sunday Letter. It is not inconceivable that both the pagan taboo-day and the Jewish sabbath had a part to play in early-medieval sabbatarianism; the extent of the influence in each case is no longer recoverable.

the ninth century. While this acceptance may have been limited in scope, the implications of this letter's subsequent spread to England require us to pay some attention to its nature.

The Sunday Letter in Ireland

The correspondence of Bishop Ecgred to Wulfsige identifies a copy of the Sunday Letter which was, at some later point, translated into Old English (Letters E and F).[18] Pehtred's role in the transmission is not stated; we only know that he owned a copy and apparently passed it on to others.[19]

A close relative of this version was also rendered into Old Irish in the ninth-century *Epistil Ísu*,[20] a version which received a treatment not paralleled by any other versions of our text.[21] In two manuscripts the *Epistil Ísu*, a short piece narrating three Sunday-related *Strafwunder* and a law code called the *Cáin Domnaig* ('Law of Sunday') form a mutually supportive trilogy consisting of pseudo-scriptural authentication, narrative exempla and the legal sanctions underpinning Sunday observance.[22] In several other manuscripts two of these three texts appear together. Furthermore, the *Epistil Ísu* itself is supplemented with a new section which repeats the prohibitions, provides fines for each and lists exemptions, reading very much like a legal tract.[23] No other treatment of the Sunday Letter approaches this level of attention paid to the actual implementation of its prohibitions; generally the received lists are copied with only minor changes. Ireland therefore stands out as a place where, some time before the ninth century and perhaps only in the circles influenced by the most ascetic of religious groups, Sunday observance and the Sunday Letter were taken quite seriously.

To further illustrate this, it is important to note that the *Epistil Ísu*, its legal

---

[18]   The connection between Letters E and F, the letter mentioned in the Bishop Ecgred's letter and the *Epistil Ísu* was first noticed by R. Priebsch, 'The Chief Sources', pp. 141–6.

[19]   Ecgred does not expressly say that Pehtred used the book for preaching purposes, though he accuses him of 'sowing the errors of the tares in the field of the Lord' (*zizaniorum in Dominico agro sparsit errores*), a reference to the parable of the tares sown by an enemy in Matthew XIII.24–30, and urges Wulfsige to ensure that Pehtred corrects 'others whom he deceived' (*aliosque quos decepit*); *Councils and Ecclesiastical Documents*, ed. Haddan and Stubbs, III, 616.

[20]   The arguments for this date have been most recently laid out by Breatnach in *A Companion to the Corpus iuris Hibernici*, pp. 210–12. See also Whitelock, 'Bishop Ecgred', pp. 57–8 and 66. Hull had proposed a much earlier date (first half of the eighth century), but even he – as does D. A. Binchy (as cited in Whitelock, p. 66) – raises the possibility of an 'archaizing' scribe ('Cáin Domnaig', p. 157).

[21]   The only situation that is somewhat similar is that of Old English Letter E, which has inserted a lengthy portion of a legal code into the body of the letter (lines 56–81); most of the text does not concern Sunday observance, however, and the material is not revised to fit the context.

[22]   Whitelock shows the distribution of the three texts in the manuscripts ('Bishop Ecgred', p. 52 n. 39; see also Breatnach, *A Companion to the Corpus iuris Hibernici*, p. 209). The *Cáin Domnaig* is listed among the 'four (principal) laws of Ireland' by Félire Óengusso (ibid. p. 192).

[23]   §§23–32, O'Keeffe, 'Cáin Domnaig', pp. 205–11.

appendage and the *Cáin Domnaig* are all three ultimately dependent on a Sunday Letter, as a comparison of the restrictions listed in each shows.[24] All of the *Cáin Domnaig*'s prohibitions are represented in the *Epistil Ísu* and, with only two exceptions, again in the legal tract attached to it.[25] Of the additional items in the *Epistil Ísu* and its appendage, some can be found in other Sunday Letters and may have been in its source.[26] The rest appear to be unique to the Irish versions.[27] Though it is therefore possible, as Whitelock suggests, that the *Epistil Ísu* drew on the *Cáin Domnaig*, it is more likely that both drew on a Latin Sunday Letter which contained at least the prohibitions in the *Cáin Domnaig*.[28] Otherwise one must assume that the author of the *Epistil Ísu* translated a Latin Sunday Letter, but then turned to the *Cáin Domnaig* for its list of prohibitions. The latter itself, in its final sections, states explicitly that it derives its laws from the Sunday epistle which fell from heaven onto an altar in Rome, and summarizes the curses which will befall those who violate the sanctity of Sunday.[29] Whatever the actual circulation and use of these texts may have been, it is clear that the Sunday Letter enjoyed an exceptionally high profile during this period in Ireland.[30]

The precise nature of this Sunday Letter and the date of its arrival in Ireland are less certain. Ecgred's letter fixes the journey of Pehtred's version of the letter to England some time before the 830s. Furthermore, we know that a modified version, close to that used by the *Epistil Ísu*, was known in Ireland as early as the ninth century since Whitelock identified a strikingly close fragment in the Hiberno-Latin florilegium known as the *Catachesis Celtica*.[31] Though short, the

---

24 These are listed in §1 of the 'Sunday Law' (Hull, 'Cáin Domnaig', pp. 160–3) and in §§9, 17 (the letter proper) and §§23–32 (legal tract) of the *Epistil Ísu* (O'Keeffe, 'Cáin Domnaig', pp. 194–5 and 200–11).

25 Food preparation and placing a load on an ox are omitted.

26 These are assemblies (presumably for legal purposes), gleaning by land or sea, and strife; see, for example the Recension I version in BN lat.12,270: *preceperunt ipsum diem dominicum magno studio celebrari pacita non custodientes, non iudicantes, non iurantes, mercatum non facientes, nec molentes, non uendentes, non ementes, non herbas in horto colligentes, alios non detrahentes, uenationes non facientes* (Appendix I, lines 11–14). There is some evidence that the ancestor of not only the *Epistil Ísu* and *Cáin Domnaig*, Old English Letters E and F, but perhaps ultimately also the source of Old English Letters C and D was an early Recension II version which retained several Recension I features lost in other members of the family. This was probably derived from a member of Recension I that had made its way to Ireland early on: the entry for 884 in *Annals of the Four Masters* (cited below) mentions a letter 'given from heaven at Jerusalem'; the arrival in Jerusalem is a feature of Recension I.

27 These include putting a boat in the water, swift running, horse driving, shooting spears or arrows, throwing stones or spears, yarn weaving, swimming, drying in a kiln and putting nets in the water.

28 'Bishop Ecgred', pp. 66–7.

29 These coincide neatly with those in most Recension II Sunday Letters: to have no share in heaven with Christ, the destruction of crops, 'unseasonable weathers on perverse peoples' and foreign invasion (§11, Hull, 'Cáin Domnaig', p. 171).

30 The legal tract added to the *Epistil Ísu* and the *Cáin Domnaig* also share a complex relationship. The *Epistil Ísu* tract (§23–31) has some of the restrictions unique to the letter portion and adds some of its own; in its list of exemptions (§32) it resembles *Cáin Domnaig* (§1), though it is shorter and contains two items (a house fire, a field being plundered) which do not appear in the *Cáin Domnaig*.

31 Vatican City, Biblioteca Apostolica Vaticana, Reg. lat. 49, edited by R. E. McNally in *Scriptores*

correspondences are remarkable and provide evidence that the Sunday Letter was circulating in Ireland at an early date. McNamara thinks the Latin letter could have been in Ireland as early the seventh century, if not the sixth.[32]

Other historical sources add interesting but far from conclusive information. The entry for 811 in the *Chronicum Scotorum* mentions a Sunday Letter-like document when it records the arrival in Ireland of the first member of an ascetic group, the *céli dé*,[33] who 'came over the sea from the south, dry-footed, without a boat, and a written roll used to be given to him from Heaven, out of which he would give instruction to the Gaeidhel [Irish], and it used to be taken up again when the instruction was delivered'.[34] Two similar entries, one under 887 and one under 946, confusingly record a similar event which refers to a 'leaf' from heaven.[35] The *Annals of Ulster* note under 886 (887) that 'an epistle came with the pilgrim to Ireland, with the "Cain Domnaigh", and other good instructions'.[36] And the *Annals of the Four Masters* states for the year 884 that 'Ananloen, the pilgrim, came to Ireland with the epistle which had been given from heaven at Jerusalem, with the Cain-Domnaigh and good instructions'.[37] These dates obviously conflict with each other. All one can say with certainty is that the cumulative evidence points to an early arrival of the letter in Ireland and that it appears to have been of enough consequence to merit inclusion in some of the annals.[38] Similarly, one addition to the *Epistil Ísu* points to a desire to lend the weight of a respected name to its message in the authenticating narrative involving Conall mac Coelmaine, abbot of Inniskeel at the end of the sixth century.[39] According to the *Epistil*, Conall copied the letter while on pilgrimage in Rome and after his death revealed its location in his shrine to a priest who was to read it aloud or die within the month.[40] It is likely this story tells us less about the arrival of the letter

---

Hiberniae minores, CCSL 108B (Turnhout, 1973), 185–6. For the manuscript as a whole and its connections to other Old English texts see C. D. Wright, 'Catachesis celtica', pp. 117–18; and Wright, *The Irish Tradition*, pp. 58–9 and *passim*.

[32] *The Apocrypha in the Irish Church*, p. 62. Cf. Whitelock, 'Bishop Ecgred', pp. 64–7.

[33] See Chapter 1, pp. 17–19.

[34] *Chronicum Scotorum*, ed. Hennessy, pp. 126–7.

[35] 'The Pilgrim, with the leaf which was given from Heaven, came to Erinn, with the Cain Domnaigh, and good precepts' (887; *Chronicum Scotorum*, ed. Hennessy, pp. 170–1); 'A year of prodigies, i.e. in which the Leaf came from Heaven, and the Cele-Dé was wont to come across the sea, from the south, to instruct the Gaeidhel' (946; ibid. pp. 206–9).

[36] *Annals of Ulster, Otherwise, Annals of Senat, A Chronicle of Irish Affairs from A.D. 431 to A.D. 1540*, ed. W. Hennessy, 4 vols. (Dublin, 1887–1901), I, 404–5.

[37] *Annals of the Kingdom of Ireland, by the Four Masters*, ed. and trans. O'Donovan, I, 488–9. This pilgrim is also mentioned in the Annals of Inisfallen under 887; see *The Annals of Inisfallen*, ed. S. Mac Airt, pp. 136–7.

[38] See also the discussion of these annals in O'Dwyer, *Céli Dé*, pp. 21–4.

[39] O'Keeffe, 'Cáin Domnaig', pp. 204–5.

[40] One might compare a statement that is made at the conclusion of the Latin version in BL Add. 30,853 (Homiliary of Toledo), which reads: *Et dum essem uigilans media noctis ora pro facinora mala mea, audiui hanc uocem et inueni hanc epistolam* (*Les homéliaires du moyen âge*, ed. Grégoire, p. 227, lines 40–2). Another intriguing event, recorded in the Annals of St Bertin (first mentioned by Whitelock in 'Bishop Ecgred', p. 67), forms an interesting parallel to this authenticating vision

in Ireland, however, than about the motivation of the translator, who was probably seeking to elevate his own house by adding the abbot's name.[41]

In any case, it is clear that Ireland was especially receptive to the Sunday Letter, and perhaps this was due to the importance of Mosaic law in its theology and the influence, however limited, of certain ascetic groups.[42] Both of these resulted in a sabbatarianism which called for prohibitions which resembled those of the Jewish sabbath, particularly in its emphasis on restricting movement from place to place.[43] It is no wonder then that the Sunday Letter was not only taken up but extensively reworked and that, given the many ties between England and Ireland, it was passed on to the Anglo-Saxons, who translated it into their own language, further adapting it as they did so. Moreover, not only did they obtain at least one version of the letter from the Irish but had access to others, a fact which makes necessary some attention to the various Latin recensions available during this period.

Recension I

Several attempts have been made to group the various versions of the Sunday Letter which developed throughout the medieval period. While others had collected Sunday Letters in various languages, it was Hippolyte Delehaye who in 1899 first attempted a broad survey of those which were known to him, both Eastern and Western.[44] Though he noted some relationships among the versions he cites, he did not attempt to divide them into recensions, being content in his conclusion to observe the chronological development of the letter in the West up to modern

as well as that of Niall recorded in the version in Pehtred's book. For the year 839, the chronicler records a visit by English envoys to Louis the Pious. In a letter from the *rex Anglorum* (perhaps Æthelwulf), Louis is told of the vision of a local priest who was 'transported out of his body' (*rapto a corpore*), which urges reform in order to avoid pagan invasion, fire and sword. The only specific sin cited is the insufficient observance of Sunday: *Quod si cito homines Christiani de variis vitiis et facinoribus eorum non egerint poenitentiam, et diem Dominicum melius et honorabilius non observaverint, cito super eos maximum et intolerabile periculum veniet.* Two interesting details also reminiscent of the Sunday Letter are the statements that prior punishment had only been averted through the intercession of the souls of the saints, and that there had been a good harvest which subsequently perished because of the sins of people (cf. Vienna 1355, Appendix IIa, lines 31–4 and 72–3); *Annales Bertiniani*, ed. G. Waitz, MGH, SS rer. Germ. 6 (Hannover, 1883), 18–19.

41   Whitelock, 'Bishop Ecgred', p. 65. Westley Follett comments that 'the attribution to Conall mac Coelmaine ... is perhaps indicative of the author's connection either to Conall's church, Inniskeel in Co. Donegal, or to his kin, the Cenél Conaill, the northern claimants to the over-kingship of the Uí Néill'; *Céli Dé in Ireland*, p. 154.

42   See above, pp. 17–19.

43   See Chapter 1, p. 17. This special interest is particularly evident in the many exemptions for 'emergency travel' in the *Cáin Domnaig* (Hull, 'Cáin Domnaig', pp. 160–3).

44   In his 1899 monograph 'Note sur la légende de la lettre du Christ tombée du ciel', Delehaye drew, in part, on R. Röhricht's overview in 'Ein "Brief Christi"', *Zeitschrift für Kirchengeschichte* 11 (1890), 36–42, 619.

times.[45] In 1906, Max Bittner catalogued the Eastern versions, and the results of this study were included in Renoir's encyclopedia article on the subject in 1913.[46] Meanwhile, Robert Priebsch had been conducting a series of investigations into several vernacular versions: the Middle High German poem *Diu vrône botschaft ze der christenheit*, some of the Old English homilies, the Old Irish *Cáin Domnaig* and the late-medieval poem by John Audelay.[47] In a final monograph published in 1936, Priebsch focused on the Latin versions and their history.[48] He divided the Latin versions known to him into three recensions, and it is this basic division which, for the most part, is used in the discussion below. A new and more comprehensive study is badly needed but is unfortunately beyond the scope of this edition. Nevertheless, it is possible to summarize what is known to date and perhaps to move such a study further along by adding some discoveries made in the process.

The manuscript history begins with the above-mentioned evidence of its appearance, which offers some guide to the letter's original contents. In Licinianus' letter, the Sunday Letter is said to have fallen from heaven onto the altar of Christ and *memoria* of St Peter.[49] Licinianus mentions a few, though probably not all, of the restrictions in the letter; we find that food preparation, travel, garden work and spinning with a distaff are all prohibited. It is difficult to form much of a picture of the letter's contents from these sparse references, but the excerpt of its beginning in the records of the Lateran Synod of 745 reveals somewhat more of its nature, in particular an introduction which is characteristic of Priebsch's 'Redaction I' (which I will refer to as Recension I).[50] Its elaborate account of the letter's appearance could have been added in the intervening years or simply not mentioned by Licinianus. Members of Recension I are few and include London, BL Add. 19,725 (s. x/xi); Basel, Universitätsbibliothek, B VII 7 (s. x);[51] Paris, BN lat. 12,270 (s. xii); Vienna, Österreichische Nationalbibliothek, 1355 (s. xiv/xv); Graz, Universitätsbibliothek, 248 (s. xv); and a copy in a now lost manuscript once found in the Cathedral Library of Tarragona, Spain.[52] The narrative runs as follows: after being discovered by St Michael near the gate of Effrem or delivered

---

[45] The four time periods he identifies are 1. before the eleventh century, 2. during the period of the crusades, 3. during the time of the flagellants, 4. during the modern period (p. 211).

[46] Bittner, *Der vom Himmel gefallene Brief Christi*; Renoir, 'Christ (lettre du) tombée du ciel'.

[47] Priebsch, *Diu vrône botschaft ze der Christenheit*; 'The Chief Sources of Some Anglo-Saxon Homilies'; 'Quelle und Abfassungszeit'; 'John Audelay's Poem on the Observance of Sunday' in *An English Miscellany Presented to Dr Furnivall in Honour of his Seventy-fifth Birthday* (Oxford, 1902), pp. 397–407.

[48] *Letter from Heaven.*

[49] By *memoria* a memorial monument, tomb or shrine can be meant; the title in the Patrologia Latina edition names Rome as the city, but the letter itself does not; PL 72, cols 699–700.

[50] To this recension also belong Old English Letters A and B.

[51] The letters in BL Add. 19,725 and Basel B VII 7 are edited here as Appendix IIb and IIc.

[52] The text was apparently copied from the manuscript in the twelfth century by Petrus de Marca, archbishop of Paris; Priebsch, *Letter from Heaven*, p. 3. For ease of reference I have compiled a list (Appendix IV) of the manuscripts which contain Latin Sunday Letters, including full shelfmarks, folio numbers and the bibliographic information of available editions. Though it aims to be complete for all copies up to the fourteenth century, it seems likely that many more remain hidden in the margins of other manuscripts.

3. The Latin Sunday Letter

there, the letter is sent from one priest to another; the names of the priests and cities where they reside are roughly similar, but not surprisingly have often been corrupted in transmission.[53] The narrative continues as the letter is sent to the mountain of St Michael, Garganus – which is identified by name only in BN lat. 12,270 and Graz 248 – from where it travels to Rome and the sepulchre of St Peter. There follows a gathering of prelates or simply the people of Rome, who hold vigils, fast and pray for three days and three nights.[54] Not all the members belonging to this recension include this introduction: one early copy, Basel B VII 7, begins, apparently intentionally, with the list of restrictions found about three-quarters of the way through the text of its closest relative, Vienna 1355.

Within this recension, it is clear that Vienna 1355, Basel B VII 7, BL Add. 19,725 and Graz 248 are the most closely related; these four vary from each other in only minor details. Vienna 1355, though late, is our most complete witness, since the other three copies all omit significant sections of the text.[55] BN lat. 12,270, though generally close, includes some passages which seem extraneous to the original theme, one of which is a diatribe against women's love of fine clothing and jewellery.[56]

Finally, the rather corrupt copy once in a Tarragona manuscript, though without doubt belonging to the same family, also exhibits many details which are unique.[57] It inveighs against pagan practices such as worship at wells and in forests as well as inappropriate behaviour in church.[58] Taking the mention of pagan practices as marking an early date, removed later when they were no longer appropriate, Priebsch considers this version the archetype of this recension.[59] For

---

53 The fictitious priests are one Achor, a Talasius located in Armenia or Jeremia, a Lebonius in Ebrea, a Juras in Cappadocia and finally a Machabeus in Bethania. All of the copies mention the gate of Effrem and the priest Achor, but then they diverge, often omitting names and places. BL Add. 19,725 offers the most plausible account of these names, though Lebonius is spelled 'Libonius' and Iuras 'Iuoras'. Vienna 1355, despite its lateness, is quite close to this, only differing in the spellings of Achor (Ichor), Jeremia (Eremia) and Machabeus (Marchabeus). BN lat. 12,270 pares the list down to Achor, Ioras in Armenia and Machabeus in Bethania. Likewise Graz 248 leaves out the cities where its priests Lebeneus, Iura and Machabeus were located. Oddly, the most anomalous list of names occurs in the Lateran Synod record with Icore for Achor, Geremia for Jeremia, Arabia for Ebrea, Macrius for Machabeus, and Uetfania for Bethania. The lost Tarragona manuscript seems to have had Eros for Achor, Erim for Jeremia, and Leopas for Leobanus, omitting the other priests and the final destination of Rome.

54 The Lateran Synod, apart from its corruption of the names, stands out in this respect as well: twelve *papati* receive the letter in Rome, which is said to be *ubi claves regni caelorum constitutae sunt*; both are details not found in any other version; *Die Briefe des heiligen Bonifatius*, ed. Tangl, p. 115.

55 Basel B VII 7, as already noted, is missing the beginning, and BL Add. 19,725 most of the second half, only adding the final warning about the coming wrath in the month of November. Graz 248 omits a section in the middle of the text.

56 These revisions have been discussed in detail by Priebsch, *Letter from Heaven*, pp. 11–14.

57 Without further comment McNally suggests that 'certain aspects of [this version] suggest Irish influence' (*Scriptores Hiberniae minores*, p. 176 n. 9).

58 These practices are similar to some condemned by Caesarius of Arles; see the references in Klingshirn, *Caesarius of Arles: The Making of a Christian Community*, pp. 156–7, 163, 212 and 285.

59 Cf. Priebsch, *Letter from Heaven*, pp. 6–7. Priebsch suggests that the omissions are of the type that Aldebert might have made who himself erected crosses in the open counryside, but there is no

45

present purposes the Tarragona copy is particularly important. It contains a few elements that are not otherwise found in other Recension I texts but appear in Recension II and in Old English Letters E and F, a version that, as we shall see, appears to be a mixture of both.[60] Hence, this status as a 'hybrid' text marks the Tarragona copy as particularly valuable in determining the line of transmission that produced letters E and F.

Other features of Recension I which may have been early additions to the Sunday Letter are the admonition to fulfil the sponsorial obligations of St John;[61] the intercession of SS Mary, Peter and Paul and the archangel Michael on behalf of Sunday violators, saving them from destruction; and the warning that the present letter is the third and last of a series, with the final devastation promised in the month of November. The punishments in this version are sometimes fanciful: it is this recension which features the flying serpents which will tear at women's breasts or, in one version, suckle like infants,[62] as well as pustules or gnats in the eyes and nose and limbs. The list of prohibitions includes some domestic chores not found in Recension II – the gathering of produce in the garden, the milking of cows and the lighting of a fire – but perhaps summarized there in the phrase *si aliquid in domo sua operatur*. Readers of this version were perhaps rightly motivated to tame some of the excesses while using it as an inspiration for a relatively improved second production.

Recension II

The second recension of the Latin Sunday Letter, unlike the first, does not have a long narrative prologue but rather simply identifies itself as the letter of Christ. We are told that it arrived from heaven in the hand of a Bishop Peter, often referred to as being of Gaza, although this important piece of information is frequently found only at the end of the letter.[63] The earliest extant copy of this recension is in the margins of a tenth-century manuscript, BN lat. 8508, and remains unedited because of its fragmentary nature resulting from substantial trimming of the edges of the manuscript. Enough remains, however, to identify it as a close cousin to the eleventh-century Munich, Bayerische Staatsbibliothek, clm 9550, a text edited and discussed by Delehaye,[64] as well as a copy in Vienna, Österreichische Nationalbibliothek, 1878 (s. xii) and the now lost copy once located in Todi, Perugia (s.

---

evidence to support this. Cf. Jones, 'The Heavenly Letter in Medieval England', p. 165.

[60] See details below, pp. 48–50.

[61] Seen in Basel B VII 7, BL Add. 19,725, and Vienna 1355 as well as Old English Letter B. See commentary to B39.

[62] The origin of this horror may be a corruption of *lacerant* to *lacterent*; see commentary to A70–2.

[63] These details are sometimes altered; in the much-shortened version in BL Add. 30,853, the so-called Homiliary of Toledo, the letter falls on the altar of St Bauduli in Nîmes (*Les homéliaires du Moyen Âge*, ed. Grégoire, pp. 226–7), and in BL Royal 11 B.x the city has been changed to Cassiana (184rb).

[64] See Delehaye, 'Note', pp. 179–81.

xii).[65] Two more fifteenth-century copies which have been edited are BL Royal 8 F.vi and Hamburg, Bibliothek der Hansestadt, S. Petri-Kirche 30b.[66] The latter urges not only Sunday but also Friday observance.[67]

All of these copies, despite the fact that they were produced over a period of several centuries, show a general uniformity of content. They begin abruptly with the wrath of God, who threatens to scourge cattle and humans and to send a pagan army to devastate the land. However, apart from the wolves and *canes maligni* mentioned at the outset, the promised punishments tend more to the natural disaster such as hailstones and famine and less the fictitious beast. A final section includes an exhortation to priests to disseminate the letter, the insistence on its having been sent to Bishop Peter of Gaza from the seventh heaven or throne of God, written by the latter's own finger (like the ten commandments, Exodus XXXI.18), and the characteristic and often lengthy oath of attestation by Peter, who swears by God's might, Christ, the angels, the saints, and so on – the list varies slightly with each copy. Some of the later examples also include a Sunday List; the relationship between these two texts will be discussed in more detail below.

Recension II also has its outlier in the so-called Homiliary of Toledo (BL Add. 30,853), written in late-eleventh-century Spain in Visigothic script,[68] in which the Sunday Letter is part of a section added at the end of the homiliary proper. There is some slight evidence that the compiler also had access to Hiberno-Latin materials.[69] The text itself represents more of a summary or paraphrase of the Sunday Letter and exhibits some peculiarities. Though it is generally thought to be a member of Recension II because it lacks the prologue detailing the travels of the letter from place to place and also contains the oath of Bishop Peter (here called the bishop of Nîmes), it also retains features which are otherwise only to be found in Recension I members, such as the arrival on an altar (here, that of St Bauduli), and the punishments of locusts and winged serpents.[70] Although its condensed state does not allow for a close comparison, in its combination of these features, it resembles the source of Old English Letters E and F.

[65] The text was apparently copied from a twelfth-century manuscript located in Todi by J. C. Amaduzzi and is printed in *Anecdota litteraria ex mss. codicibus eruta* (Rome, 1773), pp. 69–74. See also the introduction and reprint in J.-P. Migne, *Dictionnaire des apocryphes, ou collection de tous les livres apocryphes relatifs à l'Ancien et au Nouveau Testament* (Paris, 1856–8), II, cols. 367–9.

[66] Royal 8 F.vi contains the closest analogue of an English poem by the fifteenth-century monk John Audelay (Priebsch, 'John Audelay's Poem', pp. 397–407).

[67] Additional copies of Recension II are listed in Appendix IV.

[68] Grégoire, *Les homéliaires du Moyen Âge*, p. 161; the sermon is edited on pp. 226–7. See also H. Delehaye, 'Un exemplaire de la lettre tombée du ciel', *Recherches de science religieuse* 18 (1928), 164–9.

[69] The other Hiberno-Latin text is the so-called 'Three Utterances of the Soul' apocryphon (see Wright, *Irish Tradition*, pp. 215–16). The compiler of the final section of the manuscript also included a sermon on Sunday observance attributed to Eusebius of Alexandria in which a Sunday List has been inserted (see below, n. 125).

[70] G. Morin ('A propos du travail du P. Delehaye sur la lettre du Christ tombée du ciel', *Revue bénédictine* 16 (1899), 217) relates Bishop Peter with Pierre Ermengaud, bishop of Nîmes from 1080–90.

The Source of Old English Letters E and F (Y¹)

Delineating the hypothetical Latin version which formed the basis for the Irish *Epistil Ísu* and the two related Old English versions, Letters E and F, is a complicated matter.[71] It is generally assumed that it had the shape of the extant Recension II versions, but, if so, it also differed in many respects. Setting aside for the moment what appear to be innovative elements in *Epistil Ísu* and Letters E/F, there are a few characteristics that can be safely attributed to this source, which I shall refer to as Y¹. Both Dorothy Whitelock and Robert Priebsch worked on this question, and both concluded that Y¹ bore at least some relationship to Recension II, as exemplified in the copy found in Munich 9550.[72] The characteristic introduction of Recension I, which follows the letter's passage from city to city and priest to priest, is gone,[73] and perhaps most telling (in E/F) is the appearance of a recipient of the letter, a Bishop Peter, and the oath he swears to confirm the letter's authenticity, a feature which identifies it, in Whitelock's words, as a 'Bishop Peter' (i.e. Recension II) letter.[74]

However, the relationship between Munich 9550 and our vernacular texts is far from straightforward. Few of the elements contained in both are verbally close to each other. The statements that are quite close are 1. when God's wrath is mentioned,[75] 2. a statement of the required time of Sunday observance followed by an anathema for disobedience,[76] 3. a promise of blessing for correct observance,[77] and 4. the biblical quotation that God created the world in six days and rested on the seventh.[78] More often the correspondence is one of distant echo

---

[71] That all three of these texts must have had the same ancestor is shown below, p. 83.

[72] Whitelock, 'Bishop Ecgred', pp. 58–60, and Priebsch, 'Quelle und Abfassungszeit', pp. 139–46.

[73] It is possible that *Epistil Ísu*'s story of Conall mac Coelmaine bringing the Sunday Letter from Rome was intended to offer similar authentication which was locally more satisfactory. One might even further speculate that it was then itself replaced by the travels of the punishing fire and the contemporary visionary Niall in E/F.

[74] 'Bishop Ecgred', p. 55.

[75] *Quia nescitis illum custodire, propter hoc venit ira Dei super vos* (Munich 9550, Delehaye, 'Note', p. 179); cf. F133–4: *and gef ge ne willaþ get healdan sunnandæges bebod and sæternes ofernon and þare monannihte, þonne becumaþ get ofer iow micel Godes erre.*

[76] *Amen dico vobis, si non custodieritis sanctum diem dominicum de hora nona sabbati usque ad horam primam secundae feriae, anathematizabo vos cum patre meo, et non habetis partem mecum neque cum angelis meis in saecula saeculorum, amen* (Munich 9550, Delehaye, 'Note', p. 180); cf. F172–6: *Soþ, soþ is, þæt ic iow sæcge, se þe ne gehealdaþ þane halgan sunnandeg, minne restandæg, þe ic of deaþe aras, mid rihte fram nontide þæs sæternesdæges oþ þæs monandæges lihtincge, þæt he biþ awerged aa in weorulde weoruld, and ic him wiþsacæ, þonne he of þisan life gewit, and he ne hafaþ næfre dæl mid me ne mid minan ænglum to heofonan rice.*

[77] *Amen dico vobis, si custodieritis diem dominicum, aperiam vobis [cataractam] caeli in omni bono, et multiplicabo fructus vestros* (Munich 9550, Delehaye, 'Note', p. 180); cf. F182–5: *Soþ ys, þæt ic iow sæcge, gef ge healdaþ þone halgan sunnandeg mid rihte . . . þonne ontyne ic iow heofenas þeodan, and ic selle iow menigfealde wæstmas.*

[78] *Notum enim est vobis quia sex diebus creavi caelum et terram, mare et omnia quae in eis sunt; septimo autem requievi ab omni opere* (Munich 9550, Delehaye, 'Note', pp. 179–80); cf. F69–71: *And soþlice on six dagum wæran geworhte heofan and eorþe and ealle þa gescæfta, þe in hiom*

rather than source,[79] or even one of mere subject matter.[80]

If the Munich text does not qualify as a source, we may profitably look to readings in other surviving Sunday Letters to bring us closer to the nature of Y[1]. As was noted in connection with the Irish Sunday Letter above, extracts of a copy which must have been very close to Y[1] are preserved in Vatican City, Biblioteca Apostolica Vaticana, Reg. lat. 49, the ninth-century Hiberno-Latin florilegium known as the *Catachesis Celtica*, where they are attached to a Sunday List.[81] Whitelock noted the striking verbal parallels in these sentences.[82] The extracts are short and corrupt and appear to have been purposely rewritten to provide only the briefest summary of the Sunday Letter and so offer only a few tantalizing glimpses into this revised branch.[83]

Furthermore, as Priebsch observed, there are correspondences with another Latin Sunday Letter which, though they complicate the picture, help to determine more clearly Y[1]'s make-up.[84] As mentioned above, the abbreviated copy in the Homiliary of Toledo offers additional parallels which the Munich version does not have.[85] These are the promised plague of locusts (*brucos et locustas*),[86] the flying/winged serpents (*serpentes pinnatas*)[87] and the notion of an altar as the place where the letter arrives (here, the altar of St Baudile at Nîmes).[88] These are

---

sindan; and þa on þæne .vii. dæg þa let drehten fram æghwilcum weorce and hine gereste þa on þam dæge (cf. E119–21 and Exodus XX.11).

[79] Such is the case, for example, when Christ speaks of his suffering: *Ego ipse hac die resurrexi a mortuis, cum passus sum pro vestra omnium salute et in ipso die resurrectionis meae eripui vos de inferno et a potestate diaboli* (Munich 9550, Delehaye, 'Note', p. 179); cf. F159–62: *Ic eom Godes sunu, and ic feola geþrowade for iow, ic wæs an rode ahangen for iow, and ic deaþ geþrowade for iow, and ic of deaþe aras for iow an þone halgan sunnandeg, and ic an heofonas astah an þone halgan eastorsunnandæg.* Another example is when he threatens to send a heathen people upon the disobedient: *Et venit gens pagana quae alios occidit, et alios in captivitatem ducit pro eo quod non observatis diem dominicum* (Munich 9550, Delehaye, 'Note', p. 179); cf. Letter F181: *and ic lete hæþen folc ofer iow, þa iow fornimaþ and iowra bearn.* Similar relationships may be seen between Munich 9550 and E/F in the (un)natural disasters (hail, etc.) which are promised (F179–80 and 194–5; E163), the list of Sunday prohibitions (F196–201; E164–8), the oath of Bishop Peter (F213–23; E194–202), and the injunction to disseminate the letter's message (F203–10; E186–93); see the commentary for the Latin parallels.

[80] See, for example, the comment on aiding the poor and strangers (F153–6) and the directive to tithe and give alms (F16–20); see commentary on these lines for the Latin parallels.

[81] Printed in *Scriptores Hiberniae minores*, ed. McNally, p. 186, lines 42–56.

[82] See 'Bishop Ecgred', pp. 59–60, where she lays out the evidence. The sections in question have been cited in the commentary to the relevant lines (E153–9, 164–9; F182–9, 196–202; cf. *Epistil Ísu* §§12 and 17). A relationship also appears to exist between the Vatican excerpts and the copy in the Tarragona manuscript (see below, n. 90).

[83] They include blessings and curses for those who observe or fail to observe Sunday, list only two prohibitions (the cutting of hair and the cleaning of one's house), and finally enjoin the message to be preached to all. No mention is made of a divine letter.

[84] See Priebsch's comparison of Old English F, *Epistil Ísu* and Munich 9550, which he supplements with the Toledo version, his S ('Quelle und Abfassungszeit', pp. 140–6).

[85] For this homiliary see above, p. 47.

[86] Cf. F128–31; *Epistil Ísu* §3–4.

[87] Cf. F180 *fleogende neddran; Epistil Ísu* §10.

[88] E148, 195, 201 and 205; F123, 214, 217, 221 and 225; *Epistil Ísu* §18: 'this Epistle was sent unto

notably elements which otherwise occur only in Recension I texts.[89] Pointing us in the same direction, the copy transcribed from the lost Tarragona manuscript, though classified as Recension I, also offers a reading remarkably close to Y^1 when it states that whatever is asked for will be given, a comment which also occurs in Vatican City, Reg. lat. 49.[90] These two copies illustrate various forms of the Sunday Letter which, like Y^1, did not belong strictly to the groupings identified as Recension I and II, but to lines of transmission which included elements from both.

Thus, the case of Y^1, a Latin Sunday Letter no longer extant but ostensibly composed some time between 600 and 800, illustrates the difficulty of tracing the transmission of a widely disseminated text which was often treated with great freedom. While it retains some features of the earlier Recension I, it also exhibits elements clearly belonging to the later, popular Recension II. Y^1's predecessor must have been (or been derived from) an earlier form of Recension II. Was Y^1 possibly a transitional text which ultimately led to the version known to us as Recension II? This is at least possible, given its early date; it may, at the very least, represent a stage of the latter's development in Ireland, though there is no reason the final transformation into what now survives as Recension II could not have taken place elsewhere.[91]

This is made more likely since we have seen two Latin homilies with similar 'transitional' features – those in the manuscript from Tarragona and in the Homiliary of Toledo – which may suggest that the Y^1 was transmitted from Spain, one of the likely places of origin for the Sunday Letter.[92] Spanish–Irish connections or lines of transmission have been proposed for the sixth and seventh centuries by several scholars, and have been traced particularly in the case of apocryphal texts.[93] It is possible, therefore, that the Irish were one of the earliest recipients of the letter; they certainly were one of the most enthusiastic.

---

the altar of Peter in Rome of Latium' (cf. §21 'the altar of Peter the Apostle in Rome'). The arrival on an altar is in fact not common to either Recension I or II. Most Recension I copies have the place as *sepulcrum sancti Petri* although Licinianus' letter reports it fell *super altare Christi in memoria sancti Petri apostoli* (PL 72, col. 700). Recension III, however, has it usually descending *super altare sancti Petri in Hierusalem* (Priebsch, *Diu vrône botschaft*, p. 41). An interesting parallel may be found in the preface to an Old English charm for a variety of ills which claims that an angel brought it from heaven and laid it on the altar of St Peter in Rome (T. O. Cockayne, *Leechdoms, Wortcunning and Starcraft of Early England*, 3 vols. (London, 1864–6), III, 288–9). The Welsh version also refers to the altar of Peter and Paul.

89 They also occur in Recension III, which is based on I.

90 See Tarragona: *et quaecunque petieritis dabo vobis* (edited by Priebsch in *Letter from Heaven*, p. 37); cf. F187–8: *swa hwæs swa ge biddaþ an minan naman, eal ic iow sille*, and E156–7: *swa hwæs swa ge me biddað on minum naman, eall ic hit eow selle.*

91 The earliest extant copy of Recension II is that in BN lat. 8508, written by an early-tenth-century hand in the margins of a late-ninth-century penitential of Halitgar.

92 See below, pp. 54–7.

93 See, for example, D. Dumville, 'Biblical Apocrypha and the Early Irish: A Preliminary Investigation', *Proceedings of the Royal Irish Academy* 73c (1973), 299–338 and J. N. Hillgarth, 'Ireland and Spain in the Seventh Century', *Peritia* 3 (1984), 1–16.

3. The Latin Sunday Letter

The Source of Old English Letters C and D

One complete reworking of the Recension II-type Sunday Letter is particularly important to this study since it is the source of Old English Letters C and D. It survives in two Latin copies, Vienna, Dominikanerkloster 133 (s. xv) and, partially, in Kassel, Murhardsche Bibliothek der Stadt Kassel und Landesbibliothek, theol. 39 (s. xiv), hereafter jointly referred to as VK.[94] VK's most easily identified attribute is that Peter is said to be the bishop of Antioch. This particular detail has led to the discovery of three other vernacular Sunday Letters belonging to this line, an Old French, a Welsh and a fifteenth-century Middle English sermon.[95] The Old French and Welsh versions are particularly interesting since they name this location while remaining close to other copies of the Recension II line; they are therefore useful in establishing that the 'Antioch' addition was an early change in the development of VK. The Welsh letter represents an additional step towards VK, offering a version of Bishop Peter's oath which is very close to its own.[96]

The subsequent refashioning of this Sunday Letter into VK reveals a unique approach to the text.[97] The most significant changes are the following: 1. a Sunday List is added to the beginning;[98] 2. an angel is said to have written the letter, recording the words of Christ, unlike the other members of Recension II, which either insist that it was written by 'the finger of God/the Lord' or leave this element out;[99] 3. a segment on the destruction of Jerusalem under Titus and Vespasian is added to provide another instance of an earlier punishment for not

---

94 These are edited in Appendix III. Enough of that version's features remain (many verbally identical) to establish that it must be derived from it. They are the threat of foreign invasion, the promise of the same fate as Sodom and Gomorrah, the expression *flagellabo vos duris(simis) flagellis*, the same prohibitions (trade, cutting of hair, washing of clothes, baking of bread), the phrase *contentionem et detractionem* for the restriction on disputes, the biblical expression *gens prava atque perversa*, the notion that free and slave (*tam liberi quam serui*) persons should rest from work and the oath of Bishop Peter.

95 The Welsh version, found in BL Cotton Titus D.xxii (s. xv), is edited and translated by T. Powel, 'Ebostol y sul', *Y cymmrodor* 8 (1887), 162–72; the Old French is printed from BL Sloane 3126 (s. xiv) by C. Brunel in 'Versions espagnol, provençal et française de la lettre du Christ tombée du ciel', *Analecta Bollandiana* 68 (1950), 383–96 at 394–5. The Middle English sermon is located in Durham University Library, Cosin V.IV.2 (125r–128v), and is edited by V. M. O'Mara, *A Study and Edition of Selected Middle English Sermons*, Leeds Texts and Monographs, n.s. 13 (Leeds, 1994), 115–21.

96 Curiously it is also the Welsh copy which retains a reference to the letter's arrival on 'the altar of the church of Peter and Paul in Rome' and, later, 'the altar of Peter, the Apostle' ('Ebostol y sul', ed. Powel, p. 169) which connects it with Recension I and suggests that this line may be an early offshoot in the development of Recension II.

97 The Middle English translation, though a rather free adaptation, was clearly derived from a version of VK after this revision had taken place; see O'Mara, *Selected Middle English Sermons*, pp. 113–36.

98 Its sources are discussed below, pp. 96–8.

99 Appendix III, lines 2–3: *quam angelus suo digito scripsit*. The Middle English translation shows, however, that the original revision probably did not have this change; it states: *þis same wrytyng was wryttyng with þe holy hand of allmyghty God* (line 15, *Selected Middle English Sermons*, ed. O'Mara, p. 115). The final oath which restates the origin of the letter has been omitted.

observing Sunday;[100] 4. a passage from Isaiah warning against debauchery is expounded upon; and 5. a reference to the biblical Dathan and Abiram episode joins Sodom and Gomorrah as an example of God's punishment. Also, there are also many minor additions which add explanations or further emphasis to various parts of the letter. While VK generally follows the order of Munich 9550, it discards certain elements.[101] On the whole it may be said that the compiler was reasonably learned, as can be seen in his knowledge of scripture and history and his confidence in assembling a new text.

Two links suggest that this person was based in the British Isles. The first revision listed above, the Sunday List, contains some items which VK holds in common with the *Epistil Ísu*, the Irish version of the Sunday Letter. Whitelock notes the following similarities: 1. the giving of languages at Pentecost, 2. the creation of 'unformed matter' on Sunday and 3. twelve baskets of fragments left over at the feeding of the 5000. This suggests that this version, or at least its Sunday List came to England by way of Ireland.[102] In addition, there is a curious connection to Y¹, by way of Old English Letters E and F, in the reference to the Dathan and Abiram episode. Since these additions seems unlikely to have been made in both VK and E/F independently, they may derive from a common ancestor; alternatively, there may have been some influence from one on the other at some later stage of transmission. Either way, the Old English translations of VK confirm that it had been shaped no later than the eleventh century.

Recension III

Brief mention should also be made of a third recension of the Sunday Letter, a version widely translated and distributed in the High Middle Ages, and which appears to have been a development of Recension I.[103] It is characterized by a greater emphasis on the promise of foreign invasion and captivity, now sometimes identified as Saracens, and the mention of a patriarch as the recipient of the letter, which suggests it may have been filtered through the East or at least influenced by contact with the East during the period of the crusades.[104] Its opening narrative has the letter, written on marble tablets, falling onto the altar of St Peter in Jerusalem, where an angel conveys it to the populace. Like the first recension, it includes the intercession of Mary and the angels to forestall punishment. The only specific

---

[100] See commentary, note to C106–14.

[101] The author has excised the ravaging wolves and dogs, the reference to Exodus XX.11 (the sabbath commandment) and most of the promised rewards.

[102] Whitelock, 'Bishop Ecgred', pp. 62–3.

[103] A succinct description of this recension may be found in R. Stübe, *Der Himmelsbrief. Ein Beitrag zur allgemeinen Religionsgeschichte* (Tübingen, 1918), pp. 19–24.

[104] This version is closely related to the Greek, Armenian, Syriac, Garshuni, Arabic and Ethiopian copies edited and studied by Bittner. He suggests that a Latin version was brought to the East during the period of the crusades (*Der vom Himmel gefallene Brief Christi*, p. 3). Most of the members of Recension III are from the fifteenth century and later.

prohibited Sunday activity is legal proceedings, but otherwise this version is full of condemnation for those who do not observe Sunday by going to church and performing good deeds as well as for a host of other sins including usury. This strain of the Sunday Letter would appear to be a later development: the earliest manuscript copies of this recension – Munich, Bayerische Staatsbibliothek, clm 21,518 and Vienna, Österreichische Nationalbibliothek, lat. 510 – date from the twelfth century although the copy in a thirteenth-century Toulouse manuscript appears to reflect the original shape of this recension more accurately since it does not contain a lengthy and wholly repetitive section found in the others.[105]

An abbreviated version of this recension was used in England at the beginning of the thirteenth century, when a French abbot, Eustace of Flay, went to England to preach the Fourth Crusade, among other things.[106] A significant part of his campaign, which was recorded by the thirteenth-century chronicler Roger of Hoveden, was the exhortation to revere Sunday and to abolish Sunday markets in particular.[107] Eustace made two visits to England, the first meeting with a good deal of opposition from various authorities and with little success.[108] He returned a year later armed with an effective weapon, the Sunday Letter, a Latin copy of which is included in Roger's account,[109] though presumably Eustace delivered his message to the people in the vernacular. The French abbot is reputed to have caused a sensation with his letter and Sunday-related miracles, but there is no evidence that his success had any lasting effect.[110]

Furthermore, it was this version which was used by the flagellants, adapted as a sermon which was preached as they made their way throughout the countryside during the plague-years of the fourteenth century.[111] Such appropriation mirrors

---

[105] Munich 21,518 is printed by Priebsch as the source of a Middle High German poem (*Diu vrône botschaft*, pp. 41–70). Toulouse, Bibliothèque Publique, 208 is edited by E. M. Rivière, 'La lettre du Christ tombée du ciel', pp. 600–5. Additional copies are listed in Appendix IV.

[106] In this version the letter descends upon the altar of St Simeon on Golgatha and a patriarch and a Archbishop Akarias are mentioned. Two useful accounts of Eustace's mission and his use of the Sunday Letter are Jones, 'The Heavenly Letter in Medieval England', pp. 166–72; and Cate, 'The English Mission of Eustace of Flay', pp. 67–89.

[107] *Chronica magistri Rogeri de Houedene*, ed. W. Stubbs, 4 vols., Rolls Series (London, 1868–71) IV, 123–4 and 167–72.

[108] Cate, 'The English Mission of Eustace of Flay', p. 73; Jones, 'The Heavenly Letter in Medieval England', p. 168.

[109] Cate, 'The English Mission of Eustace of Flay', p. 74; Jones, 'The Heavenly Letter in Medieval England', p. 168. Apart from the letter as found as part of Roger de Hoveden's Chronicle, this version (listed under Recension IIIa in Appendix IV) is also preserved independently in Bodl. Lyell 12 and Lat. th. f. 19, BL Add. 6716, and Graz, Universitätsbibliothek, 248. In all of these it is found combined with an additional section, and in the first three a version of Recension II, closely resembling BL Royal 8. F. vi, follows.

[110] Cate, 'The English Mission of Eustace of Flay', p. 76.

[111] According to Priebsch, Vienna, Österreichische, Nationalbibliothek, lat. 510 (s. xii) and Erlangen, Universitätsbibliothek, 306 (444) (s. xiv) – the latter a shorter form which leaves out the same sections as Toulouse 208 – are the Latin versions closest to this Middle High German sermon (*Diu vrône botschaft*, pp. 33–9). It is printed in C. U. Hahn, *Geschichte der Ketzer im Mittelalter, besonders im 11., 12. und 13. Jahrhundert*, Geschichte der Waldenser und verwandter Sekten (Stuttgart, 1847), pp. 537–50. See also H. Pfannenschmid, 'Die Geißler des Jahres 1349 in Deutschland und

that of Aldebert in the eighth century, and the letter was, as in the latter's case, condemned by a contemporary, Hugo of Reutlingen.[112]

The Origin of the Sunday Letter

The external evidence examined at the beginning of this chapter – letters by Ecgred and Licinianus and the records of the Lateran council of 745 – is our earliest witness to the letter's existence and therefore a valuable indicator of its origins. The date and origin of the Sunday Letter's composition have elicited a variety of opinions, most of which are based on an only partial view of the material.[113] Not surprisingly, the most comprehensive studies have also yielded the most convincing suggestions for a place of origin, which Delehaye and Priebsch would place in Africa, Southern Gaul or Spain.[114] Licinianus' letter was written in Spain, and if we search for clues in the letter itself, we note that its requirements are consistent with the sabbatarianism developing, particularly in Visigothic Spain and Gaul, during the sixth century.

den Niederlanden', *Die Lieder und Melodien der Geißler des Jahres 1349 nach der Aufzeichnung Hugo's von Reutlingen. Nebst einer Abhandlung über die italienischen Geisslerlieder von Heinrich Schneegans und einem Beitrage zur Geschichte der deutschen und niederländischen Geissler von Heino Pfannenschmid*, ed. P. Runge (Leipzig, 1900), pp. 145–56.

[112] *Hecque gravis clero fuerat justo quoque vero, per cartas falsas et doctrinas male salsas, marmorea tabula dicens doctrina quod illa Jerusalem claram Petri venit super aram, aram qui nullam sibi servat ibi societam*; Hugo von Reutlingen, 'Chronicon', in *Die Lieder und Melodien der Geißler des Jahres 1349*, ed. Runge, p. 41.

[113] The various proposals are summarized in Delehaye ('Note', pp. 207–13) and Deletant, who himself postulates Rome as a possibility ('The Sunday Legend', pp. 449–50). As Delehaye notes, the issue has often been distorted by scholars who based their conclusions on the particular copy or recension known to them rather than on information of the broader history of the letter. Thus, those studying the Eastern recensions often postulate an Eastern origin, while Delehaye maintains that those versions were later developments, a fact that was confirmed by the thorough examination by Max Bittner ('Note', p. 7). Delehaye makes the point that, although the localization at Rome was often subject to change or omission, it would hardly have been the choice of a writer located in the East. At the same time, the use of the word *memoria* for the Basilica of St Peter, according to Delehaye speaks against an origin at Rome ('Note', p. 212). For another hypothesis concerning an Eastern origin, see Van Esbroeck, 'La lettre sur le dimanche'.

[114] See Delehaye, 'Note', p. 212 and Priebsch, *Letter from Heaven*, pp. 33–4. The link to Africa is made by a text which has been cited as a predecessor of the letter, a curious Coptic fragment (s. x/xi), possibly composed some time in the sixth century and once attributed to Peter of Alexandria. It commands Sunday rest and peace and anathematizes those who refuse to abide by this and other laws. While a portion of it in some ways resembles the Sunday Letter, it does not claim to be a letter written by Christ – the author identifies himself as Peter the Martyr – or to have fallen from heaven, and its fragmentary nature (the beginning is missing), doubtful dating and limited scope reduce its value for a study of the letter's origins. It should, however, be noted that this text also underscores the exhortation of resting on the Lord's day with Old Testament-style curses. See C. Schmidt, 'Fragmente einer Schrift des Märtyrer-Bischofs Petrus von Alexandrien', *Texte und Untersuchungen zur Geschichte der altchristlichen Literatur* 20.4b (1901), 1–50 at 4–7; and Bittner, *Der vom Himmel gefallene Brief Christi*, p. 217. For the authenticity and dating of this text, see the note on Schmidt's edition by H. Delehaye (*Analecta Bollandiana* 20 (1901), 101–3).

The prohibitions Licinianus mentions – food preparation, travel, garden work and spinning – while probably only a sampling of what he found in the letter, are easily found in the sixth-century evidence on the subject examined in Chapter 1. In particular one might note the admonishments of Martin of Braga in his *De correctione rusticorum*, written *c*. 574:

> Opus servile, id est agrum, pratum, vineam vel si qua gravia sunt, non faciatis in die dominico, praeter tantum quod ad necessitatem reficiendi corpusculi pro exquoquendo pertinet cibo et necessitate longinqui itineris. Et in locis proximis licet viam die dominico facere, non tamen pro occasionibus malis, sed magis pro bonis, id est aut ad loca sancta ambulare, aut fratrem vel amicum visitare, vel infirmum consolare, aut tribulanti consilium vel adiutorium pro bona causa portare.[115]

While Martin allows the cooking of food, his emphasis on travel restrictions and forbidding of field work echo Licinianus' letter,[116] and his encouragement of good deeds is paralleled by passages from extant Sunday Letters.[117] In 681, King Ervig takes for granted that spinning and weaving are forbidden on Sundays since a directive of his mentions specifically these chores as signifying customary Christian practice to which the Jews in his kingdom were to adhere.[118] If, in fact, Jewish influence was at work in the development of an increasingly restrictive Sunday observance, Visigothic Spain would be an obvious candidate as a place where the tensions produced through this change may have occasioned the composition of the Sunday Letter.[119]

---

[115] 'Servile work, that is, [work in] in field, meadow, or vineyard, or what is heavier [work], you should not do on the Lord's day, except what pertains to the necessity of cooking for the refreshing of the puny body with food or for the needs of a long journey. It is permitted on the Lord's day to make a journey to nearby places, not for evil purposes, but rather for good, that is to walk to the shrines of saints, or to visit brothers or friends, to console the sick, or to bring counsel or aid to one afflicted for a good cause'; *Martini episcopii Bracarensis opera omnia*, ed. Barlow, p. 202.

[116] Licinianus notes that the Sunday Letter says that *nullus . . . viam ambulet*, and opines that *meliusque erat viro hortum facere, iter agere, mulieri colum tenere, et non, ut dicitur, ballare, saltare* (PL 72, col. 699).

[117] The version in a manuscript from Todi (Perugia) states: *Et ambulaverit in alium locum in diem sanctum dominicum nisi ad ecclesiam aut ad alia loca sanctorum. uel loca martyrum aut infirmum visitare, uel mortuos sepellire aut discordantes ad concordiam revocare uel viduis et orphanis et peregrinantibus subvenire* (*Dictionnaire des apocryphes*, ed. Migne, II, col. 368). The Tarragona manuscript states: *Nihil alius operantes in die Dominico nisi ad Ecclesiam concurrere, solemnitates Domini audire. Et post haec infirmos visitare, mortuos sepelire, tribulantes consolare, discordantes pacificare* (Priebsch, *Letter from Heaven*, p. 35).

[118] See Chapter 1, p. 6 n. 27. At the same time, it is worth noting that Caesarius of Arles reprimands women who will not spin or weave on Thursday in honour of Jove (*Sermo* LII.2; ed. Morin, CCSL 103, pp. 230–1).

[119] As already noted, two extant Latin Sunday Letters may be associated with Spain: the copy found in the so-called 'Homiliary of Toledo', which, while a manuscript of the eleventh century, contains primarily material going back to seventh-century Spain; see Grégoire, *Les homéliaires du moyen âge*, p. 161; another copy, made in the twelfth century from a now lost manuscript in the Cathedral Library of Tarragona, is regarded by Priebsch as the letter's earliest form (*Letter from Heaven*, pp. 3, 33).

On the other hand, it is possible to look elsewhere for similar impetus. As previously noted, the works of Gregory of Tours, writing at the same period in Merovingian Gaul, illustrate that there too sabbatarianism was already far advanced, restricting farm work and common household activities such as the baking of bread.[120] Furthermore, the Council of Orleans of 538 condemns the popular belief that it is forbidden to travel, prepare food or tend to home or person (while itself forbidding all rural labour).[121] The Council of Mâcon in 585 provides several parallels to the ideas of the Sunday Letter, most importantly the prohibition of all court cases and the suggestion that compliance will prevent death and sterility.[122] Similarly, the *Lex Baiuvariorum* states outright that those who work on Sunday will incite God's wrath and be punished with crop failure.[123] Both Caesarius of Arles and Gregory of Tours suggest that children conceived on Sunday run the risk of being born with various afflictions.[124] Clearly, what these ordinances and menacing narratives have in common is a desire, not much in evidence before the sixth century, to exert pressure on the populace to comply with Sunday regulation. Such an environment seems fertile ground for an apocryphal letter written in support of the growing movement against more traditional views of Sunday. Its extreme rhetoric and bold claim to divine authorship reflect the uncertainty of the time. Our author used his general knowledge about Sunday prohibitions and possible threats, elaborating on the latter by means of a variety of scriptural sources to form a kind of prophetic message for his contemporaries.

The question of whether he drew on a specific literary source remains unresolved. Texts which combine the kind of sabbatarian impulses within the context of a diatribe against offenders are rare in this period. One example may be a sermon by Eusebius of Alexandria dated to the sixth or seventh century.[125] The Greek homily, while it does not indulge in the full imprecation seen in the Sunday Letter, yet castigates the violators of Sunday, first for illicit entertainments, but also for the judicial proceedings which cause dissension. Similarly, a sermon once ascribed to Ephrem the Syrian (d. 373) issues a series of warnings to those who sit in the marketplace on Sundays instead of going to church.[126] Such writ-

---

[120] See Chapter 1, pp. 12–14.

[121] See above, pp. 8–9.

[122] See above, p. 9.

[123] See above, pp. 7–8.

[124] See above, pp. 11 n. 49, 13.

[125] PG 86, cols. 413–22. See Rordorf, *Sabbat und Sonntag*, p. 135 n. 4 and Huber, *Geist und Buchstabe*, pp. 93–8. The sermon was translated into Latin at an early date, since one version of it appears in the Homiliary of Toledo – BL Add. 30,853 – which also contains a shortened copy of the Sunday Letter (see above, p. 47). For the Toledo version, see G. Morin, '*Sermo de dominincae observatione*: Une ancienne adaptation Latine d'un sermon attribué a Eusèbe d'Alexandrie', *Revue bénédictine* 24 (1907), 530–4. Cf. Priebsch, *Letter from Heaven*, pp. 32–3.

[126] *Sancti Ephraem Syri hymni et sermones*, ed. T. J. Lamy (Mechlin, 1882–1902), III, 156. For a German translation, see E. Beck, *Des heiligen Ephraem des Syrers Sermones*, Corpus Scriptorum Christianorum Orientalium 320–1, Syr. 138–9 (Louvain, 1972), pp. 77–8. Beck notes that the sermon has elements which may belong to Ephrem, but doubts whether the sermon in its present form is by him (ix). See also Priebsch, *Letter from Heaven*, p. 32.

ings may have been known to our author and may, in fact, point to some Eastern influence in its composition, but they cannot in any way be termed a 'source' of the Sunday Letter. In truth, for much of the content of the text one need look only as far as scripture.

Content and Biblical Sources

The basic framework which surrounds the letter of Christ has already been discussed above: while the earliest copies (and probably the original) rely on the mention of an important city (Jerusalem, Rome) or holy place (the sepulchre of St Peter) and the narrative of a succession of obscure priests who (it is implied) believed its message and passed it along to others, later recensions dispense with this formula in favour of other kinds of attestations such as oaths sworn by either Christ himself or by a bishop or pope. With few exceptions, however, the text insists that it has a divine origin, was written or dictated by God/Christ and came straight from heaven or the throne of God. In order to boost the urgency of the message, Recension I includes references to two earlier letters which have gone unheeded and claims that only the intercession of various saints has prevented punishment in the past. Most letters end with an admonition to the clergy, on pain of being anathematized, to preach and disseminate the letter. It is clear that all of these elements of the frame are intended to heighten the significance and authority of the message.

The epistolary portion itself is ingeniously and boldly devised. Whatever else one might say about the original author, it is obvious that he certainly had some knowledge of scripture. He did all he could to lend authenticity to his work by liberally quoting and alluding to biblical texts and imitating an Old Testament prophetic style. While the use of the first person is not always consistently maintained, the phrase *Amen dico vobis*, well-known from the Gospels, reminds one of the speaker.[127] The account of Christ's passion in words which echo an apocryphal speech that was circulating at the time, is featured in some versions.[128]

Most of the Sunday Letter, however, harks back to the Old Testament prophets in tone as well as the actual adaptation of some appropriate texts. Association with the sabbath is established with partial quotations from the decalogue. However, this is a mere allusion to the six days of creation, and the seventh of rest. Only one version adds 'in die sancto dominico requievit'; in most others the difficulty of the seventh day being the sabbath is not noticed.[129]

---

[127] Cf. Matt. VI.2, 16 etc.

[128] For example, this speech by Christ detailing what he did on behalf of mankind was incorporated into one of Caesarius of Arles' sermons; *Sermo* LVII.4, ed. Morin, CCSL 103, 251–4. A passage in Basel B VII 7 illustrates this use of the speech: *Amen dico uobis. Propter uos ueni autem in mundum, propter uos fl[age]llatus, propter uos spineam coronam ac[cepi] et suspensus in ligno et resurrexi diem sanctum [dominicum]* (Appendix IIc, lines 9–11).

[129] Graz 248 (133rb): *in die septimo, in die dominico requievit*; cf. Exodus XX.11: *et requievit in die septimo*.

Most of the biblical borrowings are of this kind; they appear to be drawn from memory or perhaps by way of other sources rather than being exact copies. For example, Leviticus XXVI, which begins with a reference to the sabbath, offers many of the very elements found in the Sunday Letter: the blessings are abundance of the field (vv. 4–5), peace (v. 6), the elimination of *malas bestias* 'harmful beasts' (v. 6), the routing of enemies (vv. 7–8), and multiplying of the people (v. 9); and for disobedience, the threats are terror (v. 16), unfruitfulness of the land (vv. 16, 20), plague (vv. 21, 25) and beasts who will consume cattle (v. 22). Other passages may also provide verbal sources for the blessings such as the *cataractas caeli* ('floodgates of heaven') or the fruitfulness of the land.[130]

Additional punishments seem also to be drawn from scripture such as the *brucos et locustas* ('bruchus and locusts') and the *scyniphes* of the plagues of Egypt,[131] or the threat to blot the names of violators from the book of the living.[132] Later versions of the Sunday Letter prefer to focus on the threat of foreign invasion, which may be drawn from the following passage in Jeremiah:

> Ecce ego adducam super vos gentem de longinquo domus Israhel, ait Dominus, gentem robustam gentem antiquam gentem cuius ignorabis linguam nec intelleges quid loquatur.[133]

On the whole, the impression created by the Sunday Letter is that of a collection of statements which are meant to sound like scripture while they do not, in fact, quote it directly. They are assembled without any particular attention to order in the main body of the text, and therefore all the varying versions suffer to a greater or lesser extent from a lack of logical coherence, since they rely on exhortation and invective rather than argument. Quickly the narrative elements give way to the collection of curses and blessings, and short lists of prohibitions, and the text ends with authenticating formulas such as oaths sworn to confirm its origin and warnings to clergy who would not disseminate the letter. The point does not seem to be clarification of the precise nature of Sunday observance but to give the

---

[130] See Malachi III.30 for the *cataractas caeli*; BL Add. 19,725, Appendix IIb, lines 31–3: *si emendaueritis aperiam uobis cataractas celi et dabo <uobis frumentum>, uindemiam, <et> pomam arborum et amplificabo uitam eternam et uiuetis in seculum*; cf. Deuteronomy VII.13: *et diliget te ac multiplicabit benedicetque fructui ventris tui et fructui terrae tuae frumento tuo atque vindemiae* ('And he will love thee and multiply thee, and will bless the fruit of thy womb, and the fruit of thy land, thy corn, and thy vintage').

[131] For *brucos* and *locustas*, see Psalms LXXVII.46 and CIV.34–5 (Vienna 1355, Appendix IIa, lines 53–4: *mitto super vos locustas et brucos qui comedunt fructus vestros*) referring to the events of Exodus X.13; for the *[s]cinifes* ('stinging insects') see Exodus VIII.16 (BN lat. 12,270, Appendix I, lines 33–4: *et mittam in os vestrum sive in oculos vel in aures bestiolas quas vocant scyniphes venenatas pessimas ad devorandum vos*).

[132] Ps. LXX.29 *deleantur de libro viventium* (BN lat. 12,270, Appendix I, lines 52–3: *delebo nomina vestra de libro vite si per penitentiam non emendaveritis*).

[133] Jeremiah V.15: 'Behold, I will bring upon you a nation from afar, O house of Israel, saith the Lord: a strong nation, an ancient nation, a nation whose language thou shalt not know, nor understand what they say' (Vienna 133, Appendix III, lines 37–8: *Et inducam super vos gentem devastandum cuius linguam nescitis*). Cf. Deuteronomy XXVIII.49–50.

impression, in a general way, that cessation of secular labour and church attendance were urgently required to avoid imminent disaster, prompted by God's wrath.
On the other hand, its very flaws may have encouraged adaptation to whatever
the circumstances seemed to require: names were changed, Sunday prohibitions
added and dropped, other misdeeds were addressed. And, not surprisingly, new
materials were brought in to strengthen its case.

Related Texts: the Sunday List and Visio Pauli

One text in particular appears frequently in association with the Sunday Letter,
since it also has the Lord's day as its theme. This is the 'Sunday List' – also known
as *Dies dominica* or the *Dignatio diei dominici* – which is a straightforward enumeration of various (mostly biblical) events which were known or supposed to
have occurred on Sunday, providing a rationale for the sanctity of that day. In
some respects, it was a very fluid tradition in which few lists are exactly alike,
suggesting that this was a text subject to frequent adaptation.[134]

Clare Lees has examined the history and transmission of the Sunday List and
compared the various versions from the early medieval period in connection with
their appearance in the Sunday Letter.[135] For example, in an early and relatively
short list in a section concerned with the distinction between sabbath and Sunday
in his *De ecclesiasticis officiis*, Isidore of Seville enumerates the first day of the
world, the creation of the angels, the first manna given from heaven, the Resurrection and Pentecost as events which occurred on a Sunday.[136] Similar lists were also
embedded in sermons: Lees notes its presence in sermons by Eusebius of Alexandria and Hrabanus Maurus, as well as in two pseudo-Augustinian sermons.[137]

---

[134] No later than the twelfth century, the list also becomes a sermon, which is found in some manuscripts
immediately preceding or following a Sunday Letter. A frequent Latin *incipit* is *Veneranda est nobis
haec dies*, and examples may be found in the following manuscripts: 1. without an accompanying
Sunday Letter: Munich, Bayerische Staatsbibliothek, 15,831 (s. xii), 131v–133v; Köln, Historisches
Archiv der Stadt Köln, W I 37 (s. xii), 72r–73v; and 2. with a Sunday Letter: Michaelbeuern,
Stiftsbibliothek, 97 (s. xv), 174v–175r; Innsbruck, Stiftsbibliothek Wilten (s.n.) (s. xv), 154ra–154vb,
and many other manuscripts of the same time period. See also a Latin/early Middle English macaronic
sermon entitled *In die dominica* in a manuscript from the end of the twelfth century, London, Lambeth
Palace 487; *Old English Homilies and Homiletic Treatises*, ed. Morris, pp. 138–45.

[135] 'The "Sunday Letter" and the "Sunday Lists"', *Anglo-Saxon England* 14 (1985), 129–51 and see the
section 'Les Bénédictions du Dimanche' in Dumaine, 'Dimanche', cols. 985–90; see also Charles
D. Wright, 'Dies dominica', *Sources of Anglo-Saxon Literary Culture*, ed. F. Biggs, pp. 93–4; and
McNamara, '52C. Two Hiberno-Latin Texts on the Lord's Day', *The Apocrypha in the Irish Church*,
p. 63.

[136] Book 1, c. 25 (PL 83, col. 761); see Lees, 'Sunday Lists', pp. 138–9.

[137] Pseudo-Augustine, *Sermones de tempore*, CLXVII (PL 39, col. 2070); Hrabanus Maurus, *Homilia*
XLI (PL 110, col. 76); Pseudo-Augustine, *Sermones de diversis*, CCLXXX (PL 39, col. 2274); for
the Eusebius sermon, see G. Morin, 'Sermo de dominicae observatione: une ancienne adaptation
latine d'une sermon attribué à Eusèbe d'Alexandrie', *Revue Bénédictine* 24 (1907), 530–4 (found
in the well-known Homilary of Toledo which also contains a Sunday Letter, see above, p. 47).
The latter three are clearly related to each other and to the lists in Isidore, Hrabanus Maurus' *De*

As regards its appearance in the Sunday Letter, Lees confirms that the list was an interpolation since none of the earliest Latin letters contain one. She has furthermore discovered that only the Insular Sunday Letters feature a Sunday List. Her tables comparing elements found in all the lists reveal that the Insular versions are also quite different in character from those which have no Insular connections.[138] The Insular lists are significantly longer, having been expanded with additional items, some biblical (though not always identified in scripture as occurring on Sunday) and some apocryphal.[139] As will be seen in the discussion of the Old English Sunday Letter in the next chapter, many of these entries and additional details also appear in the lists which are part of the Old English versions and point to a Hiberno-Latin source for the vernacular letters which include them.

Another natural association seems to have been with the *Visio sancti Pauli*, translated into Latin from the original Greek between the fourth and sixth centuries.[140] The two apocrypha must have been in circulation at roughly the same time and the influence appears to have gone both ways. In later shortened versions of the *Visio*, the final climactic scene of this text involves the intercession of St Paul and the archangel Michael on behalf of those in hell, with the result that a Sunday respite from suffering is granted. Both the intercession and the Sunday respite find their way into the Sunday Letter, perhaps by way of the *Visio*, but the connections are not as clear as they have sometimes been made out to be.[141] It should be stressed from the start that the two motifs are entirely independent of each other in the Letter and were likely added at different points in its transmission. The Letter's version of the intercession simply involves the statement that the threatened punishment would have been meted out earlier had it not been for the intercession of SS Mary, Michael, Peter and, in some versions, Paul.[142] It has been suggested

---

clericorum institutione (PL 107, col. 356) and Pseudo-Alcuin's *Liber de divinis officiis* (PL 39, col. 2274).

138 As a comparison of Tables 1 and 2 (non-Insular) with Tables 3 and 4 (Insular) shows; Lees, 'Sunday Lists', pp. 138–44. Though Lees does not label the three lists in Table 3 – those in Pseudo-Augustine 167, Sermo XXXII in Cambridge, Pembroke College 25, and in the Bobbio Missal (ed. E. A. Lowe, Henry Bradshaw Society 58 (London, 1919), pp. 150–1) – as Insular, this is likely to be the case for at least the first two which exhibit striking textual links to the Insular lists; see Chapter 4, note 172.

139 The lists in Lees's tables 1 and 2 contain no more than six entries each, which may be compared to the extreme case of the list in the Old Irish *Epistil Ísu*, which has more than twenty. Moreover, it is not just length that characterizes the Insular lists; the details added to individual entries can establish links among this group.

140 Silverstein, *Visio sancti Pauli*, pp. 5–6.

141 The connection between the *Visio* and the Sunday Letter was first noted by R. Willard in 'The Address of the Soul to the Body', *Publications of the Modern Language Association of America* 50 (1935), 957–83 at 966–73. In discussions of two other Old English homilies which also feature an intercession scene, Mary Clayton describes the connection more cautiously: 'It is probable . . . that an *Apocalypse of Mary* has also had some influence on this version of the Sunday Letter' ('Delivering the Damned', p. 100). In a similar comparison to the two Old English homilies, Richard Johnson notes that 'the ultimate aims of the intercessions differ and therefore rule out any direct relationship between the scenes'; *St. Michael the Archangel*, pp. 91–5.

142 See, for example, BL Add. 19,725, Appendix IIb, lines 28–31: *Ego uero dico uobis, quia mense*

that the intercession in the Sunday Letter, part of the first recension, is ultimately derived from the *Visio sancti Pauli*, perhaps by way of the very similar *Apocalypse of Mary*. In the latter it does not take place during a tour of hell as it does in the two other apocrypha, the favour granted is not of a respite from hell's torment, and there are no distinctive verbal echoes. The association with the *Apocalypse of Mary* is suggested primarily by the fact that Mary is one of the intercessors, as she is not in the *Visio*.[143] Given that the intercession motif is fairly common in both Christian and Jewish literature, it seems that the influence of the *Visio* or the *Apocalypse of Mary* must remain possible but uncertain.[144]

We are on more solid ground with the second feature, the Sunday Respite itself. According to Silverstein, a growing sabbatarianism was responsible for the more central role played by this respite and the veneration of Sunday in general in the later redactions, beginning with Redaction III.[145] The time period specified for the observance of Sunday is from none on Saturday to dawn on Monday.[146] These are the perimeters whenever the various versions of the Sunday Letter do specify the time of observance.[147] Because of the lateness of its appearance in the *Visio* – the earliest copy of these redactions dates from the twelfth century – it is possible that this detail was taken from the Sunday Letter itself.[148] Strengthening a case for the widespread use of the formula in the Sunday Letter before this period we have the eleventh-century Old English translations.[149] However, while it is possible

iste Nouembri proximo qui fuit, perire debuistis, si deprecacio fuisset sancte Marie uirginis et beati archangeli Michaeli necnon et beatorum apostolorum Petri et Pauli et per oracionem eorum liberi fuistis. In one, all the angels, and the cherubim and seraphim, are substituted for Peter and Paul (Graz 248, 133r). In Recension III, there may be a remote echo of the motif in that Mary and the angels are said to pray daily for those addressed.

[143] See Clayton, 'Delivering the Damned', p. 98.

[144] As Silverstein notes, such intercessions are found in biblical narratives (Abraham pleading on behalf of Sodom and Gomorrah) and elsewhere (*Visio sancti Pauli*, p. 87 and n. 25). For the role of St Michael as intercessor, see Johnson, *St. Michael the Archangel*, p. 93 and Appendix C. Mary, and SS Michael and Peter are also often invoked in protection clauses in Anglo-Saxon charters (ibid. p. 95 n. 47).

[145] Silverstein, *Visio sancti Pauli*, pp. 79–81.

[146] Silverstein, *Visio sancti Pauli*, p. 190 (discussion on pp. 80–1).

[147] The earliest surviving copy of known date – Paris 8508, s. x (60r) – has *de ora nona sabati usque ad i[i] feriam ora prima*.

[148] See the manuscripts listed by Silverstein, *Visio sancti Pauli*, pp. 220–1. Two members of this redaction add excerpts of the Sunday Letter and the Sunday List (Silverstein, *Visio sancti Pauli*, pp. 194–5); The possibility of such influence was first suggested by Willard, 'The Address of the Soul to the Body', pp. 971–2. In addition to the Latin versions of the *Visio* there is also the twelfth-century homily in London, Lambeth Palace Library, 487 called *In diebus dominicis*, an adaptation of the *Visio* which also uses this formula; *Old English Homilies and Homiletic Treatises*, ed. Morris, pp. 40–7. Morris maintains that the texts in Lambeth 487 are copies of eleventh-century exemplars (p. xi).

[149] So the Old English adaptations of second recension copies, for example, *fram sæternesdæges none oð monandæges lihtinge* (C26) and *fram þære nigoðan tide þæs sæternesdæges oð ðone morgen on monandæg* (D78–9) and frequently in E and F (e.g. E44, F101–2). However, the formula was probably already part of the first recension: though late (s. xiv/xv), Vienna 1355 and the Old English translation of a closely related predecessor together provide evidence for its inclusion as early as

that the *Visio sancti Pauli* was influenced by the Sunday Letter, it is still uncertain where the formula itself originated.[150]

Underscoring the textual evidence is that of the manuscripts: the two texts appear side by side in several late manuscripts, sometimes with no obvious break in the text to signal that we are moving from one to the other.[151] One copy of the *Visio* is supplemented with an extract from the Sunday Letter, apparently in order to further strengthen the theme of Sunday veneration.[152] Moreover, another fourteenth-century copy ends with a Sunday List.[153] This particular list was very likely copied from a Sunday Letter since the preceding biblical quotation is also found in members of Recension II, and the *Visio* list itself is strikingly similar to that found at the end of several Sunday Letters.[154] The Sunday Letter, in both its Latin and vernacular versions, was a mutating text with shifting concerns. Some common distinguishing features allow us to see a continuity during the Middle Ages, beginning with its composition before the end of the sixth century, but there were many revisions of its text. With only a few exceptions, we do not know what its reception may have been. Its persistence in populist preaching endeavours is matched only by continuing condemnation, ranging from its first appearance, to the fourteenth-century Hugo von Reutlingen, to modern-day pastoral concerns about the use of the letter as *Schutzbrief* in many German homes.[155] With six surviving vernacular versions, Anglo-Saxon England provides us with one of the earliest views of its use in a particular place and time. It is therefore valuable not only to the appreciation of eleventh-century homiletic literature, but also to the spread and transmission of the Sunday Letter itself.

---

the eleventh century and likely somewhat earlier. See B116: *fram nontide þæs sæternesdæges oð monandæges lihtinge* (Vienna 1355: *in die sabbati de hora nona usque lucescente die lune feriatis*).

[150] The closest earlier reference may be from an eighth-century Bavarian law code: *Et [siquis] in itinere positus cum carra vel cum nave, pauset die dominico usque in secunda feria*; *Die Gesetze des Karolingerreiches, 714–911*, ed. K. A. Eckhardt (Weimar, 1934), II, 114–16. In England the first mention of the formula is in the laws of Edgar, see Chapter 2, p. 22. Earlier references such as those in the laws of Wihtræd have the time period, like the Jewish sabbath, from evening to evening (see Chapter 1, p. 16)

[151] This is true of Budapest University Library, lat. 39 (s. xiv/xv); Uppsala, Universitätsbibliothek C212 (s. xiv); and Wilhering, Stiftsbibliothek, IX 162 (s. xv), for example, while in BL Royal 11 B.x (s. xiv/xv) and Royal 8 F.vi (s. xv) the Sunday Letter follows the *Visio*, and in Munich, Bayerische Staatsbibliothek, clm 2625 (s. xiii) the *Visio* occurs later in the manuscript (cf. Appendix IV). Royal 8 F.vi also has a Sunday List which is close to the one appended to the *Visio* in Vienna 1629.

[152] This is Munich, Bayerische Staatsbibliothek, clm 12,005 (s. xv); the Sunday Letter extract (from a copy of Recension II), which Silverstein identifies only as 'a warning . . . to those on earth who do not keep Sunday properly' (*Visio sancti Pauli*, p. 44) is printed by him on p. 194.

[153] Vienna, Österreichische Nationalbibliothek, 1629, printed in Silverstein (*Visio sancti Pauli*, p. 195).

[154] For example, BL Royal 8 F.vi, 24r.

[155] See above, nn. 103 and 111.

4

The Old English Sunday Letters

The Sunday Letter in its Anglo-Saxon context represents some of the earliest evidence for its widespread use in the West. Six copies survive, representing four distinct lines of transmission.[1] If it is remarkable that we encounter the letter so often in Old English, it is even more striking that it appears to have been acceptable in a variety of environments. The most learned minds of the age may have rejected it, but its placement in manuscripts compiled at respected centres and the evidence of active use suggest that it was found to be a suitable vehicle for instruction in certain contexts.

Manuscripts

Cambridge, Corpus Christi College 140 (Letter A)

Letter A was copied into CCCC 140, a West Saxon version of the Gospels written at Bath Abbey in the first half of the eleventh century.[2] The Sunday Letter was added later (s. xi²) at the end of the Gospel of Mark and is written in the same hand as some of the manumissions added at Bath in the blank spaces of the manuscript; all of these mention Abbot Ælfsige (1075–87), which provides a convenient way to assign a defined time period to the work of the scribe.[3]

The text follows the end of Mark without a break and with an only slightly enlarged capital *h*. The scribe edited (perhaps for oral delivery) the first line, adding an introductory *Men þa leofestan, halie* before *gewrit* and *soðlice* to the beginning of the second sentence. The placement of this Sunday Letter is remarkable.

---

[1]   Another copy existed in a now lost manuscript; see below, BL Cotton Otho B.x (see below, p. 72). The Old English Sunday Letters have previously been edited in the following places: Letter A by R. Priebsch in 'The Chief Sources', pp. 135–8; Letters B, C, E and F as Napier XLV, LVII, XLIII and XLIV, respectively by A. Napier in *Wulfstan*, pp. 205–15, 215–26, 226–32 and 291–9; and Letter D by Napier in 'Contributions to Old English Literature: 1. An Old English Homily on the Observance of Sunday', in *An English Miscellany Presented to Dr. Furnivall*, ed. W. P. Ker and A. S. Napier (Oxford, 1901), pp. 357–62.

[2]   See the detailed manuscript description by R. M. Liuzza in *The Old English Version of the Gospels*, I, xxv–xxxiii. A colophon names one of the scribes, Ælfric, who presented the book to a certain Brihtwold; neither figure is known from other sources (ibid. I, xxvi). Due to the loss of leaves between Mark, Luke and John, Liuzza has suggested that the individual Gospels 'spent some time as unbound booklets' (ibid. I, xxi). See also Ker, pp. 47–9 (No. 35).

[3]   This scribe wrote four manumissions: one on folio 1r and three on one of two additional leaves which formerly belonged to this manuscript and are now bound in CCCC 111 (Liuzza, *The Old English Version of the Gospels*, I, xxvi–ix). See D. Pelteret, *Catalogue of English Post-conquest Vernacular Documents* (Woodbridge, 1990), pp. 90–3 (nos. 73–6 and 81). The last seven words of a confraternity agreement of 1077 were also added by this scribe (*The Old English Version of the Gospels*, I, xxix–xxx).

The addition of non-canonical text to books of scripture is not unique,[4] but the Sunday Letter is a very unconventional text, raising the unanswerable question of whether the writer placed it in this context simply because the empty space was available, or because he in fact thought that the letter had near-canonical status, since it does, after all, claim to have been written by the Saviour's own hand (*þurh þæs hehstan hælendes handa gewriten*).[5] In other Old English versions of the Sunday Letter, the text is called a *godspell*, though not in this particular one; however, as mentioned above, *halie* is supplied before *gewrit*, possibly in an effort to add some authority to the piece.[6]

Cambridge, Corpus Christi College 419 (Letters B and E)

CCCC 419 is part of a two-volume collection of homilies that is in many ways unique. Its format is unusually small for a homiliary, apparently designed for portability.[7] Written by one scribe in the first half of the eleventh century, its origin has been placed at Canterbury or possibly at a monastery in the south-east which was closely associated with Canterbury.[8] Less uncertain is its later history: some time later the manuscript found its way to Exeter where corrections were made. Its contents are diverse, and it uses an unusual amount of non-Ælfrician material for a homiliary of this date.[9] CCCC 419 contains a broad selection of eight anonymous homilies, one of them compiled from Ælfric's work,[10] as well as six

---

4   Tom Hall provides examples in connection with such a placement of the Gospel of Nicodemus in 'The *Evangelium Nichodemi* and *Vindicta Salvatoris* in Anglo-Saxon England', p. 50 n. 48.

5   A85.

6   E188, F208. The word *godspell* is not commonly applied to texts other than the four written by the evangelists or their contents. The *DOE* notes its (rare) use in reference to 'homilies [or] explications of the Gospels' (sense 2.a.iv), in reference to (early) accounts of Christ's life written by others (sense 2.b), in texts 'erroneously attributed to Christ' (sense 2.c, as used in Letters E and F), and of texts 'perhaps thought to be based on the Gospels' (sense 4).

7   In addition to Ker's description (nos. 68–9, *Catalogue*, pp. 115–18), CCCC 419 and 421 have been extensively examined by Wilcox, 'The Compilation of Old English Homilies in MSS Cambridge, Corpus Christi College, 419 and 421'; idem, *Wulfstan Texts and Other Homiletic Materials*, pp. 1–13; and by Budny, *Insular, Anglo-Saxon, and Early Anglo-Norman Manuscript Art*, I, 525–33. Budny describes it as a 'handy and rather attractive portable copy of homilies' (I, 526). The leaves measure approximately 206 mm x 128 mm.

8   Pope vol. I, p. 82; *CH* II, introd., lxxii; *CH* I, introd., p. 159. The connection to Canterbury is made through Cambridge, Trinity College B. 15. 34, a manuscript written at Canterbury which shows close textual affinities with CCCC 419 in the Ælfrician items common to both. Wilcox, in the most thorough analysis of the manucript to date, also suggests Ramsey or Winchcombe as possibilities, since these were less centralized scriptoria with strong Canterbury influences. Wilcox, 'Compilation', pp. 238–42; see also Pope vol. I, pp. 80–3. It may be worth noting that the closely related Letter F also appears in a south-eastern manuscript probably written at Christ Church, Canterbury (BL Cotton Tiberius A.iii; see below).

9   Godden has described it as a 'general purpose collection', *CH* II, introd., lxxi. Scragg notes that the compiler has drawn upon a broad selection of works by Wulfstan and Ælfric and has put together his collection 'with care and authority'; 'The Corpus of Vernacular Homilies', pp. 252–3.

10   These are Napier XLII (Ker, art. 1), Letters E and B (arts. 2 and 3), Napier XL (art. 8), Belfour VI,

by Archbishop Wulfstan[11] and an Ælfrician sermon for Rogationtide.[12] The latter homily is the only one for which the occasion is specified; otherwise the topics are general and cover the basics of the Christian faith, the Anti-Christ and Judgement Day, among other things.

Most remarkable for the present study is that the manuscript contains two Old English Sunday Letters (E and B) back to back as the second and third items, together occupying some fifty-seven pages. Their location at the beginning of the manuscript means that they formed an integral part of its design. The subject of Sunday observance was no doubt seen to fit in with the manuscript's overall emphasis on general themes related to Christian faith and practice, and like several pieces in the manuscript, Letter E incorporates some material from Wulfstan's work, which appears again later in the manuscript, and draws on some of the sources which are also used in the Vercelli Book for its conclusion.[13] The selection of the former, in this case a pertinent extract on Sunday and tithing, is not surprising since the manuscript as a whole is, according to Bethurum (p. 1), one of the two archetypes for Wulfstan's homilies.

CCCC 421, a companion volume written in the same hand, originally contained six Ælfrician homilies and one sermon by Byrhtferth (Napier XLVIII), and again some anonymous compositions.[14] Two sections now bound with CCCC 421 were written at Exeter; they consist of five Ælfrician and two Wulfstanian homilies.[15] Although it is not definitely known where these portions were added to CCCC 421, Wilcox sees some clues in the corrections and accent marks which are probable characteristics of Exeter scribes and occur in both the original and added portions; while these point to Exeter as the place where the manuscript was augmented, it is not known when the collation took place.[16]

Wilcox has meticulously laid out the various corrections and additions to each sermon in the manuscript. He divides these into changes made during the original

Assmann XI (arts. 13 and 14), Napier XLVI (art. 11); Napier XL, XLII and XLVI are composites which include excerpts from Wulfstan's work, and Ker's article 15 is compiled of Ælfrician material though it is probably not by him (Pope vol. II, pp. 799–803).

11   Ker, articles 4–7, 9–10 contain Bethurum XX, VIIIc, VI, VII, Xc, XIII.

12   This is *LS* XVII, *De auguriis*, here entitled *Sermo in letanie maiore uel quando uolueris*.

13   See details below, pp. 88–93. Other sermons in CCCC 419 and the original portions of 421 which include Wulfstan extracts are Napier XL, XLVI, XLVII.

14   The Ælfrician pieces are Pope XI, for the Octave of Pentecost (Ker, art. 6); *CH* I, XVIII, Rogationtide (art. 12); *CH* I, XIX on the Lord's Prayer (art. 13), *CH* I, XX on the Catholic Faith (art. 14), and *CH* I, XXI on the Ascension (art. 15), and a piece now lost (*De duodecim abusivis*, art. 16). The anonymous items are Napier XLVII, a composite combining Wulfstan and Byrhtferth excerpts (art. 8), and Vercelli X / Blickling IX (art. 9).

15   These were added to the manuscript in two groups; at the beginning of the volume, following Ælfric's homily on Pentecost (art. 1, *CH* I, XXII), and are for the celebration of the saints, apostles, martyrs, confessors and virgins (Ker, arts. 2–5, *CH* II, XXXV–XXXIX); in a separate section are Wulfstan's eschatological homily Bethurum III (art. 10), and a piece compiled of the archbishop's material, though perhaps not by him (art. 11, Napier L, see Bethurum, pp. 39–40). It has been suggested that Lambeth 489, which contains another Sunday Letter (Letter C), was intended to be a companion volume to these sections (see below, pp. 67–8).

16   The corrections are the *i* to *y* change mentioned below (Wilcox, 'Compilation', p. 31).

production, signs of early use and alterations made at Exeter once it had arrived there.[17] The latter two categories provide significant evidence for the reception of Letters B and E.[18] While the manuscript was still in Canterbury, several readers worked through and corrected Letter E (which precedes B in the manuscript), including a very careful reader whom Wilcox labels 'hand 13'. This person, nearly all of whose interventions occur in E, made frequent verbal substitutions (*yrfe* for *ceap*, *æftemesta* for *nexta*, *gereste* for *ablan*, for example), and added clarifications to the text (such as *fram þæs sæternesdæges none* to complete the time reference, and *gereorda* to *twa and hundseofontig*). He reveals his knowledge of other texts on the subject by adding *and wifunga* to a list of Sunday proscriptions.[19] The Exeter corrections reveal a very different focus. Here one scribe (Wilcox's 'hand 20') frequently changed *i* to *y*, and another ('hand 22') made many linguistic modifications, altering non-West Saxon spellings to conform to standard late West Saxon, frequently changing *in* to *on* and *heo* to *hi*, for example.[20] All of these changes, in one way or another, point to a continued interest and possibly use of Letter E. The same cannot be said for Letter B. It may be that it, too, was consulted, but there are almost no traces of this.

Letters E and B are two very different versions of the Sunday Letter, based on two separate Latin recensions. Wilcox speculates that they were copied from the same exemplar, which is possible, but the evidence is slight.[21] It is difficult to see the rationale for devoting so much space to these two pieces. Was instruction on the subject seen as a priority, in particular with a view towards increasing church attendance? A more mundane explanation may be that the title of Letter B, *Sermo angelorum nomina*, led the compiler to believe that this piece was on a separate subject, since Letter E is entitled *Sunnandæges spell*.[22] The latter suggestion, however, seems less in keeping with the active engagement with the texts otherwise in evidence throughout the manuscript.[23] In any case, the survival of two Old English Sunday Letters in CCCC 419 expands our understanding of its significance in the late Anglo-Saxon milieu.

---

[17] The corrections to E made in production are listed in tables 8–10 in Wilcox ('Compilation', pp. 26–7). These include the possibly significant deletion of *me* in lines 140 and 157 (see commentary).

[18] These are listed in tables 11–12, 17 and 19–20 in Wilcox ('Compilation', pp. 28–36).

[19] The addition could have been taken (or remembered) from the source of Napier XXIII, which was copied again later in CCCC 419 (see commentary for line 72).

[20] See discussion of Letter E's language below.

[21] It is based on the similarity of decoration in the initial letter and the fact that B 'ends with greater finality than the other homilies (its last letters are in capitals and touched in red)' (Wilcox, 'Compilation', p. 20).

[22] Jost speculates that the title is somehow associated with one of Aldebert's heretical prayers which included exotic names of angels (*Wulfstanstudien*, p. 227, and above, p. 38), though Letter B's introduction with its no doubt unfamiliar-sounding names of priests receiving the letter may be just as likely an occasion for the rubric. On Aldebert's angel names see Jeffrey Russell, 'Saint Boniface and the Eccentrics', *Church History* 33 (1964), 235–47, at 236–8.

[23] See Scragg, 'Corpus of Vernacular Homilies', pp. 252–3.

London, Lambeth Palace 489 (Letter C)

Lambeth Palace 489 was produced at Exeter by scribes who were active during the time of Bishop Leofric (1046–72), and like CCCC 419 it is relatively small in size.[24] It is generally agreed that it once formed part of or was a companion to another collection of sermons, BL Cotton Cleopatra B.xiii (part 1).[25] Five different hands have been distinguished, and there is evidence that parts of it were written simultaneously; in addition, Robinson has pointed out that it was probably produced in two booklets with the first three Ælfrician homilies forming the first, and the balance, the second.[26] The manuscript has been damaged, probably as it was put together, and some of the letters in its gutter are no longer visible.

Lambeth 489 was very likely produced for use by a bishop.[27] It begins with three Ælfrician homilies for major festivals (Christmas, Easter day, All Saints' day), includes Sunday Letter C and a reworking of Ælfric's homily on the Lord's Prayer, and concludes with three homilies for the dedication of a church, two of which, again, use Ælfric's work.[28] Its companion volume Cleopatra B.xiii contains similar items, including, among other things, another homily on the dedication of a church, a homily on the consecration of a bishop and a coronation oath, all likewise pointing to its episcopal functionality.[29]

The appearance of the Sunday Letter in such a collection raises some intriguing questions. Whether it was copied under a bishop's (Leofric's?) specific direction or merely selected by a compiler collecting pieces to be used by a bishop, the fact remains that there is no indication that its orthodoxy was in any way suspect. A person clearly influenced by Wulfstan's phraseology troubled to extensively

---

24 The leaves measure 191mm x 118mm (Wilcox, *Wulfstan Texts*, p. 79).

25 Ker, *Catalogue*, pp. 182, 345. Ker notes that the hand which wrote Letter C is 'closely similar to and perhaps identical with the hand of Cleopatra B.xiii . . . art. 10' (*Catalogue*, p. 345). The manuscript has also been described by T. A. M. Bishop, 'Notes on Cambridge Manuscripts; Part III: MSS Connected with Exeter', *Transactions of the Cambridge Bibliographical Society* 2 (1954–8), 192–9, and Wilcox, *Wulfstan Texts*, pp. 79–82.

26 P. R. Robinson, 'Self-Contained Units in Composite Manuscripts of the Anglo-Saxon Period, *Anglo-Saxon England* 7 (1978), 231–8. The two final lines of Letter C are added as extra lines at the bottom of 30v and 31r showing that the next text had already been written (Wilcox, *Wulfstan Texts*, p. 80).

27 See Godden's assessment that it was compiled 'probably for the use of a bishop' (*CH* II, introd., xlii). Clemoes divides the manuscript into three units at least two of which (including the one containing C) he considers 'intended for the use of a bishop' (*CH* I, p. 22); cf. Wilcox, 'Compilation', p. 34.

28 The first three are *CH* I, II, XV, XXVI. The composite which follows Letter C is based on *CH* I, XIX, but also uses *CH* I, IX, *CH* II, I, *LS* XII, Wulfstan excerpts, a passage also found in Vercelli II, and a passage which also concludes Letter C. The three homilies on the dedication of a church are edited as 1. *CH* II, XL, parts of *LS* XIII and XIX, and Brotanek, *Texte und Untersuchungen*, II, 2. Brotanek II, and 3. Brotanek I, by Ælfric.

29 Its entire contents are Napier XL (on Judgement Day), Ælfric, *CH* I, XVII (Second Sunday after Easter); *CH* I, I (*De initio creaturae*); Wulfstan, Bethurum XVIII (on the dedication of a church); Bethurum XVII (on the consecration of a bishop); a composite homily using *CH* I, XVIII and Vercelli XIX (rogationtide); a coronation oath and sections on royal duties; the beginning of Pope VIII (mainly on prayer); the end of Napier XXVII (a selection of sentences from Bethurum XX); and Ælfric's translation of the Lord's Prayer and the Creed.

rework the Latin source of Letter C, and the likelihood that some if not all of this took place at Exeter is increased by the concluding sentences reappearing in the homily which follows our text in the manuscript.[30] Letter C is entitled *Sermo ad populum [de] dominicis diebus*, and begins with a prelude, which improves on its Latin source in that it offers an introduction of the subject matter and a reasoned accounting for the letter's unusual arrival. The writer of this passage addresses his audience as bishops and mass-priests, which may be an indication of his own status, particularly as he refers to *us bisceopum*.[31] If we add to this the arrival in Exeter of two more Old English Sunday Letters (in CCCC 419) during this same period, we must conclude that these pieces were acceptable, at least at this time and place, to some of the highest ecclesiastical authorities in England.[32]

Cambridge, Corpus Christi College 162 (Letter D)

The earliest Old English letter (Letter D) was copied into CCCC 162, a carefully assembled sermon collection written by one scribe at the beginning of the eleventh century.[33] The manuscript was produced in the south-east at either Rochester or Canterbury, possibly St Augustine's Abbey.[34] A mid-sized homiliary that was thoughtfully compiled and produced, CCCC 162's contents can be divided into two sections: an initial collection of homilies which are designated for any occasion, and a *temporale* which begins with the second Sunday after Epiphany

---

30   For the borrowing of a list of sinners (C147–54) from Wulfstan, see Wilcox, 'Dissemination', p. 212. For additional details about the changes made to C, see below, pp. 78–82.

31   *Leofan men, us bisceopum and eallum mæsse-preostum is swiðe deope beboden þæt we æfre sculon mynegian and tyhtan eow, læwede menn, georne to eowre sawla þearfe, and hu ge agan her on life rihtlice to libbanne* (C1–4). It is true that the Latin urges the letter to be disseminated to all kings, bishops and Christian folk, but the introduction has been so thoroughly changed that there seems to be no reason why the author would feel compelled to include this reference to similar groups if they were not appropriate to his context.

32   It may be worth noting that these three Sunday Letters represent one of each of the three versions known to have been available in Anglo-Saxon England.

33   Budny suggests a date as early as the end of the tenth century (*Insular, Anglo-Saxon, and Early Anglo-Norman Manuscript Art*, I, p. 465). Extensive descriptions of CCCC 162 may be found in Ker, *Catalogue*, pp. 51–6 (No. 38); Scragg, 'Cambridge, Corpus Christi College 162', pp. 71–83; and Budny, pp. 463–73 (No. 28). Part of CCCC 178 was bound with CCCC 162 (pp. 139–60) by Archbishop Parker.

34   Ker, *Catalogue*, p. 56; Scragg, 'Cambridge, Corpus Christi College 162', p. 71. Godden posits Rochester as 'the most likely place of origin . . . though Canterbury is possible' (*CH* II, introd., xxxii) while Richards suggests that it was acquired (along with Bodley 340/342) from a southeastern source, 'possibly St Augustine's, Canterbury' (*Texts and their Traditions*, pp. 89–90). The collection concludes with the beginning of a homily for the feast and deposition of St Augustine with the title and initial in the main hand (Budny, *Insular, Anglo-Saxon, and Early Anglo-Norman Manuscript Art*, I, 463 and 469). The piece ends in the middle of sentence with the verso of the leaf left blank which may imply that it was copied from another collection containing this homily but was abandoned as not being appropriate for the intended recipient. Script and decorated initials resemble those in BL Royal 6 C.i which belonged to St Augustine's (Ker, *Catalogue*, p. 56; Budny, p. 466).

and follows the Church year.[35] The latter is constructed from mainly Ælfrician homilies, but includes two sets of anonymous homilies for Holy Week and Rogationtide as well as an additional homily for Lent.[36] The remaining homilies are by Ælfric, merging *CH* I and II and exhibiting a familiarity with his earlier rather than later work.[37]

The first part of this homiliary, however, may have been put together in stages, according to Donald Scragg's analysis.[38] It begins with a group of three general catechetical sermons by Ælfric: *De initio creaturae*, *De dominica oratione* and *De catholica fide* (*CH* I, I, XIX and XX). Letter D follows and the compiler selected three more Ælfrician homilies of a general nature (*CH* II, XIX; *LS* XIII; *CH* II, XII), and two for the second and third Sundays after Epiphany (*CH* II, IV; *CH* I, VIII).[39] Scragg has suggested that the last two homilies were an afterthought, independently copied in order to supplement the *temporale* to follow. Furthermore, he notes that the quire containing the beginning of Letter D may not originally have been intended to, since it consists of three bifolia and an added

---

35 Textual and palaeographical analyses have established that CCCC 162 is closely related to Bodl. Bodley 340/342 (Scragg, 'Cambridge, Corpus Christi College 162', pp. 71–4; Richards, *Texts and their Traditions*, p. 89) with the same corrections made in both in texts that they have in common (*CH* II, xxxii).

36 The first group consists of an anonymous sermon for Palm Sunday (Cameron B3.2.18), Assmann XIII (Maundy Thursday), Vercelli I (Good Friday), and anonymous sermons for Holy Saturday (Cameron B3.2.25) and Easter day (Cameron B3.2.27 with extracts from *CH* II, XV); the second group includes Vercelli XIX (Rogation Monday), Vercelli XX (Rogation Tuesday), Bazire/Cross III (Rogation Wednesday), and Tristram III (Ascension day). Vercelli III supplements Ælfric's homily for the second Sunday in Lent. To these one should add the anonymous appendage to *CH* I, XXXV (edited by Franz Wenisch in '*Nu bidde we eow for Godes lufon*: A Hitherto Unpublished Old English Homiletic Text in CCCC 162', in *Words Texts and Manuscripts: Studies in Anglo-Saxon Culture Presented to Helmut Gneuss on the Occasion of his Sixty-Fifth Birthday*, ed. Michael Korhammer (Cambridge, 1992), pp. 43–52) and the beginning of a homily for the Feast of the Deposition of St Augustine (H. Tristram, ed., 'Vier altenglische Predigten aus der heterodoxen Tradition' (Ph.D. diss., University of Freiburg, 1970), p. 428), at the end of the collection.

37 See Pope, vol. I, p. 22, and Scragg, 'Cambridge, Corpus Christi College 162', pp. 72, 80. The Ælfrician homilies are *CH* II, V (Septuagesima); *CH* II, VI (Sexagesima); *CH* I, X (Quinquagesima); *LS* XII (Quinquagesima); *CH* I, XI (1st Sunday in Lent); *CH* II, VII (1st Sunday in Lent); Pope II (Friday following); *CH* II, VIII (2nd Sunday in Lent); Pope III (Friday following); Pope IV (only 4 words, 3rd Sunday in Lent); Pope V (Friday following); *CH* I, XII (4th Sunday in Lent); Pope VI (Friday following); *CH* II, XIII (5th Sunday in Lent); Assmann V (Friday following); *CH* II, XIV (Palm Sunday); Assmann XIII (Maundy Thursday); *CH* I, XVI (1st Sunday after Easter); *CH* I, XVII (2nd Sunday after Easter); *CH* I, XXII (Pentecost); *CH* I, XXIII (2nd Sunday after Pentecost); *CH* II, XXIII (3rd Sunday after Pentecost); *CH* I, XXIV (4th Sunday after Pentecost); *CH* II, XXV (8th Sunday after Pentecost); *CH* II, XXVI (9th Sunday after Pentecost); *CH* I, XXVIII (11th Sunday after Pentecost); *CH* II, XXVIII (12th Sunday after Pentecost); *CH* II, XXXI (16th Sunday after Pentecost, expanded); *CH* I, XXXIII (17th Sunday after Pentecost); *CH* I, XXXV (21st Sunday after Pentecost, expanded with an anonymous portion); *CH* I, XXXIX (1st Sunday in Advent); *CH* I, XL (2nd Sunday in Advent).

38 Scragg, 'Cambridge, Corpus Christi College 162', pp. 75–6.

39 Two of the three homilies which follow Letter D concern Moses, the Ten Commandments, and the battle of Joshua, topics which parallel this letter's references to Dathan and Abiram as well as Titus and Vespasian.

69

singleton, rather than a quaternion as found throughout the rest of the manuscript.[40] This would mean that the section was built up in stages, and that Letter D was not necessarily part of the original plan.

There is a good deal of evidence that CCCC 162 was in regular use during the eleventh century and beyond. Several hands made interlinear and marginal alterations and additions, and many of them point to an active use of the manuscript.[41] In Letter D, there are several minor corrections as well as more significant additions, one of which indicates that the reader was correcting against another copy of the sermon.[42] Perhaps the most remarkable alteration, though of course undatable, is the erasure of punctuation throughout the Letter D, which hardly seems worth the effort except to enhance the readability of the text.[43]

Letter D's place in CCCC 162 is our only evidence for the relationship of the Sunday Letter to the Ælfrician tradition. Since its subject matter has no definite function within the cycle of the Church year – it is simply entitled *Be þam drihtenlican sunnandæg folces lar* – one expects it to appear as a supplement, to be used whenever needed as, in fact, it does in CCCC 162. As with some of the other anonymous sermons in a collection dominated by Ælfrician material, it was likely seen as filling a perceived lacuna in Ælfric's output, and one would therefore probably not be too far off the mark in supposing a significant interest in the matter of Sunday observance from the early years of the eleventh century onwards.

London, British Library, Cotton Tiberius A.iii (Letter F)

Cotton Tiberius A.iii was written around the middle of the eleventh century. It has been most recently and thoroughly described by Helmut Gneuss.[44] Its contents are diverse, but the collection begins with several monastic texts: the Benedictine Rule (with supplements) and the *Regularis concordia*, both glossed in Old English. Thereafter the book was used to collect a variety of texts, among which are prognostics, confessional prayers and penitential texts, Ælfric's *Colloquy* and *De temporibus anni*, his homily for Palm Sunday (*CH* II, XIV), a letter to Wulfstan, a life of St Margaret, homiletic pieces based on Wulfstan material, an *Examinatio in ordinatione episcopi*, a text on monastic sign language, a lapidary, charms and an office of the Virgin.[45] Letter F's place in this collection may have been as part

---

40   Scragg, 'Cambridge, Corpus Christi College 162', p. 76.
41   For example, in a passage on p. 516 (at the end of *CH* II, XXVIII), a reader changes *ge* to *we* and *eow* to *us* which seems to indicate a new audience or perhaps a change in the status of the reader.
42   In the 'Sunday list' portion of the letter, this hand adds *and acenned wearð seo geleaffulle gesamnung*, above the line following *on Sunnandæg tosleap Iudea gesamnung* (line 24); the addition renders the Latin *et nata est ecclesia katholica*. In line 82, this time independently of the Latin, the comment *and eow secgað eowre sawle þearfe, hwæt ge for Godes lufon don scylon. and ge þæt forhogiað* amplifies an exhortation to listen to wise teachers.
43   I indicate where I am reasonably certain these erasures occur in the apparatus to Letter D.
44   Helmut Gneuss, 'Origin and Provenance of Anglo-Saxon Manuscripts'.
45   One description that may be convenient is that it was a 'type of reference book'; Clayton and

of three texts – along with the Life of St Margaret and the 'Devil's Account of the Next World' – which have to do with otherworldly visions or messages, since, in addition to its divine attribution, Letter F is a version of the Sunday Letter that includes the attestation of the Irish deacon Niall, who had allegedly returned from the dead.[46]

There is no doubt that Cotton Tiberius A.iii was written in the south-east, and Gneuss has been able to confirm with some certainty the place of origin as Christ Church, Canterbury, based on the cumulative evidence of various external and internal clues.[47] In particular, the presence and wording of the *Examinatio episcopi* indicates, according to Gneuss, that the manuscript was made at 'an archbishop's church in England where a monastic community existed, and this, in the eleventh century and later on, could only be Christ Church, Canterbury'.[48]

It is not surprising, then, to find that many of the Old English pieces in this manuscript bear traces of distinctive south-eastern linguistic features.[49] By Gneuss's count, this is true, to a greater or lesser extent, for roughly forty of the seventy-three Old English items. Three texts in which the Kentish characteristics are particularly pronounced are the Old English Sunday Letter F, 'The Devil's Account of the Next World' and Ælfric's Palm Sunday homily, all copied by Ker's scribe 3.[50] The dialectal traits of the Ælfrician piece are especially significant

Magennis, *The Old English Lives of St Margaret*, p. 86. See the list of contents in Gneuss, 'Origin and Provenance', pp. 14–15 and in Ker, *Catalogue*, pp. 240–7 (No. 186). See also M. Förster, 'Beiträge zur mittelalterlichen Volkskunde', *Archiv für das Studium der neueren Sprachen und Literaturen* 121 (1908), 31–46.

[46] Gneuss, 'Origin and Provenance', p. 15. Another topic of interest to those compiling the manuscript may have been arcane knowledge about Noah and the Flood, which is featured in the first part of Letter F and also in items 8 (a) and 14.

[47] These include early manuscript catalogues, the two proper names and illustrations found in the manuscript, textual relationships to other manuscripts of known origin, the names of saints mentioned in liturgical texts, the hymns in the Marian office, and finally, the *Examinatio episcopi*.

[48] Gneuss, 'Origin and Provenance', pp. 33–6; cf. *CH* II, introd., lvi. The textual associations of Tiberius A.iii can be seen in Letter F's use of excerpts from texts also found in the Vercelli Book (Vercelli IX and X), another manuscript associated with Canterbury although they were not taken from the Vercelli Book itself, but rather from a manuscript more closely related to Bodl. Hatton 116; see discussion below, pp. 88–91. The Ælfrician homily which precedes it also contains an excerpt from Vercelli I, a version most closely related to that in Bodl. Bodley 340/342 (*CH* II, introd., lvi); cf. Scragg, *Vercelli Homilies*, introd., xxxi.

[49] 'Origin and Provenance', p. 40. See especially the comments in the following editions: Kluge, 'Zur Geschichte der Zeichensprache', p. 130; H. Logeman, *The Rule of S. Benet: Latin and Anglo-Saxon Interlinear Version*, EETS os 90 (London, 1888), introd., xliv–lxiii; M. Förster, 'Vom Fortleben antiker Sammellunare', pp. 64–9; Herbst, *Die Altenglische Margaretenlegende*, pp. 9–18 and 46; Clayton and Magennis, *The Old English Lives of St Margaret*, pp. 97–101; Sauer, 'Spätaltenglische Beichtermahnungen', pp. 17–20; and Kornexl, *Regularis concordia*, cxcvii–ccxii.

[50] These are included in the discussion of the language below, pp. 103–9. Items in the manuscript which were written by this scribe are the Old English gloss to the *Regularis concordia*, the prognostics on 37v–42v (Ker's item 7 (h)–(q)), the Old English gloss to Ælfric's *Colloquy*, Ælfric's translation of Bede's *De temporibus anni*, the commonplaces on 3rv, the life of St Margaret, Ælfric's Palm Sunday Homily, 'The Devil's Account of the Next World', the twelve Wulfstanian homiletic pieces, the *Examinatio episcopi*, and the directions for a confessor on 94v–95v.

because we know that it was first issued in standard West Saxon, and we can therefore be sure that the non-West Saxon forms were introduced within the first half of the eleventh century.[51] But the fact that many of the items copied by the same scribe exhibit few to no Kenticisms[52] leads one to believe that it is not the scribe's dialect that is reflected in the other texts, but rather that these were drawn from a south-eastern repository of texts with such features, and, in the case of the three pieces just mentioned, perhaps even from the same exemplar.

This supposition is strengthened by the observation that scribe 3 seems to have mechanically (though not very carefully) copied whatever was before him.[53] Though he made some corrections to his own work, often of single letters added above the line, he did not usually trouble himself with erasure of faulty portions. The corrections seem to be of the type made during the copying of the text; had the scribe gone over his text after he was finished, he might have discovered and corrected the many additional errors which remain.[54] The text received no perceptible attention after it was copied, and the person who provided alterations and additions to some of the surrounding items in the manuscript left our text untouched.[55]

London, British Library, Cotton Otho B.x (Wanley)

We know of yet another Old English Sunday Letter from Wanley's description of a manuscript, Cotton Otho B.x (s. xi[med]), containing predominantly saints' lives, which was once in the Cotton collection but was destroyed in the fire at Ashburnham house. According to Ker, the leaves in question did not belong to this collection but were originally part of an independent manuscript, which, unlike the rest of Cotton Otho B.x, was glossed by the 'tremulous hand' of Worcester.[56] This section of twelve leaves included one other item, Ælfric's retelling of the story of Judith and Holofernes, and Malchus, of which two leaves survived the fire and which appears to have a few south-eastern spellings similar to those recorded by

---

[51] Godden states that the homily, which he edits from BL Cotton Tiberius A.iii separately in an appendix (*CH* II, pp. 381–90), is a 'confused and corrupt version, incorporating a vast number of small additions and alterations', a version that had gone through at least two stages of non-authorial alterations (*CH* II, introd., lv–lvi).

[52] This is true of the Old English gloss to Ælfric's *Colloquy*, his *De temporibus anni*, and the Wulfstanian homiletic pieces, for example.

[53] See details in the discussion of the language of Letter F below, pp. 103–4.

[54] For the numerous errors in Letter F, see pp. 103–4.

[55] This person, writing in a 'small upward-sloping hand' (Ker, *Catalogue*, p. 240), worked on two confessional texts (somewhat earlier in the manuscript), the Life of St Margaret, and the twelve homiletic pieces by Wulfstan, but not the Palm Sunday homily by Ælfric which immediately precedes Letter F and the 'Devil's Account' which follows it; cf. Clayton and Magennis, *The Old English Lives of St Margaret*, p. 86.

[56] Ker, *Catalogue*, p. 229 (No. 178). Before the fire, the remainder of BL Cotton Otho B.x contained saints' lives (mostly by Ælfric), some general sermons, synodal canons and penitential texts.

Wanley for the Sunday Letter.[57] Wanley's incipit and explicit run as follows:

> Her onginneð þæt gewrit þe com of heofonum to Hierusalem, and biforan þam
> geate þe is gecweden Effrem on eorðan afeoll. . . . Ðis gewrite soðlice in ðam
> halgan burh Hierusalem of heofenu dun afeal. And to sancte Petres sepulchrum
> becom. Ðis is þæt ðridde gewrit þæt wæs asend of heofonum. And æfter ðisson
> ne cymeð nefre nan oðer. Ge bisceopes and mæssepreostas cyðað gelomlice ðis
> gewrit eallum folce. And sendað fram anre burhscire to oðre and hi biddon and
> geornlice læron þæt hi gelyfon þæt hit nis afunden fram ænigan eorðlice men.
> Ac gewriten fram handum ðes haligan hælendes.[58]

These remaining segments show that this letter belongs to the same recension
as Letter A (Recension I), and is closest to its source, a copy in BN lat. 12,270,
though its final sentences differ in some respects, following Letter A more closely
than the Latin.[59]

Simply looking at the context of the Old English versions we can derive some
conception of how the Anglo-Saxons who copied it may have viewed their texts.
Not surprisingly, given the topic, the Sunday Letter is never assigned to an occasion in the Church year and is therefore often found in the company of catechetical or miscellaneous sermons. Where one is provided, the title it is given – *Be þam
drihtenlican sunnandæg folces lar* (Letter D), *Sermo ad populum [de] dominicis
diebus* (Letter C) and *Sunnandæges spell* (Letter E) – confirms its intended audience to be general rather than monastic.

The manuscript contexts can be seen as falling into two groups: those in which
the letter(s) forms an integral part of the collection (CCCC 162, CCCC 419 and
Lambeth 489), and those to which it was added later or as an accretion (CCCC
140, Cotton Tiberius A.iii). But even taking into consideration the latter group,
where it is added it to a gospel-book and to a florilegium, one must come to the
conclusion that there is no evidence that the Sunday Letter was viewed as anything but orthodox and suitable for delivery.

Since all of these copies date from the eleventh century, one might speculate
that part of its legitimacy derived from its similarity, in some respects, to the
work of Wulfstan, whose sermons also speak of the national disasters about to be
visited upon the English for their many sins. It is probably significant that Letters
C and E have been augmented with his writings and adopt some of his phrases,
and Letters B, E and F are found side by side with his authentic works. The letter's apocalyptic sermonizing would not have sounded excessive to any audience
familiar with Wulfstan's style and substance.

The precise way in which the Anglo-Saxons made the Sunday Letter their own

---

57 Though scant, they are *nefre* (for *næfre*), *ðes* (for *ðæs*) and perhaps *afeal* (for *afeoll*). The piece is
edited in B. Assmann's *Angelsächsische Homilien und Heiligenleben*, pp. 102–16.

58 *Librorum veterum septentrionalium catalogus, 2: Linguarum veterum septentrionalium thesaurus*,
ed. G. Hickes (Oxford, 1705), p. 192. The text is numbered in the *Dictionary of Old English Corpus*
as Cameron B3.5.6.

59 BL Cotton Otho B.x omits Letter A's final two sentences, however.

73

will be shown in their many adaptations, which, as will be seen, range from the addition of 'sermon markers' (*Men þa leofestan*) to a wholesale rewriting (Letter C). In the following, it will be important to distinguish their work as much as possible from that of earlier revisers of the Latin versions, and it should become clear that the Anglo-Saxon reception of the Sunday Letter often went well beyond the preservation of a curiosity, and can be characterized in terms of a lively engagement with a fascinating text.

Transmission of the Old English Sunday Letters

Letters A and B

Letter A is an Old English Sunday Letter which draws on a Latin version of Recension I-type, a twelfth-century manuscript from Corbie (BN lat. 12,270).[60] The translator was generally faithful to his source, but several changes should probably be attributed to him. He added Old English sermon markers and a few explanatory phrases to the text, and, in two instances, seems to have made alterations based on his recollection of biblical passages echoed in the text.[61] Two longer passages in BN lat. 12,270 are omitted in Letter A; they condemn swearing by the cross and women's pride in their dress.[62] The latter section is briefly touched on by the translator, which suggests that the section was indeed in his source and deliberately excised as being extraneous to the subject of Sunday observance.

The nature of Letter A's source and its relationship to BN lat. 12,270 as well as to other Latin Sunday Letters is more difficult to explain. That the actual source of Letter A differed in several respects from BN lat. 12,270 can be seen by certain discrepancies, several of which point to a text which included a few elements paralleled in other copies of Recension I.[63] These may have been removed from some earlier version of BN lat. 12,270.

But BN lat. 12,270 and Letter A also include elements which are otherwise

---

[60] The Old English Sunday Letter in BL Cotton Otho B.x, destroyed in the 1731 fire, was of the same recension as this one; see above, pp. 72–3. BN lat. 12,270 was edited by Delehaye, 'Note', pp. 181–4. Priebsch originally printed another Latin version, Vienna, Österreichische Nationalbibliothek, 1355 (provided in Appendix IIa as a parallel to Letter B), as the closest source, but then discovered Delehaye's article and revised his earlier statements in his 1935 monograph *Letter from Heaven* (p. 10). Priebsch thought that this version came to England during the time of Æthelwold (d. 984) who brought monks from Corbie to Abingdon where he was Abbot, a theory which is hardly provable though not inconceivable (*Letter from Heaven*, pp. 10–11).

[61] These are the two instances of direct address of the audience (*Men þa leofestan*, lines 1, 59), a phrase common in Old English sermons (lines 33–4), the substitution of *þeowan hiwe* (line 23) and a biblical quotation for the conclusion of the homily (lines 87–9); see the commentary.

[62] The omissions occur at lines 68 and 77.

[63] These are the exhortation to place (or make the sign of) the cross in one's house (lines 27–8), naming the Ninevites in connection with fasting (line 29), a threatened plague of beetles and grasshoppers (lines 40–1), and the exhortation to go to church (lines 67–8); see the commentary.

only found in the members of Recension II and which point to a separate line of transmission. For example, a sentence in which God swears by the Cherubim and Seraphim is not found in Recension I copies:[64]

> Ic eom soð God and soð ic eow secge and þus swerige þurh me sylfne and þurh mine halgan englas Cherubin and Seraphin þæt min yrre cymð ofer eow ær on lytlan fyrste. (A48–50)[65]

> And ic swerige þurh mine mihte and þurh mine englas, cherubin and seraphim. (E159–60)

> Soþ is, þæt ic iow sæcge, þæt ic swerige þurh minne miht and þurh mine þa halgan ænglas, cherubin and særaphin. (F190–1)

In Letter F this statement is followed by Recension I's promise of punishment to come at a particular time (here in September or October) which Letter A seems to have modified to the less specific *on lytlan fyrste* ('in a little while'). A similar correspondence may be seen in another part of the text, the warning concerning a heathen invasion, which is again closely paralleled by similar statements in Letters E and F and also in Letter B:

> ic asende ofer eow hæðen folc þæt fornimað eow and eowre bearn. (A42–3)

> ic sende hæðen folc ofer eow, þe eow ofnimað eowre æhte and eower lif and eowere wif and cild. (B119–20)

> ic sende hæðen folc ofer eow, and þa eow benimað eowres eðles and eowres lifes. (E47–8)

> ic lete hæþen folc ofer iow, þa iow fornimaþ and iowra bearn. (F181)

These sentences must derive from a single statement in a Latin source which included the elements of a heathen people who will take life or property and children. In particular, the closeness of Letters A and F, two letters normally associated with two entirely different recensions, is in need of an explanation. While heathen enemies appear in both recensions, there is nothing which looks like a true source for the Old English versions.[66] The conclusion which should be drawn

---

64 Graz 248 names them along with Mary in the following sentence concerning the latter's intercession on behalf of mankind.

65 'I am true God and I tell you the truth and thus swear by myself and by my holy angels, Cherubim and Seraphim, that my wrath will come over you in a little while.'

66 Tarragona (Recension I): *propter hoc tradam vos in fame et in manus gentium . . . incredulorum paganorum* (Priebsch, *Letter from Heaven*, p. 36); Munich 9550: *Et uenit gens pagana quae alios occidit, et alios in captiuitatem ducit pro eo quod non obseruatis diem dominicum* (Delehaye, 'Note', p. 179). Cf. D45: *And ic tradam vos in ælþeodigra handa* (Lat. (VK): *Et tradam vos in manus alienorum*); C82–3: *and swa bysmorlice bringan of heora eðle and betæcan eow teonlice syððan on hæðenra hand heries lafe.* The Irish *Epistil Ísu* has 'and heathens shall come to you from me . . . even a race of pagans, who will carry you into bondage from your own lands, and will offer you up to their own gods' (O'Keeffe, 'Cáin Domnaig', p. 197).

from this is that an early version of Recension I was circulating in the British Isles and was the ancestor of the sources of Letters A, B and E/F. A version then derived from it shows what might be seen as transitional features, omitting the initial travels of the letter from priest to priest and including an oath by a Bishop Peter (thus making it fall broadly into the Recension II category), but yet also exhibiting elements belonging to Recension I which were apparently excised later in the process of becoming Recension II. It may have been related to the copy in the Homiliary of Toledo (BL Add. 30,853, s. xi) which also exhibits some of these 'transitional' characteristics as noted in Chapter 3; to parallel the above statement, for example, it has *misi super uos gentes malas, qui ducunt filios et filias uestras in [captiuitate] et labores uestros in exterminatione*. In the following, it will be seen that Letter B has additional signs that such a version existed, and that it was a version much like this that developed into the source of the Latin VK (translated in Old English Letters C and D).

The closest Latin version to Letter B is the rather late copy of the Sunday Letter in Vienna, Österreichische Nationalbibliothek, 1355 (s. xiv/xv). It is part of a sub-group of Recension I which includes the obligations associated with the co-parenthood or sponsorship of St John.[67] Three other members of this group are BL Add. 19,725 (s. x/xi), Basel, Universitätsbibliothek, B VII 7 (s. x), and Graz, Universitätsbibliothek, 248 (s. xv), which are even closer to Letter B at some points but are missing portions of the text.[68] These copies can offer a better idea of the translator's source; for example, the statement in Vienna 1355 *Suspiciosa non sit epistola ista* ('this letter should not be suspect') appears in the Letter B (line 36) as *underfoð þyssum drihtnes ærendgewrite* ('receive this message of the lord') which is more likely a translation of BL Add. 19,725 *et suscipite epistolam istam*.[69]

The Anglo-Saxon translator often treats his source with a great deal of freedom, which may have been due to his difficulty in making sense of the Latin, but at times may also be an attempt to improve upon the original. He omits all but one of the references to the co-parenthood of St John, probably because this was not a contemporary practice in England.[70] The use of typical Old English homiletic phraseology may signal that the additions were made during translation.[71]

---

67 See commentary for B39.

68 BL Add. 19,725 and Basel B VII 7 are edited in Appendix IIb and IIc, respectively; the Sunday Letter in Graz 248 is on 133rb–133va. J. H. Lynch maintains that the co-fatherhood or co-parenthood of St John appeared on the Continent before the tenth century (*Christianizing Kingship: Ritual Sponsorship in Anglo-Saxon England*, p. 124). Another Sunday Letter alludes to sponsorial obligations in general; see BN lat. 12,270 *et propter fidem quam non observastis inter amicos et vicinos vestros et conpatres et omnes fideles Christi* (Delehaye, 'Note', p. 183). Recension III letters also refer to sponsors; see, for example, the copy in Toulouse, Bibliothèque publique, 208 (s. xiii): *Vos autem non estis fratres, sed inimici, et uos facitis compatres, et tamen eos non tenetis, sicuti decet* (Rivière, 'La lettre du Christ tombée du ciel', p. 603).

69 Appendix IIb, line 25. Other correspondences with these copies are noted in the commentary.

70 These are excised at lines 59, 73, 113 and 116. See note to lines 38–9 and Wilcox, 'Compilation', p. 79.

71 See, for example, *heofona rices wuldor* (lines 35, 48, 50 and 72) and also additions described in notes to lines 16–17, 31–2, 53–4, 54–6, 66–7 and 85.

In several of these additions, one detects an added emphasis on God's mercy, not usually a feature of the Sunday Letter, and perhaps meant to alleviate the unrelenting condemnation of the letter.[72]

In some of the changes, another influence may also be seen at work, though not necessarily to be attributed to the translator. Expressions such as *word and wedd* and *wanung and granung* and *mid rihte* or *on riht* are perhaps not surprising in a manuscript which contains much Wulfstanian material. That the scribe himself could have made minor changes based on his familiarity with it is shown in a remarkable circumstance: while no extant Latin Sunday Letter states that the missive was written in golden letters, Letter B does so twice, and Letters E and F, which belong to a separate line of transmission, do as well. The best explanation for this is that the scribe, having just copied Letter E into CCCC 419, inserted this detail into Letter B, which follows. Since the golden letters do not appear in the Irish *Epistil Ísu*, this addition is unlikely to go back to the 'transitional' ancestor mentioned above.

A few other details in Letter B, however, do support the notion of a common ancestor. In two places (lines 2 and 132), Letter B has *of þam seofoðan heofone* as the place from which the letter fell, where the Latin has *de caelo* or *de septimo throno*; this is also so in Letters E (38, 179) and F (40). While all the Latin members of Recension I mention the letter's eventual travel *ad sepulcrum sancti Petri* or *sanctum Petrum* (BN lat. 12,270 *ad sepulcrum sanctum*) in the conclusion, the common ancestor of Letters A, B and E, F must have included both an altar and a tomb, the latter featuring in a dramatic story of its opening on the letter's arrival in Letters E and F.[73] In addition, the conclusion contains an added section which reads like a precursor to the oath of Bishop Peter in Recension II, in which the audience is urged to believe the letter:

> And gelefað þissum gewrite þurh drihten sylfne and þurh englas and heahenglas for þæra mihte and anweald, þurh heahfæderas and witegan, þurh apostolas and martyres and confessores and þa halgan fæmnan and ealle Cristes þa halgan, þæt ge fullice þysum gewrite gelyfan.[74]

Although Letters E and F have truncated versions of the oath, other Recension II texts are clearly in the same line of transmission as this one.[75] Finally, the Sunday

---

72 These occur at lines 71 and 78.

73 *On Sanctus Petrus hehaltare hit wæs funden þus awriten mid gyldenum stafum . . . þis gewrit becom on Sanctus Petrus weofod, þæt eall seo stow wearð onrered, and heo abifode eall, and seo byrgen wæs open geworden and unhlidod, þær Sanctus Petrus lichama inne læg* (E201–2 and 205–7). Letter A has only a tomb, but Letter B has St Peter's altar where BN lat. 12,270 has a tomb (line 11) and later refers to a tomb where the Latin has *sanctum Petrum*. Letters E and F (and the Irish *Epistil Ísu*) repeatedly state that the letter fell on St Peter's altar (see above, p. 49 n. 88). Cf. BL Add. 30,853 *super altare sancti Bauduli* (Grégoire, *Les homéliaires du moyen âge*, pp. 226 and 227); Recension III letters also fall on an altar.

74 'And believe this writ for the sake of the Lord himself and for the sake of the angels and archangels and for their might and power, for the sake of the patriarchs and prophets, for the sake of the apostles and martyrs and confessors, and the holy virgins and all the saints of Christ, that you fully believe this writ.'

75 See BL Add. 30,853: *Nam iuro, ego Petrus episcopus de ciuitate Nimaso, omnibus legentibus hanc*

List, a catalogue of events said to have occurred on Sunday, reveals a similar pattern. It too is not a part of BN lat. 12,270, but shows significant simililarities to the lists in the other Old English Sunday Letters which have one. The Sunday Lists will be examined as a group below in order to clarify the relationships among them.

Letters C and D

These two copies of the Sunday Letter are translations of a distinctive version of Recension II (designated VK in the previous chapter), which cites a Bishop Peter from the church in Antioch as the recipient of the letter. Two Latin copies of this recension survive in manuscripts of the late fourteenth and early fifteenth centuries.[76] As is evident by the close correspondence of Old English Letter D, a text very much like this must have been available to the translators of C and D, and these Latin letters are therefore edited here for the first time and printed as Appendix III.[77]

Letter D only rarely strays from its source. The only notable alterations are occasional additions of typical sermon addresses (*Men þa leofestan*), a comment which comes after a list of sins and which helpfully clarifies that these are not fobidden only on Sundays but at all times,[78] three sentences on obeying God's word,[79] and a transitional sentence which introduces the passages from Isaiah, specifically referring to the rich.[80] It also adds the prohibition of trade.[81] Otherwise the additions are minor in nature, but indicate that the translator was occasionally keen to add familiar vernacular homiletic modes of expression, such as the characteristic benediction at the end.

Letter C, however, represents a very different approach to the Sunday Letter. Although it follows the Latin enough to be able to see the relationship to its source quite clearly, its author freely expands on the material. A new introduction (lines

---

epistolam, per crucifixum dominum nostrum Iesum christum filium dei et patrem omnipotentem et trinitatem inseparabilem, et sancta quattuor euangelia, quia non est hac ępistola ab homine abtata nec subtracta (Grégoire, *Les homéliaires du moyen âge*, pp. 226–7). The list closest to the one in Letter B is the one in the Welsh version; see Powel, 'Ebostol y sul', p. 169 and note to D123.

[76] These are Kassel, Murhardsche Bibliothek der Stadt Kassel und Landesbibliothek, theol. 39 (a partial copy) and Vienna, Dominikanerkloster 133; the relationship of VK to the other Latin versions is discussed in Chapter 3, pp. 51–2.

[77] The Latin text was also available in England later in the Middle Ages since it (or a translation) was used as the basis for a Middle English sermon. O'Mara edits this version and discusses its relationship to Letters C and D in *Selected Middle English Sermons*, pp. 100–7.

[78] D32: *And þas þing sindon eallum tidum forbodene.*

[79] D53–6: *And be þysum ylcan andgyte drihten cwæð: Se ðe of Gode bið, he Godes word gehyrð. Þa yfelan þwyran men hyt gehyrað, ac hi hyt healdan nellað. Forði þe hi þæs deofles syndon, gif hi yfeles geswican nellað and þam gelyfan þe we eow herbeforan ær sædon.*

[80] D102–3: *Gemunað ge weligan þæt ge eowre wiste rihtlice gehealden, and ondrædað eow þæt þæt awriten is þurh þone witegan.*

[81] D32–3: *And healdon ge þone sunnandæg wið ælce ceapunga.*

1–11) remarkably refers to the speaker (and audience) as 'we bishops and priests' which, coupled with the fact that this manuscript (Lambeth 489) was copied for a bishop, perhaps Leofric, may suggest a greater degree of acceptance for the Sunday Letter than one might have expected.[82] Letter C introduces the topic as *sunnandæges halignysse*, and a short and sensible narrative is provided which explains that after Christ's life on earth and ascension, mankind was not observing Sunday properly thus necessitating a further message from heaven.

The ending also includes an extensive addition replacing that in VK, which takes as its starting point the concept in the Latin source that if one participates in sin, sin is one's lord or god. For this, Letter C substitutes the more concrete dichotomy of serving either God or the devil, providing a long list of sinners who are God's enemies. This theme then prompted the compiler to use yet another source, the distinctive lists of the three ways in which the devil deceives a person, followed by the three ways in which a person reaches hell and the three ways in which a person reaches heaven, enumerative topoi which have been identified as being of Irish provenance.[83] The closest Latin source for Letter C's passage is Munich, Bayerische Staatsbibliothek, clm 14,364 (fol. 37), a ninth-century manuscript,[84] but the sequence also occurs in other early manuscripts containing texts associated with the Irish tradition,[85] and the second half of this section uses a form of the 'thought, word and deed' triad, which has been likewise seen as a peculiarly Irish mode of expression.[86] Letter C concludes with a general exhortation without returning to the theme of Sunday observance or the Latin source, which at this point launches into the admonition to learned men to disseminate the letter, a reiteration of the origin of the message and Bishop Peter's oath. Whether by design or not, these omissions in Letter C greatly reduce the letter's apocryphal character.

In addition to his effort in furnishing the text with a new beginning and conclusion, the freedom and confidence with which this adapter approached his source is felt in many ways throughout Letter C. He rearranges the elements of the Sunday List so that they appear, with one exception, in chronological order.[87] Two additions to the list may indicate that he knew of other Sunday Lists.[88] He corrects details that seem erroneous, such as the statement that the Red Sea was divided into twelve paths (lines 33–5), and he wisely leaves out the repellent threat of

82   See notes on the manuscript above, pp. 67–8.
83   This text was identified by J. E. Cross and explored by Wright in 'The Irish "Enumerative Style"', pp. 54–6 and again in *The Irish Tradition*, pp. 81–4.
84   Reprinted in the commentary for Letter C from Wright, *The Irish Tradition*, pp. 82–3.
85   Wright lists Munich, Bayerische Staatsbibliothek, clm 19,410, clm 22,053, and, for the first part only, Einsiedeln, Stiftsbibliothek, 281, Bodl. Laud Misc. 129 as well as an Irish homily in the Leabhar Breac (Dublin, Royal Irish Academy 32. P. 16) (*The Irish Tradition*, pp. 82–4).
86   P. Sims-Williams, 'Thought, Word and Deed: An Irish Triad', *Ériu* 29 (1978), 78–111; cf. Wright, 'The Irish "Enumerative Style"', p. 54.
87   The moved items are the nativity, Pentecost and perhaps the Resurrection, though the Kassel version lists that last item in the correct spot.
88   These are Christ's baptism and the rare item of Christ's revealing himself to Peter after the Resurrection which is only paralleled in an Old English Easter homily (see below, n. 191). Other details also appear to have been supplied from another list (see below, p. 97).

children being born with disease or handicap (D89–91). An example of his treatment of the material can be seen in a passage on aiding the poor and needy in which the author is at pains to stress that such relief is only required of those who are able to do so (lines 66–71; his additions are italicized):

> Ic eow wylle eac eallswa cyðan, þæt man ah seoce men to geneosianne and deade bebyrian, earmingas, *þam þe onhagað*, fedan and scrydan. And, *loca hwa þære mihte age*, he mot gehæftne man alysan, wreccan and ælþeodige underfon, and *ælc be his mihte* welwyllendlice heom god don, wudewum and steopcildum and utancumenum froferlice fylstan to rihte.

Not only was the writer of Letter C someone who actively reshaped his raw material, he had also learned something of his craft by reading (or listening to) a master homilist of his time, Wulfstan of York. The exact nature of the influence is more complex than simple borrowing, however. The evidence of Letter C as a whole shows that, as was seen in his reworking of his Latin source, our author was eager to use Wulfstanian formulas in creating his own text. Examining the introduction one finds several of these expressions (italicized below):

> Leofan men, us bisceopum and eallum mæsse-preostum is *swiðe deope beboden* þæt we æfre sculon mynegian and tyhtan eow, læwede menn, georne to eowre sawla þearfe, and hu ge agan her on life *rihtlice* to libbanne. And, gif we swa ne doð, þonne beo we *swyðe scyldige wið God* ælmihtigne. Nu wylle we eow secgan be þæs haligan sunnandæges halignysse, hu se ælmihtiga God hine gehalgode, and hu he wyle, þæt he freols beo fram eallum *unrihtdædum* and þeowetlicum weorcum, for ic wat, þæt hit is eow uncuðre, *þonne ge þearfe ahton*. Hit wæs, þæt, siððan Crist þæs ælmihtigan Godes sunu wæs astigen up to heofena rice, syððan he hæfde her gewunad onmang mannum þreo and .xxx. wintra and healf gear, þæt men forgymdon *Godes laga swyðor*, þonne heora þearfa wæron, and þæs halgan sunnandæges freols *wyrs* heoldon, þonne hit Gode licwyrðe wære. (C1–11)

The ideas of the first two sentences are often found in Wulfstan and are probably adapted from his work, though no exact match survives.[89] However, Letter C's version also exhibits a syntactical feature rarely found in Wulfstan, yet occurring several more times in Letter C: *agan* with *to* and the inflected infinitive (*agan . . . to libanne*).[90] This suggests that the author echoes Wulfstan's phraseology but is composing the text himself. This is further confirmed when the introduction

---

[89] The closest parallel is in Bethurum VI (lines 3–5, 10–12). Jost thought that the final admonition to disseminate the letter (*forðan ðe swa hwilc sacerd swa ne gebodað þam folce heora synna, huruþinga on domes dæge heora blod bið fram him asoht, and he scildig þonne stent be heora synnum on Godes andweardnysse*, D115–18) was moved to the beginning, possibly using Bethurum VI to reformulate the idea. Without benefit of the Latin source, he speculates that the reference to bishops and priests was already in the Latin (*Wulfstanstudien*, pp. 229–30); VK has *sacerdos* in the final admonition (Appendix III, line 87).

[90] The other occurrences in C are *ah to forganne* (60), *ah . . . to secanne . . . and . . . to gebidanne* (63–4), *ah . . . to geneosianne* (67), *ah . . . to gesibsumianne* (71–2).

then turns to Sunday observance, still using the occasional Wulfstan expression, but providing the plausible background to the Sunday Letter mentioned above.[91] Moreover, Wulfstan's influence is felt throughout the entire homily in the many expressions characteristic of his style, especially the use of intensifiers and alliteration.[92] While it is never possible to recover the exact extent of such borrowing, one can see that our adapter was a thoughtful author in his own right and that he made some effort to effect a rhetorical update using an admired orator as his guide.

A few other passages may have even been lifted whole from the work of Wulfstan and others. The first is the list of sinners found near the end of the sermon in an elaboration on the theme of the devil's works.[93] Such lists are ubiquitous in both the homilies and legal texts written by Wulfstan, though none that survive match that in Letter C exactly. The closest is one in a passage taken from Wulfstan which is inserted in Napier XLII and which also includes the elaboration on the unjust judges who take bribes (203.21–204.4).[94] Another possible borrowing, though probably not from Wulfstan, is the conclusion of the sermon (lines 173–80) which also appears in the very next item in Lambeth 489 (Ker's item 5), a composite homily which ends in a catena from several sources. The two passages are almost identical and were probably drawn from a third copy available to the compiler.[95]

The inclusion of this borrowed text supports other evidence that Letter C was composed not long before the manuscript was compiled in a location where Wulfstan's sermons had some currency, possibly in the same scriptorium where Lambeth 489 was assembled. A second aspect of its literary environment is the

---

91   One might compare the way another homily, in the companion volume to Lambeth 489, BL Cotton Cleopatra B.xiii, was put together, using a new introduction which uses Wulfstan formulas, but was apparently not written by him (Scragg, *Vercelli Homilies*, pp. 49, 66). Scragg suggests that it is the work of 'an eleventh-century adapter or adapters of homiletic material very well versed in Wulfstan's phraseology' (p. 51), a statement that applies to Letter C as well.

92   Intensifiers such as the use of *swiþe* in *swiðe deope*, *swyðe scyldige*, and phrases such as *georne to eowre sawla þearfe, swyðor þonne heora þearfa wæron* are just a few examples. A passage elaborating on the horrors of foreign invasion is particularly alliterative (romanized here): *Þæt is, þa þe ahte syndon, hi sculon* fleonde *on* gefeohte *beon ofslagene, and þa* ealdan *sculan* earmlice *licgan* heapmælum *æt ham hungre* acwolene. And man sceal þa *geoguðe geomorlice* lædan *gehæft heanlice* mid *heardum bendum* and swa *bysmorlice bringan* of heora eðle and betæcan eow teonlice *syððan on hæðenra hand heries* lafe. And syððan æfter þære *earmlycan eowre geendunge,* ic besence *eowre* sawla *on susle* on helle, swa swa ic hwilon dyde þa twa burh Sodomam and Gomorram, þe mid heofonlicum *fyre* her wurdan *forbærnde, and ealle þa, þe him on eardodon, æfre byrnað on* hellegrunde *on* hatan fyre, *forþan hi þone* mildan *God* manfullice gremedon *(lines 79–88). See Wilcox ('Dissemination', p. 216) for these kinds of echoes of Wulfstan's style which suggest a kind of internalization of his ideas and modes of expression.

93   Lines 147–54.

94   Other close parallels are listed by Bethurum (p. 309) and in Wilcox, 'Dissemination', p. 212. Cf. Jost, *Wulfstanstudien*, p. 228.

95   The only significant change is that Ker's article 5 has *heofonlice rice* instead of Letter C's *uplice rice*, but *l uplice rice* is added above the line. Wilcox suggests that the composite homily borrowed the passage from Letter C ('Dissemination', p. 213 n. 65), but then one would expect to find that phrase in the body of the text.

Hiberno-Latin influence indicated in the borrowings mentioned above. Additional details found in the Latin source VK as well as in both Letters C and D suggest that even prior to translation, this version was composed under Hiberno-Latin influence. For example, one unusual motif found in the Sunday List portion is that Moses divided the Red Sea into twelve paths (one for each tribe) instead of one. Thomas Hall remarks on the appearance of this figure in Psalter glosses with Irish connections.[96] Furthermore, the introduction of the Dathan, Abiram and Korah story, however briefly, into the Sunday Letter is conspicuous because it otherwise occurs only in the Old English Letters E and F (there fully narrated), which have demonstrable Irish connections.[97] Such correspondences point to an environment where, at the very least, Hiberno-Latin materials were readily available.

Although our author borrowed from multiple sources, he yet creates a well-shaped sermon which does not feel like the patchwork that it is. Through judicious editing, the author manages to place less emphasis on the apocryphal aspects of the letter, adding instead more conventional condemnations of sins of the day.[98] Perhaps it was these emendations that allowed it to find a place in a bishop's sermon collection, side by side with the works of Ælfric.

Letters E and F

The version preserved in Letters C and D represents a bold revision of the Sunday Letter. In a similar fashion, that presented in Letters E and F is a wholesale reworking, though a less successful one, of the Sunday Letter material, perhaps revealing something about the context in which it was made. Unlike the previous Old English Sunday Letters, there is external evidence for the transmission of Letters E/F in the correspondence of Bishop Ecgred.[99] There is no doubt that the version which Bishop Ecgred mentions in his letter is closely related to these Old English versions. Peculiar to Pehtred's version and E/F alone are the authenticating story of Niall, a fictitious Pope Florentius[100] and the message having been written in golden letters.[101] All of these elements occur in no other version of the letter and serve to identify this peculiar adaptation and date its arrival in England to no later than the early ninth century.

Even more fortuitous and informative is the survival of the Old Irish *Epistil Ísu* which establishes a connection to Ireland and confirms an early date.[102] It was

96 See commentary to line D35.
97 See details below.
98 Priebsch calls it 'a thundering philippic against the evil customs . . . of the time' ('Chief Sources', p. 146).
99 See discussion in Chapter 3, p. 39.
100 The *Epistil Ísu* does refer to an abbot of Rome (i.e. the pope), but does not name him (§1 and §18, O'Keeffe, 'Cáin Domnaig', pp. 192–3 and 202–3), perhaps recognizing that such information could send up a red flag, as it did for Ecgred.
101 Old English Letter B also mentions golden letters.
102 See Chapter 3, pp. 40–3.

Priebsch who first observed a relationship between our Old English E/F and *Epistil Ísu*, and Dorothy Whitelock explored the links between the two even further.[103] While the Irish text is clearly at some remove from the Old English, the two share important details not found in other versions: 1. the trembling of the earth and opening of St Peter's tomb when the letter appears;[104] 2. an identical oath sworn by Bishop Peter and a Pope Florentius in EF and the abbot of Rome in *Epistil Ísu*, mentioning only God's might and Christ's cross where others include a host of characters such as prophets and martyrs;[105] 3. a threat of 'five beasts' which will come up from the sea;[106] and perhaps 4. the idea that souls in hell receive rest on Sunday.[107] In general, *Epistil Ísu* and E/F treat the same topics though the order differs, pointing to a common Latin source, which was discussed as Y[1] in the previous chapter.

At the same time, E/F and *Epistil Ísu* are independently derived from Y[1] because there are significant differences in the treatment of the material. The *Epistil Ísu* augments the Latin with extensive elaborations[108] and also with additional items in the list of prohibitions and in the Sunday List.[109] Where E/F has the story of Niall, the Irish translation offers a similar authentication in the tale of Conall mac Coelmaine (d. *c.* 590), abbot of Inniskeel, who, so the *Epistil Ísu* claims, copied the Sunday Letter while on pilgrimage in Rome, informing a cleric in a vision many years after his death that the writ was to be found in his shrine.[110] As previously noted, it is followed by a legal tract providing specific fines and penalities for violations.[111]

None of these elements are to be found in E/F, which has its own peculiar character. Thus, at some point Y[1] was revised to form Y[2], the version mentioned in Bishop Ecgred's letter and owned by Pehtred:

---

[103] Priebsch, 'Quelle und Abfassungszeit'; Whitelock, 'Bishop Ecgred', pp. 53–7.

[104] E205–7, F225–7, *Epistil Ísu* §1.

[105] E198–200, F217–19, *Epistil Ísu* §18. For an example of the longer oath, see the end of D123–9. *Epistil Ísu* has no Bishop Peter, therefore it is possible that this figure was not in their common source but was added later in the branch that produced E/F. It is not difficult to see how the altar in St Peter's church, or perhaps his sepulcre (see note 73) might give rise to a Bishop Peter.

[106] F146 (not in E), *Epistil Ísu* §11.

[107] E138–40, F99–101, *Epistil Ísu* §9. The idea occurs in different contexts in the Old English and Irish; in the former it is in the Sunday List and in the latter in an early paragraph which seems to draw on another source (see Whitelock, 'Bishop Ecgred', p. 57 and n. 69). The respite also turns up in two Middle High German sermons which are related to both the Sunday Letter and the Sunday List (see discussion below, pp. 93–6).

[108] One colourful example is the elaborate description of the activities of one of the pestilences threatened, the *bruchus*: 'Their hairs are pins of iron, and they have fiery eyes. They go into the vineyards and cut the branches of the vine so that they fall to the ground; thereupon they roll about in the fruit, so that the grapes of the vine stick in these pins, and they bear them away to their abode'; O'Keeffe, 'Cáin Domnaig', 193. See J. Borsje, 'The *Bruch* in the Irish Version of the Sunday Letter', *Ériu* 45 (1994), 83–98.

[109] The Sunday List is discussed separately below.

[110] O'Keeffe, "Cáin Domnaig," 204–5. See Chapter, 3, n. 73.

[111] See Chapter 3, p. 41.

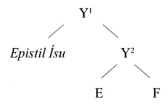

In Y^2, the basis for Old English Letters E and F, the most prominent departure from Y^1 is the figure of Niall, who bears a close resemblance to a historical person, Niall mac Ialláin, whose death is recorded in a variety of Irish annal entries, which place it between 854 and 860.[112] The *Annals of Ulster*, which records his death for 859 (860), says the following: 'Niall son of Iallán, who suffered from paralysis for thirty-three years, and was disturbed by frequent visions, both false and true, rested in Christ.'[113] The *Annals of the Four Masters* seem to corroborate one element of the account in E/F, by recounting for the year 854 that 'Niall, son of Gillan, after being thirty years without food or drink, died'.[114] The dates provided for Niall's death would thus appear to indicate that he was still alive when Ecgred complains that 'Pehtred . . . says with foolish falsehood that Nial the deacon was dead for seven weeks and came to life again, and partook of no food afterwards',[115] since, according to Whitelock, Ecgred's letter was written around 835,[116] and it appears that information about Niall's brush with death (*c.* 824) was quite current when the author of Y^2 added it to the Sunday Letter. Whatever the historical facts of Niall's life, visions and death may have been, the notoriety gained through his alleged miraculous existence provided our author with a contemporary reference point to enhance the Sunday Letter's authenticity.

Remarkable is the creativity with which the Niall story is interwoven in the text. The way he is introduced indicates that the author anticipates some scepticism on the part of his audience.[117] He thus fashions Niall into a Noah-type figure, a special messenger sent by God ostensibly due to the fact that the heavenly letter was not at first believed:

---

112 Whitelock, 'Bishop Ecgred', p. 49 and n. 20.

113 S. Mac Airt and G. Mac Niocaill, ed., *The Annals of Ulster (to A.D. 1131)* (Dublin, 1983), pp. 318–19. For 825 (826) it also records the following: 'Great terror in all Ireland, i.e. from warning of plague given by Iellán's son of Mumu' (pp. 282–3).

114 *Annals of the Kingdom of Ireland*, ed and trans. O'Donovan, pp. 488–9. But a similar entry for four years later (858) says 'Niall, son of Giallan, died, after a good life, after having been twenty-four years in oppressive sickness' (pp. 492–3). Cf. the *Chronicum Scotorum* for 856: 'Death of Niall, son of Gillan, after having been thirty years without food or drink' (ed. Hennessy, pp. 154–5).

115 Whitelock, *English Historical Documents*, p. 876. Whitelock places the composition of the letter around 835, but no later than 836 based on Archbishop Wulfsige's dates. It is however possible that Wulfsige lived into the 840s, which would give the Niall story (or a Sunday Letter incorporating it) more time to reach England; cf. Whitelock, 'Bishop Ecgred', p. 47 n. 4.

116 Whitelock, 'Bishop Ecgred', p. 47.

117 The fact that Ecgred refers to Niall as a liar (Whitelock, *English Historical Documents*, p. 876) and the reference in the *Annals of Ulster* to his having false as well true visions suggest that his reputation had been called into question before.

And nu doð men þam gelicost syððan, swylce hit wære idel spell and unsoð. Nu he þonne gyt hine to ðam geeadmedde, þæt he Nial þone diacon of deaðe awehte, to ðam þæt he mihte cyðan Godes folce þæt towearde yrre.[118]

However, as with Noah, Niall's predictions have been doubted:

Ðonne Noe þis mannum sæde be ðam flode, þæt he wolde ealle synfulle menn adrencan, þonne hlogen men his worda on bysmer and cwædon þæt he luge. Swa þonne wenað nu manige men, þæt þes diacon leoge be þam fyre, þe drihten sylf hine secgan het manna bearnum.[119]

The comparison with Noah is an apt one, for Noah was seen as a preacher of coming disaster to an unconcerned audience.[120] Like Noah, Niall warns of an apocalyptic destruction, one that may only be avoided through a turning from sin.

While the mention of the Irish deacon points to Ireland as the place of composition for Y^2, this element could also have been added in England by someone who had heard stories of the deacon.[121] What speaks in favour of an Irishman (wherever he was located) making this addition is another characteristic feature of this version, the path taken by the threatened fire as it arrives first in Ireland, moves on to Wales (in E) and only then reaches England and finally the Continent.[122] On balance, it seems less likely that an Anglo-Saxon would trouble to insert a story about an Irish deacon or bother to launch the punishing fire in Ireland.

Apart from Niall, Noah and the apocalyptic fire that will journey from country to country, Y^2 features several other innovations. While we saw but a brief mention of the Dathan and Abiram story in Letter C and D, here the narrative is fully developed and their punishment is attributed to the violation of Sunday though

---

[118] E179–82. 'And now men act just as if it were an empty tale and untrue. Now then he has yet humbled himself to that extent, that he awakened Niall the deacon from death, in order that he might make known to God's people the coming wrath.'

[119] E20–4. 'When Noah spoke to these men about that flood, that it would drown all sinful men, then men laughed to scorn at his words and said that he lied. So now many men think that this deacon lies about the fire, concerning which the Lord himself commanded him to tell the children of men.'

[120] See Matthew XXIV.37–9 for an analogy of the period of the Flood with the sudden arrival of the end times. Anlezark explores the use of Noah in Letters E and F in *Water and Fire: The Myth of the Flood in Anglo-Saxon England*, connecting the Noah figure with the broader theme of an apocalyptic devastation which takes the form of a punishing fire in the case of E/F (pp. 112–21).

[121] Based mainly on the five beasts found in F (*þa sænde dryhten v deor up of se*, line 146) and *Epistil Ísu* ('five huge beasts and hideous in the depths of hell', §11), Priebsch postulates another stage of development. He argues that because of the similarity of these beasts to those in Napier XLII 200.8–10 (*þonne cumaþ up of helle egeslice mycele deor swylce swa næfre ær gesawene wæron oð ðone timan*), and some correspondence in subject matter with Pehtred's book, that the latter was the author and the addition was made in England with a revised version making its way back to Ireland ('Quelle und Abfassungszeit', pp. 147–50, 153–4). Whitelock shows this complex scenario to be entirely unnecessary ('Bishop Ecgred', pp. 55–6). Indeed, there is no reason why the five beasts could not have been one of the several additions made when Y^1 was initally composed.

[122] See Priebsch, 'Chief Sources', p. 144. For examples of contacts between the Irish and the English, see K. Hughes, 'Evidence for contacts between the Churches of the Irish and English from the Synod of Whitby to the Viking Age', in *England before the Conquest: Studies in Primary Sources Presented to Dorothy Whitelock*, ed. P. Clemoes and K. Hughes (Cambridge, 1971), pp. 49–67.

the biblical account has nothing to suggest this. One possible explanation for its incongruous appearance is that it was initially introduced into an earlier version as an additional example of dramatic divine punishment; such a use in Letters C/D supports this origin. Then the author of Y^2 expanded the reference with more details, some biblical, others conveniently altered to suit the theme of Sunday observance. Its inclusion may also have prompted the more pertinent story of the man executed for gathering wood on the sabbath, which precedes that of Dathan and Abiram in the book of Numbers.[123] The Y^2 version also exhibits unique details such as the golden letters with which the letter is said to have been written, a date of September or October for the coming destruction, and a Pope Florentius, who joins Bishop Peter in the final oath. Much of this letter, judging particularly from its form in F, is an unfortunate expansion of the usual contents of the Sunday Letter, resulting in a rambling piece which was subsequently modified to produce the different versions which survive in Letters E and F.

Some suggestions have been offered in regard to the date when this translation of Y^2, the common ancestor of the Letters E and F, was made. Dorothy Whitelock notes that the formula which E/F apply to the time period for Sunday observance (midday Saturday to dawn on Monday) does not occur prior to the laws of Edgar and therefore believes a date after 962 is required.[124] However, it is also possible that it was merely following its Latin source, or that this formula was commonly in use for some time before Edgar enshrined it in his law code.[125] Another consideration, this time of a linguistic nature, is Janet Bately's discussion of E and F in connection with the use of the term *Scotta ealond* or *Scotland* to refer to Ireland. According to Bately, this term came to be used exclusively for Scotland in the tenth century, and consequently, while noting the possibility of the translator's using an outdated term, she would suggest a date of 'before the second quarter of the tenth century' for our text.[126] Given that Y^2 could have been available at any time after the first quarter of the ninth century, this leaves us with a roughly hundred-year time span for the production of Letters E and F.

Differences between Letters E and F

Letter F preserves most of the source text from what we can surmise from a comparison with Letter E. Two longer sections are neither in E, nor in other Sunday Letters, but were probably in the Letter F's source. The first, an expansion of the provision of manna to the Israelites in their wanderings, occurs in the Sunday List. It quotes a scriptural passage on the sabbath, which it strategically refers to

---

123 Numbers XV.32–6.

124 Whitelock, 'Bishop Ecgred', p. 51; see also Chapter 3, p. 61.

125 So it is listed whenever a time period is mentioned in the Sunday Letter, though admittedly none of the manuscripts predate the middle of the tenth century.

126 'Old English Prose before and during the Reign of Alfred', *Anglo-Saxon England* 17 (1988), 93–138 at 114–18.

as the 'rest-day'.[127] Another addition is the story of the man gathering wood on the sabbath, noted above, which may have been inspired by the Dathan and Abiram story. The remainder, with the exception of the conclusion (see below), has some basis in various Latin versions of the letter.[128]

In Letter E, we find a more attentive approach to the unwieldy material at hand, one which becomes bolder as the text progresses. Initially, the author follows his source closely; in fact, he retains a portion not found in F.[129] But beginning with a comparison of the Deacon Niall and Noah, which he may have rewritten in order to make connections between the two more explicit, he begins to modify the text.[130]

Shortly after that passage, the author of Letter E inserts a lengthy section on tithing and the observance of Sunday and other feast days drawn from Wulfstan's work.[131] It is not clear whether this was meant to substitute for a few sentences on tithing in Letter F which are not in E, or whether it was simply prompted by the availability of material on the subject of Sunday. While the selection includes a great deal of text that is extraneous to the topic at hand, such as a description of hell, it does provide a momentary glimpse into the reception of the letter, showing that it brought to mind the legal injunctions of the time.

The most dramatic editorial activity by Letter E's author occurs in one particularly extended and tedious section, in which Letter F rambles on about successive periods of disobedience and punishment by God, echoing the ten plagues of Exodus (so much so that at one point he inserts a comment that these events took place in Egypt). Here the author of E cuts ruthlessly and reorders the material. He leaves out all references to locusts and grasshoppers (which repeatedly figure in F) as well as flying serpents.[132] Episodes of previous human disobedience are conflated into a single instance (E171) which refers to unnamed forebears (*yldran*)

---

127 F54–71; the passage is Exodus XXXI.12–15 and is oddly interrupted by a Sunday List item, perhaps copied from a marginal note. The biblical quotation also receives two explantory notes in Letter F (see commentary).

128 There are, however, many details and flourishes only to be found in Letter F: 1. the floodwaters rose sixteen cubits above the highest mountain (F31), 2. 14,000 died in the rebellion by Dathan, Abiram and Korah (F80), 3. and the plagues mentioned happened in Egypt (F144). On the other hand, it is Letter E that retains the names of Noah's sons (E32–3).

129 E44–55, 99–109. Some of the same ground is covered in later sections of F – for example, the heathen invaders (F181, E47–8) – but lines 102–9 are the introduction to the Sunday List which begins rather abruptly in F.

130 E (16–30; cf. F13–28) tightens this section, making the connection between the reception of Noah and Niall more explicit. A similar editorial cut occurs when F (58–63) alludes to the biblical command to punish sabbath-breaking by death (Exodus XXXI.14–15) and explains that this is the death of hell-fire; E retains only the final verse. One wonders whether E's omission of a sentence (at F71–3) that claims that God established how Sunday should be observed by resting on the seventh day (the sabbath) was motivated by the suspect nature of the argument.

131 See below, pp. 91–3.

132 In this cut, E also omits mention of five beasts, reprimands for not taking care of the poor and foreigners, a first-person reproach by Christ, an explanation of how Saturday has now become Sunday because of the Resurrection, an obscure mention of rest for beasts, additional hailstones and flying serpents and a general exhortation to give alms and go to church on Sunday.

who suffered burning fire and terror. But after God repents and removes the fire, and mankind falls into sin again, God responds by writing the Sunday Letter as a warning, which brings us swiftly to the author's present concern. From there he moves on to Niall, the need to believe and the framework of the letter's arrival and the command to disseminate it. The result, if not exactly elegant, is a much improved sequence of ideas, which leads logically to the conclusion.

In other, minor ways, E's composer shows a comprehensive approach to the Sunday Letter. He gives it a title (taken from the body of the text): *Sunnandæges spell*. He may be responsible for adding Wales to the path taken by the fire.[133] Letter E also resists setting a specific deadline for the threats. The statement that the fire will come in September or October occurs twice in F, both retained by E minus the specific date.[134] Both Letters E and F make changes to the conclusion of the letter, some of which may have been accomplished in their common vernacular source. These draw on texts known to us from other vernacular sources, particularly those preserved in the Vercelli Book.

Additions from the Vercelli Homilies

One of the additions to E/F can be traced back to materials which were used by several other Anglo-Saxon sermon writers. The sermon preserved in Vercelli IX and its analogues in other manuscripts contains several extracts, sometimes mere snippets, which were used by E and F.[135] Oddly, Letters E and F preserve different selections from Vercelli IX, with only two short segments being common to both. For this reason, there has been some question as to whether an earlier version of E/F contained all the portions from Vercelli IX with differing cuts being made in later transmission, or whether each added its selections independently.[136] The difficulty probably cannot be resolved definitively, but a fresh look at the changes may clarify the process.

All of the borrowings appear in the conclusions of E and F. Both sermons, after they have recorded the oath of Bishop Peter and Pope Florentius concerning the divine origin of the letter, then pose a rhetorical question:

> Hwylc man is þonne æfre, butan his heorte sy eall mid deofles strælum awrecen, þæt he wene, þæt se halga papa and se biscop dorston swerian mænne að þurh swa miclan mægenþrymme?[137]

---

[133] E4–5: *hit þonne færð on Brytwealas.*

[134] F196 and F211 (cf. E164 and 193).

[135] These are indicated in the commentary. Versions of Vercelli IX also appear in Bodl. Bodley 340 and Hatton 115, printed as E and L respectively in Scragg's edition.

[136] See the discussions in Scragg, 'Vernacular Homilies', pp. 248–51; idem, *Vercelli Homilies*, pp. 154–7, and Wright, *Irish Tradition*, pp. 222–4.

[137] E202–4. 'What man is there unless his heart be utterly pierced with the arrows of the devil, that he would believe that the holy pope and the bishop dared to swear a false oath by such great might.' Cf. F222–4: *Men þa leofestan, hwilc man is þonne efre, butan his heorte se eal mid deofles strealum*

The image of the heart pierced by the devil's arrows clearly parallels the last phrase in the statement about hell in Vercelli IX.117–18 that 'Se nama is to geþenceanne ælcum men butan hwæs heorte sie mid diofles stræle þurhwrecen'.[138] There is no doubt that this was part of the source of E and F since it is well integrated into the Sunday Letter material and occurs at the same point in both texts. It is, however, a memorable image which may have been more widespread than the surviving evidence suggests and could have even been borrowed by the writer of Vercelli IX from E/F or one of its sources. The second sentence is the last that Letters E and F have in common, and it, too, appears in somewhat different form in Vercelli IX:

And gif ge nellað gelefan, men þa leofestan, þæs ærendgewrites, þonne ne geþencað ge na, hu þæt deofol þam ancre sæde, hwylc hit in helle wære to wunianne (E).[139]

And gef eorþlice men nu agemeleasiaþ þisæs gewrites bebodes, þonne ne geþæncaþ hio na, hu strang hit biþ an helle to bionne (F).[140]

Hwæt, we nu gehyrdon secgan hwylc hit is on helle to bionne (Vercelli IX.222).

The correspondence here is perhaps less compelling, but the source of E and F seems to have had a version of this sentence. It may be just a coincidence that it also appears in Vercelli IX.[141]

From here on, Letters E and F exhibit separate uses of the material. E's author uses the above reference to hell as a launching pad to allude to the popular 'Devil's Account of the Next World' story which forms a significant part of Vercelli IX. He introduces the subject of the narrative, an anchorite who once forced a devil to tell him about hell, using some wording reminiscent of the beginning of the independent narrative, oddly found in F's manuscript (BL Cotton Tiberius A.iii) immediately following the Sunday Letter.[142] However, instead of continuing with the expected description, he then provides an 'inexpressibility topos', one also

awrecan, þæt he wæne, þæt se halga papa and se biscup dorstan swerigan menne aþ þus micel megen?

[138] 'The notoriety (of hell) should be remembered by every man whose heart is not pierced with the devil's arrow' (trans. Scragg, *Vercelli Homilies*, p. 188). Wright believes that this overlap suggests that all the borrowings from Vercelli IX were once in the common ancestor of E and F (*Irish Tradition*, p. 223).

[139] E207–9. 'And if you will not believe, dearest people, this letter, then you are not considering how that devil spoke to the anchorite, what it would be to dwell in hell.'

[140] F227–9. 'And if earthly men now neglect the commandment of this letter, then they are not considering how severe it will be to be in hell.'

[141] Less likely is a relationship between the statements in E and F that no one can tell the torments of hell in both. E212: *ne mæg nænig man wordum asecgan fram þam susle, þe in þære helle is* and F247–9: *þær biþ sar butan frofre and ærmþo butan are and wæana ma, þonne hit eniges mannes gemet sie, þæt hit asecgan mege*; the latter is very close to Vercelli IX.30–1 (L, Hatton 115).

[142] This version has been edited by F. Robinson in 'The Devil's Account of the Next World: An Anecdote from Old English Homiletic Literature', in *The Editing of Old English* (Oxford, 1994), pp. 196–205. Scragg maintains that 'it is probable that N [Letter E] should be seen as related to [the 'Devil's Account' in Cotton Tiberius A.iii]' (*Vercelli Homilies*, p. 155)

found in Vercelli IX, but used in another context.[143] E (220–5) then concludes with a selection from the beginning of Vercelli IX, an Old English commonplace which states the need to confess sins and the hope of forgiveness and eternal life in heaven.[144]

F has other correspondences with Vercelli IX. Perhaps because a full 'Devil's Account' narrative follows Letter F in the manuscript, there is no reference to it in the letter. Though, like E, it threatens that those who disregard the letter are insufficiently mindful of a destiny in hell, it then provides a more general conclusion, taken from the beginning of Vercelli IX, which refers to the Last Judgement when we must give account of our wrongdoing, followed by a brief description of hell.[145] While E seems to have taken its borrowings entire, F rewrites the extracts to suit the current subject matter, Sunday observance.[146]

Several scenarios for the borrowings from Vercelli IX have been proposed. The simplest proposes that all were present in the common ancestor of E and F and were later excised in divergent ways.[147] Another possibility is that the author of F discarded most of the ending now found in E and selected an alternate passage from Vercelli IX to conclude his sermon.[148] Finally, it is possible that E and F selected much, if not all, of their borrowings independently.[149]

Two factors should be taken into account when evaluating these propositions. Firstly, the two borrowings from Vercelli IX (noted above) that both E and F have in common certainly do point to a stage when the common ancestor incorporated these phrases, though it should be said that, unlike the more extended borrowings, they could have been borrowed from or simply remembered from some other text. Secondly, the two conclusions are quite sufficient as they stand. If, presuming a single borrowing from Vercelli IX, one were to combine them, the ending would be unusually long and repetitive, particularly taking into consideration that E and F are already rather lengthy sermons. It therefore seems more likely that they were constructed independently, with the author of F replacing the conclusion of their common ancestor with his own, as suggested in the second scenario above, though this presupposes two stages of borrowing from Vercelli IX. Furthermore, the assumption that some earlier version of Vercelli IX was the source of all the added portions is also open to question; they could have been gleaned from else-

---

143 Vercelli IX.108–13. This is the well-known image of the 'Men with Tongues of Iron'.

144 Vercelli IX.10–14. The text is also found in a confessional piece in Cotton Tiberius A.iii (Scragg's m), the same manuscript that has F; see H. Logeman, 'Anglo-Saxonica minora', *Anglia* 12 (1889), 497–518 at 513–15.

145 Vercelli IX.1–27. Another version of Vercelli IX, a later copy of which may be seen in Hatton 115 (Scragg's L), is somewhat closer to Letter F (Scragg, *Vercelli Homilies*, p. 155).

146 The added phrases are readily seen in Scragg's edition where they are italicized (*Vercelli Homilies*, pp. 158–61).

147 Wright, *The Irish Tradition*, pp. 222–4.

148 This is suggested by Wilcox, 'Compilation', p. 77.

149 Scragg refers to 'two brief (and different) extracts incorporated separately into [E and F]' (*Sources of Anglo-Saxon Literary Culture*, ed. Biggs, p. 126). However, in a previous statement acknowledging the complexity of the situation, he had noted that 'the order of the composition of XLIII [E] and XLIV [F] is probably now beyond recovery' ('Vernacular Homilies', p. 250).

where, perhaps in some other form and sequence. At least some of them appear in other contexts, and Vercelli IX itself seems to be at some remove from the texts as they appear in E and F. In any case, it is clear that the borrowings were made from Old English texts: the verbal correspondences between E and F and the analogues mentioned above as well as the use of distinctively Old English phrases in both prove that the texts had already been translated into the vernacular.[150]

Another relationship that is difficult to track is that of an insertion much earlier in E and F. Both sermons make the comparison that those who will not believe the letter or keep Sunday are like learned men who refuse to preach the gospel to the people. The context is completely different in each; in E the comment comes after a reference to Niall, and in F it follows the Dathan and Abiram narrative. Letter F, as always, provides the fuller example with a biblical quotation and the detail that fifty sins will be forgiven those who listen to the gospel and a hundred for those who preach it. Letter E has pared the section down to a much simpler statement.[151] Similar passages appear in Vercelli IX and X,[152] but in both of these, it is a later insertion.[153] The relationship in this case seems to be that F preserves the original reading while E has reduced and edited the material.

Additions from a Wulfstan Law Code and Sermons

As mentioned above, one lengthy addition to E (lines 56–98) is taken from Wulfstan's works and is therefore datable within certain parameters. The passage is comprised of an adaptation of some of his legal writings as well as a selection from one of his sermons. Both of these pieces were copied again later in the same manuscript as part of a longer sermon, and a comparison shows that a common

---

150 Distinctive phrases include the reminder to be mindful of 'our soul's need' (*ure saule þearfe* F230–1), expressions like *siþ oþþe ær* ('at any time' F235) and *weagesiþ* ('companion in woe' F243) and the alliterative pair *magan and motan* (E222), all also found in the analogues.

151 F84–90: *Hiom weorþ swa, swa swa þare bocere sawle biþ, þe nellaþ godspel sæcgan Godes folce for hiora gemeleaste and for weoruldgalnesse. Forþon þe Crist selfa cwæþ: þeah mann anum men godspyl secge, þonne bio ic an hiora midle; and þæm biþ, þe þæt godspel sagaþ, forgefen .c. synny, and þam fiftig, þe hit for Godes naman lustlice gehereþ; and þam biþ wa æfre geborenum, þe hit secgan can and ne wile; forþan men sculan þurh þa godspellican lare becuman to liues wige*; E182–5: *And þa ðe nu get ne gelefað þisses, þonne bið heom, swa swa þam bocerum bið, þa ðe nellað heora boccræftas Godes folce wel nytte gedon. Forðon þæt Godes folc sceal becuman to lifes wege þurh þa godspellican lare.*

152 Vercelli X.3–8: *þeah man anum men godspel secge, þonne bio ic þæronmiddan. And þam bioð synna forgifene þe ðæt godspel segð and gecwið, and synna þam bioð forgifene þe hit for Godes naman lustlice gehyreð, and þam bið wa æfre geworht þe secgan can and nele, for ðam men sculon þurh ða godcundan lare becuman to life* (cf. Vercelli IX (L).99–113). See Scragg, 'Vernacular Homilies', p. 230 and n. 8. Vercelli X's version is very close to that in F, but excludes the number of sins forgiven; Vercelli IX also has some distinctive words in common with F (see note to these lines in Scragg's edition).

153 It only occurs in Vercelli IX (L), does not appear in the other versions in manuscripts A or E and seems quite out of place in L. In Vercelli X it was added as part of a new introduction, which again is not found in the other versions of that sermon.

source must have been used for both occurrences because they are textually very close.[154] The legislative portion which is only slightly adapted into a sermon is a piece edited as Napier XXIII and found in three manuscripts apart from its appearance in the Sunday Letter.[155] Two of them, in BL Cotton Tiberius A.iii and CCCC 201, bear the title *To eallum folce* followed by the text as it stands in Napier;[156] in CCCC 419, however, it is entitled *Larspell* and has been supplemented with the conclusion of Wulfstan's 'Pastoral Letter', Bethurum XIII (Napier XXI–XXII) and Napier XXIV, all together representing Napier XXI–XXIV. In all three contexts it is part of a collection of Wulfstan material. The source for the piece was obviously a law code, a version quite close to I Cnut, though it retains some elements from earlier laws; it was therefore produced no earlier than the second decade of the new millennium.[157]

The selection from Napier XXII which follows in the legal portions in Letter E, again textually very close to the copy later in the manuscript, is a reminder of the coming judgement and the horrors of hell. It is difficult to see why this was appended here since it has the ring of a common type of conclusion found in Old English sermons and no attempt is made at providing a transition with what follows in the Sunday Letter. In fact, the placement of the Wulfstan material is puzzling, coming as it does between the prediction of the fire and a Sunday List and not where one would expect, as a replacement for the prohibitions which are found much later in E. The rationale for the borrowing as a whole, however, seems obvious enough: the compiler had to hand some contemporary, authoritative material regarding Sunday observance and tithing and found it more or less germane to the Sunday Letter. Tithing is frequently mentioned in Latin Sunday Letters and seems to have been often treated in conjunction with Sunday observance in general.[158] At the same time, the familiarity with Wulfstan's work in evidence throughout the manuscript as a whole would encourage the blending of legal extract and sermon.[159] In any case, it seems likely that the person who added this section had access to the same materials as the compiler of CCCC 419, and

---

[154] For example, the clauses *ðær is benda bite and dynta dyne, þær is wyrma slite and ealra wædla gripe* (E93–4; Napier XXII, p. 114) occur only in the two copies in CCCC 419. The few changes are perhaps such as any copyist might make: *cornteopung* (E60) vs. *eorþwæstm, beon geeastrode* (E74) vs. *ofer eastran*, and the addition of honouring mother and father in Napier XXIII, 119.3 and omission from E of a general statement on the cessation of conflict during holy days at Napier XXIII, 119.1–3.

[155] See P. Wormald, 'Archbishop Wulfstan and the Holiness of Society', in *Legal Culture in the Early Medieval West* (London, 1999), pp. 225–51 at 243 and nn. 66–7 and Wilcox, 'Dissemination', p. 207 and n. 37.

[156] These two texts are of a slightly later date (s. xi^med) and more closely related to each other than to that in CCCC 419. All three differ in their introductions and conclusions.

[157] See Chapter 2, p. 26. The relevant laws are cited in the commentary to Letter E. One Sunday proscription, sexual relations, is listed in CCCC 419, and is added marginally in Letter E, but does not appear in the later versions of Napier XXIII, perhaps providing evidence of the fluctuating view on this matter (see commentary for E72).

[158] See Munich 9550: *Iterum iterumque moneo atque praecipio uobis ut detis mihi decimas iustas et sacerdotibus meis; et qui decimam meam defraudauerit, non uidebit uitam aeternam.*

[159] See above, p. 65.

may have been the scribe himself.[160]

The treatment of the Sunday Letter in Old English Letters E and F once again shows that the Anglo-Saxons were not merely copying it as a curiosity or simply for the sake of preservation. The extent and types of modifications indicate a desire to fit the letter into the vernacular homiletic and legal traditions of the time. That these two lengthy versions were part of manuscripts, each of which has been described as designed for a bishop, contributes to the perhaps surprising conclusion that they were an accepted part of the homiletic canon of the day.

The Sunday List in the Old English Letters

A distinctive feature of the Old English Sunday Letters is that all but one incorporate a Sunday List. For two of them, C and D, the evidence is quite clear that the list was already part of the Latin source text, one of the earliest pieces of evidence for the combination of Letter and List at this early date.[161] For two others, E and F, this was probably also the case, since they are derived from the same Latin source (the version owned by Pehtred) and their lists reflect this relationship. The Latin version closest to Old English B, however, has no Sunday List, and there is no external evidence which would indicate at what point in the transmission it was added, requiring a comparison to other lists to determine its possible origin. In fact, tracing the relationships among all of these lists yields valuable information about their origins and, by extension, that of their host letters.

As already noted, one type of Sunday List is relatively short, restricting its entries to biblical events, most of which occurred on a Sunday according to scripture.[162] Such lists may be found in Old English texts apart from the Sunday Letter. The *Theodulfi capitula* lists the creation of light, the giving of manna,[163] the Resurrection and Pentecost.[164] A list in a short passage entitled *Incipit de Sabbato*, possibly written by Ælfric but found in what has come to be known as Wulfstan's canon-law collection, has Sunday as the first day of the world, the day of the Resurrection and of Pentecost.[165] In his *Enchiridion*, Byrhtferth lists the creation of the angels, the Annunciation, the Resurrection and Pentecost.[166]

---

160 See Scragg, 'Vernacular Homilies', p. 250.

161 Another possible witness to an early integration of the two texts is a Latin list in Vatican City, Biblioteca Apostolica Vaticana, Reg. lat. 49 (s. ix/x, McNally III, see Chapter 3, n. 81), which is followed by a short excerpt from a Sunday Letter.

162 See discussion in Chapter 3, pp. 59–60.

163 The notion that Sunday was the first day on which manna was given from heaven was provided with a lengthy explanation in the traditional list which included it; cf. the related lists in Pseudo-Alcuin, Hrabanus' *De clericorum institutione*, and in an addition to a sermon in the Homiliary of Toledo (see Chapter 3, n. 137).

164 C. 24 (*Theodulfi capitula*, ed. Sauer, pp. 336–7). The Latin text was probably available in England no later than the second half of the tenth century (Sauer, p. 74).

165 Listed by Lees as the *Excerptiones Egberti* ('Sunday Lists', pp. 140–1), but since identified and edited by Cross and Hamer as *Wulfstan's Canon Law Collection*, pp. 127–8.

166 *Byrhtferth's Enchiridion*, ed. P. S. Baker and M. Lapidge, EETS ss 15 (Oxford, 1995), p. 72.

It is the expanded list, however, as observed by Lees, that finds its way into the Sunday Letter.[167] That the transformation and lengthening of the Sunday List took place in a Hiberno-Latin environment is proved by three examples of such amplified lists, conveniently collected and edited by McNally.[168] All three occur in manuscripts of the ninth and tenth centuries.[169] New items featured in these lists include the infusing of spirit into the soul of Adam (III), the resting of Noah's ark after the Flood (II, III), Moses striking the stone in the desert (II, III), the adoration of the magi (II), the giving of the law at Mount Sinai (II), Judgement Day (III), the end of the Jewish 'synagogue' and the beginning of the Christian Church (I) and the Apocalypse of John (II), among other things. Moreover, McNally III is the earliest Latin example of the joining of Sunday Letter and Sunday List.[170]

McNally's lists, because of their early date and established Hiberno-Latin connections,[171] may be regarded as the gauge by which one may assess the probable origins of other Sunday Lists. Indeed, we discover that all of the Latin lists in which corresponding items or details concerning those items occur have such connections, and may therefore be seen as members of a broader Hiberno-Latin and, in the vernacular, Insular tradition.[172]

---

[167] Lees, 'Sunday Lists', pp. 143–51.

[168] *Scriptores Hiberniae minores*, ed. McNally, pp. 175–86; hereafter these will be referred to as McNally I, II, and III. See also M. Lapidge and R. Sharpe, *A Bibliography of Celtic-Latin Literature, 400–1200* (Dublin, 1985), p. 247 (Nos. 903–5).

[169] Orléans, Bibliothèque municipale, 221 (193), Brittany, s. viii/ix (McNally I); Paris, BN lat. 3182, Brittany, s. x² (McNally I); Vatican City, Biblioteca Apostolica Vaticana, Pal. lat. 220, Middle Rhineland, s. ix¹ (McNally II); and Vatican City, Biblioteca Apostolica Vaticana, Reg. lat. 49, Brittany, s. ix/x (McNally III). Wright ('Dies dominica', p. 93) identifies two more manuscripts with copies of McNally II: Karlsruhe, Aug. CCLV (s. ix), fol. 8 and St Gall, Stiftsbibliothek 682 (s. ix), pp. 330–4. That such lists were available in Ireland as early as the ninth century (and probably earlier) is illustrated by the one incorporated into the Old Irish *Epistil Ísu* (see above, p. 40). Another Irish text has been associated with the tradition, the hymn *Precamur Patrem* which has been dated to the seventh century and which lists many of the same events; cf. M. Herren and S. A. Brown, *Christ in Celtic Christianity: Britain and Ireland from the Fifth to the Tenth Century* (Woodbridge, 2002), pp. 284–8; and M. Lapidge, '"Precamur Patrem": An Easter Hymn by Columbanus?' in *Columbanus: Studies on the Latin Writings*, ed. M. Lapidge (Woodbridge, 1997), pp. 255–63.

[170] Lines 42–56 are from a reworked version resembling Recension II and are closely related to the Old Irish *Epistil Ísu*; see discussion above, p. 49.

[171] These connections are made by McNally in *Scriptores Hiberniae minores*, pp. 177–9; by B. Bischoff, 'Wendepunkte in der Geschichte der lateinischen Exegese im Frühmittelalter', *Mittelalterliche Studien* I (Stuttgart, 1966), pp. 205–73 at 269; and finally by C. D. Wright in *Irish Tradition, passim*. In addition, for Vat. Reg. lat. 49 see P. Grosjean, 'A propos du manuscrit 49 de la Reine Christine', *Analecta Bollandiana* 54 (1936), 113–16; and for Vat. Pal. Lat. 220 see R. McNally, '"In nomine dei summi": Seven Hiberno-Latin Sermons', *Traditio* 35 (1979), 121–43.

[172] These are the Old Irish *Epistil Ísu* (O'Keeffe, 'Cáin Domnaig', pp. 196–201); an Old English Easter homily in CCCC 162 (see next note); and sermon XXXII in the Pembroke Homiliary (77r–79v), a copy of a ninth-century sermon collection containing several texts with Hiberno-Latin connections (see T. Hall, 'The Early Medieval Sermon', in *The Sermon*, ed. B. M. Kienzle (Turnhout, 2000), p. 223; and *Cambridge Pembroke College Ms. 25: A Carolingian Sermonary Used by Anglo-Saxon Preachers*, ed. J. E. Cross (London, 1987), pp. 64–87). The latter has an unusual item in common with the *Epistil Ísu*: the statement that on Sunday *omnis creatura reformabitur in melius et sol et luna septuplum lumen accipient* ('all creation will be transformed to the better and the sun and

4. The Old English Sunday Letters

Apart from those in the Sunday Letter, only one Old English example of such an expanded version survives: that in the Easter Homily in CCCC 162.[173] This list includes the creation of earth, the seven heavens, the nine orders of angels and man, and Christ's baptism in the River Jordan, the beginning of his forty-day fast, the vision of St John on the island of Patmos (greatly elaborated), Christ's revealing himself to Peter, the Resurrection and the Harrowing of Hell. It is a good illustration of the type of list that shows Hiberno-Latin connections.[174]

Such lists are characterized not only by their greater length, but by the free use of extra-biblical items, both tendencies which are in keeping with the Irish penchant for enumeration and the embrace of apocryphal materials. In order to show the interrelation of the Old English Sunday Letters and this tradition, a third factor, the propensity for elaboration by means of added literal detail, will also be considered.[175]

As the Old English Letters with the clearest connection to Ireland, we may expect E and F to exhibit the above features, and this is indeed what we find.[176]

---

moon will receive a seven-fold light', 79r); cf. *Epistil Ísu* §15: 'On Sunday there shall be a renewal of every element in a form fairer and better than at present, as they were made at the first Creation, when the stars of Heaven will be as the moon, and the moon as the sun, and sun as the light of seven summer days' (O'Keeffe, 'Cáin Domnaig', p. 201). This notion is ultimately derived from the *Liber de ordine creaturarum*, a seventh-century Hiberno-Latin work (*Liber de ordine creaturarum: Un anónimo irlandés del siglo VII*, ed. M. C. Díaz y Díaz (Santiago de Compostella, 1972), p. 114; cf. D. Whitelock, 'Bishop Ecgred', p. 64 and J. E. Cross, '*De ordine creaturarum liber* in Old English Prose', *Anglia* 90 (1972), 132–40). A portion of the Pembroke sermon with an almost identical list (including the item just mentioned) is edited as the Pseudo-Augustinian sermon XLVII (PL 39, col. 2070). The list in the Bobbio Missal should also be included in this group (*The Bobbio Missal*, ed. E. A. Lowe, Henry Bradshaw Society 58 (London, 1919), pp. 150–1); for the missal's (at times perhaps overstated) Irish connections, see Y. Hen, 'Introduction: the Bobbio Missal – from Mabillon onwards', in *The Bobbio Missal: Liturgy and Religious Culture in Merovingian Gaul*, Cambridge Studies in Paleography and Codicology, ed. Y. Hen and R. Meens (Cambridge, 2004), pp. 1–18 at 2–3, and C. D. Wright and R. Wright, 'Additions to the Bobbio Missal: *De dies malus* and *Joca monachorum* (6r–8v)', ibid., pp. 79–139 at 96, n. 65. Some later texts clearly derive from the same tradition and will be included in the discussion below. These are two Middle High German texts, one edited by J. Kelle in *Speculum Ecclesiae* (Munich, 1858), pp. 176–8, and the other by P. Strauch ('Altdeutsche Predigten', *Zeitschrift für deutsche Philologie* 27 (1895), 148–209 at 149, lines 55–6). M. Tveitane has proposed Hiberno-Latin connections for these in 'Irish Apocrypha in Norse Tradition?' *Arv: Tidskrift för nordisk folkminnesforskning* 22 (1966), 111–35 at 114–16.

173 The homily has been edited and discussed by C. Lees in 'Theme and Echo in an Anonymous Old English Homily for Easter', *Traditio* 42 (1986), 115–42; the list is located at lines 31–75 (Lees, pp. 118–19).

174 The fasting of Christ (Lees, 'Theme and Echo', p. 118, lines 46–7) occurs elsewhere only in the Hiberno-Latin *Catachesis Celtica* (McNally II, p. 185, lines 34–5). The Vision of St John occurs only in McNally II (p. 183, lines 39–40) and in the Old Irish *Epistil Ísu* (O'Keeffe, 'Cáin Domnaig', p. 201). The creation of the seven heavens, particularly the statement *þone seofoðan [heofon] he geworhte him sylfum on to sittene* ('the seventh heaven he made for himself, to dwell in [it]' (Lees, p. 118, lines 37–8)), points to the Irish interest in the seven heavens; see Wright, *Irish Tradition*, pp. 218–21, and R. Willard, 'The Apocryphon of the Seven Heavens', *Two Apocrypha in Old English Homilies* (Leipzig, 1935), pp. 6–30.

175 Both characteristics are well documented in Wright's *The Irish Tradition*.

176 The list is found in E at lines 102–42 and F at lines 47–107 (somewhat shortened) and includes the

95

One might particularly single out the creation of Adam,[177] the detail of the Isra-elites crossing the Red Sea 'with dry feet' (E only),[178] the statement that their enemies drowned,[179] the addition to the Pentecost entry of the speaking of many languages,[180] and the entry for Judgement Day, including the detail (echoing the Nicene Creed) that Christ will judge the living and dead.[181] The use of an apocry-phal motif about the River Jordan, which states that it will not flow on Sundays, the day on which Christ was baptized in it, is probably another item which should be seen as derived from Hiberno-Latin materials.[182] Though lengthy, the lists in E and F are considerably shorter than that in the related *Epistil Ísu*, and it seems likely that the latter either drew on another list to supplement its source or used a different list altogether.[183]

The list in Old English Letters C and D can be readily linked to the same tradition.[184] In the entry listing the creation of the angels, it refers to 'heavenly

first day (E only), the Resurrection (E only), Judgement Day, the creation of Adam, turning water into wine at Cana (F only), the crossing of the Red Sea, the giving of manna, the belief that the Jordan does not flow on Sunday because Christ was baptized in it on that day, Pentecost, and the Sunday respite for souls in hell or purgatory.

[177] Also in McNally III (p. 185): *dies dominicus dies beatus, in qua die spirauit Deus animam in Adam*. The Genesis account obviously places the creation of man on the sixth day. Cf. Old English Letter C and D based on the Latin VK which states that God created the soul of man on Sunday (see below).

[178] E110–11 *And on þone dæg Moyses oferfor þa readan sæ mid his werode drygum fotum*; cf. *Epistil Ísu*, 'Israel passed dryshod through the Red Sea' (O'Keeffe, 'Cáin Domnaig', p. 199). In Latin lists the dry feet (*siccis pedibus*) occur in McNally III (p. 185, line 19), where the phrase is also applied to the crossing of the Jordan River, and in Pembroke 25's *Sermo XXXII*. B97 has *drium fotum*. C35–6 has *and þæt folc for betwux þam twam wæterum on þam grunde ealle drygsceode*, but this is not in D or the Latin source (VK) and may be an addition by the Anglo-Saxon translator. Dry feet curiously also turn up in the entry for 811 in the *Chronicum Scotorum*, which records that the first *céli dé* 'came over the sea from the south, dry-footed, without a boat, and a written roll used to be given to him from Heaven' (*Chronicum Scotorum*, ed. Hennessy, pp. 126–7). The expression is used regularly in Insular texts, not only for the crossing of the Red Sea, but for the crossing of the Jordan River by Joshua as well as Christ's and Peter's walking on water. It is much less common elsewhere.

[179] Also in B98 and, of Pharaoh alone, in a Middle High German sermon of the twelfth century (*Speculum ecclesiae*, ed. J. Kelle, p. 177).

[180] The *Epistil Ísu* states that Christ 'distributed the many tongues of the earth to His disciples' (O'Keeffe, 'Cáin Domnaig', pp. 200–1). Cf. C50–3: *And on þam dæge sende God þone halgan gast ofer þa apostolas ealle þær þær hi wæron on anum huse inne belocene, and tæhte heom, þæt hi cuðan ealle þa spræca, þe syndon swa wide, swa middaneard is*. Again, the detail is not in the parallel text D nor in the Latin source (VK).

[181] Judgement Day occurs in the *Epistil Ísu* (O'Keeffe, 'Cáin Domnaig', pp. 200–1), McNally III (p. 186, line 40), *Sermo 32* of Pembroke 25 (without the added detail from the Nicene Creed), and in the two Middle High German sermons, see note 172.

[182] See Hall, 'The Reversal of the Jordan', pp. 53–86, and the commentary to E131–4.

[183] There are no details or events that belong exclusively to these three lists and which might confirm their use of a common source. One of the two Irish manuscripts (N) which, according to O'Keeffe ('Cáin Domnaig', p. 190), have the oldest readings contains no Sunday List, perhaps an indication that it was not in the Latin source.

[184] Whitelock noticed the links between C/D and EF as well as the Irish *Epistil Ísu*, stating that C and D 'have all the events shared by *Epistil Ísu* and Pehtred homilies [EF]. . . except that Hom. D omits Christ's baptism' ('Bishop Ecgred', p. 63).

orders';[185] it mentions the creation of the soul of man;[186] it specifies that manna was provided for forty years;[187] it lists the nativity of Christ,[188] the biblical but rarely mentioned detail that twelve baskets of bread remained after the feeding of the five thousand,[189] the languages known at Pentecost (C only), an entry for Judgement Day, and perhaps most remarkably, the statement that Sunday brought the end of the Jewish 'synagogue' and the beginning of the Christian Church[190] and Christ's revelation to Peter (C only).[191] D also features an unusual apocryphal motif: that the Red Sea was divided into twelve paths instead of one.[192]

Old English Letter C, in keeping with its generally more expansive treatment of the source, has several items which do not appear in either the Latin VK or in D, leaving open the possibility that its author may have known of other lists. The added items are the detail of the dry feet for the crossing of the Red Sea, Christ's baptism, Christ's revelation to Peter and the mention of languages in connection with Pentecost. He also rearranges the list to follow the historical order, moving the nativity of Christ, the Resurrection and Pentecost to their proper chronological places.[193] This thoughtful engagement with the Sunday List is a good witness to the activity that produced the many varying lists extant from this period. What appears to be an unpromising enumeration to the modern reader was obviously viewed by Insular writers as an opportunity to edit and expand.

Having observed the points which relate these two sets of lists to the Hiberno-Latin tradition, we are now able to tackle the list added to Old English Letter B. It, too, has the Israelites crossing the Red Sea with dry feet, and adds that their enemies drowned, calls manna the 'heavenly food',[194] and states that it was given for forty years. Furthermore, it mentions the ark's resting on Mount Armenia,[195] the Nativity, and, in connection with the feeding of the five thousand, that the

---

[185] Cf. the Easter Homily in CCCC 162: *mid nigon engla endebyrdnyssum* (Lees, 'Theme and Echo', p. 118, lines 36–7); and McNally II: *in die dominica creati sunt angeli et archangeli ab ore Dei, uirtutes et potestates, principationes, dominationes, throni, cerubim et seraphim* (p. 183, lines 8–10).
[186] See note 177.
[187] Cf. the *Epistil Ísu* (O'Keeffe, 'Cáin Domnaig', pp. 198–9), McNally I (p. 182, line 28), II (p. 183, line 14) and, where it mistakenly reads *XL dies*, III (pp. 185, line 21). The detail also occurs in Old English Letter B and in both Middle High German sermons.
[188] Also in McNally I, II, II, the *Epistil Ísu* (O'Keeffe, 'Cáin Domnaig', pp. 198–9), both Middle High German Sermons, and the Bobbio Missal.
[189] Also in the *Epistil Ísu* and the two Middle High German sermons.
[190] Only in Old English Letters C and D, its Latin source (VK), and McNally I: *Die uero dominica sinagoga Iudeorum fugit et in die dominica nata est eclesia* (p. 181, lines 17–18). Cf. Jerome, *Epistola* 29: *haec est qua Synagoga finitur et Ecclesia nascitur* (PL 30, col. 224).
[191] This item is in C49–50 but not in D or the Latin source VK; its only other occurrence is in the Easter Homily in CCCC 162 (Lees, 'Theme and Echo', lines 66–7). It is perhaps a borrowing from another list, the ten manifestations of Christ after the crucifixion; see Lees, 'Sunday Lists', p. 145 and n. 67.
[192] See note to D17; C (line 35) corrects the number to the more usual figure.
[193] The only item that remains out of place is the added entry of Christ's baptism (line 43) which should come before the changing of the water into wine in Cana.
[194] In the *Epistil Ísu* and Old English Letters E and F.
[195] Also in the *Epistil Ísu* and in the two Middle High German sermons.

count does not include women and children.[196] It also has a paraphrase of the Psalter verse for the harrowing of hell,[197] the detail that after his resurrection Christ is seated at the right hand of the Father,[198] and that at Pentecost the Holy Spirit came in the likeness of fire.[199] Many of these elements are scriptural or traditional and could conceivably have been added independently to any one of these lists, but their cumulative effect leaves little doubt that the list in Letter B was derived from the same tradition as that found in the other Old English letters. Whether it was added in the Latin or in the Old English versions cannot be answered; we simply do not know if the Sunday List was ever regarded as a discrete text in Old English or if it was always translated as part of a larger composition.

The appearance of the Sunday List in nearly all of the Old English Sunday Letters confirms the suspicions concerning Old English Letters B, C and D, already noted in the discussion above, that their sources were probably moulded in an environment where Hiberno-Latin materials were available, perhaps in Ireland itself. The evidence of the Sunday List in its textual relationships and its association with Insular versions of the Sunday Letter at an early date is critical in establishing the latter's paths of transmission.

While it is difficult to settle definitely on a place of origin for each copy of the Sunday Letter that made its way to England, it is perhaps possible to say that they were, with the possible exception of Letter A's source, all Insular productions. We can be more certain of the reception that our text enjoyed in the specifically Anglo-Saxon milieu. All the evidence points to an active engagement with the letter, from its respectable place in the manuscripts to the level of revision and adaptation that most of the Old English versions underwent. It may not have inspired a legal tract, as it did in Ireland, but the attention evidenced in the surviving textual materials suggests the possibility that it was indeed preached to the English in the their own language.

The Language of the Old English Texts

Due to the complexities of examining six different texts scattered in five manuscripts, this discussion of the language of the Old English Sunday Letters will focus primarily on the dialectal features which may be helpful in determining the transmission and possibly the origin of each text and, to a lesser extent, on the indications of their lateness.[200] As might be expected, given the relative age of

---

[196] Also in McNally II and in the Middle High German sermon edited by Strauch (see note 172).

[197] *And on sunnandæg cwæð se hælend: openiað þas geatu and þa fæstan scytelsas, and ic wille gan þæron* (lines 106–7). McNally I has: *Die uero dominica dixit Christus ad anglos: Aperite portas iustitiae. Et ingresus in eas confitebor Domino* (p. 181, lines 15–16) from Psalm CXVII.19.

[198] A detail likely taken from the Nicene Creed but found only here and in McNally II, Pembroke 25, and the Middle High German homily edited by Strauch.

[199] Also in Old English E and F and the *Epistil Ísu*.

[200] The usual grammars have been consulted: A. Campbell, *Old English Grammar* (Oxford, 1959), and Karl Brunner, *Altenglische Grammatik. Nach der angelsächsischen Grammatik von Eduard Sievers,*

the manuscripts, all of the texts, to a greater or lesser degree, were written in the language of late Anglo-Saxon England known as late West Saxon. Five out of the six also bear traces of being influenced by or perhaps even originally written in another dialect.

Letter A

Letter A alone shows no traces of having been written in or transmitted through a non-West Saxon environmont.[201] Its late West Saxon features are as follows:

(1.1) *e* for earlier WS *ea* due to Late West Saxon smoothing (Cmpb. §312, S–B §§121, 123):[202] e.g. *fex* (A79), *hehstan* (A85), *neheboras* (A66)

(1.2) the falling together of the vowels in unstressed syllables (Cmpb. §§377–81):[203] e.g. *buton* (A67), *cildra* (A73), *demon* (A15), *eagon* (A32, 74), *eallon* (A33), *forwyrðon* (A29), *gaton* (A2), *handon* (A74), *asendæ* (A40), etc.

(1.3) for WS *þā*, one example of the demonstrative *þæge* (A46), a form derived from Old Norse *þeir* according to Campbell; it also appears five times in the main text (Gospels) of the manuscript (Cmpb. §713).[204]

Common in Late West Saxon but also attested in Early West Saxon and other dialects is:

(1.4) vocalization of *g*, resulting in *ī* = *ig* (Cmpb. §§267–72, S–B §126.2): e.g. *adylgie* (A66), *bileofan* (A41), *halie* (A1, 9), *mynegie* (A25).

Letter B

To these Late West Saxon features,[205] Letter B adds the spelling *ht* for earlier *ct* (Cmpb. §484, S–B §210 A.4) in *lehtune* (B18, 122) and *h* for syllable-end WGmc *g* (Cmpb. §446) in *fuhlas* (B117).[206] But it also contains a number of traces of a

---

3rd ed. (Tübingen, 1965). These are occasionally supplemented by Richard Hogg's *A Grammar of Old English* (Oxford, 1992), Karl Luick's *Historische Grammatik der englischen Sprache* (Leipzig, 1921), and Ursula Kalbhen's extensive analysis of the Kentish dialect in her edition of the Kentish Glosses in *Kentische Glossen und kentischer Dialekt im Altenglischen* (Frankfurt am Main, 2003), pp. 241–71.

[201] It is one of the additions to CCCC 140, a copy of the West Saxon Gospels made in Bath in the second half of the eleventh century; see above, pp. 63–4, and Liuzza, *The Old English Version of the Gospels*, I, xxvi.

[202] Anglian smoothing (see 2.1 below) is not likely in *hehstan* since there are no other Anglian features in the text; it is rather due to a Late West Saxon smoothing of analogical *ea* (Cmpb. §658, n. 6).

[203] These include, for example, *on* for *an*, *um* or *en*, *æ* for *e*, *a* for *u*, and *an* for *on* or *en*.

[204] See Liuzza, *The Old English Version of the Gospels*, II, 153.

[205] Examples include (1.1) *fex* (B82); (1.2) *sohtan* (B13), *scoldan* (B42).

[206] The language of Letters B and E has been examined in some detail by J. Wilcox in his unpublished dissertation on CCCC 419 and 421; much of what follows has already been discussed there. See 'Compilation', pp. 200–202 and 220. Letter B follows E in CCCC 419 but did not receive the

non-West Saxon, possibly Anglian, origin. These possibly include:

(2.1) *e* for *ea* due to Anglian smoothing (Cmpb. §§222 and 225, S–B §119): e.g. *þeh* (for *þeah*, B18), *lehtune* (B18, 122); however, such spellings could just as likely be due to Late West Saxon smoothing; see (1.1) above.

More definitely non-West Saxon are the following spellings:

(2.2) *e* for WS *y/i*

(2.2.1) (EWS *ie/īe*) from the i-umlaut of *ea/ēa* (Cmpb. §200.2 by breaking, §200.5 from PGmc *au*; S–B §§104–6; Hogg §5.82): e.g. *awerged* (B129), *gecerrað* (B70, 79), *ermingas* (B34), *geherað* (B57, 65), *hersumiað* (B133), *gelefan* (5x), *gelefað* (B72, 136), *leg* (B135)

(2.2.2) (EWS *ie/īe*), the result of diphthongization of Gmc *e* after palatals *c, g, sc* (lacking in Mercian and Kentish, irregular in Northumbrian) (Cmpb. §§185–7, 743; S–B §§91a and A.1, 91c, and A.6; Hogg §§5.53–5):[207] e.g. *begetenne* (B19), *begetene* (B40)

(2.2.3) in the *sel-* group (LWS *syl-*, EWS and nWS *sel-*) (Cmpb. §§325–6; S–B §124): e.g. *sellað* (B67)

(2.3) *eo* for WS *y/i* (EWS *ie/īe*)

(2.3.1) due to palatal diphthonization of *e* (lacking in non-West Saxon which shows back mutation instead) (Cmpb. §§185, 210; S–B §§370, 391 A. 4):[208] e.g. *ageofan* (B40, etc.), *ageofað* (B110), *begeotað* (B35), *geofena* (B140), *ongeotað* (B24, etc.)

(2.3.2) breaking before *r* (Anglian) (Cmpb. §§155, 459 (1); S–B §§84 A.3, 386 A.2): e.g. *beornendne* (B135), *eornenne* (B21)

(2.3.3) by i-umlaut of Gmc *io* (Mercian *eo*, Kentish and Northumbrian *io / eo*) (Cmpb. §§201 and 294–5; S–B §107):[209] e.g. *eorre* (B58, 84), *feond* (B98), *heo* (9x, for WS *hy*), *seo* (B140, for WS *sy*)

(2.4) *æ* for WS *e*

(a) the i-mutation of *æ* < *a* before a nasal (? non-West Saxon) (Cmpb. §193 (d); S–B §96.5 A.8): e.g. *beþænce* (54), *sænde* (72)

(2.5) *ea* for WS *eo* (non-West Saxon) (Cmpb. §§275–81 and 768 (d); S–B §§35 and A.1–2, 427.1): e.g. *eam* (B79)

(2.6) 3rd person singular preterite and participles of weak II verbs end in *-ad(e)* (Anglian and Kentish) (Cmpb. §757): e.g. *adilegad* (B82, 129), *gefullad* (B23), *gemyngad* (B126), *þrowade* (B92)

(2.7) *eo* for WS *o* or *e* due to back mutation: the spelling *weorold-* (*weoroldgestreona*, B32) is more common in Mercian/Kentish whereas in West Saxon and Northumbrian combinative u-umlaut results in *woruld* (Cmpb. §§205 and 210.1–3, S–B §§110 A.3 and 113 (b); Kalbhen §7.3.7).

---

attention of E's correctors, perhaps because it covers the same subject matter and was passed over.

[207] Hogg argues that it is lacking in Northumbrian as well (§5.54).

[208] Mercian back mutation may also be present in *geatu* (B46, for WS *gatu*), but the diphthong may just as well have been transferred from the singular form (Cmpb. §206, S–B §§108 A.4, 109 A.8).

[209] Cmpb. §§703 (*hēo*), 768 (d) (*sēo*); S–B §§334 A.2 (*hēo*), 427 A.3 (*sēo*).

The possibility that Letter B was Anglian in origin has been proposed by Franz Wenisch. The evidence for this is two-fold. Wenisch points to the Anglian vocabulary item *leactun* (spelled *lehtune*) for WS *wyrtun* and the use of *in* rather than *on*.[210] Secondly, many of the non-West Saxon spellings discussed above are characteristic of the Anglian dialects (Mercian and Northumbrian).[211]

Letter C

In addition to the Late West Saxon features already mentioned,[212] Letter C also has *waxe* (C98) for earlier *wasce* (Cmpb. §440, S–B §204.4) and *eorne* (C24) for WS *georne*, caused by a shift of stress (Cmpb. §303, S–B §212 A.2). Its non-West Saxon elements are sparse and yet enough to give rise to speculation that it, too, was copied from an Anglian original.[213] They include the verbal endings in *-ad(e)* (as in 2.6 above): *geendad* (C53), *gereordade* (C43), *þrowade* (C47), *gewunad* (C9). Wenisch notes the use of *forgripe* (C157), and *forhwon* as an interrogative adverb (C106; cf. D67 *forhwi*).[214] In addition, the word *oferhygd* (*oferhigde*, C90) has been associated with Anglian dialects.[215]

Letter E

Letter E presents the strongest case for an Anglian original.[216] Like Letter B and the related Letter F, it exhibits signs of an Anglian origin, many of which were noticed and altered by subsequent readers.[217] The details for E will be given in the

---

[210] Wenisch, *Spezifisch anglisches Wortgut*, pp. 298–9; *cf.* A17 *wyrtune*.

[211] These are *ageofan* (3x), *ageofað* (B110), *awerged* (B129), *begeotað* (B35), *begetenne* (B19), *begetene* (B40), *beornendne* (B135), *gecerrað* (B70, 79), *eornenne* (B21), *ermingas* (B34), *geofena* (B140), *geherað* (B57, 65), *hersumiað* (B133), *gelefan* (5x), *gelefað* (B72, 136), *leg* (B135), *ongeotað* (3x), and perhaps *þeh* (for *þeah*, B18) and *lehtune* (B18, 122) (ibid.). Wenisch also notes the 3rd person singular preterite and past participles of weak II verbs ending in *-ad(e)* (listed under point 2.6). See also Wilcox's assessment that Letter B was 'copied from a dialectal exemplar' ('Compilation', p. 220).

[212] Letter C's examples are (1.1) *scel* (C100, 140, 144, 146); (1.2) *be hwan* (C104), *for hwan* (C106), *an* (for *on*, C105); and (1.4) *heries* (C83), *hig* (6x), *lifiendan* (C156), *geþingie* (C178).

[213] Wenisch, *Spezifisch anglisches Wortgut*, pp. 153, 286 and n. 74.

[214] Pp. 152–3 and 285–7.

[215] Wenisch, *Spezifisch anglisches Wortgut*, p. 153; H. Schabram, *Superbia: Studien zum altenglischen Wortschatz* (Munich, 1965), pp. 101–2.

[216] Late West Saxon features are (1.1) *ehta* (E20, 32), *fex* (E165), *genehhe* (E189), *geseh* (E175), *wexes* (E62); (1.2) the preterite plural of verbs (16x).

[217] Wilcox distinguishes twenty-two hands making alterations to CCCC 419/421 (pp. 24–37). In Letter E, these often involve changing non-West Saxon to Late West Saxon spellings (see details in notes below), primarily by Wilcox's Hand 21, as well as altering *i* to *y* (Wilcox, 'Compilation', pp. 35–6). Other readers made more substantive additions. Worth noting here are the lexical alternatives, *yrfe* for *ceap* (E100), *æftemesta* for *nexta* (E103), and *gereste* for *ablan* (E120), by Hand 13 (Wilcox, 'Compilation', pp. 28–30).

following, and a summary of these will follow the discussion of F.[218]

Following the numbering in Letter B, examples of non-West Saxon features are as follows:

(2.1) e.g. *hehaltare* (E201)

(2.2.1) e.g. *acerrede* (E146), *alefed* (E114), *awerged-* (E42, 46, 168, 192), *gemeleas* (E191), *gelefan* – (5x), *gelefað* (E17, 183), *leg* (E173), *scerð* (E166)[219]

(2.2.2) e.g. *get* (4x)

(2.3.1) e.g. *eorlicum* (E38), *eorre* (E172), *feond* (E111), *forbeornað* (E37)[220]

(2.3.2) e.g. *beornende* (E173)[221]

(2.5) e.g. *eam* (E158)

(2.6) e.g. *bodade* (E19), *gefullad* (E132), *þrowade* (E188, 200)

To these should be added the failure to distinguish forms of *þry* (m.) and *þreo* (f. and n.),[222] and *haldan* (E150) for WS *healdan* due to retraction of *æ*, rather than breaking before *l* followed by a consonant, both considered Anglian.[223] In addition to these phonological elements, Wenisch has also identified Anglian vocabulary, which is discussed together with that in F below, since they are derived from a common source which used these words.[224]

Letter D

In the final two texts which remain to be examined, another element is at work, that of a south-eastern or Kentish influence. In Letter D the evidence is more broadly non-West Saxon, which may, however, point to some southern influence:[225]

(2.2.1) e.g. *hæftned* (D44, 71, WS *hæftnyd*), *hæftnedlingas* (D37)

(2.6) e.g. *geendad* (D25)

Letter D also has one occurrence of *yo* for WS *eo*, *twyon* (D115), which has been

---

[218] See pp. 108–9.

[219] Of these, Wilcox's Hand 21 corrects *alefed* to *alyfed*, *awerg-* to *awyrg-* and *gelef-* to *gelyf-* (Wilcox, 'Compilation', p. 36).

[220] Wilcox's Hand 21 corrects *eorre* to *yrre*, *feond* to *fynd*, and *forbeornað* to *forbyrnað* (Wilcox, 'Compilation', p. 36). Wilcox suggests that *eorlicum* 'escaped the attention of the corrector because he mistook the sense for "manly"' (p. 199).

[221] Hand 21 corrects to *byrn-* (Wilcox, 'Compilation', p. 36).

[222] In *þreo suna* (E32) and *ðreo ealdormen* (E123) (Cmpb. §683). Hand 21 corrects to *þry* (Wilcox, 'Compilation', p. 36).

[223] Cmpb. §143. Wilcox's Hand 5 has added an *e* above the line (Wilcox, 'Compilation', pp. 27, 199).

[224] See p. 108. Except for changing *in* to *on* (9x), these remain untouched by the correctors.

[225] Late West Saxon features are (1.1) *fex* (D60); (1.2) *buton* (3x), *healdon* (D32); (1.4) *lufien* (D9), *þeowien* (D9), *myngie* (D94). One might also note that the spellings *wirignysse* (D64) and *wyricð* (D60) perhaps show the development of a Late West Saxon parasite vowel (Cmpb. §296) and that the appearance of both *þweore* (D67) and *þwyran* (D54) may likewise be a sign of lateness in the coalescing of *-wyr-* and *-weor-* in *-wur-* (Cmpb. §324).

regarded as a south-eastern phenomenon.[226] The use of the word *ofermodignys* (D107) is also southern, according to Schabram (p. 130). These two points may indicate that Letter D's nWS spellings which are listed above are the result of Kentish or perhaps more general Southern influence rather than that of other non-West Saxon dialects. This conclusion accords well with the supposition that the manuscript, CCCC 162, was written in either Rochester or Canterbury.[227]

Letter F

The language of Letter F presents a much more complex picture and therefore requires a more detailed treatment. In the consideration of the manuscript (BL Cotton Tiberius A.iii) above, it was observed that this Old English Sunday Letter was probably copied from the same exemplar as its immediate neighbours in the codex – Ælfric's Palm Sunday homily and a piece referred to as 'The Devil's Account of the Next World'.[228] Not only do these texts all show a similar admixture of late West Saxon and Kentish, they also exhibit idiosyncracies which are not dialectal in nature. In the following discussion, I will therefore occasionally refer to them for the sake of comparison.

The scribe who copied our text was probably not responsible for most of its linguistic characterics.[229] He appears to have copied mechanically, producing numerous errors, which sometimes obstruct a clear view of what should be taken as dialectal variation.[230] These include the omission of single letters (*gospel* for *godspel, swelic* for *sweflic, mildheornesse* for *mildheortnesse, getanad* for *getacnad, gorenestan* for *gecorenestan, geyngode* for *gemyngode, heofelican* for *heofenlican, genihtsumes* for *genihtsumnes, stranlice* for *stranglice*),[231] reversal

---

[226] See discussion in A. Healey, *The Old English Vision of St Paul* (Cambridge, MA, 1978), pp. 36–8; cf. Cmpb. §296.

[227] See above, p. 68.

[228] Malcolm Godden has helpfully edited the Cotton Tiberius A.iii version of this homily in an appendix to his edition of the Catholic Homilies (*CH* II, pp. 381–90). The 'Devil's Account' has been edited by Fred Robinson in 'The Devil's Account of the Next World', in *The Editing of Old English*, pp. 196–205. These will be referred to as XIVct and DANW respectively in the present discussion; what follows is by no means a complete analysis of these texts.

[229] Other texts copied by him do not have these features; see above, p. 72.

[230] The poor quality of the work of scribe 3 in Cotton Tiberius A.iii has been remarked on by several editors of his work: Garmonsway refers to the glossator of *Ælfric's Colloquy*'s 'gross errors' and 'scribal carelessness . . . of which there is a good deal in the text' (p. 17), and notes that he 'makes frequent mistakes' (pp. 4 n. 1, 17,15); Herbst mentions a 'vielzahl von Fehlern' (*Die altenglische Margaretenlegende*, p. 6) in the *Life of St Margaret*, while Kornexl finds that some errors in the Old English gloss to the *Regularis Concordia* are only to be explained by 'eine äußerst oberflächliche, mechanische Arbeitsweise' (*Regularis concordia*, cxx). No doubt Ker was including Letter F in his assessment of the manuscript when he says that 'some of the OE pieces are very corrupt' (*Catalogue*, p. 240). Even Napier states: 'Bei der verderbtheit der sehr abweichenden überlieferung habe ich es vorgezogen, die [homilie] genau nach der [handschrift] abzudrucken, indem ich keinen versuch machte . . . einen korrekten text wider herzustellen' (*Wulfstan*, p. 215).

[231] In the case of *gospel, mildheornesse* and *stranlice*, scribal carelessness may not be the only

103

of letters (*reng* for *regn*, *freni* for *frein* (from *frignan*)), substitutions of letters (*abolgel* for *abolgen*, *stod* for *stow*, *wille* for *sille*, *weorþaþ* for *weorpaþ*, *ryrt-edæg* for *rystedæg*), intrusion of letters (*gemerlease* for *gemelease*, *andged* for *onget*), and the misleading formation *Angelcing* (for *Angelcynn*).[232] The unthinking copying of the scribe may be best illustrated in his peculiar word-division. For example the manuscript shows *micel ne beo leofan* for *micelne beoleofan*, *on deghwilcan* for *ond eghwilcan*, *þas alestan* for *þa salestan*, *mana þus* for *manaþ us*, and *swing gæþ* for *swin(g)gæþ*. In some cases, the scribe seems to have mindlessly taken glosses and corrections from his exemplar into the text, writing *ger-shoppan stapan* and *ælþeoðiodige* for *ælðiodige* and a superfluous *weorþan* in *beon geedstaþoled weorþan*.[233] Simple dittography also occurs occasionally.

The language of the text is therefore that of a copyist(s) at a prior stage in the transmission. On the whole, it is late West Saxon,[234] a fact which is especially evident in the falling together of the vowels of unstressed syllables, which is quite advanced.[235] To the features already encountered above, Letter F adds *g* for WS *h* (Cmpb. §447) in *hegestan* (F32), *hegre* (F31, 32);[236] *d* for *þ* in *fædman* (F31, for *fæðman*) (Cmpb. §424); and *u* for *f* in *liues* (F90) (Cmpb. §60).[237] The spelling *me*

explanation. Due to its frequency in the Kentish Glosses, it has been suggested that the reduction of groups of three unlike consonants is characteristic of the Kentish dialect; see Kalbhen, §7.3.12, Cmpb. §477 and I. Williams, 'A Grammatical Investigation of the Old Kentish Glosses', *Beiträge zur Anglistik* 19 (1905), 92–166 at 129. For similar occurrences in the same manuscript, see Kornexl (*Regularis concordia*, ccvi) and Kluge ('Zur Geschichte der Zeichensprache', p. 130); Cf. XIVct *gaslicum* (for *gastlicum*, 225).

[232] Spellings ending in *-ng* are attested elsewhere (see *DOE* s.v. *cynn*, noun). It also occurs in DANW in the compound *wyrmcyncg*, where it has been interpreted as *cyning*.

[233] Similarly, XIVct has *æteowde eteowde* in the main body of the text (311).

[234] Late West Saxon features are (1.1) *angen* (F28, 30), *anget* (F137), *andged* (F139), *ongen* (F75), *age* (F75), *gerum* (F149), *scel* (F183); cf. DANW *scel* (16), *geseh* (44), XIVct *scel* (258), *scep* (240), *scette* (75), *togenys* (97), ? *forgefan* (212), *agef* (306, 320), *gescefte* (361); (1.4) *hig* (F104), *restandæig* (F184), *sig* (F103), *sige* (F116). *Wige* (F90) may also belong here if it is merely an error for *weige* (cf. XIVct *weig*, 4x); however, the form is also attested in the Kentish Glosses (*wiferend*, *wig-*, 4x); see Cmpb. §266–7 and n. 4. Kalbhen suggests that the *g* may have effected this raising in Kentish (p. 172). *Freni* (F111) is a unique spelling of WS *frægn* (preterite sg. of *frignan*), possibly showing Kentish *e* for *æ* (see below) and Kentish or Late West Saxon vocalization of *g*.

[235] Examples are that (a) *æ* is found for earlier *o* and *a*: e.g. *þæne* (F70, for *þone*), *sunnændæg* (F167); *hioræ* (F80); (b) *a* for *æ*: e.g. *þare* (7x), *þaræ* (F203), *þar* (F104); (c) *a* for *e*: e.g. *iowar* (F58), *gehealdaþ* (F172), *sagaþ* (F1, 87); (d) *a* for *o*: e.g. *þane* (16x), *þanne* (13x), *wundarlic* (F36), *wuldar* (F250); (e) *æ* for *e*: e.g. *þaræ* (F203), *þisæs* (F228), *wiþsacæ* (F175); (f) *o* for *u*: e.g. *helo* (F219), *helletintrego* (F243), *ærmþo* (F248); (g) *u* for *o, eo*: e.g. *bescup* (F213), *biscup* (F224); (h) *e* for *o*: e.g. *þene* (F232, for *þone*); (i) *an/am* for *on* and *um*: e.g. *adruncan* (F48), *cwædan* (F27), *earman* (F18); *hæfdan* (F44), *suman* (F1), *þisam* (F101), *þisan* (F1), *wæran* (F33), *wurdan* (F37), etc.; (j) *an* for WS *on* occurs also in the preposition *on* and prefix *on-*: e.g. *ancerrede* (F118), *angan* (F150), *anget* (F137), *ansende* (F95), etc. According to Campbell, some of these processes began as early as the ninth century in Kentish (Cmpb. §§377, 396). Cf. XIVct *an* (11, etc.), *angunnan* (166), *hwane* (98), *modar* (289), *swustar* (290), *þane* (132), *þare* (13, etc.), *wundar* (184), DANW *an* (18, etc.), *andune* (10), *angan* (3), *anhrine* (37), *anmiddan* (60), *ansittaþ* (27), *deofal* (73, etc.), *dohtar* (65), *þane* (11, etc.), *þanne* (36, etc.), *þare* (60, etc.), *þarto* (15), *wuldar* (77), *wurdan* (52).

[236] Cf. DANW *hegest* (8), *hegran* (50).

[237] Cf. XIVct *liue* (189, 192), *liuigendan* (224), *kauertune* (148).

for *man* (F113) indicates a transition to early Middle English.[238]

The following features are broadly non-West Saxon:

(2.2.1) e.g. *agemeleas-* (F208, 228), *alefed* (F64), *ancerrede* (F118), *awerg-* (3x), *hegestan* (F32), *hegre* (F31, 32),[239] *gehereþ* (F88), *gelefan* (F15), *gelefdon* (F14), *gemeleaste* (F85), *gemerlease* (F120), *leg* (F141, 180), *unalefedlice* (F114, 199)[240]

(2.2.2) e.g. *ageldan* (F232, 235), *forgef-* (F87, 178), *get* (7x)[241]

(2.2.3) e.g. *self-* (14x, *sylf-* 2x), *sellan* (F17), *selle* (F185)[242]

There are also inverted spellings of *y* for *e* (found in both accented and unaccented syllables):[243] e.g. *æryst-* (F47, 172), *deaþy* (F59, for *deaþe*), *elmyssan* (F17), *frecynysse* (F121), *godspyl* (F86, 208), *rystedæg* (F55, 57, 67), *wy* (F236)

(2.3.3) e.g. *beoleofan* (F4), *eorlicum* (F40), *feond* (F48), *seon* (F118, for WS *sȳn*)[244]

(2.3.4) failure to distinguish forms of *þry* (m.) and *þreo* (f. and n.) in *þreo sunu* (F22, 34) (Anglian) (Cmpb. §683)[245]

(2.5) confusion of *ea* and *eo*:[246] e.g. *eam* (F56, 189), *scealan* (F247, for WS *sceolon*), *heoldan* (F45, 170, for WS *healdan*), *wudebeorwas* (F136, for WS *wudubearwas*)

(2.6) e.g. *wudade* (F112), *bodade* (F20), *gefulwad* (F91), *getanad* (F113), *geþrowade* (F160, 161), *þrowade* (F205), *aþrowade* (F219)[247]

(2.7) e.g. *feola* (F160), *weorold* (6x)[248]

(2.8) *e* for WS *æ*

(2.8.1) *æ* from WGmc *ā*, PGmc *æ* (Cmpb. §128; S–B §§62 and 98; Kalbhen

---

[238] See Fernand Mossé, *A Handbook of Middle English*, trans. James A. Walker (Baltimore, 1952), p. 63 and *Middle English Dictionary* s.v. *me* pron. (1), *Oxford English Dictionary* s.v. *me* pron.²

[239] The *ē* in *hegestan* and *hegre* could also be the result of Anglian smoothing or Late West Saxon smoothing of analogical *ēa* (Cmpb. §658, n. 6).

[240] See also Kalbhen §7.3.6.1. Cf. E *acerrede* (146), *awerg-* (3x), *gemeleas* (191), *gelef-* (7x), *leg* (173), *scerð* (166), DANW *hehstan* (7), *hegest* (8), *hegran* (50).

[241] See also Kalbhen §7.3.5. Cf. E *get* (4x), XIVct *forgefenessæ* (62), DANW *get* (50).

[242] Cf. E *selle* (157), XIVct *self-* (69, 116, etc.), *sellenne* (54).

[243] Cf. XIVct *fyt* (36), *geryste* (362), *twylfa* (21), DANW *fyt* (8), *hyllewite* (46), *gehylpan* (25), *gesyte* (40), *yft* (for *eft*, 16), *wexbryde* (33).

[244] See Kalbhen §7.3.6.2. Cf. E *eorlicum* (38), *eorre* (172), *feond* (111), XIVct *gefreond* (188), *heorde* (158); some of these spellings, notably *feond-*, also occur in West Saxon. In the case of *erre* (F134) *e* likely replaces a WS *y*; this suggests the Kentish spellings were introduced into a West Saxon text rather than the other way around.

[245] Cf. E *þreo suna* (32), *ðreo ealdormen* (123).

[246] Cf. XIVct *forleagan* (136), *þreogende* (278).

[247] See also Wenisch, *Spezifisch anglisches Wortgut*, pp. 298–9 and n. 155. Cf. XIVct *geofrade* (80), *gelogad* (175), *gewitegad* (263).

[248] In the case of a short diphthong between *w* and *r* with a following consonant, F has several *weorþ-* spellings rather than the common Late West Saxon spelling *wurþ-*; e.g. *weorþunge* (F91, 99), *weorþment* (F250), *weorþmendum* (F184) (Cmpb. §§320–1, S–B §113). Northumbrian has *worþ-* (by retraction, Cmpb. §147, S–B §113 and A.3), though some *weorþ-* spellings occur. Cf. XIVct *weorulde* (140), DANW *weorulda weoruld* (77).

§7.3.1):[249] e.g. *brecan* (pret. pl., F145), *ded-* (noun, F235, 238), *lete* (pres., F181), *misdeda* (F236), *neddran* (F180), *redaþ* (F11)

(2.8.2) *æ* (i-umlaut of PGmc *a*), retained in West Saxon (due to metathesis of vowel + *r*), but raised in non-West Saxon before nasals (Cmpb. §193(d); S–B §96 A.7): e.g. *forbernan* (F12), *anberned* (F195)

(2.8.3) *æ* (i-umlaut of *a*), instead of expected *e* (i-umlaut of *æ*, due to analogy with related forms) (non-West Saxon) (Cmpb. §193(c); S–B §96.3b):[250] e.g. *awecnigan* (F36), *hebbe* (pres. subj., F205), *gemeccan* (F35), *stepe* (F92)

(2.9) *o* for *a* before a nasal (Anglian) (Cmpb. §130, S–B §79):[251] e.g. *gegongeþ* (F38), *lichoman* (F231), *mon* ('man', F8, 135, 207, 209 (*mynstermon*)), *noman* (F203)

(2.10) unsyncopated 3rd person, present verbs (Anglian and early Kentish) (Cmpb. §733 (a–b); S–B §358):[252] e.g. *sagaþ* (F1, 87), *sægeþ* (F150), *cymeþ* (F1, 194) *hafaþ* (F175), *gehealdaþ* (F172)

Specifically Kentish are the following spellings:

(3.1) *e* for WS *y/i* from the i-umlaut of PGmc *u/ū* (Cmpb. §§199 and 288; S–B §§31 A.1 and 102–3; Hogg §§5.194–5; Kalbhen §7.3.10.3):[253] e.g. *afelled* (F63), *behedan* (F236), *gededan* (F154), *dede* (F110, 113), *dreht-* (23x), *fer* (F195), *geld(e)num* (F43, 127, 222), *letl-* (F139, 145), *mengaþ* (F238), *sceldige* (F66), *senleas* (F114), *unnet* (F208), *(ge)werc-* (verb, F114, 233, 241)

(3.2) *e* for WS *æ*

(3.2.1) *ǣ* from i-umlaut of OE *ā*, PGmc *ai* (Cmpb. §§197 and 288; S–B §97 and A.1):[254] e.g. *efre* (F223, 235), *nefre* (F9), *eghwilcan* (F203), *egþer* (F215), *elces* (F35), *eniges* (F248), *nenig-* (F221, 238), *erest* (F49), *gegeð* (F200), *helo* (F219), *mende* (F61, 94, 164), *menne* (F224), *mestan* (F62), *se* (F49, 146, for WS *sæ*)

(3.2.2) *æ* from WGmc *a*, PGmc *æ* (Cmpb. §§193 (c) and 288; S–B §52):[255]

---

[249] Cf. XIVct *aletan* (118), *dedum* (279), *forletan* (238), DANW *dedum* (75), *lete* (10).

[250] Cf. XIVct *hebbe* (53), DANW *hebbe* (37, 41).

[251] While there are earlier Kentish and West Saxon spellings with *o*, Clayton and Magennis note that these spellings are 'likely to reflect Anglian influence in the period of our manuscript' (*The Old English Lives of St Margaret*, p. 100); cf. Herbst, *Die Altenglische Margaretenlegende*, pp. 9–10.

[252] Campbell (§734) notes, however, that such forms also occasionally occur in West Saxon. See also A. Campbell, 'An Old English Will', *Journal of English and Germanic Philology* 37 (1938), 133–52 at 151.

[253] Cf. XIVct *dede* (163), *drehten* (86), *efele* (67), *gefelled* (205), *senna* (62), DANW *afelde* (39), *dede* (50), *smetegelden* (58).

[254] According to Cmpb. §292 and S–B §97.1, these spellings also turn up in Anglian texts before dental or palatal consonants. Cf. XIVct *elc* (35), *er* (65), DANW *eghwylcum* (37), *elcan* (39).

[255] Cf. XIVct *cweþ* (303), *nes* (260), *sede* (60, 105, etc.), *simbeldege* (28), *gesprec* (34, 92), *þunresdeg* (30), DANW *asegd* (73), *meg-* (40, 43, etc.). The spellings in 2.8 and 3.2 are less likely to be related to the second fronting primarily found in the Vespasian Psalter (Cmpb. §§164–9, Kalbhen §7.3.10.1) because *ǣ* (due to i-umlaut and from PGmc *ǣ*) is also affected (Cmpb. §§169, 290), as are words with weak stress (Cmpb. §166). See also R. M. Hogg, 'On the Impossibility of Old English Dialectology', in *Luick Revisited: Papers Read at the Luick Symposium at Schloß Lichtenstein*, ed. D. Kastovsky and G. Bauer (Tübingen, 1988) pp. 183–203 at 193–8.

e.g. *bocblece* (F220), *cweþ* (pret., F209), *-deg-* (40x), *elmyssan* (F17), *ger-shoppan* (F130, 138), *megan* (pres.subj.pl., F180, 236, 242), *mege* (pres. subj.sg., F249), *megen* (noun, F224), *se(g)de* (F7, 116, 212), *sprec* (pret., F6), *wes* (4x), *nes* (F8, 146)

Less reliably Kentish but probably to be considered as such in this context are the following items:

(3.3) *æ* is frequently found for WS *e*. While some of these spellings could have other causes, the most likely, given the variety of environments in which *æ* appears in F, is that they are inverted spellings and the result of the graphic equivalence of *æ* and *e* which in some cases has been associated with the Kentish dialect or, alternatively with Late West Saxon.[256] They occur in both accented and unaccented syllables; for the latter, see note 235 above: e.g. *æc-* (3x), *sæcgan* (F85), *sæcge* (7x, beside *secge*, 3x), *sæcgaþ* (F219), *særaphin* (F191).

(3.3.1) This is perhaps also the case for *æ* for *e* before nasals (Cmpb. §§193 (d) and 291; S–B §96.5 A.8):[257] e.g. *mæn* (F72, for *men*), *besæncte* (F81), *ængl-* (F176, 190), *geþæncaþ* (F228), *ænde* (F186, 202), *anwændaþ* (F170) *sænd* (pret., F16), *asænde* (pret., F15), *ansænde* (pret. F43), *sænde* (pret., F129, 138, 146), *sænde* (pres., F132), *wæne* (F223).

(3.3.2) *æ* also appears for *e* as the first element of the diphthongs *ea* and *eo*:[258] e.g. *wæan* (F52), *wæana* (F248), *ęasprencguum* (= *æa-*, F30), *wæorc* (F66).

(3.3.3) By extension, the spellings *æ* for WS *i/y* are probably best explained as inverted spellings for nWS *e*:[259] e.g. *ærmþo* (F248), *cwælmed* (F62), *gedægeþ* (F121), *gehære* (F177) (cf. *gehereþ* at 88), *gehwærfede* (F186), *læg* (F132, cf. *leg* at 141, 180).

---

[256] Kornexl, *Regularis concordia*, cxcix–cc; Cmpb. §§193 (d), 288. Cf. XIVct *æhteras* (163). Campbell points out that, after the ninth century, 'the symbols become increasingly confused' (Cmb. §289; S–B §§55 A., 62 A.2 and 97 A.1). Cf. Dobbie, *The Anglo-Saxon Minor Poems* (lxxxi) and Förster, 'Vom Fortleben antiker Sammellunare' (pp. 65–6 and n. 2). In the case of the spellings of *secgan*, the issue may just be analogical replacement of a related form (Cmpb. §193 (c)).

[257] However, see 2.4 above for examples of its more general non-West Saxon use. Cf. DANW *æncgel* (48), *ænde* (61, 76). The spelling *æ* for WS *e* before nasals (where *e* is the result of i-umlaut of Gmc *a* and a subsequent raising) has elicited much comment. Rather than seen as specifically south-eastern, it has been associated with a broader southern region. See also Luick, *Historische Grammatik*, §§186, 363 A.2; Hogg §5.78 (1); Sauer, 'Spätaltenglische Beichtermahnungen', p. 18; H. Gneuss, *Hymnar und Hymnen im englischen Mittelalter*, Buchreihe der Anglia 12 (Tübingen, 1968), pp. 160–1; idem, 'Origin and Provenance', p. 41; and C. and K. Sisam, eds., *The Salisbury Psalter*, EETS os 242 (London, 1959), who comment that the spelling is 'generally regarded as a mark of South-Eastern colouring' but was probably 'tolerated over a wide area of Southern England' (pp. 13–14).

[258] Cf. DANW *æal* (36), *gesæald* (63), *sæon* (67), *wæalle* (35); and XIVct *æac* (371), *æal* (344), *æaþy* (115), *awæarp* (31), *dæage* (227), *wæardum* (381). These spellings also occur in the gloss to the *Regularis concordia*; Kornexl lists *ðwæan*, *hæaldan*, and *þæah* (*Regularis concordia*, cciii).

[259] Cf. XIVct *alæsednesse* (57), *gehæraþ* (16), *gehærsum* (229), *wæterscætan* (32), DANW *gehærdan* (13). See Herbst (*Die Altenglische Margaretenlegende*, p. 11 n. 40) and Kluge, 'Zur Geschichte der Zeichensprache', p. 130. Similarly, *gescæfta* (F70, for WS *gesceafta*) may also be an inverted spelling of *gescefta* due to Late West Saxon smoothing.

(3.4) *io* for WS *eo*: F shows a great number of *io* spellings where Late West Saxon normally has *eo*.[260] Though not conclusive in themselves, these are consistent with other Kentish spellings mentioned above, particularly in the case of *io* for historical *ēo, eo*; e.g. *abiofode* (F226), *ation* (F112), *diopnesse* (F67, 81, 83), *iorþe* (F79), *nioh* (F141), *tioþunge* (F17), *þiotan* (F27).[261] *io* also occurs for historical *īo, io*; e.g. *ælþeoðiodige* (F156), *betwioh* (5x), *bioþ* (7x), *hio* (23x), *hiom* (9x), *iow-* (40x), *gestrionum* (F19), *þiode* (F74), *wiofode* (F214).[262] Of particular interest is the uncorrected duplication in *ælþeoðiodige* (F156), which would appear to indicate that a scribe not far removed from the extant copy was, perhaps mechanically, substituting *io* forms for *eo*.[263] In addition, the spelling *sion* (F119, 230) for WS *syn, sin* (EWS *sien*) also appears to be a Kentish feature.[264]

(3.5) Use of the symbol *ę*:[265] *Noę* (F20, 22, 23, 34), *ęasprencguum* (F30)

There is no doubt that Letter F was at some point copied by a scribe who introduced Kentish spellings into the text. The fact that F's neighbours, the 'Devil's Account of the Next World' and the Ælfrician Palm Sunday homily, show a similar Kentish influence suggests that these modifications were made no earlier than the beginning of the eleventh century. In addition, a comparison of Letter F as a whole with just those sections that were inserted from other sources confirms that the entire text was probably modified with the Kentish features noted above after these portions were added since the additions also show these spellings, whereas parallel texts in other manuscripts do not.

As for the earlier history of F, Wenisch has suggested that the common ancestor of E and F was Anglian in origin. This may be seen in the use of *in* rather than *on*, *nænig*, *aræfnan* (E), *carcern* (F), *frignan* (F) and *gærshoppa* (F).[266] In addition,

---

260 Exceptions, due to West Saxon developments are *nioh* for WS *neah* (Cmpb. §145, S–B §86.4) and *abiofode* for WS *abifode* by analogy with the present tense (S–B §111 A.1).

261 From PGmc *eu* (Cmpb. §§275 and 293–7; S–B §§38 and 77; Luick, *Historische Grammatik*, §260), and by breaking of Gmc *e* (Cmpb. §146; S–B §§84 and 86). In Kentish *ēo, eo* were raised to *īo, io*, although this was less pronounced for the short diphthong (Cmpb. §297). In West Saxon *io, īo* and *ēo, eo* fell together into *ēo, eo* (Cmpb. §296); in Northumbrian the historical spellings were retained. In Mercian some *īo* spellings for historical *ēo* occur (Cmpb. §294–5), so that theoretically, they may reflect either Kentish or Mercian influence. The spelling *fillon* (F79), if an error for *fiollon* (WS *feollon*), may also belong here. Cf. Kalbhen §7.3.9; XIVct *liorningcniht-* (43, 81), DANW *diopnesse* (54).

262 From PGmc *iu* (Cmpb. §§275 and 293–7; S–B §§38 and 78; Luick, *Historische Grammatik*, §§125 and 261), breaking of Gmc *i* (Cmpb. §§148 and 277, S–B §§86 A.5 and 88). Cf. XIVct *bioþ* (83), *hiom* (97, 105, etc.), *iow* (35, 36, etc.), DANW *bioþ* (72), *hiom* (27).

263 This may also be supported by the spelling *erre* (F134) for WS *yrre* instead of the expected non-West Saxon spelling *iorre* (cf. *yrre* at line F125).

264 Cmpb. §768 (d). According to Sievers-Brunner, it is based on analogy with *bio* (§427 A.3); cf. *seon* at line 118. Cf. DANW *ansione* (72).

265 Cf. DANW *ęlc* (36). See Dobbie's observation that the use of the tailed *e* is 'frequent in most Kentish texts' (*Anglo-Saxon Minor Poems*, lxxxi) and I. F. Williams's article 'The Significance of the Symbol *ę* in the Kentish Glosses', *Otia Merseiana* 4 (1904), 81–3.

266 Wenisch, *Spezifisch anglisches Wortgut*, pp. 115, 117, 157, 159, 174–5, 193, 197 and 298–9. The sequence *gershoppan stapan* (F138) seems especially significant to Wenisch in that *stapan* appears to be a West Saxon gloss (taken into the main text by a copyist) to an Anglian word (p. 117); Wenisch cites

some of the spellings discussed above confirm this thesis, and enough of these are shared by E and F for Wenisch's suggestion to be a distinct possibility.[267] This would not be surprising, given this version's transmission through the north of England.

H. Rauh, 'Der Wortschatz der altenglischen Übersetzungen des Matthaeus-Evangeliums untersucht auf seine dialectische und zeitliche Gebundenheit' (Ph.D. diss., Berlin, 1936), p. 27 and H. Rubke, 'Die Nominalkomposita bei Aelfric. Eine Studie zum Wortschatz Aelfrics in seiner zeitlichen und dialektischen Gebundenheit' (Ph.D. diss., Göttingen, 1953), p. 123.

[267] These are listed in the discussion of E under 2.1, 2.3.2 and 2.6. The non-West Saxon spellings which E and F have in common are *alefed* (E114, F64), *awerg-* (E and F), *eorlicum* (E 38, F40), *feond* (E111, F48), *forgef-* (F87, 178), *get* (E and F), *geme(r)leas-* (E and F), *gelef-* (E and F), and *leg* (E173, F141, 180). Wenisch also mentions the unsyncopated 3rd person present verbs (listed in 2.10, only in F) and the 3rd person singular preterite and past participle of weak II verbs ending in *-ad(e)* (listed under 2.6 above, Wenisch, *Spezifisch anglisches Wortgut*, p. 298 and n. 155); the latter, however, also occur in the Ælfrician homily, and one should also note that some of the spellings in F for which there are no parallels in E may be due to the later Kentish influence.

Editorial Conventions

Punctuation, capitalization and word-division follow modern conventions.
Accent marks have not been recorded. The following symbols and abbreviations
have been employed:

< >	indicates an editorial addition
:::	indicates a missing or illegible letter (or letters)
` ´	indicates letter(s) which were added suprascript
<	in the apparatus, indicates an alteration (altered form < original form)
[ ]	indicates damage to the manuscript
***	indicates a lacuna in the text
††	indicates a corrupt or unreadable portion for which a conjectured reading is not possible
∂	indicates erasure of punctuation

THE OLD ENGLISH

SUNDAY LETTERS

Text and Translation

LETTER A

Cambridge, Corpus Christi College 140 (71r–72v)

[71r] ᵃMen þa leofestanᵃ, herᵇ onginð þæt halieᶜ gewrit þe com fram heofenan
into Hierusalem. Soðliceᵈ¹ hit gefeol beforan þam gaton Effrem, and þær hit wæs
funden þurh anes preostes handa, þæs nama wæs Achorᵉ. And he hit sende to anre
oðre byrig² to oþrum preoste, þe genemned is Ioram, þe hit asende fram Bethania
5 byrig to oðrum preoste, þe genemned is Machabeus. And he hit asende to monte
Garganum þær sancte Michaeles circe is þæs heahengles. Soðlice þæt ylce gewrit
þurh Cristes ᶠwillan uresᶠ hlafordes com to Rome to sancte Petres byrgene. And
ealle þa men þe wæron on þam burgum þær þæt gewrit to com, dydon þreora
daga fæsten and halie gebedu and ælmessan, þæt ure milda hlaford heom fultum
10 sealde and geopenode gewitt on manna heortan to oncnawenne uresᵍ drihtnes
hælendes Cristes mildheortnesse. Eac hit segð for hwilcon þingumʰ þis gewrit
com to Hierusalem and to oðrum burgum þus gesutelod.³ And hit com on þone
halgan sunnandæg, and þæt folc soðlice budon þone ylcan dæg to mærsianne mid
micelre gecyrrednesse and geleafan.
15   On sunnandæg nan man ne healde gemot, ne ne demon domas [71v], ne aðas ne
swerion, ne grindan, ne hlafas bacan, ne bicgan, ne syllon on þone halgan sunnandæg, ne wyrtan on wyrtune ne gaderion, ne nanne ne tælon, ne nane huntunge
nabbon forþam soðlice þurh þas þing bið þes middangeard forworden and cymð
Godes yrre ofer eow.⁴
20   Eala yrmingas, nyte ge þæt God geworhte heafenas and eorðan, sæ and eal þæt
þæron is on syx dagum,⁵ and syððan geworhte þone forman man Adam, and for
his agægednesse fif þusend and twa hund and viii and twentig geara rihtwise and
synfulle on helle forlet.⁶ Crist com for us on þisne middaneard on þeowan hiwe⁷
and micel for us þolode, and æfter his æreste to heofena rice rihtwise clypode.
25 Ic eow bidde and mynegie, abysegiað eow þa hwile ge þæs fyrstes habbon on
eowrum gebedum and on fæstenum and on wæccan and on ælmessan and on
mycelre forhæfdnesse eoweres lichaman. Gað to cirican gelomlice and settað
rodetacn geond eower hus.⁸ And ic eow beode, fyliað Criste on axan and on
hæran mid þreora daga fæstene, ealswa Niniuete dydon þæt ge ne forwyrðon.⁹
30 Eala yrmingas, þreagað eow and begitað Cristes rice þe eow is gegearwod fram
frymðe middaneardes,¹⁰ forþam þe dæghwamlice deað gegearwað beforan

a–a `Men þa leofestan´
b *initial* h *slightly larger*
c `halie´
d `Soðlice´
e i *between* h *and* o *erased and underlined*
f–f willa ure
g ure
h þin, *at end of line*

LETTER A

Dearest people, here begins that holy letter which came from the heavens into Jerusalem. Truly, it fell in front of the gates of Effrem, and there it was found through the hands of a certain priest whose name was Achor. And he sent it to another town, to another priest, who is called Joram, who sent it on from the town of Bethany to another priest, who is called Machabeus. And he sent it on to Mount Garganus where the church of St Michael the archangel is. Truly, that same letter by the will of Christ our Lord came to Rome to the tomb of St Peter. And all the men who were in those cities where the letter arrived engaged in a three-day fast and holy prayers and almsgiving, that our merciful Lord might give them aid and open understanding in the hearts of men to know the mercy of our Lord Saviour Christ. Moreover, it says for which reasons this letter came to Jerusalem and was revealed thus to other cities. And it came on holy Sunday, and indeed they bade that people honour that same day with great conversion and faith.

On Sunday let no man hold an assembly, nor determine sentences, nor swear oaths, nor grind, nor bake bread, nor buy, nor sell on holy Sunday, nor gather plants in the garden, nor charge anyone, nor hold a hunt, because truly on account of these things this world will be destroyed and God's wrath will come over you.

O wretched ones, do you not know that God created the heavens and the earth, the sea and all that is therein in six days, and afterwards created the first man, Adam, and because of his transgression he [God] forsook the righteous and sinful in hell for 5228 years. Christ came for us into this world in the form of a servant and suffered much for us, and after his resurrection he called the righteous to the kingdom of the heavens. I beseech and admonish you: busy yourselves while you have time in your prayers and in fasts and in vigils and in almsgiving and in great abstinence of your body. Go to church often and set the sign of the cross throughout your house. And I command you: follow Christ in ashes and in haircloth with a three days' fast, just as the Ninevites did, so that you will not perish. O wretched ones, chastise yourselves and obtain Christ's kingdom, which has been prepared for you from the beginning of the world, since daily death is made ready before

eowrum eagon. And ic kyðe eow þurh þis gewrit, gif ge nellað eow gerihtlæcan
and sunnandæg ne healdað and eower teoðunge getrywlice syllað of eallon þam
þe eow drihten alæned hafað,[11] na þæt an of eowrum geswince ac eac ge agon
35 eowerne cræft ealswa teoðian and of ealre eowre cypinge and of eallum þam
þingon þe ge æfre agan and on eowrum[i] flæsce þurh forhæfdnesse eoweres lichaman, and gif ge nellað gelyfan, ge sculon þolian micel wite on helle.

Drihten segð and eow soðlice cyð be þisum bufancwedenum þingum þe ge
me ne aguldon, doð dædbote on þissere worulde. And gif ge nellað geswican and
40 betan, ic asendæ ceaferas on eowre wudas and gærshoppan on eowerne hwæte
þæt fornimað eowerne bileofan.[12] And ic asende hearde stanas and oðre fela
frecednessa, and ic asende ofer eow hæðen folc þæt fornimað eow and eowre
bearn, gif ge ne healdað þone sunnandæg mid rihte ne ne gelyfað on me and on
min bebod. And ic asende ofer eow hunger and hreohnesse and byrnende ren and
45 sweflenne lig and fela ungelimpa. And ic asende on eowrum muþum [72r] and on
eowrum nosum and on eowrum eagum and on earan þæge wyrrestan gnættas and
þa geættrode eow to amyrrenne.[13]

Ic eom soð God and soð ic eow secge and þus swerige þurh me sylfne and þurh
mine halgan englas Cherubin and Seraphin þæt min yrre cymð ofer eow ær on
50 lytlan fyrste.[14] And fela frecednessa synd gegearwod togeanes eow and gefyrn
wære gif minre leofan moder þingung nære Sancta Marian and sancte Michaeles
and sancte Petres and þæra .xii. apostola.[15] And soðlice ic eow secge gif ge wyllað
geswican eowre yfelra dæda, ic geopenige eow heofena renscuras[16] and ic sylle
eowre eorðan wæstmbærnesse and genihtsumnesse and ic gelenge eower lif and
55 ge beoð libbende on ealra [j]worulda world[j].

Eala ge mine getrywestan, ic secge eow, þurhwunige mid eow,[17] waciende and
gebiddende and ælmessan syllende and ealle yfele dædan forlætende, and ælc
unrihthæmed forfleon and ælcne mansliht forbugan. Healdað mine bebodu þæt
ge geearnian[k] eow þæt ge habban ealra halgena geferræddene. Men þa leofestan,
60 fyliað me and gelyfað on þone dæg and þæt þis gewrit is gesend of minre agenre
mihte and of þam þrymsetle.[18] Geclænsiað eow fram eowrum horwum synna[l][19]
and geglengað eowre sawle[20] þæt ge magon eow geahnian þæt ece lif. Witað, la
yrmingas, þæt for eowre teoðunge þe ge me ætbrudon and for eower untimlican
geswince þe ge dydon on sunnandagum and on þam halgum freolsdagum, and
65 for eower untrywleaste[21] þe ge ne heoldon ongean eowre frynd þæt synd eower
neheboras and godsibbas[22] and ealle geleafulle, ic adylgie eower naman of þære
liflican bec[23] gif ge þurh dædbote nellað gebetan and buton ge gelomlicor eowere
cirican secean and þær underfon andetnesse and gecyrrednesse.[24] Soðlice eower
wif þe ne wurðiað þone halgan sunnandæg and þa freolsdagas on geare, ic asende
70 næddran to slitenne heora flæsc and hangiende to heora breostan and sucende hi
ealswa heora bearn, hi to witniende eal for þære unclænnesse þe ge ne heoldon
þone halgan sunnandæg.[25]

i eower
j–j world aworld
k geearn`i´an
l synnū

114

your eyes. And I make known to you through this letter: if you do not wish to amend yourselves and do not keep Sunday and give your tithes faithfully from all those things that the Lord has lent you – not only of your labour but also your skill you must likewise tithe, and of all your trade and of all these things which you at any time own and in your flesh, through your body's abstinence – and if you will not believe, you will have to suffer great torment in hell.

The Lord says and indeed makes known to you concerning the above-mentioned things which you did not render to me, do penance in this world. And if you will not cease and repent, I will send beetles upon your forests and grasshoppers on your wheat, which will destroy your sustenance. And I will send hard stones and many other perils, and I will send upon you heathen peoples, who will seize you and your children, if you do not keep Sunday rightly nor believe in me and in my commandment. And I will send upon you hunger and storms and burning rain and sulphurous fire and many disasters. And I will send into your mouths and into your noses and into your eyes and into ears those worst and poisonous gnats to destroy you.

I am true God and I tell you the truth and thus swear by myself and by my holy angels, Cherubim and Seraphim, that my wrath will come over you in a little while. And many perils are prepared against you and would have happened long ago were it not for the intercession of my dear mother St Mary and St Michael and St Peter and the twelve apostles. And truly I say to you, if you will cease from your evil deeds, I will open for you the rain showers of the heavens, and I will give fruitfulness and abundance to your soil, and I will prolong your life and you will live for ever and ever.

O you my most faithful, I say to you, may it remain with you in watching and praying and giving alms and forsaking all evil deeds, and may you flee any fornication and refrain from any manslaughter. Keep my commandments, so that you may earn for yourselves the fellowship of all the saints. Dearest people, follow me and believe in that day and that this letter is sent by my own might and from the throne. Cleanse yourselves from the impurities of your sins and adorn your souls that you may obtain for yourselves that eternal life. Know, O wretched ones, that because of the tithes which you withheld from me and for your untimely labour which you did on Sundays and on the holy feast-days and for your faithlessness, that you did not keep [faith] with your friends, who are your neighbours and fellow sponsors and all believers, I will blot out your name from that book of life if you do not want to atone through penance and unless you visit your church more often and there receive confession and conversion. Certainly your women who do not honour that holy Sunday and the feast days in the year – I will send serpents to bite their flesh, hanging on their breasts and sucking them just like their children, to afflict them entirely on account of that uncleanness, that you did not keep that holy Sunday.

And þa cildra þe beoð begiten on sunnanniht and on þam halgan freolsnihtum, hi sceolan beon geborene butan eagon and butan fotum and butan handon and eac
75 swilce dumbe,[26] forþam þe ge ne heoldon [72v] mid clænnesse þa halgan niht and ne wiðtugan[m] mid eowre tungan to cursiende, and beoð gemodegode on eowrum scrude.[27] Ic eow bidde þæt ge healdon þone restedæg fæstlice and ic eow beode þurh þis gewrit þæt ge ne wahson on þam sunnandæge ne on þam freolsdagum eower heafod, ne ne sceran ne efsian eower fex.[28] Soðlice, þa þe gehyrað þas word
80 and nellað gelyfan, hi beoð amansumod. Soðlice þis gewrit feol of heofenum into Hierusalem and swa com to Rome to sancte Petres byrgene,[29] and æror comon twa and þis is þæt ðridde and æfter þison ne cymð næfre ma.

Ge bisceopas and mæssepreostas kyðaþ þis gelomlice eallum folce and sendað þis gewrit geond ealle scira þæt eal folc hit geornlice underfoo and his gelyfan þæt
85 hit nis þurh [n]nanne man[n] geworht, ac þurh þæs hehstan hælendes handa gewriten. And þa men þe þis gewrit habbað and eow kyþað, healdað hi and hi underfoð mid ealre geornfulnesse and lufe and blisse for Cristes lufon forþi se þe underfehð rihtwisne on þæs rihtwisan naman, he underfehð þæs rihtwisan mede. And se þe underfehð witigan on þæs witigan naman he underfehð þæs witigan mede.[30]
90 AMEN.

m wiðtuga
n–n nanū, ū *expuncted*, `ne´, mæn, æn *expuncted*, `an´

And those children which are conceived on Saturday night and on the vigils of holy feasts, they shall be born without eyes and without feet and without hands and also mute, because you did not keep with chastity those holy nights and did not refrain from blaspheming with your tongue, and you are filled with pride in your dress. I beseech you to keep that day of rest steadfastly, and I decree to you through this letter that you not wash your head on Sunday nor on feast days, nor shave, nor cut your hair. Truly, those who hear these words and do not want to believe, they are accursed. Truly, this letter fell from the heavens into Jerusalem and so came to Rome to St Peter's tomb, and two came earlier, and this is the third, and after these never will more come.

You bishops and mass-priests, make this known frequently to all the people and send this letter throughout all the districts so that all the people may receive it eagerly and believe of it that it was not made by any man, but was written by the hands of the most exalted Saviour. And those men who have this letter and make it known to you, support them and receive them with all diligence and love and joy for the love of Christ, because he who receives a righteous man in the name of a righteous man, he will receive the reward of a righteous man. And he who receives a prophet in the name of a prophet, he will receive the reward of a prophet. Amen.

LETTER B

Cambridge, Corpus Christi College 419 (pp. 73–95)

[p. 73] [a]Sermo angelorum nomina[a]. [b]Her onginð[b], men ða leofestan, ymb [p. 74]
ures drihtnes ærendgewrite be ðære halgan þrynnesse, þe feoll of þam seofoðan
heofone þurh þone halgan heahengel Michael and wæs funden in þam geate, þe
hatte Effrem. And he hit sende þam mæssepreoste, þe hatte Achorius. And he hit
5   underfeng and sende hit to ðære ceastre, þe hatte Ieremiam, and to þam mæssepreoste. And he hit asende Talasius. And Tala soðlice hit asende to Ebream þære
ceastre and to þam mæssepreoste, þe hatte Lebonum. [p. 75] Lebonum soðlice hit
asende to Cappadociam þære ceastre and to þam mæssepreoste, þe hatte Machabium. And Machabium soðlice hit asende to þære stowe Sanctus Michael þæs
10   heahengles. And þanan hit becom to Rome and in ða burh and þær wæs funden
on Sanctus Petrus weofod[1] and þus wæs awriten mid gyldenum stafum.[2] And
soðlice þa, ðe in þære ceastre wæron, heo ða dydon, swa heo þær gewearð,[3] þæt
heo fæsten þreo dagas and to Gode and to Sancte Petre georne sohtan [p. 76]
mid ælmessum, and mid fæstenum, and mid wæccum, and mid halgum gebedum
15   þone intingan þysses halgan gewrites, forðan þis ærendgewrit in þissum ceastrum
becumen wæs. And hit wæs forðan, þæt on þam halgan sunnandæge þæt nan man
hine to unnytnesse to swiðe ne geþeodde.[4] Ðæt is, þæt nan man on þysne dæg
on dome ne sitte, ne að ne swerige, ne wyrte in lehtune ne fatige; and þeh hwam
gebyrige, þæt his fyr ut gewite, nis þæt alyfed to begetenne.[5]
20   And nan wif hire yrfe ne meolcige,[6] [p. 77] butan heo ða meolc for Godes
lufan sylle. Ne mylnum nis alyfed to eornenne[7] ne on huntað to ridenne ne nan
unalyfedlic weorc to wyrcenne. Forðan þe for ðyssum yfelum weorcum forweorðað þas eorðlican þing, and se bifigenda dom cymð ofer gefullad folc. And
ongeotað, ge earmingas synfulle, þæt on six dagum wæron geworhte heofonas
25   and eorðan, sunne and mona, sæ and fixas and ealle þa ðe on hym syndon; and
æfter eallum þissum swa gewordenum he gesceop Adam þone ærestan man[8] of
þam lame. [p. 78] And þa ðy seofoðan dæge he hine gereste æfter his six daga
weorcum.[9] And swa gedafenað ælcum men to habbenne restendæg,[10] swa ða
halgan englas reste habbað on heofonum[c].[11] Ac ic halsige on Godes naman and
30   eornostlice hate, þæt ge gecyrran to Gode mid gebedum and mid wæccan and
mid fæstenum and mid synna andettnesse eowrum scriftan and mid hreowsunge
dædbota and mid teoðunge ealra ura æhta weoruldgestreona.[12] And mid þære
halgan rode he us gesenað.[13] And þæt fæsten, [p. 79] þe ða[d] Niniuete fæston,
fæstað þa. And gif ge swa doð, þonne ahreddeð us drihten. Ge ermingas, efestað
35   and begeotað heofena rices wuldor, forðan dæghwamlice se deað cymð beforan

a–a sermonem angelorum nomina, *red rustic capitals*
b–b H *red, ornate initial, 5 lines deep; rest of letters black square capitals*
c heofonnm
d ðe

118

LETTER B

A sermon on the names of the angels. Here begins, dearest people, [that which is] about our Lord's message by the holy Trinity, which fell from the seventh heaven, through the holy archangel Michael and was found in that gate which was called Effrem. And he sent it to the mass-priest, who was called Achorius, and he received it and sent it to that city which was called Jeremia and to the mass-priest, and he sent it to Talasius. And indeed, Tala[sius] sent it to Ebrea, the city, and to the mass-priest who was called Lebonus. Lebonus indeed sent it to Cappadocia, the city, and to the mass-priest who was called Machabius. And Machabius indeed sent it to the place of St Michael the archangel. And thence it came to Rome and into that city and there was found on the altar of St Peter, and was written out thus with golden letters. And truly those who were in that city, they then did as they there agreed, that they should fast for three days and from God and St Peter with almsgiving and fasts and with vigils and holy prayers earnestly seek the purpose of this holy writ, for which this message had come to these cities. And it was for the reason that no one should apply himself too greatly to that which is unprofitable on holy Sunday. That is, that no one on this day should sit in judgement, nor swear an oath, nor fetch herbs in the garden; and though it should happen to someone that his fire should go out, it is not permitted to obtain [that].

And let no woman milk her cattle, except she give the milk for the love of God. It is not permitted for mills to be run, nor to ride on a hunt, nor to do any unlawful work. Because on account of these evil works these earthly things will perish, and terrible judgement will come over baptized people. And consider, you sinful wretches, that in six days were made the heavens and the earth, sun and moon, the sea and fish, and all things that are in them. And after all these things thus made, he created Adam, the first man from clay. And then on the seventh day he rested himself after his six days of work. And so it is fitting for each man to have a rest-day, just as the holy angels have rest in the heavens. But I entreat in God's name and earnestly command that you turn to God with prayers and with vigils and with fasting and with the confession of sins to your confessors and with the sorrow of penance and the tithing of all the worldly riches of our possessions. And with the holy cross he will bless us. Fast then the fast which the Ninevites fasted. And if you do so, then the Lord will save us. You poor wretches, strive to attain the glory of the kingdom of the heavens, because daily death comes before your eyes, and accept this message of the

eowrum eagum, and underfoð þyssum drihtnes ærendgewrite. And gif ge nellað gebetan eowre misdæde and healdan þone halgan sunnandæg mid rihte fram non-tide þæs sæternesdæges oð monandæges lihtincge,[14] and gif ge nellað healdan þa godsibbrædenne, þe ge habbað for Gode and for Sancte Iohannes[15] [p. 80] dæle
40 begetene and ure teoðunge on riht ageofan: and gif ge þæt nellað, ic sende ofer eow hagelstanas, and ælc an hagelstan wegeð fif pund.[16]

Ic sæcge, þæt on þam monðe, þe hatte Nouembris, þæt ge scoldan ealle for-weorðan, nære þære halgan Sancta Marian gebed and þæs halgan heahengles Michahel and þara haligra apostola Petrus and Paulus.[17] And þurh heora bene
45 ge wæron alysde of þam witum, ða þe towearde wæron. Ic cweðe to eow, gif ge willað fon to dædbote, þonne beoð eow opene heofena [p. 81] geatu, and ic sylle eow hwæte and win and ele[18] and <in> eowrum bernum[e][19] blæde and gemanigfealde[f][20] god in eowrum husum; and ic eow sylle heofona rices wuldor aa on ecnesse soðlice[g]. And ic cweðe to þissum folce minum þam holdan and
50 þam leofan: gewislice ge becumað to heofona rices wuldre mid gebedum and mid wæccum and mid ælmessa sylenum, gif ge willað ealle yfelu[h] forlætan, ge on manslihte ge on mænum aðum, and fylstan widewum and fæderleasum and moderleasum cildum, þæt ge motan beon mid eowrum [p. 82] broðrum Godes bearn gecigede.[21] Beþænce se fæder þone sunu and se sunu þone fæder butan yrre
55 and butan werignesse, þæt ge þurh þæt ne synd fordone ne to deaðe forlorene, þe ge mid yfele onginnað[i] and þæt næfre wel ne geendiað.[22] Ic cweðe to eow: gað to minum cyricum mid ælmessum and mid leohte and geherað þone halgan sang and forlætað eorre and druncennesse and unrihthæmed and healdað þone halgan sunnandæg.[23] And beþencað þone bifigendan domes dæg simle beforan eowrum
60 [p. 83] eagum.[24] Ic sende eow gehadode beforan Gode simble, and gif ge hym willað gelefan.[25]

Ic eow halsige, min getreowe folc, þurh Iordane þa ea,[26] þær Sanctus Iohannes me þone halgan fulluht asende mid ele and mid crisman me þurhsmyrede.[27] And þonne he se engel cwæð to me: þis is min leofa sunu, on þæm ic me wel gelicode[j],
65 geherað him wel.[28] And þurh þis halige gewrit ic eow halsige, þæt ge þysum gele-fan; and ic hate, þæt ge gangen to minum cyricum, and þær ge eower geswinc sellað.[29] And gif ge nellað [p. 84] swa don, þonne bende ic minne bogan, and ic sende mine flan ofer eow, and þonne forweorðað synfulle men. And ic sende ofer eow fleogende nædran, þa þe fretað eowre breost and eowre blæde, þe ge big
70 libban scylon.[30] Ac þeahhwæðere gecerrað to me, ge synfulle, and forlætað yfelu[k], forðam þæm ic mildsiende eom, minum þam getreowum, and heo onfoð heofona rices wuldre.[31] Gelefað þyssum wordum <þe> ic sænde to eow for þam halgan sunnandæge, þæt ge ageofan ða teoðunge to Godes cyrican, forðam, gif ge nellað

e bearnum
f gemanigfealdum
g 'soðlice' *insertion mark after* ecnesse
h yfel
i onginneð
j gecleopode
k yfel a

Lord. And if you do not want to atone for your misdeeds and keep holy Sunday properly from the ninth hour on Saturday until dawn on Monday, and if you do not want to uphold the co-parenthood which you have obtained for the sake of God and St John, and pay our tithe rightly – and if you do not wish [to do] that, I will send hailstones over you, and every single hailstone will weigh five pounds.

I say, that in that month which is called November, that you should have all perished, were it not for the prayer of holy St Mary and of the holy archangel Michael and the holy Apostles Peter and Paul. And through their supplication you were delivered from those torments which were facing you. I say to you, if you will undertake penance, then the gates of the heavens will be opened for you, and I will give you wheat and wine and oil, and crops in your barns, and I will multiply goods in your homes. And I will give you the glory of the kingdom of the heavens, truly for ever in eternity. And I say to this my faithful and beloved people: truly you shall enter the glory of the kingdom of the heavens with prayers and vigils and by the giving of alms, if you will forsake all evils, both in respect to manslaughter and in respect to false oaths, and help widows and fatherless and motherless children, that you may be called with your brothers children of God. May the father consider the son and the son the father, without anger and without weariness, that you will not be brought to ruin nor condemned to death because you begin with evil, and that never ends well. I say to you: go to my churches with alms and with a light, and listen to the holy song and forsake anger and drunkenness and fornication and keep holy Sunday. And pay heed to the terrible day of judgement, [keeping it] always before your eyes. I have continually sent to you those [who are] ordained before God, if you wish to believe them.

I entreat you, my faithful people, in the name of the River Jordan, where St John administered holy baptism to me and anointed me with oil and the chrism. And then he, the angel, said to me: 'This is my beloved son, in whom I am well pleased, obey him well.' And through this holy writ I entreat you to believe in these things, and I command that you go to my churches, and give there [the product] of your labours. And if you will not do so, then I will bend my bow, and I will send my arrow upon you, and then sinful men will perish. And I will send upon you flying serpents, which will devour your vitals and your crops by which you must live. But nevertheless, return to me, you sinful, and forsake evil things, because I am merciful to them, my faithful ones; and they will partake of the glory of the kingdom of the heavens. Believe these words [that] I have sent to you for the sake of holy Sunday, that you may pay the tithe to God's Church, because, if you do not wish to give it to God and his priest (he is my brother and my son), to

121

[p. 85] hy ageofan Gode and his preoste – he is min broðor and min sunu þam,

75 ðe to me wendað, and þam, þe hit forhealdað, beo he fram me and fram minum
bebodum – ic sende ofer eow wedende wulfas and wedende hundas, þe etað eowerne lichaman to deaðes tocyme. Ic sende on eowre hus biternesse and wanunga
and granunga; and ic þa eft nime fram eow for minre mildheortnesse. And gað to
minum cyricum and gecerrað to me, and ic to eow,[32] forðam ic eam mildsiende,

80 and ic mildsige ælcum þara, þe mine be[p. 86]bodu healdað, a in ecnesse.

Ic hate and ic halsige, þæt ge on sunnandæge eowre heafdu ne þwean ne eower
fex ne efesian; and gif ge swa doð, þonne beo ge adilegad, ge and eowre sawle, of
lifigendra bocum. And gif ge nellað betan, þæt ge to wo gedon habbað, ic sende
yfel on eower hus and eorre. And ic hæbbe asend þis gewrit to eow, þæt ge him

85 gelefan. And gif ge nyllað healdan eower word and eower wedd,[33] ge þonne beoð
adilegode of ealra lifigendra bocum, forðan ic hæbbe aboden eow [p. 87] tuwa
þurh twam gewritum ær þissum, and þis is þæt ðridde, þe ic sende nu to eow. And
gif ge nellað healdan min bebod, ic sende ofer eow geswinc and mettrumnesse[l] on
andwlitan and on eagum and on earum and on eallum limum, þa eow habbað oð

90 deaðes tocyme swiðe hearde.

Soð is, soð is, þæt ic eow secge, þæt ic wæs for eow on rode genægled, and þær
ic þrowade for eow, and ic aras on sunnandæg[34] of deaðe, forðan þe se sunnandæg
is restendæg and wuldorlic dæg and lihtnesse dæg, [p. 88] and forðan þe on ðam
sunnandæge gescop drihten heofonan and eorðan and ealle þa gesceafte, þe on

95 hym syndon.[35] On sunnandæg wæron englas gesceapene. And on sunnandæg
reste Noes earce on þære dune, þe Armenia hatte, æfter ðam miclan flode.[36] On
sunnandæg lædde drihten his folc of Egyptum þurh ða readan sæ drium fotum,
and his feond adruncon in ðære sæ. On sunnandæg let se hælend rinan mannan,
þone heofonlican mete, þe he his folc mid fedde feowertig wintra [p. 89] on þam

100 westenne. On sunnandæg is seo acennednes ures drihtnes hælendes Cristes. On
sunnandæg worhte drihten win of wætere in architriclines huse.[37] On sunnandæg
gefylde se hælend of fif hlafum and of twam fixum fif þusend manna butan wifum
and cildum. And on sunnandæg aras drihten of deaðe.

And on sunnandæg he asende his apostolum þone halgan gast on fyres ansyne.

105 And on sunnandæg gesæt se hælend on ða swiðran healfe þæs heahfæder. [p. 90]
And on sunnandæg cwæð se hælend: openiað þas geatu and þa fæstan scytelsas,
and ic wille gan þæron.[38] Forðan ongeotað ge þis bebod: ic bebeode eallum minum
cyriclicum larum,[39] þæt heo beþencen drihtnes ærendgewrit; and behealdað þone
halgan sunnandæg and þa fæstendagas,[40] þe men eow beodað to healdenne; and

110 eowre teoðunge ageofað to Godes mynstrum, forðan[m] þe ge fulluhte onfengon;
and healdað eowre clænnesse, swa ge geheton æt fulluhtes bæðe; and gebiddað
me [p. 91] swa georne, þonne eow becymeð yfel, þonne do ic mine bletsunge on
eow, þe me biddað. And þa hæðenan soðlice heo ne synd cristene, ne heo God ne
lufiað ne his bebodu healdan ne willað, ne heo na on hine ne gelyfað.

l mettrunesse
m and forðan

those who turn to me, and to those who withhold it, may he be [far] from me and from my commandments – I will send over you raging wolves and raging dogs who will eat your body to the arrival of death. I will send on your house hardship and lamentation and groaning. And I will then again take them away from you because of my mercy. And go to my churches and turn to me, and I [will turn] to you, because I am merciful, and I show mercy to each of those who keep my commandments, for ever in eternity.

I command and entreat [you] that you do not wash your heads on Sunday, nor cut your hair, and if you do so, then may you be blotted out, you and your soul, from the books of the living. And if you will not atone for what you have wrongly done, I will send evil and wrath on your house. And I have sent this writ to you so that you may believe it. And if you will not keep your word and your pledge, then you will be blotted out of the books of all the living, because I have twice proclaimed to you through two writings before this one, and this is the third, which I am now sending to you. And if you will not keep my commandment, I will send over you affliction and sickness – on the face, and in the eyes, and in the ears, and in all limbs – which you will have very severely until the approach of death.

Truly, truly I say to you that I was nailed on the cross for you, and there I suffered for you, and I arose on Sunday from death, because Sunday is the day of rest and a glorious day and the day of brightness, and because on Sunday the Lord created the heavens and the earth and all those creatures which are in them. On Sunday the angels were created. And on Sunday Noah's ark rested on the mountain which is called Armenia, after the great Flood. On Sunday the Lord led his people away from the Egyptians through the Red Sea with dry feet, and his enemies drowned in that sea. On Sunday the Saviour caused it to rain manna, that heavenly food with which he fed his people for forty years in the desert. On Sunday is the birth of our Lord Saviour Christ. On Sunday the Lord made wine from water in the house of the governor of the feast. On Sunday, with five loaves and two fish, the Saviour satisfied five thousand men apart from the women and children. And on Sunday the Lord arose from death.

And on Sunday he sent his apostles the Holy Spirit in the form of fire. And on Sunday the Saviour sat down at the right hand of the high Father. And on Sunday the Saviour said: 'Open these gates and the fastened bolts and I will go in.' Therefore consider this command: I command with all my ecclesiastical teachings that they should consider the message of the Lord; and keep that holy Sunday and those fast days which men have commanded you to keep. And pay your tithe to God's minsters because you received baptism. And maintain your purity as you were commanded at the bath of baptism and thus pray to me earnestly when evil befalls you; then I will send my blessing on you who ask me. And truly the heathens are not Christians, nor do they love God nor wish to keep his commandments, nor do they believe in him at all.

115 Soð is, soð is, þæt ic eow secge, þæt eow is þearf, þæt ge healdan þone halgan
sunnandæg mid rihte fram nontide þæs sæternesdæges oð monandæges lihtinge.
And gif ge nellað þyssum gewritum gelefan, ic sende ofer eow wyrmas and fuhlas
wedende,[41] and þa fordoð eowre [p. 92] blæde, þe ge bi libban scylan, and heo
beoð eow æteowode.[42] And ic sende hæðen folc ofer eow, þe eow ofnimað eowre
120 æhte and eower lif and eowere wif and cild,[43] butan ge þa teoðunge syllan to
Godes cyrican for minum lufan. Soð is, soð is, þæt ic eow secge, gif ge lesað in
lehtune wyrte on sunnandæg, ic sende nædran gefiðrede, þe etað eowre breost
oð deaðes tocyme,[44] gif ge ne healdað þone halgan sunnandæg. Ðonne beoð on
eowrum husum[45] acennede cild, þe ne geseoð ne ne gehyrað [p. 93] ne ne gað, and
125 ge forweorðað.

And geþencað, þæt ge synd þæs oft gemyngad[46]; and gif ge healdað mine
beboda, ealle god ic gehate and swa soðlice gelæste þurh me. And swa hwylc
mæssepreost, swa hæbbe þis gewrit and nelle cyðan Godes folce, þonne cweð
se hælend, þæt his sawel wære awerged, and his nama bið adilegad of lifigendra
130 bocum. Ðis gewrit wæs afunden in Hierusalem, and þanan hit becom to Rome
and to Sancte Petres byrgenstowe for ure þearfe,[47] and þus wæs awriten mid
gyldenum[n] [p. 94] stafum, and of þære seofoðan heofone us to becom, þæt ge þy
fæstlicor gelyfdon. Ongeotað ge Godes word, and his larum hersumiað, forðan
þe eow nealæcð se deað toweardes. And gif ge nellað gelefan, ic sende to eow
135 beornendne ren and sweflene leg, and eow fordeð and eowre bearn butan ende.
And æfter þyssum gewrite ne cymð eow nan oðer fram me. And gelefað þissum
gewrite þurh drihten sylfne and þurh englas and heahenglas for þæra mihte and
anweald, [p. 95] þurh heahfæderas and witegan, þurh apostolas and martyres and
confessores and þa halgan fæmnan and ealle Cristes þa halgan, þæt ge fullice
140 þysum gewrite gelyfan.[48] Seo him drihtne simle þanc ge þæs ge ealra his geofena,
lof and wuldor a in ecnesse a °butan ende, amen°.

n gylgenum
o–o -n ende amen, *rustic capitals*

Truly, truly I say to you that there is need for you to keep Sunday correctly from the ninth hour on Saturday until dawn on Monday. And if you do not want to believe these writings, I will send worms upon you and raging birds, and they will destroy your harvest, by which you must live, and they will be shown to you. And I will send a heathen people over you, who will take from you your property and your life and your wife and child, unless you give those tithes to God's Church for love of me. Truly, truly I say to you, if you gather produce in the garden on Sunday I will send winged serpents, who will devour your breasts until the approach of death, if you do not keep that holy Sunday. Then children will be born in your houses who neither see, nor hear, nor walk, and you will perish.

And consider that you are often reminded of that, and if you keep my commandments, I promise every good, and thus truly [it] will be accomplished through me. And whichever mass-priest may have this writ and may not want to make it known to the people of God – then says the Saviour that his soul will be accursed, and his name will be blotted out from the books of the living. This writ was found in Jerusalem and from there it came to Rome and to St Peter's burial place for our benefit, and was for that reason written with golden letters, and came to us from the seventh heaven that you through it might believe the more steadfastly. Understand God's word and obey his teachings, because death is drawing near to you. And if you do not want to believe, I will send to you burning rain and sulphurous flame, and [it] will destroy you and your children without end. And after this writ no other will come from me. And believe this writ for the sake of the Lord himself and for the sake of the angels and archangels and for their might and power, for the sake of the patriarchs and prophets, for the sake of the apostles and martyrs and confessors, and the holy virgins and all the saints of Christ, that you fully believe this writ. To him, the Lord, be always thanks both for that and for all his gifts, praise and glory for ever in eternity, for ever without end. Amen.

LETTER C

London, Lambeth Palace Library, 489 (25r–30v)

[25r] ªSermo ad populum <de> dominicis diebusª. ᵇLeofan menᵇ, us bisceopum and eallum mæssepreostum is swiðe deope beboden þæt we æfre sculon mynegian and tyhtan eow, læwede menn, georne to eowre sawla þearfe, and hu ge agan her on life rihtlice to libbanne. And, gif we swa ne doð, þonne beo we swyðe scyldige wið God

5   ælmihtigne. Nu wylle we eow secgan be þæs haligan sunnandæges halignysse, hu se ælmihtiga God hine gehalgode, and hu he wyle, þæt he freols beo fram eallum unrihtdædum and þeowetlicum weorcum, for ic wat, þæt hit is eow uncuðre, þonne ge þearfe ahton. Hit wæs, þæt, siððan Crist þæs ælmihtigan Godes sunu wæs astigen up to heofena rice, syððan he hæfde her gewunad onmang mannum þreo and .xxx. wintra

10   and healf gear, þæt men forgymdon Godes laga swyðor, þonne heora þearfa wæron, and þæs halgan sunnandæges freols wyrs heoldon, þonne hit Gode licwyrðe wære.¹

    Ða asende se ælmihtiga God an ærendgewrit ufan of heofenan be anum halgan engle to anum bisceope, se hatte Petrus; se wæs biscop on Antiochia² þære burh, þær þær Sanctus Petrus se apostol ærest gesæt his biscopsetl.³ [25v] On þam

15   gewrite stod eall be þæs dæges halignesse; and þæt gewrit ne awrat nan eorðlic manᶜ, ac Godes agen ængel,⁴ swa swa seo halige þrynnys hit sylf gedihte. And eac se ængel bebead þam biscope, þæt he hit sceolde cyðan eallum cristenum mannum, þæt men geswican heora unrihtes, þe hi on þam halgan dæge druganᵈ and gyt to swiðe dreogað. Nu is þis þæt angin þæs engles spræce, þa þa he þæt

20   gewrit þam bisceope on hand sealde. He cwæð: Ic, Godes engel, middaneardes hælendes boda, beode and hate, þæt ægðer ge cyningas ge eorlas and gerefan, þe

a–a *red rustic capitals*
b–b *large green initial* L, *two and a half lines deep*, leofan men *in very small script above the line*
c *followed by* þe him to com, *expuncted*
d dreogan, eo *expuncted*, u *above line*

LETTER D

Cambridge, Corpus Christi College 162 (pp. 44–52)

[p. 44] ªBe þam drihtenlican sunnandæg folces larª. ᵇMen ða leofestan, her onginð ðætᵇ ærendgewrit ures drihtnes, middangeardes hælendes, be þam forebode ealra yfela and be þam embegange ealra goda. Þæt awrat drihtnes engel⁴ mid his sylfes fingrum and hit sealde Petre þam bisceope on ðære Antiochiscan² cirican, bebeodende

5   and halsigende [p. 45] þurh naman þæs lifigendan Godes þæt he gewidmærsode þas drihtnes word eallum cynegum and bisceopum and eac swilce eallum cristenum folce. Þillic is þonne se fruma þæs ærendgewrites: Ic, ærendraca and boda drihtnes

a–a *red rustic capitals*
b–b M *green ornate initial, two lines deep, remainder in black rustic capitals*

126

LETTER C

Sermon to the people concerning Lord's days. Dear people, it is very solemnly commanded to us bishops and all mass-priests that we should ever admonish and exhort you, the lay people, earnestly for the benefit of your souls, and how you must live rightly here in life. And if we do not do so, then we will be very guilty before God almighty. Now we wish to speak to you about the sanctity of holy Sunday, how almighty God hallowed it, and how he wishes that it be free from all evil deeds and servile works, for I know that it is more unknown to you than you have need. It happened that after Christ, the Son of the almighty God, had ascended to the kingdom of the heavens, after he had dwelled here among men thirty-three and a half years, that men disregarded the laws of God more than was to their benefit and kept the festival of holy Sunday worse than was pleasing to God.

Then almighty God sent a message from the heavens above, by means of a certain holy angel to a certain bishop who was called Peter. He was bishop in the city of Antioch, where St Peter the Apostle first established his bishopric. In that writ stood everything concerning the holiness of that day. And no earthly man wrote that letter, but God's own angel, just as the holy Trinity himself dictated it. And also the angel commanded that bishop that he should make it known to all Christian people that people should forsake their wickedness, which they engaged in on that holy day and still engage in too much. Now this is the beginning of the angel's speech, when he gave that writ into the hand of the bishop. He said: I, the angel of God, messenger of the Saviour of the world, bid and command that both kings

LETTER D

An exhortation of the people concerning the Lord's Sunday. Dearest people, here begins that message of our Lord, the Saviour of the world, concerning the prohibition of all evils and the performance of all good things. An angel of the Lord wrote that with his own fingers and gave it to Peter the bishop in the church of Antioch, commanding and entreating by the name of the living God that he should spread abroad these words of the Lord to all kings and bishops and likewise to all Christian people. Such is then the beginning of the message: I, messenger and emissary

mæst unriht dreogað, and eac ealle men ægðer ge gehadode ge læwede, þæt hi
lufian rihtwisnysse on wordum and on worcum and on eallum þingum, and þæt hi
hyran drihtne hælende Criste eorne on eallum ege, forþan þæt is ealles wisdomes
25   angin, þæt man habbe ege to Gode.[5]

And ic beode,[6] þæt men healdan þone drihtenlican dæg fram eallum þeowetlicum weorcum, þæt is, fram sæternesdæges none oð monandæges lihtinge,
forþan þe se dæg wæs se forma dæg,[7] þe se soða scyppend, þæt is God ælmihtig,
gesceop, þa þa he ealle þing gesceop, and eac[e] syððan fela wundra on þam dæge
30   geworhte[f] [26r] ægðer ge ær þan þe he menniscnysse underfenge, ge eac syððan.
Ðæt is þonne, þæt he gesceop heofenan and eorðan and englas and heahenglas
and ealle heofenlice miht and endebyrdnysse on þam dæge; and eac on þam dæge
he gesceop manna sawla. And, þa þa Moyses se heretoga lædde Godes folc of
Egipta lande, þa on þam dæge he hit lædde ofer þa readan sæ, swa þæt he sloh
35   mid anre gyrde on þa sæ, and heo toeode on twa,[8] and þæt folc for betwux þam
twam wæterum on þam grunde ealle drygsceode, oð hi coman to þam lande up.
And on þam dæge com ærest se heofenlica mete ufan of heofnan þam ylcan folce
to bilyfan, and God hi mid þam afedde .xl. wintra on þam westene, þe hi to foron;
and se mete hatte manna. And on þam dæge wæs Crist þæs lifigendan Godes sunu
40   geboren of Sancta Marian innoðe soð man, ealswa he is soð God, middaneard to
alisanne of deofles anwealde, þe his ær geweald ahte for Adames gylte.

e ea:
f geworh::

hælendes Cristes, betæce and bebeode þam bisceopum and þam cynegum and eallum
geþungenum mannum þæt hi lufien rihtwisnysse on eallum þingum and þeowien
10   drihtne on eallum ege, and þæt ge gehealdan sunnandæg fram eallum woruldlicum
weorcum, forðan ðe God geworhte manega wundra on ðam sunnandæge.[7]

Þæt is þonne ærest, þæt he on þam sunnandæge geworhte heofonas and eorðan
mid eallum heofonlicum endebyrdnyssum and þæt ungehiwedlice andweorc.
On sunnandæg he[c] geworhte ealle[d] þa ðing þe witudlice syndon gesewene and
15   wuniað. On ðam dæge he gesceop ealra manna sawla. And on ðam dæge Crist
wæs acenned þisne[e] middaneard to alysenne. And on ðam dæge he todælde þa
readan sæ on twelf[f] dælas.[8] And on ðam dæge aras ure drihten of deaðe. And on
ðone dæg he asende haligne gast ofer his ærendracan. And on ðone dæg he let
rinan wundorlice andlyfene of heofonum ofer þæt Israhela folc, and hi on ðam
20   fedde feowertig wintra.

c *erasure of about eight letters*
d `and on sunnandæg :::´
e y > i
f `.xii.´ *added above* twelf *by another hand*

and noblemen and reeves, who engage in the most wickedness, and likewise all people, both those in orders and lay persons, that they love righteousness in words and works and in all things, and that they eagerly obey the Lord Saviour Christ in all fear, because that is the beginning of all wisdom, that one have fear of God.

And I command that men keep the Lord's day from all servile works, that is from the ninth hour on Saturday to dawn on Monday, because that day was the first day, which the true Creator, that is God almighty, created when he created all things, and also afterwards [he] did many miracles on that day both before he assumed a human nature and also afterwards. That is then that he created the heavens and the earth and the angels and archangels and all the heavenly powers and orders on that day; and also on that day he created the souls of men. And then, when Moses the chieftain led the people of God from the land of the Egyptians, then on that day he led them across the Red Sea, so that he struck the sea with a rod, and it parted in two, and that people travelled between the two waters on the ground, all of them dry-shod, until they came up onto the land. And on that day the heavenly food came first from the heavens to that same people as nourishment, and God fed them with it for forty years in that desert to which they travelled; and the food was called manna. And on that day Christ the son of the living God was born of the womb of St Mary, a true man, just as he is true God, in order to deliver the world from the power of the devil, who before had control

of the Lord Saviour Christ, enjoin and command bishops and kings and all noble men that they love righteousness in all matters and serve the Lord in all fear, and that you keep Sunday from all worldly works because God performed many miracles on Sunday.

That is then the first, that on Sunday he made the heavens and the earth with all the heavenly orders and unformed substance. On Sunday he made all those things which are truly seen and exist. On that day he created the souls of all people. And on that day Christ was born to redeem this world, and on that day he divided the Red Sea into twelve parts. And on that day our Lord arose from death. And on that day he sent the Holy Spirit over his apostles. And on that day he let rain wondrous sustenance from the heavens over the people of Israel, and they fed on that for forty years.

And syððan he acenned wæs, he awende on þam dæge wæter to wine. And on þam dæge he wæs gefullod. And on þam dæge he gereordade æt anum mæle fif[g] þusend manna of fif berenum hlafum and twam [26v] fixum, syððan he hæfde

45 þone bilyfan mid heofoncundlicre bletsunge þam ylcan dæge gebletsod; and, þa þa hi ealle fulle wæron, þa bær man þær up of þan, þe hi læfdon, twelf leapas fulle. And on þam dæge aras Crist of deaðe, syððan he þrowade on rode for mancynnes hæle. And on þam dæge wæs þæra iudeiscra manna geleafleasnys gewiten fram mannum, and riht geleafa asprang onmang Godes gelaðunge, syððan Crist

50 æteowode hine sylfne Sancte Petre æfter his æriste of deaðe. And on þam dæge sende God þone halgan gast ofer þa apostolas ealle þær þær hi wæron on anum huse inne belocene, and tæhte heom þæt hi cuðan ealle þa spræca þe syndon, swa wide swa middaneard is. And on þam dæge wyrð middaneard eall geendad. And on þam dæge cymð God to demanne eallum mancynne ælcum be his agenum

55 gewyrhtum, and farað þonne þa godan and þa rihtwisan into ecere myrhðe mid Gode and his englum, and þa arleasan farað to helle mid deofle and þær beoð gecwylmede on cwicsusle and eardiað þær[h] a butan ende mid him.

Nu forþam bebead drihten God eow, þæt ge healdan þone sunnandæg [27r] fram ælcum geswinclicum worce and swyðost fram þam, þe ic eow nu secgan

60 wylle. Ðæt is, þæt man ah to forganne ealle fulnyssa, þe Gode laðe syndon, þæt is forliger and druncennys, mannsliht and leasung, reaflac and stalu, unrihthæmed and geflit, æfest and ælc þæra mandæda, þe mannum forboden is, and ælc gemot ænig mann to fremmanne.[9] Ac man ah cyrican and haligdom to secanne and þær

g ::: þusend
h þæ:

And on ðam dæge he gecyrde wæter [p. 46] to wine on Chana, þære Galileiscan byrig. And on ðam dæge God gebletsode[g] .v. berene hlafas and .ii. fixas, and of þam he afedde .v. þusend manna, and þær to lafe wæron .xii. cypan fulle on þam gebrytsnum. and on sunnandæg tosleap Iudea gesamnung[h]. And on þam dæge bið þes

25 middanerd geendad, and on ðam dæge God demð menniscum cynne. and þa ðe her rihtlice lybbað, hi gewitað on þæt ece lif, and þa ðe her on woh libbað, hi gewitað on þæt ece fyr[i], and hi beoð cwylmede on ecum bryne mid þam deofle[j] and his gesiðum.

Þi þonne eow bebeodeð drihten God þæt ge þone sunnandæg healdan[k] fram eallum woruldlicum weorcum, þæt is þonne fram unclænnysse and fram forligre

30 and fram druncennysse and fram manslihte and fram leasunge and fram reaflace and fram stale and fram unrihthæmede and fram geflite and fram andan and fram eallum mane. And þas þing sindon eallum tidum forbodene. And healdon ge þone

g `ge´bletsode, *insertion mark after* God
h `and acenned wearð seo geleaffulle gesamnung´, *by another hand*
i *raised punctus over erasure*
j, k ð

of it because of Adam's sin.

And after he was born, he turned water into wine on that day. And on that day he was baptized. And on that day he fed at one meal five thousand men from five barley loaves and two fish after he had blessed that nourishment with a heavenly blessing on that same day. And then, when they were all full, then one there carried away from that which they left behind twelve baskets full. And on that day Christ arose from death, after he suffered on the cross for the salvation of mankind. And on that day the unbelief of the Jewish people departed from men, and the right belief sprang up among the Church of God, after Christ revealed himself to St Peter after his resurrection from death. And on that day God sent the Holy Spirit over all the apostles there where they were shut up inside a house, and showed them that they understood all those languages which there are, as wide as the world is. And on that day the world will be brought to an end entirely. And on that day God will come to judge all mankind, each according to his own deeds, and the good and righteous will then go to eternal bliss with God and his angels, and the wicked will go to hell with the devil and there will be tortured in a living torment and dwell there for ever without end with him.

Now therefore the Lord God commanded you that you keep Sunday from every laborious work and above all from those of which I will now tell you: that is that one should abstain from all impurities which are hateful to God, that is adultery and drunkenness, manslaughter and deceit, robbery and theft, fornication and strife, envy and each of those evil deeds which is forbidden to men, and [it is forbidden]

And on that day he turned water into wine in Cana, that Galilean city. And on that day God blessed five barley loaves and two fish, and from those he fed five thousand men, and there were twelve baskets full from those pieces as a remainder. And on Sunday the assembly of the Jews dissolved (and the believing assembly was born). And on that day this world will be ended, and on that day God will judge mankind. And those who live here rightly, they will depart into eternal life, and those who live here in error, they will depart into the eternal fire, and they will be tormented in the eternal conflagration with the devil and his companions.

Therefore then the Lord God commands you that you keep Sunday from all worldly works, that is then from uncleanness and adultery and drunkenness, manslaughter and deceit, and from robbery and theft and fornication and discord and

hine georne inne to gebiddanne and mid eadmodnysse hlystan loca hwæt þa
65 lareowas heom þær to Godes lage tæcan, and þa godan weorc, þe God us beboden
hæfð to adreoganne on þam drihtenlican dæge. Ic eow wylle eac eallswa cyðan,
þæt man ah seoce men to geneosianne and deade bebyrian, earmingas, þam þe
onhagað, fedan and scrydan. And, loca hwa þære mihte age, he mot gehæftne[i]
man alysan, wreccan and ælþeodige underfon, and ælc be his mihte welwyllend-
70 lice heom god don, wudewum and steopcildum and utancumenum froferlice fylstan to rihte. And, loca hwylc cristen man sy ungesibsum, man ah on þam dæge
hine to gesibsumianne.

  Þas[j] syndon þa weorc, þe Gode syndon anfenge on ælcere tide, and swyðost hig
syndon to healdenne[k] [27v] on sunnandagum, forþan se sunnandæg is se forma
75 dæg ealra dagena, and he bið se endenyhsta æt þyssere worulde ende. And, gif
ge þis nellað healdan, cwæð God, ic wylle swingan eow mid þam smeartestum
swipum, þæt is, þæt ic witnige eow mid þam wyrstan wite, swa þæt ic sende ofer
eow min yrre on feower wisan, þæt is, hunger and sweordes ecge, cwyld and hæft-
nunge.[10] Þæt is, þa þe ahte syndon, hi sculon fleonde on gefeohte beon ofslagene,
80 and þa ealdan sculan earmlice licgan heapmælum æt ham hungre acwolene. And
man sceal þa geoguðe geomorlice lædan gehæft heanlice mid heardum bendum
and swa bysmorlice bringan of heora eðle and betæcan eow teonlice syððan on
hæðenra hand, heries lafe.

i gehæf`t´ne
j þis
k heald::::

sunnandæg wið ælce ceapunga. On ðam dæge sy þæt eower æreste weorc þæt ge
eow geemtigen on gebedum, and þæt ge gehyren on cirican halige bodunga fram
35 eowrum lareowum, and secað halige stowe and geneosiað untrumra manna and
deade bebyrgeað. And on ðan dæge ge sceolon þearfan fedan and nacode scrydan
and þurstigum[l] drincas [p. 47] syllan and hæftnedlingas alysan and ælþeodige
wilsumlice onfon and wreccan helpan and wædlan and wudewan frofor gearwian
and gesibsumian þa ungesehtan cristenan.
40   Þas æðelan weorc sint to healdenne on eallum tidum beforan Gode, þeahhwæðere swiþost on sunnandæg, forðan ðe sunnandæg is se forma and se yte-
mysta dæg ealra daga. Gif ge þonne elles doð butan þas forespræcenan þing,
þonne swinge ic eow þam heardostan swinglan, þæt is þæt ic asette on eorðan
mine feower wyrrestan domas: hungor and hæftned and gefeoht and cwelm.[10]

l þurstige, ū *above* e

132

for any man to hold any meeting. But one should visit church and holy place and there within eagerly pray and with humility attend to whatever the teachers instruct him as God's law and to those good works which God has commanded us to do on the Lord's day. I likewise want to make known to you that one should visit sick people and bury the dead, and those for whom it is possible [should] feed and clothe the poor. And whoever has the power, he may set free the captive, receive strangers and foreigners, and each according to his ability benevolently do good for them, [and] rightly give aid to widows and orphans and strangers consolingly. And whatever Christian man may be quarrelsome, one should on that day reconcile him.

These are the works which are acceptable to God at all times, and they are above all to be observed on Sundays, because Sunday is the first day of all days, and it will be the last at the end of this world. And if you will not keep this, said God, I will afflict you with the most painful scourges, that is that I will punish you with the worst torment, so that I will send my wrath over you in four ways: that is, hunger and the edge of the sword, pestilence and captivity. That is, those who are good for anything, they shall be slain fleeing in battle, and the old ones must wretchedly lie in heaps at home, dead from hunger. And one will sadly lead the youth abjectly fettered with strong bonds, and so shamefully lead [them] from their homeland and afterwards deliver you with reproach into the hands of heathens, as the spoil of the army.

malice and from all wickedness. And these things are forbidden at all times. And keep Sunday from any trade. On that day, may your first work be that you free yourselves for prayers and that you listen in church to the holy teachings from your teachers, and seek out holy places and visit sick people and bury the dead. And on that day, you should feed the poor and clothe the naked and give drink to the thirsty and set captives free and willingly receive strangers and help outcasts and the needy and provide comfort to widows and reconcile Christians at odds.

These noble deeds are to be practised at all times before God, nevertheless especially on Sunday, because Sunday is the first and last day of all days. If then you do anything other than the aforesaid, then I will scourge you with the most severe affliction, that is I will place on the earth my four worst judgements: hunger, captivity, war and pestilence.

And syððan æfter þære earmlycan eowre geendunge, ic besence eowre sawla
85 on susle on helle, swa swa ic hwilon dyde þa twa burh Sodomam and Gomorram, þe mid heofonlicum fyre her wurdan forbærnde, and ealle þa, þe him on
eardodon, æfre byrnað on hellegrunde on hatan fyre, forþan hi þone mildan
God manfullice gremedon. And ealswa hit gelamp on Moyses dagum, mines
gecorenan, þæt wæron^l [28r] twegen men, þa wæron genemnode Dathan and
90 Abiron; hi ic besencte mid sawle and mid lichaman on hellegrund for heora oferhigde, and forþan hig spræcon bysmorlice be me and be minum sacerdum.[11] And
ic sende ofer eow þa þeode eow to hergianne and eower land to awestenne, þe ge
heora spræca ne cunnan, forþan þe ge ne healdað sunnandæges freols, and forþan
þe ge me forseoð and mine beboda noldon healdan.[12] Ac wite ge gewislice and
95 gemune ge wel georne, þæt ic æfre fram frymðe bebead þone drihtenlican dæg
to healdenne.

Swa hwa swa ænige cypinge on þam dæge begæð oððe oðre þing, þæt man
claðas waxe, oððe ænig cræftig man him on his cræfte tylige, oððe man efesige
oðerne man oððe bread bace oððe ænig ungelyfed þing bega on þam dæge, he
100 scel beon utlaga wið me and ealle þa, þe him to þam unrihte fylstað and him þæt

l wæro:

45 And ic eow gesylle to ælþeodigra handa, and ic eow fordo and besence eow,
swa ic dyde Sodoman and Gomorran, and ic dyde Dathan and Abiron, þa yfelan
þe wiðsocon minum naman and forsawon mine sacerdas.[11] And ic eow gelæde to
hergienne on þa ðeode þe ge heora gereord ne cunnon, and hi gegripað ongean
eow scyldas and flana.[12] And þære þeode stefen angryslice fram norðdæle
50 ofer eow swegð, and heora hlisa eow gebregð ær ðan ðe he to eow cume, and
geswenceð mid sare and gegripeð eow swa þæt eacnigende wif,[13] forþi ðe ge ne
healdað þone halgan sunnandæg, and forðan ðe ge onscuniað me and ge nellað
mine word gehyran. And be þysum ylcan andgyte drihten cwæð: Se ðe of Gode
bið, he Godes word gehyrð. Þa yfelan þwyran men hyt [p. 48] gehyrað, ac hi hyt
55 healdan nellað. Forði þe hi þæs deofles syndon, gif hi yfeles geswican nellað
and þam gelyfan^m þe we eow herbeforan ær sædon. Drihten sylf cwæð, wite^n ge
gewislice and on gemyndum habbað þæt ic fram frymðe bebead þone sunnandæg
to healdenne.

And swa hwa swa ænig woruldlic weorc^o on sunnandæg wyrcð, oððe hrægel
60 wæsceð oððe ænigne cræft^p wyricð, oððe he his fex efsige oððe hlafas bace oððe
ænig unalyfed þing þurhtihþ, ic hine fornime and his gewyrhtan and his gefylstan

m ∂
n witu:, *final letter erased*
o ∂
p cræf t´

And after your wretched end, I will plunge your souls into torment in hell, just as I once did to the two cities Sodom and Gomorrah, which were burned here with heavenly fire, and all those who dwelled in them ever burn in the abyss of hell in a hot fire, because they wickedly provoked the merciful God. And likewise it happened in the days of Moses, my chosen one, that there were two men, who were called Dathan and Abiron. I plunged them with soul and with body into the abyss of hell because of their pride and because they spoke shamefully about me and my priests. And I will send over you people, to harry you and lay waste your land, those whose language you will not understand, because you do not keep the feast of Sunday, and because you despise me and did not want to keep my commandments. But know for certain and consider earnestly that I ever from the beginning commanded the Lord's day to be kept.

Whoever engages in any trading on that day or any other thing – that one washes clothes, or any craftsman toils at his craft, or one cuts another person's [hair] or bakes bread or does anything which is not permitted on that day – he shall be an exile to me and [likewise] all those who aid him in that wickedness and allow him [to do] that. Because those people who do such things will not

And I will give you into the hands of foreigners, and I will destroy you and plunge you down, as I did to Sodom and Gomorrah and I did to Dathan and Abiram, those evil ones who denied my name and scorned my priests. And I will bring a people to harry you whose language you will not understand, and they will take up shields and arrows against you. And the voice of that people will resound terribly over you from the north, and their repute will frighten you before it comes to you and afflicts [you] with suffering and seizes you as [it does] a pregnant woman in labour, because you would not keep that holy Sunday, and because you reject me and do not wish to obey my word. And with the same meaning the Lord said: He who is of God, he obeys God's word. Evil, perverse people hear it, but do not want to keep it. For that reason, they are of the devil if they do not want to cease from evil and believe that which we said to you before. The Lord himself said: Know for certain and keep in mind that I from the beginning commanded Sunday to be kept.

And whoever does any worldly work on Sunday, or washes clothes or performs any craft or cuts his hair or bakes bread or carries out any illicit thing, I will deprive him and his accomplice and his helper of my kingdom. And those who do

geþafiað. Forþan þa men, þe swylc þing begað, ne begytað hi na mine bletsunge
ne mine myltse, ac heom becymð færlice min grama ofer for þæs dæges forsewennysse. And ic asende ofer eow mancwealm and orfcwealm, swa þæt þa lybbendan nyton, be hwan hig lifian, [28v] and þa deadan man nat, hu man delfe,
105 for þære untrumnysse, þe heom an becymð eal for minra beboda forsewennysse.

For hwan nele þeos wyðerwearde þeod and þas unrihtwisan men geþencan þa
yrmða, þe towearde syndon æt þyssere worulde ende, and hu ic geþafode, þæt
twegen cyningas[14] foran of Rome mid here to Hierusalem þære burh, þe me wæs
burga leofost, ær þan þe hig mine beboda tobræcon, þe þære burge þa geweald
110 ahton. Ðæt wæs, þæt Titus and Uespasianus tobræcon þa burh and ofslogon þær
hund þusend manna, and .xi. siðan hund þusenda hi læddon þanon ealle gebende.
Þis wæs gedon on þam halgan easterdæge, forþan hig forsawon ær to healdenne
þone halgan dæg mid rihte, swa swa ic sylf ær and syððan mine boceras heom
beboden hæfdon. And, gif ge gyt nellað healdan þone halgan sunnandæg,
115 ægðer ge freoh ge þeow, fram sæternesdæges none oð monandæges lihtinge, ic
amansumige eow ætforan minum fæder, þe on heofenan is, swa þæt ge ne sculon
habban nænne gemanan mid me ne mid minum englum æfre to worolde.

of minum rice. And þa ðe þis doð, hi minre bletsunge ne onfoð[q] ne næfre ne
gemetað. Ac for þære bletsunge þe hi forhogodon on þam sunnandæge buton
yldinge wirignysse hi gemetað. And ic asende on heora hiwrædene unarimedlice
65 untrumnysse[r] and cwealmas, ægðer ge ofer hi ge ofer heora bearn and ofer heora
hired and ofer heora nytenu, forði ðe hi min word oferhogodon.

La forhwi ne geman[s] seo þweore[t] þeod and seo wiðerwearde, þe nu wunað on
ðære ytemestan tide þises middaneardes, hu ic het Romana cyningas[14] faran to
Hierusalem þære ceastre[u]; seo me wæs ofer ealle oðre ceastre seo[v] gecorenesste.
70 And ic hi het ut alædan on þone halgan easterdæg of ðære ceastre .xi. siðum
hundred þusenda on hæftned, and hi hundred þusenda [p. 49] þærinne ofslogon,
forði mine leofan Hierusalem ceasterware me forhogodon and mine lareowas,
and hi ne heoldon[w] þone drihtlican sunnandæg swa ic him bebead. Gif ge þonne
on þam halgan sunnandæge on ænigum geflite standað oððe on ænigum fullicum
75 weorcum oððe on unnyttum, ic þonne onsende yfela gehwilc. And hi todrifene
weorþað and geteoriað mid arleasra sawlum, forði þe hi min gebod forhogodon.
Soðlice, gif ge þus[x] ne healdað[y] þone halgan sunnandæg fram eallum weorcum,
ægðer ge þeowe ge frige, fram þære nigoðan tide þæs sæternesdæges oð ðone
morgen on monandæg[z], ic eow amansumige fram minum fæder, and ge dæl
80 nabbað mid me ne mid minum englum.

q, r ∂   w ∂
s -man, *over erasure*   x þis
t, u ∂   y ∂
v þeo   z *raised punctus over erasure*

obtain my blessing nor my mercy, but my anger will come on them suddenly for the contempt of that day. And I will send over you pestilence and cattle-plague, so that the living will not know by what means they might live, and one will not know how one should bury the dead, because of the disease which will come upon them all because of contempt for my commandments.

Why does this perverse people and these unrighteous men not consider those miseries which are approaching at the end of this world, and how I permitted that two kings advanced from Rome with an army to the city of Jerusalem, which was dearest to me of cities before those who ruled that city broke my commandments? That was, that Titus and Vespasian destroyed that city and slew there a hundred thousand men, and eleven times a hundred thousand they led all bound from there. This was done on the holy day of Easter, because they previously refused to keep the holy day rightly, just as I myself before and my learned men afterwards had commanded them. And if you still do not want to keep holy Sunday, both free and slave, from the ninth hour on Saturday until dawn on Monday, I will curse you before my father who is in the heavens, so that you shall not have any fellowship with me nor with my angels for ever.

this, they will not receive nor ever find my blessing. But for that blessing which they despised, without delay they will meet with a curse on that Sunday. I will send on their household countless diseases and pestilences, both upon them and upon their children, and upon their household and upon their cattle, because they scorned my word.

Lo, why does that perverse and that rebellious people, which now dwells in the last age of this world, not remember how I commanded kings of the Romans to travel to the city of Jerusalem; it was above all other cities the choicest to me. And I commanded them to lead out from that city on that holy Easter day eleven times a hundred thousand into captivity, and they slew a hundred thousand therein, because my beloved inhabitants of Jerusalem despised me and my teachers, and they did not keep the Lord's Sunday as I commanded them. If you then on that holy Sunday continue in any dispute or in any disgraceful or unnecessary works, then I will send every evil. And they will become scattered and will waste away with the souls of the wicked, because they despised my commandment. Truly, if you thus do not keep holy Sunday from all labours, both servile and free, from the ninth hour of Saturday until Monday morning, I will separate you from my father and you will have no part with me nor with my angels.

And, gif ge nellað teoðian [29r] ælc þæra þinga, þe eow God lænð, on swa hwylcum þingum, swa ge hit begytað mid rihte, and to Godes cyrcan hit getrywe-
120 lice bringan, ic benæme eow þæra .ix. dæla, and ge sculon þæs teoþan dæles mid teonan brucan.[16] Þæt is, þæt ic asende ofer eower land ælcne untiman, þæt bið egeslice great hagol, se fordeð eowre wæstmas, and unasecgendlice þunras and byrnende ligræscas, þa forglendriað eowre wæstmas ægðer ge on wuda ge on felda. And drugoða eow cymð, þonne ge renas behofedan, and ren, þonne eowre
125 wæstmas wederes beþorftan. And gyt, þæt is egeslicost eow eall to geþafianne: þæt is, þæt ungecyndelic fyr cymð færunga on eowre burga and on tunas and forbærnð þone betstan dæl, þe ge big[m] sceoldon libban.

Nu we habbað eow gesæd be þæs halgan sunnandæges freolse, swa swa ge habbað gehyred[n]. Nu, swa hwa swa hæfð ænigne hyge to Gode, he wile hlistan
130 þyssera worda, ac ic adræde, þæt ge willan heora læs gyman, þonne ge þearfa ahton, forþan þe ge gremiað God ælmihtigne[o] grimlice oft mid yfelum worcum.[18]

m g *added by main hand*
n gehyr`e´d
o ælmihtig

Ac gyf ge þis forhicgað and sacerdum ne gehyrað and eowrum yldrum and wisum lareowum, þe eow swuteliað þisne weg[a], þonne onsend ic ofer eowerne eard[b] ysta and ligræscas and wilde[c] fyr on eowrum ceastrum and on eowrum tunum and mistida hreognysse and ungemetlice[15] hætan and unwæstmbærnysse æcera
85 and treowa and wingearda and ealra [d]eorðan blosmena[d]. And gif ge getreowlice and rihtlice þa frumsceattas eowre teoþunga of eallum eowrum geswincum, oððe on landes teolunge, oððe on ænigum cræfte, on ælmihtiges Godes naman to ðam [p. 50] cyrican ne bringað þe eow mid rihte to gebyreð, þonne anime ic eow fram þa nigon dælas.[16] And ic þærtoeacan gedo þæt on eowrum husum weorðað
90 acennede[e] blinde bearn and deafe and anhende,[16] hreoflan and laman, and eow þonne gewyrð swa micel hungor[f] þæt se welega ne mæg þam wædlan gehelpan.

Men ða leofestan, ge habbað genoh gehyred be ðam sunnandæge, forðan ðe se ðe of Gode is, he Godes word gehlyst and þa wel gehylt.[18] For ures drihtnes, hælendes Cristes lufon ic myngie eow and eac halsige þæt ge georne þis eall

a `and eow secgað eowre sawle þearfe, hwæt ge for Godes lufon don scylon. and ge þæt forho-giað´, *above the line by another hand, insertion mark after* weg
b ∂
c y > i
d–d eorðana blosman
e, f ∂

138

And if you do not want to tithe each of those things which God has granted you, in whatever circumstances you rightfully obtain it, and bring it faithfully to God's Church, I will take from you those nine parts, and you shall partake of the tenth part with injury. That is, that I will send over your land every misfortune, that is terribly large hail, which will destroy your produce, indescribable thunder and burning lightning, which will consume your abundance both in wood and field. And drought will come to you when you had need of rain, and rain when your fruits had need of fair weather. And yet what is altogether the most frightening for you to suffer is that an unnatural fire will come unexpectedly upon your towns and villages and will burn up the best portion, by means of which you must live.

Now we have told you about the festival of holy Sunday, just as you have heard. Now whoever has any thought for God, he will attend to these words, but I fear that you will heed them less than you have need because you severely provoke almighty God often with evil works.

But if you scorn this and do not listen to priests and to your elders and wise teachers, who show you this way (and tell you the need of your soul, what you must do for the love of God, and you rejected that), then I will send upon your land storms and lightning and wildfire on your cities and on your villages and the tempests of evil times and immense heat and the barrenness of fields and of trees and of vineyards and of all the fruits of the earth. And if you do not bring faithfully and rightly, in almighty God's name, the first-fruits of your tithes from all your labours, or in the cultivation of the land, or in any trade, nor that which it rightly behoves you [to bring], then I will take from you the nine parts. And I will, in addition to that, bring about that in your houses will be born blind, deaf and weak children, leprous and lame, and such great hunger will befall you that the wealthy will not be able to help the poor.

Dearest people, you have heard enough about Sunday, because he who is of God, he listens to God's words and keeps them well. For the love of our Lord

139

And, ge rican men, geþencað, þæt þeos woruld is neah þam ende, geswicað
eowra[p] unþeawa and ne awende ge ne[q] [29v] þone dæg to nihte ne þa niht to dæge.
Forþan wa eow, þæt ge æfre gewurdon men, buton ge geswicon, ge þe awendað
135 riht to woge and ælc woh for lyðran medsceatte gelætað to rihte.[19] Ge syttað ealle
niht and drincað oð leohtne dæg and swa awendað dæg to nihte and niht to dæge,
swa ic ær cwæð, eall for druncennysse and oferfylle, and swa ge eowerne beorscipe
brucað on unriht. Ac wite ge mid gewissan, þæt eow wurðað þa mycclan bollan
bytere forgoldene æt eowrum endedæge, butan ge geswican. Nyte ge ful georne,
140 þæt ælc man scel hyran his hlaforde and don, þæt he hine hæt, and be þan man wat,
þæt he bið his hlaford? And swa man mot oðrum[r] twegra hyran, Gode ælmihtigum
and his beboda healdan, oððe þan earman deofle anrædlice fylian. Forþan nis na
ma hlafordinga on worulde, þonne twegen, God ælmihtig and deofol. Forþan, se
þe Godes beboda hylt, he is Godes man, and he mid Gode scel habban ece blisse
145 on heofena rice æfter þison life. And, se þe deofles worc begæð, he is deofles man,
and he scel mid deofle wunian on helle æfter þison life a to worulde[s].

p eowre
q n:
r oðra
s woruld:

95 understandan[g] þe ic eow gesæd hæbbe, forðan þises middaneardes ende[h] is swiðe
neah, and eower geara gerim ys gescyrt. Ðonne is eow micel neadþearf[i] þæt ge
gebeton þa þing þe eow fram Gode forbodene wæron and on ðære ealdan cyðnysse
þurh heahfæderas and witegan and on ðære niwan þurh Godes sunu ænne and
þurh þa apostolas and þa witigan and þurh þa wundru þe God dæghwamlice on
100 middaneard ætyweð, ægþer ge on eorðan ge on heofonum ge on steorran ge on sæ
ge on eallum gesceaftum.
  Gemunað ge weligan[j] þæt ge eowre wiste rihtlice gehealden, and ondrædað
eow[k] þæt þæt awriten is þurh þone witegan: Wa eow þe wyrcað dæg to nihte
and niht to dæge, and wendað swete on biter and biter on swete.[19] Wa eow þe
105 fram morgen oð æfen and fram æfen oð morgen mid missenlicra gliwa oferfylle[l][20]
[p. 51] druncennysse neosiað[m] on eowrum gebeorscipum oð wambe fylnysse.
Nyte ge þæt ofermodignys bið þæs god þe[n] hyre filigð, and gytsung is þæs god þe
hyre þeowað[o]. Se ðe þeowað gyfernysse and oferdruncennysse, hi him beoð for

g -an < -un, ∂
h `ende´, *by another hand, insertion mark after* middaneardes, *followed by erasure of six letters*
i neadþ- *over erasure*
j, k ∂
l oferfiligað and *(see commentary)*
m ∂
n ðe *erased after* þe
o -eo- *over erasure*

And, you rich men, consider that this world is near to the end; cease from your evil practices, and do not turn day to night and night to day. Therefore, woe to you, that you ever became men unless you desist, you who turn right to wrong, and each wrong you permit as right for a vile bribe. You sit all night and drink until bright day and so turn day into night and night into day, as I said before, all for drunkenness and gluttony, and so you enjoy your carousing wickedly. But know with certainty that for you the large cups will be bitterly paid for at your end-day, unless you desist. Do you not know full well that every man shall obey his lord and do what he commands him, and by that one knows that he is his lord? And so one must obey one of two, God almighty, and keep his commandments, or constantly follow the wretched devil, because there are no more than two masters in the world, God almighty and the devil. Therefore, he who keeps God's commandments, he is God's man, and he shall have eternal bliss with God in the kingdom of the heavens after this life. And he who does the devil's work, he is the devil's man and he shall dwell with the devil in hell after this life for ever.

Saviour Christ, I admonish you and entreat that you understand all this well which I have told you, because the end of the world is very near and the number of your years is shortened. There is then a great need for you to repent of those things which were forbidden you by God and in the Old Testament through the patriarchs and prophets and in the New through God's only Son and through the apostles and prophets and through the wonders which God daily displays in the world, both on the earth and in the heavens and in the stars and in the sea and in all creatures.

Remember, you rich, that you possess your abundance rightly, and fear what is written by the prophet: Woe to you who make day into night and night into day, and turn sweet to bitter and bitter into sweet. Woe to you who from morning until evening and from evening until morning with an excess of various amusements seek out drunkenness at your carousings up to the fullness of the stomach. Do you not know that pride is the god of the one who follows it, and greed is the god of the one

Þæt syndon Godes wiðersacan: morðwyrhtan, hlafordswican and manswaran, manslagan[t] [30r] and mægslagan, cyrchatan and sacerdbanan, hadbrecan and æwbrecan, þeofas, ryperas and reaferas, unrihthæmeras, þa fulan, þe forlætað
150 heora cwenan and nimað oðre and þa þe habbað ma, þonne heora rihtæðel-cwene, wyccan and wælcyrian and unlybwyrhtan, unrihtdeman, þe demað æfre be þam sceatte and swa wendað wrang to rihte and riht to wrange, and þa, þe lufiað þa mycclan druncennysse æfre and oðra[u] unrihta fela, þe nu syndon lange to areccanne.[23] And butan tweon, þæs worc þe man begæð, þam hlaforde man hyrð;
155 and, se þe swylc begæð, swylc ic nu rehte, he forsihð þone soðan God. Forþam ic bidde eow and halsige þurh þone lifiendan God, þæt ge geswicon eowres unrihtes, ær þan se earmlica deað eow endemes ealle forgripe and eowre sawla on helle besence.

And, se ðe nele nu ne ne recð Godes lare, ac hi forsihð and nele hi gehyran, ac
160 læt him eaðelice ymbe þæt and ælce dæge cunnað, hu he mæst mage gesyngian ongean Godes wyllan, and nele his synna andettan, ac þencð se unwara on his geþance, eallswa deofol hine lærð, þe ælc yfel of cymð.[24] Þæt[v] is, ærest he hine

t manslaga:
u oðre
v Þæt, *faded*

hlaford getealde, and ælc man bið swa fela leahtra þeow swa he underþeod bið.
110 Geornostlice se ðe swilcum leahtrum filigð, hi þone soðan God forlætað. Þi ic eow þonne halsige þæt ge ealle þas uncysta forlæton, ær þan se deað eowre sawle on helle cwicsusle teo.

Gif þonne hwilc bisceop oððe hwilc gelæred man, æfter þan ðe he[p] þis ærend-gewrit him on handa hæfð and hit næle þam folce underþeodan ne him rædan[q],
115 buton twyon anrædlice he þolað Godes domes, forðan ðe swa hwilc sacerd swa ne[r] gebodað þam folce heora synna, huruþinga on domes dæge heora blod bið fram him asoht, and he scildig þonne stent be heora synnum on Godes andweard-nysse.[21] Gif he him þonne bodað heora synna and heora mane, ne byð geþæf mid him, he unscildig byð of heora synnum. Men ða leofestan, þis gewrit næs æt
120 fruman awriten ne amearcod þurh nanes eorðlices mannes handa, ac Godes engel hit awrat[s] mid his agenum fingrum, swa ic eow ær herbeforan sæde, and hit Petre sealde, þam bisceope. And he [p. 52] hit swutele mid aðsware geæðe and geswor, þus cwæðende:[22] Ic Petrus and[t] bisceop on þære Antiochiscan cyricean geæðe and

p `he´, *insertion mark after* ðe
q ::rædan, *two letters erased*
r ne *over erasure of* ge
s ∂
t a *over erased* p

Those are God's enemies: murderers, traitors and perjurers, man-slayers and kin-slayers, persecutors of the Church and priest-slayers, the one who injures someone in holy orders and adulterers, thieves, robbers and plunderers, fornicators, the impure, those who leave their wives and take others and those who have more than their lawful wife, magicians, and witches and sorcerers, unjust judges who always judge according to the bribe and so turn wrong to right and right to wrong, and those who ever love much drunkenness and many other evils, which are now [too] long to recount. And without a doubt, according to the work which one does, that [is] the lord one obeys, and he who does such as I have now recounted, he scorns the true God. Therefore I bid you and entreat you by the living God that you forsake your wickedness before wretched death seizes you all together and plunges your souls into hell.

And he who does not want to be concerned for God's teaching now, but scorns it and does not wish to obey it, but takes the matter lightly and every day seeks to know how he may transgress against God's will the most, and does not want to confess his sins, but the heedless one thinks in his mind just as the devil teaches

who serves it? He who serves gluttony and drunkenness, they will be considered his lord, and each man is the slave of as many sins as he is subject to. Accordingly, he who pursues such sins, they forsake the true God. Therefore, I entreat you that you abandon all those vices, before death drags your soul into the living torment of hell.

If then, any bishop or any learned man, after he has this message in his hand, does not want to submit it to the people nor read it to them, without a doubt he will definitely endure the judgement of God because whichever priest does not preach to the people their sins surely on the day of judgement their blood will be sought from him, and he will then stand guilty on account of their sins in the presence of God. If he preaches them their sins and their wickedness, and he is not in agreement with them, he will be guiltless of their sins. Dearest people, this message was not at first written nor laid out through the hands of any earthly man, but God's angel wrote it with his own fingers, as I told you before, and gave it to Peter the bishop, and he confirmed it openly with an oath and swore, saying thus: I, Peter and bishop in the Antiochian Church, make an oath and

lærð, þæt he his synna ne andette, forþam þe he iung is; eft he cwæð to [30v] þam
men: oðre syngodon hefelicor, þonne þu, and þeahhwæðere hig leofedon[25] lange
165   hwile. He cwyð þryddan siðe: do swa yfele, swa þu do, Godes mildheortnys is
swiðe mycel, and he wyle þe forþi þine synna forgifan. And þurh þas unwærnysse
he gebringð hine on helle. Ðreo þing syndon, þe gebringað þone ungesæligan on
hellegrunde: þæt is, unclæne geþanc and idele word and yfele dæda. And oðre
þreo þing syndon, þe gebringað þone gesæligan to heofenan rice: þæt is, halig
170   geþanc and god spæc and fullfremed worc.

    And þreo þing syndon, þe ne beoð forgifene ne on þissere worulde ne on
þam toweardan life: an is, þæt man God to tale habbe; oðer, þæt man ærestes
ne gelyfe; þrydde, þæt man ortruwige Godes mildheortnysse. Uton nu forþyg
habban trumne geleafan to Gode and hine biddan, þæt he us geunne æfter urum
175   forðsiðe, þæt we moton becuman to his mildheortnysse, swa swa he eallum þam
behaten hæfð, þe hine lufiað and his beboda healdað, þæt is þæt uplice rice, þe he
sylf wunað on mid eallum his halgum a butan ende. And eac we sceolon biddan
þa halgan fæmnan Sancta Marian ures drihtnes moder, þæt heo us geþingie[w] to
hyre leofan[x] bearne, hyre scippende, and to urum scippende[y] [31r] þæt is God
180   ælmihtig, forþam ðe heo mæg abiddan æt him eall þæt heo wyle.[26]

w geþing`i´e
x leof::
y scipp::::

---

swerige[u] þurh þone lifigendan Godes sunu, þæs ðe gesceop heofonas[v] and eorðan
125   and ealle gesceafta[w], and þurh þa halgan þrynnysse and annysse[x], and þurh þa
eadigan fæmnan sancta Marian and þurh ealra engla endebyrdnysse and þurh
ealra haligra lichoman, þæt þas word þe on þis ærendgewrite awritene syndon on
fruman[y] næron of nanes mannes handa gehiwode, ac hi wurdon onsende of Godes
þrymsetle and mid engles fingrum awritene. Gyf ge[z] þonne þysum gelyfan willað[a]
130   þe þis gewrit us segð and bodað, þonne sylþ us God ece lif mid his englum in
worulda woruld, a buton ende, a on ecnysse. Amen.

u, v, w, x ð
y fruma
z `ge´, *by another hand, insertion mark after* Gyf
a ð

---

him, from whom comes every evil. That is, first he teaches him that he should not confess his sins because he is young. Also he says to that man: Others have sinned more grievously than you, and nevertheless they lived a long while. He says a third time: Do as evilly as you do; God's mercy is very great, and he will therefore forgive you your sins. And through this heedlessness he brings himself into hell. There are three things which bring the accursed one into the abyss of hell: that is impure thought and empty words and evil deeds. And there are three other things which bring the blessed one to the kingdom of the heavens: that is, holy thought, and good speech, and perfect works.

And there are three things which will not be forgiven either in this world or in the future life: one is that one hold God in derision, another, that one not believe in the Resurrection; a third, that one despair of the mercy of God. Let us now, therefore, have a firm belief in God and ask him, that he grant us after our death that we may attain to his mercy, just as he has promised to all who love him and keep his commandments, that is that celestial kingdom in which he himself dwells with all his saints for ever without end. And we also should ask the holy Virgin St Mary, the mother of our Lord, that she intercede for us to her beloved child, her Creator, and to our Creator, that is God almighty, because she may ask from him all that she wishes.

swear by the son of the living God, him who created the heavens and the earth and all creation, and by the holy Trinity and Unity, and by the blessed Virgin St Mary, and by the order of all the angels, and by the bodies of all the saints that these words which are written in this letter were not at first formed by the hand of any man, but they were sent from God's throne and written with the fingers of an angel. If you then will believe that which this writ tells and commands us, then God will give us eternal life with his angels, for ever, always without end, ever in eternity. Amen.

LETTER E

Cambridge, Corpus Christi College 419 (pp. 38–73)

[p. 38] ^aSunnandæges spell^a. ^bHer sægð^b on þisum^c drihtnes ærendgewrite, þæt fyr cymð sume^d þissa hærfesta ofer manna bearn.¹ And hit gefeald ærest on Sceotta land,² and hit þær forbærnð ealle ða fyrenfullan^e, þa ðe nu God gremiað mid sunnandæges weorcum and sæternesdæges ofernon.³ And hit þonne færð on
5 Brytwealas and gedeð þær þæt ilce. And þonne hit færð on Angel[p.39]cyn and gedeð þær þæt ilce, þe hit dyde þam oðrum þeodum twam. Ðonne hit færð suð ofer sæ geond þæt þeodland, and hit þær forbærnð þæt mancyn, swa hit her ær dyde. Forðam, men þa leofestan, geþencan we, þæt an diacon wearð forðfered on Sceotlande, and he wæs fif wucan dead and onwoc þa eft of deaðe and spræc to
10 mannum. And he sæde fela wundra, þe he geseah on ðære oðre weorulde. And næs ænig word, þæt ænig man on hine funde, butan [p.40] hit wære eall soð, þæt þæt he sæde. And næs syððan, þæt he æniges eorðlices metes abyrigde, ne he næfre syððan butan cyrcan ne com. And þæs diacones nama wæs Nial haten. And se diacon sæde fram þysum fyre, emne swa we rædað on sunnandæges spelle, ðæt
15 drihten sylf gewrat iu gewrit, þæt he wolde ealle synfulle men forbærnan.

a red rustic capitals   d sum
b–b square capitals, H large initial, 3 lines deep   e y < i, by a later hand
c þises

LETTER F

BL Cotton Tiberius A.iii (83r–87r)

[83r] Her sagaþ an^a þisan drihtnes ærendgewrite, þæt fyr cymeþ on suman hærfeste.¹ And hit gefeallaþ ærest on Scotta land² and syþþan on Angelcing and deþ þær^b ælc yfel. And þonne færþ hit suþ ofer sæ on þa þeodland and forbærnþ ægþer ge mancynne man and eac ^cmicelne beoleofan^c. [83v] An diacan wæs dead
5 nu an unmenigum geare, þæs nama wæs Nial. He wæs an Scotta ealonde, and he wæs .v. wucan dead; and he þa eft of deaþe aras þurh Cristes mihte and sprec to mannum and hiom sede fela wundra, þæs he geseah in þare oþran weorulde, þæs þe ^dænig^d mon an hine anfindan mihte butan eal soþ, þæt he sægde^d. And nes siþþan, þæt he ænige eorþlices metes anbergde, ne nefre siþþan he butan cirican
10 ne com. And þæs diacones nama^e wæs haten Nial. And se diacan sægde be þam fyre, ealswa we redaþ an sunnandeges spelle, þæt drihten self awrat, þæt he wolde mid fyre ealle synfulle forbernan.

a a over erasure   d–d words omitted through homœoteleuton
b þær twice   (see commentary)
c–c micel ne beo leofan   e naman

146

LETTER E

A Sermon of Sunday. Here it says in this letter of the Lord that fire will come upon the children of men one of these harvests. And it will fall first on Ireland, and there it will consume all the sinful who now provoke God with Sunday and Saturday afternoon labours. And it will then go to the Britons of Wales and will do the same there. And then it will come upon the English people and do the same there as it did to the two other nations. Then it will advance south over the sea throughout the continent, and there it will consume mankind, just as it did here previously. Therefore, dearest people, let us consider that a certain deacon passed away in Ireland, and he was dead for five weeks, and then he awoke again from death and spoke to men. And he told of many marvels which he saw in that other world. And there was no word that any man might find in him but it was all true, that which he said. And afterwards he did not partake of any earthly food, nor did he ever thereafter come out of the church. And that deacon's name was Niall. And that deacon said about this fire, just as we read in the sermon of Sunday, that the Lord himself formerly wrote that message, [and] that he would burn up all the sinful.

LETTER F

Here they say in this letter of the Lord that fire will come during a certain harvest. And it will fall first on the land of the Irish and afterwards on the English and will do every evil there. And then it will go south over the sea onto the continent and will burn up both mankind and also much livelihood. There was a deacon, dead not many years now, whose name was Niall. He was on the island of the Irish, and he was dead for five weeks, and then he arose from death again, through the power of Christ, and spoke to men and told them many marvels, according as he had seen in that other world, after which there was no [*from E*: word that] any man might find in him, but [it was] all true, what he said. And after that he did not partake of any earthly food, nor ever afterwards did he come outside the church. And the deacon's name was Niall. And the deacon said about that fire, just as we read in the Sunday sermon which the Lord himself wrote, that he would burn up all the sinful with fire.

And þonne sæde se diacon, þæt þæt fyr cymð forðan ofer manna bearn þy þe
men gelefað to hwon drihtnes [p. 41] sylfes ærendgewrites, þe he sylf to Sanctus
Petrus cyrican asende. Ac heo^f him wiðsacað, swa sume men iu geara dydon þam
heahfædere, þa he ðone miclan flod bodade menniscum cynne huru hundtwelft-
20 igum wintrum,⁶ ær he come and ealle men adrencte butan ehta mannum. Ðonne
Noe þis mannum sæde be ðam flode, þæt he wolde ealle synfulle^g menn adrencan,
þonne hlogen men his worda on bysmer^h and cwædon þæt he luge. Swa þonne
wenað nu manige [p. 42] men, þæt þes diacon leoge be þam fyre, þe drihten sylf
hine secgan het manna bearnum. Ac men him nellað gelefan þe ma, þe heo^i Noe
25 dydon, ær þæt fyr heom on sitt, swa þonne iu men ne woldon gelefan Noes worde,
ær ealle wolcnu and ealle heofones^j þeotan wæron mid wætere gefylde, and ealle
eorðan æddre onsprungon ongean þam heofonlican flode. And hit þa ongan rinan^k
feowertig daga and feowertig nihta tosomne þy mæstan rene^l [p. 43]; and seo
eorðe weoll ongean þam heofonlican flode swa swyðe,⁷ oððæt þæt wæter wæs
30 heahre þonne ænig munt æfre wære.

And þa forðam adruncon ealle cwice wihta, þe betwyx^m heofonan and eorðan
wæron butan ehta mannum: ðæt wæs Noe and his wif and heora þreo^n suna, Sem
and Cham and Iafeth, and heora þreo wif and ælces cynnes twa gemacan, þæt

f eo *expuncted*, i *above line*   k hrinan
g y < i, *by a later hand*   l hrene
h y < i, *by a later hand*   m y < i, *by a later hand*
i eo *expuncted*, i *above line*   n eo *expuncted*, y *above line*
j heofonas

And þonne sæde þæt þes diacon, þæt þæt fyr come forþan ofer manna bearn,
forþan hie gelefdon to hwon drehtnes selfes ærendgewrites, þe he to Sancte Petrys
15 cirican asænde. Ac him wiþsacaþ menige men and nellaþ gelefan an þas halgan
lare. Forþon hiom sænd God on micelne brogan, fyr and hungor, butan hio to
Godes geleafan ær gecyrran willaþ and heora elmyssan sellan and hiora tioþunge
an riht gelæstan to Godes cirican and earman mannum, þæt biþ of cwican orfe and
of corne and of eallum þam gestrionum, þe iow drehten unne, and þonne biddan
20 drehtnen his mæran mildse.⁵ Þus bodade Noę se witega þone micel flod menniscum cynne huru hundteontigum wintrum,⁶ ær he come, and ealle men adrencte
se micela flod butan eahta mannum: þæt wæs Noę and his wif and his þreo sunu
and heora þreora wif. And þonne Noę þis mannum sæde be þam flode, swa þes
diacon dyde nu be þysum fyre drehtnes selfes worde he bodode mannum, and þæt
25 þæt fyr wille cuman and ealle synfulle swyþe geunrotsian^f. Þonne hlogan men
Noes worda, þonne he þis folce sæde be þam flode, and^g bismerodan hine, and hi
cwædan to him, þæt he luge, oþþæt ealle wolcen and eall heofenes þiotan wurdan
mid wætere gefyllede, and ealle edran asprungan angen þam heofenlican flode.

And hit agan þa rinan .xl. daga and .xl. nihta tosomne þæm mæstan rene, and
30 sio eorþe rinde ealswa swiþe of hire ęasprencgum^h angen þam heofelican flode,⁷

f geunro`t´sian   h ęasprencguum
g an

And then the deacon said that that fire will therefore come upon the children of men because men believe too little of the Lord's own message, which he himself sent to St Peter's church. But they reject him, just as certain men long ago did the patriarch, when he announced that great flood to mankind for at least a hundred and twenty years, before it came and drowned all except for eight people. When Noah spoke to these men about that flood, that it would drown all sinful men, then men laughed his words to scorn and said that he lied. So now many men think that this deacon lies about the fire, concerning which the Lord himself commanded him to tell the children of men. But men do not want to believe him any more than they did Noah, before that fire oppresses them, just as men formerly would not believe the word of Noah, before all the clouds and all the channels of heaven were filled with water and all the streams of the earth rose towards that heavenly flood. And then it began to rain for forty days and forty nights together with the greatest rain, and the earth welled up towards that heavenly flood so fiercely, until that water was higher than any mountain has ever been.

And then therefore all living beings drowned which were between heaven and earth except for eight people: that was Noah and his wife and their three sons, Shem and Ham and Japheth, and their three wives, and of each kind two mates, so

And then this deacon said that that fire would therefore come upon the children of men because they believed too little of the Lord's own message which he own sent to St Peter's church. But many men reject him, and will not believe in this holy teaching. Therefore God will send upon them a great terror, fire and hunger, unless they will turn to belief in God beforehand and give their alms and their tithe rightly to God's Church and to poor people, that is of live cattle and of grain and of all that property which the Lord may grant you, and then ask the Lord for his great mercy. Thus Noah, the prophet, announced the great flood to mankind for at least one hundred years before it came, and the flood drowned all except for eight people: that was Noah and his wife and his three sons and their three wives. And then Noah told this to the people about the flood, as this deacon now announced to people about the fire with the word of the Lord himself, and that that fire will come and will greatly grieve all the sinful. Then the people laughed at Noah's words, when he told this people about that flood, and mocked him, and they told him that he lied, until all the clouds and all the channels of heaven were filled with water, and all the streams rose up against the heavenly flood.

And then it began to rain for forty days and forty nights together with the greatest rain, and the earth rained just as greatly from its springs towards the heavenly

þeos weoruld mihte of hym awæcnian. Ac þæt is lang and wundorlic to sæcganne,
35 hu þa wurdon generede in þære [p. 44] Noes earce, þa ðe þær to lafe oðstodon.
Ðonne nu gegangeð þam mannum, þe þyses fyres cyme nellað gelefan, þæt heo°
ealle forbeornað[p]. Hwæt, Crist sylf hine to ðan geeadmedde, þæt he wrat gewrit
on ðam seofoðan heofone swyðe eorlicum wordum for sunnandæges weorcum
and sæternesdæges ofernon.[9] Forðan se an dæg wæs swiðe[q] oft gehalgod eallum
40 Godes gesceaftum to reste butan deoflum and hæðenum sawlum, þa næfre reste ne
onfoð.[10] And þis he [p. 45] awrat eall mid gyldenum stafum[11] menniscum cynne.

And forðam men habbað heo[r] sylfe swyðe stranglice wið God awerged and wið
ealle his halgan, forðan þe heo[s] nellað healdan þone halgan sunnandæg mid rihte
fram nontide þæs sæternesdæges oð monandæges lihtincge. Forðan drihten Crist
45 swor þurh his þa halgan þrynnesse and þa soðan annesse: se man, se ðe ne wolde
healdan þone halgan sunnandæg mid rihte, þæt he wære awerged in ða neoðemestan
hellewitu. [p. 46] And he swa cwæð[14]: ic sende hæðen folc ofer eow, and þa eow
benimað eowres eðles and eowres lifes, and ic sende on eowrum husum cwealm
and hungor and untimnesse and fyr, þæt forbærnð ealle eowre welan.[15] Hwylc fyr
50 mænde Crist elles, butan þæt ilce, þæt se diacon foresæde? And he cwæð: gif we
nu woldan swa lyt gelefan drihtnes sylfes ærendgewrites, swa men iu dydon þæs
flodes tocyme, þonne becymð þæt fyr hraðe ofer manna bearn. And se an broga
bið strengra [p. 47] to aræfnanne[t], þonne æfre ænig ær in middanearde become;
and men sweltað butan þam fyre for ðæs þunres ege anum and þære ligette and for
55 ðæm ormætlicum cwealme, þe heo[u] geseoð beforan heora eagum.[16]

o eo *expuncted*, i *above line*   s i *above line*
p eo *expuncted*, y *above line*   t aræfn`i´anne
q swiðe swiðe   u i *above line*
r i *above line*

oþþæt wæter wæs hegre beufan eorþan, þonne se munt, þe is syxtinan fædman
hegre.[8] Se flod wæs bufan þam hegestan munde, þe is an middangearde.

And þa adruncan ealle cwice wihte, þe betwioh heofonum and eorþan wæran
butan .viii. mannum: þæt wæs Noę and his wif and his þreo sunu[i] and heora þreora
35 wif, and þær wæran elces cynnes wihta twa gemeccan, þæt þeos weoruld mihte
eft beon geedstaþoled[j] and eft of awecnigan. And þæt is lang [84r] and wundarlic
to asecgenne, hu þa wurdan generede in þare Noes earce, þe þær to lafe wurdan.
Swa þonne nu gegongeþ þam mannum, þe þyses fyres cymes geleafan nellaþ,
þæt hio ealle forwyrþaþ. Hwet, drehten hine selfne to þan geeadmette, þæt he
40 awrat gewrit an þæm seofeþan heofone swiþe eorlicum wordum for sunnandeges
weorcum and seternes ofernon.[9] Forþan se sunnandeg wes gehalgod eallum
mannum to reste butan deoflum anum and hæþenum sawlum, þa næfre reste ne
onfoþ.[10] And þis gewrit he awrat mid geldenum stafum[11] and hit þa ansænde to
mankynne, forþon þe hie hæfdan hie sylfe swiþe stranglice wiþ God forgelte and
45 wiþ ealle his halgan, forþon hio nellaþ heoldan þane halgan sunnandeg and þone
drehtenlican dæg from nontide þæs sæternesdeges oþ þes monandeges lihtinge.

i sunu < suna
j geedstaþoled weorþan (weorþan *likely taken into the text from a gloss in exemplar*)

that this world might arise from them. But that is long and wondrous to tell, how in Noah's ark those were preserved, who remained as a remnant. Therefore now it will happen to those people, who will not believe in the coming of this fire, that they will all burn up. Alas, Christ humbled himself to that extent that he wrote a message in the seventh heaven with very angry words on account of the labours of Sunday and Saturday afternoon, because that one day was very often sanctified for all God's creatures as a rest, except for devils and heathen souls, who never receive rest. And this he wrote entirely with golden letters for mankind.

And therefore men have very severely damned themselves before God and all his saints, because they will not keep holy Sunday properly from the ninth hour on Saturday until dawn on Monday. Therefore, the Lord Christ swore by his holy Trinity and that true Unity: that man who would not keep holy Sunday properly would be damned into the lowest torments of hell. And so he says: I will send a heathen people over you, and they will deprive you of your land and your life, and I will send on your houses pestilence and hunger and evil times and fire that will burn up all your riches. What fire did Christ otherwise mean, but the same as the deacon foretold? And he says: If we now wish to believe so little the letter of the Lord himself, as men once did the coming of that flood, then that fire will soon come over the children of men. And that terror alone will be more arduous to endure than any that has ever come to the world before; and men will die, in addition to the fire, from the terror of the thunder and lightning alone and from the immense slaughter which they will see before their eyes.

flood, until the water was higher above the earth than the mountain, which is sixteen cubits higher. The flood was above the highest mountain which is on the earth.

And then all living creatures which were between the heavens and the earth drowned, except for eight people: that was Noah and his wife and his three sons and their three wives, and there were two mates of every kind of creature, so that this world might be again restored and arise again [from them]. And that is long and wondrous to tell how those were saved in Noah's ark, who became the remnant there. So then it will now happen to those people who will not believe in the coming of this fire that they will all perish. Alas, the Lord humbled himself to that extent that he wrote a message in the seventh heaven with very angry words on account of the labours of Sunday and of Saturday afternoon. Because Sunday was sanctified for all people as a rest, except for devils and heathen souls alone, who will never receive rest. And this message he wrote with golden letters and sent it to mankind, because they had very severely incurred guilt before God and all his saints, because they will not keep holy Sunday and the Lord's day from the ninth hour of Saturday until dawn on Monday.

151

E   La leofan men, utan us warnian georne þa hwile, þe we magon.[17] Us gebyreð[v],
þæt we ælces þinges ure geoguðe teoðunge rihtlice Gode betæcan, ure sulhælm-
essan .xv. niht onufan eastran and ure geoguðe teoðunge be Pentecosten.[18] And
sy ælc heorðpening agifen [p. 48] be Petrus mæssedæg to þam biscopstole ælce

60   geare,[19] and cornteoðung be emnihte oððe latest be ealra halgena mæssan,[20] and
æfre þone teoðan æcer, ealswa seo sulh hit gega,[21] and cyricsceattas to Martinus
mæssan,[22] and leohtgesceota þreowa on geare: ærest healfpeningwurð wexes to
candelmæssan and eft on easteræfen and þriddan siðe to ealra halgena mæssan.[23]
And healde man ælces sunnandæges freolsunga fram sæternesdæges none oð

65   monan[p. 49]dæges lihtinge and ælcne oðerne mæssedæg, swa he beboden beo.[24]
And sunnandaga cypincge we forbeodað eac eornostlice and ælc folcgemot,
butan hit for mycelre neodþearfe sy.[25] And þæt man ælc beboden fæsten healde,
sy hit ymbrenfæsten, sy hit lenctenfæsten, sy hit elles oðer fæsten, mid ealre
geornfulnesse.[26] And to Sancta Marian mæssan ælcere and to ælces apostoles

70   mæssan fæsten, butan to Philippi and Iacobi we ne beodað nan fæsten for ðam
easterlican [p. 50] freolse, and ælces frigedæges fæsten, butan hit freols sy.[27] And
we forbeodað ordal and aðas[w] freolsdagum and ymbrendagum and lenctendagum
and rihtfæstendagum and fram aduentum domini oð octabas epiphaniae[x] and fram
septuagesima, oð fiftene niht beon geeastrode.[28] And eac we lærað eornostlice, þæt

75   cristenra manna gehwylc understande, þæt he æfter forðsiðe butan sawlsceatte on
mynstre ne licge, ac gelæste man a þone sawelsceat æt openum pytte.[29] Leofan
men, eac ic bidde [p. 51] for Godes lufan, þæt ælc cristen man understande georne
his agene þearfe, forðam ealle we scylan ænne timan gebidan, þonne us wære
leofre, þonne eall þæt on middanearde is, þær we aworhton þa hwile, þe we

80   mihton, georne Godes willan; ac þonne we scylan habban anfeald lean þæs, þe
we on life ær geearnoden.[30]
        Ac utan beon on gebyrge[y] earmum wudewum and steopcildum and helpan
georne earmum mannum, ælþeodigum and utancumenum. Utan hlywan ofcalene
and wæfan nacode [p. 52] and syllan mete þam gehingredum and drenc þam

85   ofþyrstum. Utan frefrian ahwænede and hyrtan ormode, alysan gehæfte, gif us to
þam onhagige, and seoce geneosian and forðferede þearfan mildheortlice cystian
and syððan bebyrian.[31] Se ðe þus deð, he deð him sylfum micle þearfe. Forðam
an tima cymð ure æghwylcum, þæt us wære leofre, þonne eall þæt we on worulde
wiðæftan us þonne læfað, þær we aworhton þa hwile, þe we mihton, þæt Gode

90   licode. Ac þonne we scylon habban anfeald [p. 53] lean þæs, ðe we on life ær
geworhton. Wa ðam þonne, þe ær geearnode hellewite. Ðær is ece bryne grimme
gemencged, and þær is ece gryre, þær is ece ece and þær is sorgung and sargung
and a singal heof; ðær is benda bite and dynta dyne, þær is wyrma slite and ealra
wædla gripe, þær is wanung and granung, þær is yrmða gehwylc and ealra deofla

95   geþring. Wa ðam þonne, þe þær sceal wunian on wite; betere him wære, þæt he

v *second* e *expuncted, a* above line
w *and* wifunga, *by a later hand in left margin, insertion mark after* aðas
x epiphanię
y y *expuncted,* eo above line

152

Lo, dear people, let us earnestly take warning while we may. It is fitting for us to give rightly to God of each thing, a tithe of our young [animals], our plough-alms fifteen nights after Easter and our tithe of young [animals] by Pentecost. And may every hearth-penny be paid by St Peter's festival to the episcopal see each year, and the tithe of grain by the autumnal equinox or at the latest by All Saints' day, and ever the tenth acre just as the plough traverses it and churchscot at St Martin's day, and the lightscot three times a year: first, a halfpenny-worth of wax at Candelmas and again on Easter eve and the third time at All Saints' day. And one should keep the holy days of each Sunday from the ninth hour on Saturday to Monday at dawn and every other festival as it may be enjoined. And we also strictly forbid Sunday trading and every public meeting, unless it be for great necessity, and that one keep each ordained fast, whether it be the Ember fast or the Lenten fast or another fast, with all diligence. And on each festival of St Mary and on the festival of each apostle one is to fast, except for [those of] Philip and James [on which] we enjoin no fast because of the Easter festival, and each Friday's fast, except when it is a feast day. And we forbid ordeals and oaths (and sexual relations) on feast-days and Ember days and on days in Lent and on appointed fast days and from Advent to the octave of Epiphany and from Septuagesima until fifteen nights after Easter have elapsed. And also we solemnly teach that each Christian man should understand that after death he should not lie without payment for the soul in the minster, but one should always make the payment for the soul at the open grave. Dear people, I also bid you for the love of God, that each Christian man understand his own need well, because we shall all experience a time when it would be dearer to us than everything that is in the world that we had wrought God's will eagerly while we were able. But then we shall have the just reward for what we previously earned in life.

But let us be a protection for poor widows and orphans and eagerly help poor men, foreigners and strangers. Let us warm the cold and clothe the naked and give food to the hungry and drink to the thirsty. Let us console the afflicted and encourage the despairing, set free captives, if it is within our power, and visit the sick, and compassionately lay the deceased poor in a coffin and afterwards bury [them]. He who does so, he does himself a great benefit. Because a certain time will come to each of us, that it would be dearer to us than all that we then leave behind us in the world, had we done there while we were able that which was pleasing to God. But then we shall have a just reward for that which we did previously in life. Woe to the one then, who before earned the torment of hell. There eternal fire is cruelly mixed and there is eternal terror; there is eternal pain and there is sorrowing and lamentation and everlasting grief; there is the bite of bonds and the din of blows; there is the sting of serpents and the clutch of every want; there is wailing and groaning; there is every misery and the press of all the devils. Woe to the one then, who must there dwell in torment; it were better for him that he had never become

mann nære æfre geworden, þonne he gewurde; forðam nis se man on life, þe
areccan [p. 54] mæge ealle þa yrmða, þe se gebidan sceal, se ðe on þa witu ealles
behreoseð; and hit is ealles þe wyrse, þe his ænig ende ne cymð æfre to worulde.

100   Ðis gewrit sægð get forð, þæt drihten swore að swiðe, gif men ne woldon get
geswican untidweorces, þæt God wolde sendan æerest hungor and adla on manna ceap^z,
ær þæt fyr come on heo^a, and heo^b mid mislicre seocnesse æt mannum genyman^c.[32]
And þis he deð, forðam þe se sunnandæg is swiðe micelum gecoren eallum [p. 55]
Godes gesceaftum, forðam þe he wæs ealra daga se æresta, and he bið eft se nexta^d.[33]
And on þone dæg drihten of deaðe aras; and forðon he wæs syððan eall genemned
105 to sunnandæge^e oð ðæs monandæges lihtincge, forþan þe drihten on þam dæge of
deaðe aras. And þæt bið gedon, þæt þusend daga bið gedon to anum sunnandæge; and
þonne on þam dæge forbyrnð heofon and eorðe and sæ and ealle þa gesceafta, þa ðe on
hym syndon. And drihten cymð on þam dæge to us, and he us [p. 56] þonne myngað
þæs sunnandæges weorces and þæs sæternesdæges ofernon and þære monannihte.
110   And on þone dæg wæs Adam gesceapen, se æresta man. And on þone dæg
Moyses oferfor þa readan sæ mid his werode drygum fotum, and his feond^f
adruncon behindan him in^g þære sæ. And on þone dæg drihten ongan ærest Israhela ^{h}folc fedan^h mid mannan^i þone heofoncundan mete.

z `yrfe´, *by a later hand*	e `fram þæs sæternesdæges none´, *by a*
a i *above line*	*later hand*
b i *above line*	f eo *expuncted*, y *above line*
c y < i, *by a later hand*	g i *expuncted*, o *above line*
d `æftemesta´, *by a later hand*	h–h folce sendan

i mannum, *marked for deletion*, mannoc *or* manna *by a later hand in left margin*

    And an þane dæg wæs Adam gescapen, se ærysta man. And an þone dæg
Moyses oferferde þa readan sæ mid his weorude, and his feond adruncan^k beæftan
him an þare se. And an þane dæg drehten angan erest fedan Israela folc in þam
50 westenne mid manan, þam heofenlican mete.
    And swiþe oft drehten bead^l þam halgan Moyse, þæt he bude manna bearnum,
þæt hio an þane dæg ne worhtan; and mycel yfel and menigfealdne wæan drihten
gehet þurh Moyses menniscum cynde. And drehten wæs sume siþe þus sprecende
to Moyse and cwæþ[12]: sprec to Israhela bearnum and cweþ to hiom: witan ge, þæt
55 ge healdan minne þane halgan rystedæg, forþan tacen is betwioh me and betwioh
iowrum kynne, and forþon is to witanne, þæt ic eam se drihten, se iow gehalgode;
and healdaþ ge forþan minne þane halgan rystedæg. And on þam dæge he awende
wæter to wine.[13] And soþlice swa hwilc iowar, swa hine besmiteþ mid ænigre
yfelnysse an þone halgan sunnandæg, þonne biþ he deaþy^m sweltende. And swa
60 hwylc man, swa his weorc deþ an þane halgan sunnandeg, þanne weorpaþ^n þæs
mannes lif and saule of þam heape mines folces. Hwylcne deaþ mende he drehten
swiþor, þonne þæs mannes sawle scolde bion cwælmed in þæm^o mestan helle-
fyre, and þæt hio wære afelled of eallum haligan hepe?

k adru`n´can	n weorþaþ
l bead < dead	o æ < a
m deaþy < deady	

a man, when he became [one]; because there is no man alive who may relate all those miseries which he must endure who falls entirely into those torments, and it is all the worse for him that its end will never come in eternity.

This letter says yet further that the Lord strongly swore an oath, if men would still not cease from work done at an improper time that God would send first hunger and diseases to the cattle of men, before that fire comes upon them, and they will be taken with diverse sickness from men. And this he will do because Sunday is very dear to all God's creatures, because it was of all days the first, and it will also be the last. And on that day the Lord arose from death; and therefore it was afterwards universally called Sunday (from the ninth hour of Saturday) until Monday dawn, because the Lord arose from death on that day. And that will be done, that a thousand days will come to one Sunday; and then on that day heaven and earth and the sea and all those creatures which are in them will burn up. And the Lord will come to us on that day, and he will then remind us of the labours of Sunday and Saturday afternoon and Monday eve.

And on that day Adam was created, the first man. And on that day Moses crossed the Red Sea with his multitude with dry feet, and his enemies drowned behind him in that sea. And on that day the Lord first began to feed the people of Israel with manna, the heavenly food.

And on that day Adam was created, the first man. And on that day Moses crossed the Red Sea with his multitude, and his enemies drowned behind him in that sea. And on that day the Lord first began to feed the people of Israel in the desert with manna, the heavenly food.

And very often the Lord commanded holy Moses that he urge the children of men that they should not work on that day, and great evil and manifold miseries the Lord promised through Moses to mankind. And the Lord was at one time speaking thus to Moses and said: Speak to the children of Israel and say to them: Know that you should keep my holy rest-day, because [it] is a sign between me and your nation, and therefore it is to be understood that I am the Lord, who sanctified you, and keep therefore my holy rest-day. And on that day he turned water into wine. And truly whichever of you defiles himself with any evil on that holy Sunday, then he will suffer death. And whichever man does his work on holy Sunday, then may they cast out the life and soul of that man from the company of my people. What death did the Lord mean more than [that] the soul of that man should be tormented in the greatest hell-fire, and that he would be cast down from all the holy company?

And drihten cwæð þæt six dagas syndan, þæt eow is alefed[j] eowre weorc on to
115 wyrcenne, ac se [p. 57] seofoða is min se halga restendæg.[34] And ealle, þa ðe on
ðam dæge doð heora weorc, þonne beoð þa deaðe sweltende; and se deað bið on
helle deopnesse. And healdað ge, Israhela bearn, minne restendæg[k] and mærsiað
hine in[l] eowrum cynne, forðan se eca treowa is betwux me and Israhela bearnum.
And soðlice on six dagum wæron geworhte heofonas and eorðe[m] and ealle þa
120 gesceafta, þa ðe on hym syndon; and þa on þam seofoðan dæge ablan[n] drihten
fram ælcum weorce.

And þa gebyrede [p. 58] hit on sume tide, þæt Dathan and Abiron and Choreb, þa
ðreo[o] ealdormen, noldon wurðian þone halgan sunnandæg, swa swa hym beboden
wæs ægðer ge þurh Moyses ge þurh urne drihten sylfne.[35] And hy wurdon Godes
125 wyðerwinnan[p] and forheoldon teoðunge and ælc oðer þing þe to Godes handa
belimpan sceolde. And þa forwurdon hy sona, and seo eorðe þa tobærst under
hym, and hy þa feollon þurh ða eorðan nyðer[q] mid eallum heora werode, and hy
wurdon ealle besencte mid sawle and mid licha[p. 59]man in[r] helle deopnesse.

j y *above first* e
k -re *over erasure*
l i *expuncted*, o *above line*
m eorðan
n ł gereste *in right margin, insertion mark before* ablan

o y *above line*
p y < i, *by a later hand*
q y < i, *by a later hand*
r o *above line*

And drehten eft cwæþ: .vi. dagas sindon, þæt iow is alefed, þæt ge motan iower
65 weorc an wyrcan.[34] And se seofoþa ys drehtnes se halga restedæg. And ealle, þa þe
doþ heora wæorc an þam dæge, þanne bioþ þa deaþes sceldige; se deaþ biþ þonne
in helle diopnesse. Ac healdaþ, Israela bearn[p], þone minne halgan rystedæg[q] and
mærsiaþ hine in iowrum ciricum[r], forþon[s] [84v] sio æce triowþ is betwioh me and
betwioh[t] Israela bearnum. And soþlice on six dagum wæran geworhte heofan and
70 eorþe and ealle þa gescæfta, þe in hiom sindan; and þa on þæne .vii. dæg þa let
drehten fram æghwilcum weorce and hine gereste þa on þam dæge. And he þa
þær anstealde him self æryst hu mæn scoldan þone halgan sunnandæg healdan
and haligan.

Þa weran an þare þiode .iii. ealdormen on Israhela folce, and þa noldan drehtnes
75 beboda healdan, ac ciddan ongen Moyses and age Aaron[u] his broþer on Israhela
folce.[35] Dathon hatte an and Abiron and Choreb. Hi noldan weorþian þone haligan
sunnandæg, swa heom drehten bebead, ac macodan micel geflit agen Moyses on
þam Godes folce and gremedan God þearle swyþe. Þa forwurdon hi sona, and
sio iorþe tobærst undernioþan heom, and hio fillon þa þurh þa eorþan mid eallen
80 hioræ weorude, and eac wif and cild and feowertyne þusend manna,[36] and hio
wurdan þa ealle besæncte in helle diopnesse mid sawle and mid lichaman.

p b < þ
q ryrtedæg
r cir'i'cum

s *twice, repeated at the top of* 84v
t -ioh < a
u Aaron < Auron

And the Lord says that there are six days on which it is permitted for you to do your work, but the seventh is my holy rest-day. And all who do their work on that day then will suffer death, and that death will be in the abyss of hell. And keep, children of Israel, my rest-day and honour it in your nation, because there is an eternal covenant between me and the children of Israel. And truly in six days the heavens and the earth and all those creatures which are in them were made, and then on the seventh day the Lord ceased from every work.

And then it happened at one time that Dathan and Abiram and Korah, the three elders, would not honour that holy Sunday, as it was commanded to them both by Moses and by our Lord himself. And they became God's enemies and withheld the tithe and every other thing which should have belonged to God's hands. And then they perished immediately, and the earth burst apart under them, and then they fell down through the earth with all their multitude, and they were all plunged with soul and body into the abyss of hell.

And the Lord also said: There are six days in which it is permitted to you that you may do your work. And the seventh is the Lord's holy rest-day. And all those who do their work on that day then will be guilty of death; that death will then be in the abyss of hell. But keep, children of Israel, my holy rest-day and honour it in your churches, because there is an eternal covenant between me and the children of Israel and me. And truly in six days were created heaven and earth and those creatures which are in them, and then on the seventh day the Lord ceased from every work and then rested on that day. And then he himself there first established how people should observe and sanctify that holy Sunday.

Then there were in the nation, in the people of Israel, three elders, and they would not keep the commandments of the Lord, but they quarrelled with Moses and with his brother Aaron within the people of Israel. One was called Dathan, and [the others] Abiram and Korah. They would not honour that holy Sunday, as the Lord had commanded them, but they created much discord against Moses within the people of God and vexed God very greatly. Then they perished at once, and the earth burst apart under them, and then they fell through the earth with all their multitude, and women and children likewise and fourteen thousand men, and they all were plunged into the abyss of hell with soul and with body.

Swa þonne nu gegangeð manna bearnum, þæt heora sawle beoð besencte
130   in^s helle deopnesse, gif heo^t ne wyllað^u healdan þæs sunnandæges bebod and
sæternesdæges ofernon and þære monannihte. And þæt is eac cuð, þæt Iordanis^v
seo ea, þe Crist wæs on hire gefullad on sunnandæge, þæt heo getacnað þæs
dæges halgunga, forðon nis an stæpe^w, þæt heo wille oferyrnan fram nontide þæs
sæternesdæges oð ðæs monandæges lihtincge.[38] And drihten asende on sunnan-
135   dæg [p. 60] his apostolas^x þone halgan gast on fyres ansyne. And on þam dæge
wurdon todælede manna gereordu; and ær wæs eall weoruld sprecende on an
gereord, and nu synd gereord twa and hundseofontig.[39]

s o *above line*
                             v -nen *above* -is, *by a later hand*
t i *above line*
                             w æ < e
u y < i, *by a later hand*
                             x apłas, as *underlined*, on *above line*

Swa þonne nu gegangeþ manna bearnum, þæt heora sawle bioþ ascyrede in
helle diopnesse, gef hio nellaþ healdan þane halgan sunnandeg and þæs sæternesdæg ofernon. Hiom weorþ swa, swa swa þare bocere sawle biþ, þe nellaþ godspel
85   sæcgan Godes folce for hiora gemeleaste and for weoruldgalnesse. Forþon þe
Crist selfa cwæþ[37]: þeah mann anum men godspyl secge, þonne bio ic an hiora
midle; and þæm biþ, þe þæt godspel sagaþ, forgefen .c. synny, and þam fiftig, þe
hit for Godes naman lustlice gehereþ; and þam biþ wa æfre geborenum, þe hit
secgan can and ne wile forþan men sculan þurh þa godspellican lare becuman
90   to liues wige. And þæt is cuþ eac, þæt Iordane is seo ea, forþan Crist wæs in
hire gefulwad in sunnandæge, hio getacnaþ þæs dæges halgunge and weorþunge,
forþon nis nan stepe, þæt hio wile oferyrnan fram nontide þæs seternesdeges ær
þæs monandeges lihtincge.[38] Drehten cwæþ, þæt he come to demenne cwicum
and deadum an þone halgan sunnandæg; þa he mende mid þam worde þane eges-
95   lican domes dæg. And drihten ansende an sunnandege his apostolum þone halgan
gast in fyre ansyne. And an þam dege wurdan todælde ealra manna gehriorde; and
ær wæs eal weoruld sprecende an an gehriorde, and nu is ealra gehriorde twa and
hundseofentig.[39]

So then it will now befall the children of men, that their soul will be plunged into the abyss of hell, if they will not keep the command of Sunday and Saturday afternoon and Monday eve. And that is also known that the River Jordan in which Christ was baptized on Sunday, that it shows the consecration of that day because it will not flow one step from the ninth hour of Saturday until dawn on Monday. And the Lord sent to his apostles the Holy Spirit in the likeness of fire on Sunday. And on that day the languages of men were divided, and previously all the world was speaking in one language, and now there are seventy-two languages.

So then it will now befall the children of men that their soul will be banished in the abyss of hell if they will not keep holy Sunday and Saturday afternoon. It will be for them just as it will be for the soul of learned men who will not tell the gospel to God's people because of their carelessness and because of worldly lust. Wherefore Christ himself said: Though a man tell the gospel to one man, then I will be in their midst; and for the one who speaks the gospel, a hundred sins will be forgiven, and fifty for the one who gladly listens to it for God's name. And woe be to the one ever born, who is able to tell it and will not because men must come to the way of life through the gospel teaching. And that is also known that the River Jordan, because Christ was baptized in it on a Sunday, signifies the honour-ing and consecration of that day since it will not flow one step from the ninth hour on Saturday until the dawn of Monday. The Lord said that he will come to judge the living and the dead on that holy Sunday; then he meant with that statement the terrible day of Judgement. And the Lord on Sunday sent the Holy Spirit in the likeness of fire to these apostles. And on that day the languages of all men were divided, and previously all the world spoke in one language, and now the languages of all are seventy-two.

And is eac cuð þæt for þæs dæges halgunge and weorðunge ealle[y] hellware onfoð reste, gif heo[z] æfre fulluhtes onfangen hæfdon, fram nontide þæs sæternes-
140 dæges oð monandæges lihtincge.[40] And me[a] [42] þis is lang to secganne and to writanne, hu oft se an dæg wæs gehalgod, and hu oft he wæs for[p.61]boden þurh God sylfne and þurh his halgan, þæt him man on ne worhte.

And þæt is eac cuþ, [85r] þæt for þæs dæges halgunge and weorþunge þæt þa
100 sauwla onfoþ reste, þa þa beoþ on witincgstowan. Gef hi mid ænigan þingan Crist gegladodan on þisam earman life, þonne habbaþ hi reste from þære nontide þæs seternesdæges oþ þæs monandæges lihtincge. And we gelyfaþ þurh Godes gife, þæt hit swa sig, gif hi Criste her on life on ænigan þingan gecwemdon. Ac þa, þa to helle becumaþ, ne cumaþ hig næfre to reste, ah þar acwylmiaþ mid saule on
105 þam lichaman æfter domes dæge.[40] And hit is to lang eal to awritenne hu oft se an dæg wes gehalgod, and hu oft he wæs forboden þurh God sylfne and þurh Godes halgan, ðæt him nan man on ne worhte.

And þæt gelamp on Moyses dagum, þæt Moyses for þurh anne[v] wudu mid his werode; þa gesawan hie ænne ceorl, hwær he stod and wudede him.[41] Þa het
110 Moyses, þæt hine mon gebunde, and þæt hine mon dede in carcern, oðþæt he askede þone hælend, hu he me be þam ceorle don scolde. Þa freni Moyses urne drihten, hu he þane ceorl ation scolde, þe him wudade an þan halgan sunnandæg. Þa het ure drehten, þæt hine me dede of life. Hwæt, þa wes openlice getacnad[w], þæt þæt biþ senleas wite, þæt mon an þam genimþ, þe he unalefedlice werceþ
115 fram þæs sæternesdeges[x] none oþ þæs monandeges lihtincge.

v e < u
w getanad
x -deges, *twice*

And it is also known that on account of the hallowing and consecration of that day all the inhabitants of hell receive rest, if they had ever received baptism, from the ninth hour of Saturday until the dawn of Monday. And this is long for me to tell and to write how often that one day was sanctified, and how often it was forbidden by God himself and by his saints, that one work on it.

And that is also known that for the hallowing and consecration of that day, those souls receive rest who are in places of torment. If they in any way pleased Christ in this wretched life then they have rest from the ninth hour of Saturday until the dawn of Monday. And we believe by God's grace that it may be so, if here in life they pleased Christ in any thing. But those who enter hell, they will never come to rest, but will there be tormented with their soul in the body after the day of judgement. And it is too long entirely to write how often that one day was sanctified, and how often it was forbidden through God himself and through God's saints to work on it.

And that happened in the days of Moses that Moses went through a wood with his company; then they saw a certain man, where he stood and cut wood for himself. Then Moses commanded that one bind him and that one put him in prison, until he might ask the Saviour what more he should do concerning that man. Then Moses asked our Lord how he should deal with that man who cut wood for himself on holy Sunday. Then our Lord commanded that one take his life. Alas, then was openly shown that that is a sinless penalty that one take from a man what he illicitly produces from the ninth hour on Saturday until the dawn of Monday.

And Nial sæde, se diacon, se wæs fif wucan on heofonum, he sæde, þæt God
sy for sunnandæges weorcum and sæternesdæges ofernon ealra swiðost abol-
145 gen, and þæt he forðam swiðest sende misgelimpu on manna bearn. And he sæde
þæt for manna ungeleaffulnesse synd ealle þas eorðlican þing acerrede, þæt heo^b
ne syndon, swylce heo^c iu^d wæron. And drihten sende his agen handgewrit on
Sanctus Petrus heah[p.62]altare⁴³ in^e his circan, þær mæst manna færð, þæt he
get wolde his mildheortnesse on us gecyðan and us sæcgan, hu we us gehealdan
150 sceoldan wið Godes yrre, and hu he wið us gedon wolde, gif we ne woldan haldan^f
sunnandæges bebod and sæternesdæges ofernon and þære monannihte. Ða wæs
þæt gewrit þus awriten mid gyldenum stafum.

b i *above line*
c i *above line*
d ʼ**l** hwilonʼ *by a later hand*

e o *above line*
f hʼeʼaldan, *by another hand*

And Nial sede, se diacon, se wes .v. wucan an heofonum, þæt God sige sunnandeges weorcum and sæternesdeges ofernon swiþe stranlice abolgen^{y44}; and
þæt ealle þas eorþlice þing seon ancerrede for manna ungeleaffulnysse, þæt hio
ne sion swa gode, swa hio iu wæron. And hit hefþ nu ofergan eal cristen folc, þæt
120 hio sindon to gemelease^z Cristes selfes beboda and him to litelne ege to witan.
Ac hiom þæs cymþ ful ær ece hunger, ^aþam þe^a þæs fyres frecynysse gedægeþ
and þæt ofercumaþ. And drehten sende his agen handgewrit an Sancte Petres
heahaltare⁴³ in his cirican, þær mæst manna to gefereþ. And he þæt dyde, forþon
þe he wolde þa get his mildheortnesse^b an mannum gecyþan and us gecyþan, hu
125 we us gescildan scoldan wiþ Godes yrre, and hu he wiþ us gedon wolde, gef we
noldan healdan sunnandæges bebod and sæternes ofernon and þare monannihte.
And þa wæs þæt gewrit þus gewriten mid geldenum stafum.
Amen, amen, dico uobis, quod misit brucus in uobis, et non timuisti eos; soþ,
soþ is, þæt ic iow secge, þæt ic sænde ceferas an eow, and ge iow þa ne andredan.
130 [85v] Þa sende ic gershoppan anufan iowerne hwæte, and ge þa get gecyrran
noldan, þæt ge wel gehealdan woldan þone halgan sunnandeg.⁴⁵ Soþ, soþ is, þæt
ic iow sæcge, þæt ic sænde an iow birnenda renas and^c sweflen læg of heofonum,
and gef ge ne willaþ get healdan sunnandæges bebod and sæternes ofernon and
þare monannihte, þonne becumaþ get ofer iow micel Godes erre.
135 Eala hwæt, monnum iu stranglice gelamp for sunnandæges weorce, þæt
he drihten sende ceferas ofer manna bearn, þa þonne adilegedan ealle wudebeorwas for sunnandeges weorce. And þa hy drehten anget, þæt men þa get
noldan geswican untidweorca, he þa sænde wunderlice gershoppan, stapan^d
an eorþan, þæt hio^e fretan ealle eorþwæstmas butan letlan dæle. Þa andged he
140 ure drihten, þæt men noldan þa get healdan sunnandeges bebod, he sende þa
birnende regn and sweflen leg ofer manna bearn. Þa scoldan hio swiþe nioh mid

y abolgel
z gemerlease
a–a þam þe *twice*
b mild heornesse

c and, *twice*
d *likely taken into the text from a gloss*
  in exemplar
e h < þ

And Niall said, the deacon who was five weeks in the heavens, he said that God is most of all angered because of Sunday and Saturday afternoon labours, and that he therefore will most severely send exceeding misfortunes upon the children of men. And he said that because of the unbelief of men, all those earthly things are changed so that they are not such as they once were. And the Lord sent his own hand-written message onto the high altar of St Peter in his church, where the most men go, because he yet wanted to make known his mercy unto us and tell us how we should keep ourselves from God's wrath, and how he would act against us, if we would not keep the command of Sunday and Saturday afternoon and Monday eve. Then the letter was written thus with golden letters.

And Niall the deacon, he who was dead for five weeks in the heavens, said that God is very severely angered by the labours of Saturday afternoon and Sunday, and that all those earthly things have changed for man's unbelief, so that they are not as good as they once were. And it has now come upon all Christian peoples that they are too careless of Christ's own commandments and know too little fear towards them. But to them will accordingly come very soon eternal hunger, to those who survive the danger of the fire and overcome that. And the Lord sent his own hand-written message onto the high altar of St Peter in his church, where the most men go. And he did that because he still wanted to make known his mercy to men, and to show us how we may protect ourselves against God's wrath, and how he would act against us, if we would not keep the command of Sunday and of Saturday afternoon and of Monday eve. And the letter was written thus with golden letters.

Amen, amen, dico uobis, quod misit brucus in uobis, et non timuisti eos. Truly, truly, I say to you that I sent beetles upon you, and then you were not afraid. Then I sent locusts upon your grain, and yet you would not turn and keep the holy Sunday well. Truly, truly, I say to you that I will send upon you burning rains and sulphurous fire from the heavens, and if you will still not keep the command of Sunday and of Saturday afternoon and Monday eve, then there will yet come upon you God's great wrath.

Alas, severely it once befell men because of Sunday's work, in that he, the Lord, sent beetles on the children of men, who then destroyed all the groves on account of Sunday work. And when the Lord considered them, that men still would not cease from their labours at improper times, then he sent wondrous grasshoppers, locusts onto the earth, so that they devoured all the crops except a small portion. When he, our Lord, perceived that men would still not keep the command of Sunday, he sent a burning rain and sulphurous fire upon the children of men. When they would have very nearly perished entirely, then the destruction

F   ealle forweorþan, þa gehreaw him drihtne manna forwyrd, þa genam he þæt
fyr eft fram manna bearnum and his miltse let ofer manna bearnum. Þis wæs
geworden on Egipta lande.[46]

145   Hie þa heoldan letle hwile[f] sunnandeges bebod and brecan eft and noldan
geswican untidweorces. Þa sænde dryhten .v. deor up of se, and nes ænig man
þæt hiom wiþstandan mihte, ær þanne he[g] drehten eft fram mannum hi anam, þa
he geseah þæt his handgeweorc forweorþan scolde. Þa gelamp hit binnan feawe
gerum þæt menn eft oferhogodan sunnandæges bebod and sæternes[h] ofernon. Þa

150   angan drehten selfa dihtan þæt gewrit, þe her nu forþ sægeþ, and he cwæþ: soþ is,
þæt ic iow secge þæt ic iow wæs arful geworden and milde, and iow com micel of
heofonum and genihtsumes, and ge sweþeah noldan healdan be minan bebodum
þane halgan sunnandæg. Soþ is, þæt ic eow sæcge, þæt ic wæs geþyldig for iow,[47]
and ge me oft tynan gededan, þanne þearfan cleopedan to iowrum husum[i], and ge

155   hi ne noldan gehyran, ne me nane mildheortnesse noldan an heom gecyþan; and
þonne ælðiodige[j] to iow coman, þanne noldan ge hiom nan god don. Soþ, soþ is,
þæt ic iow sæcge, gef ge ne healdaþ þane halgan sunnandæg fram nontide þæs
seternesdeges oþ þæs monandeges lihtincge, þæt ealle þa yfel becumaþ eft ofer
iow, þe iow ær an becoman and her beufan gewritene sindon. Ic eom Godes sunu,

160   and ic feola geþrowade for iow, ic wæs [86r] an rode ahangen for iow, and ic deaþ
geþrowade for iow, and ic of deaþe aras for iow an þone halgan sunnandeg, and ic
an heofonas astah an þone halgan eastorsunnandæg, and ic sitte nu an þa swiþran
healfe God fæder, and ic cume to demenne cwicum and deadum an þone halgan
sunnandæg.[48] Þa he þanne mende þane egeslican domes deg. Hwæt, he drihten

165   þa openlice cydde on þam worde, þa he cwæþ, þæt an sunnandæg of deaþe arise,
þæt se sæternesdæg biþ þæs sunnandeges, siþþan hit non biþ, forþon hit wæs
sunnændæg, þa drihten self of deaþe aras. Crist selfa and ealle halgan hefdan for
sunnandeg þone dæg, þe Crist aras of deaþe.

    And from nontide þæs sæternesdæges oþ þæs monandæges lihtincge ge

170   sceolan[k] heoldan, and gef hit eorþlice men anwændaþ, þonne ne onfoþ hio næfre
dæl drehtnes wuldres. And drehten wæs þa get forþ sprecende, and he cwæþ:
soþ, soþ is, þæt ic iow sæcge, se þe ne gehealdaþ þane halgan sunnandeg, minne
restandæg, þe ic of deaþe aras, mid rihte fram nontide þæs sæternesdæges oþ þæs
monandæges lihtincge, þæt he biþ awerged aa in weorulde weoruld, and ic him

175   wiþsacæ, þonne he of þisan life gewit, and he ne hafaþ næfre dæl mid me ne mid
minan ænglum to heofonan rice.[49]

    Ealle fyþerfete nytenu[50] cleopiaþ to me, and ic hio gehære, and hiom nillaþ
reste forgefan an þone halgan sunnandeg. Soþ is iow sæcge, gef ge ne healdaþ
þone halgan sunnandeg mid rihte, þæt ic sænde gyt ofer iow micele stormas and

180   hagolstanas and fleogende neddran, þa ge abera ne megan, and sweflicne[l] leg;[51]
and ic lete hæþen folc ofer iow, þa iow fornimaþ and iowra bearn.[52]

f wile
g hie
h n < a
i h < a

j ælþeoðiodige
k a < u
l swelicne

164

of men grieved him, the Lord, [and] then he removed that fire again from the children of men and allowed his mercy [to come] upon the children of men. This happened in the land of the Egyptians.

Then they kept the commandment of Sunday for a little while, and broke [it] again and would not cease from their untimely work. Then the Lord sent five beasts up from the sea, and there was no man who might withstand them, before the Lord removed them again from men, when he saw that his handiwork must perish. Then it happened within a few years that men again neglected the commandment of Sunday and of Saturday afternoon. Then the Lord himself began to dictate that letter which now here goes on, and he said: Truly, I say to you that I had become compassionate towards you and merciful, and much came to you from the heavens and great abundance, and you nevertheless would not keep holy Sunday in accordance with my commandments. Truly, I say to you that I was patient with you, and you often did injury to me when the poor cried out to your houses, and you would not listen to them, nor would show me any mercy in them; and when foreigners came to you, then you would not do any good for them. Truly, truly, I say to you, if you will not keep holy Sunday, from the ninth hour of Saturday until the dawn of Monday, that all those evils will come upon you again which before came upon you and are here written above. I am God's son, and I suffered much for you; I was hung on the cross for you, and I suffered death for you, and arose from death on holy Sunday, and I ascended into the heavens on that holy Easter Sunday, and I sit now on the right side of God the Father, and I will come to judge the living and the dead on holy Sunday. Then he meant that terrible day of Judgement. Alas, he, the Lord, openly made known in that statement, when he said that on Sunday [he] would arise from death, that Saturday after the ninth hour belongs to Sunday, because it was a Sunday when the Lord himself arose from death. Christ himself and all the saints count Sunday as that day on which Christ arose from death.

And from the ninth hour of Saturday until the dawn of Monday, you must keep [it], and if earthly men transgress it then they will never have a part of the Lord's glory. And the Lord was then still speaking further, and he said: Truly, truly, I say to you, he who does not keep properly holy Sunday, my rest-day, on which I arose from death, from the ninth hour of Saturday until the dawn of Monday, that he will be accursed for ever in eternity, and I will reject him when he departs from this life, and he will never have a part with me nor with my angels in the kingdom of the heavens.

All four-footed beasts cry out to me and I hear them, and they will not give them rest on holy Sunday. Truly I say to you, if you do not keep holy Sunday properly, that I will yet send upon you great storms and hailstones and flying serpents, which you will not be able to endure, and sulphurous fire. And I will cause a heathen people [to come] upon you, who will destroy you and your children.

Amen, amen, dico uobis. Soð is, soð is, þæt ic eow secge: gif ge healdað þone
sunnandæg mid rihte, þonne ontyne ic eow heofona [p. 63] rices duru, and ic eow
155 sylle manigfealde wæstmas minra bletsunga on eowrum husum to nytte oð ende
eowres lifes. And gif ge beoð gehwyrfde to me and to minum halgum, swa hwæs
swa ge me^g biddað on minum naman, eall ic hit eow selle. And ic blissige on eow
and ge on me; and ge beoð halige, forþan ic eam eower drihten, and nis ænig
oðer butan me.[53] And ic swerige þurh mine mihte and þurh mine englas, cherubin
160 and seraphim, þa clypiað freabrihtum stefnum and þus [p. 64] cweðað: sanctus,
sanctus, sanctus, dominus, deus sabaoth.

    Ða cwæð drihten God: þurh heora mihte ic swerige, gif ge ne^h healdað þone
sunnandæg mid rihte, þonne cymð ren and hagolstanas ofer eow, and micel fyr
bið onæled ofer eow. And ic þonne forbærne ealle þa fyrenfulleⁱ, þa ðe foran to
165 unriht wyrceð, oððe on þam dæge him hlaf baceð oððe hine baðað oððe his fex
efesað oððe hine scerð oððe on þam dæge oðerne swingð oððe his hus feormað,
oððe he unalyfedlice gegæð on þam dæge, þæt he sy werig, oððe [p. 65] ænig
unriht gefremme on þam dæge.[55] Ða þe hit doð, þonne beoð þa awergede^j fram me
in^k þa ecan witu and heora bearn butan ende.

g me *expuncted*	j y *above first* e
h *added above line by main hand*	k o *above line*
i y < i *by a later hand*	

    Soþ ys þæt ic iow sæcge, gef ge healdaþ þone halgan sunnandeg mid rihte,
mid ælmessan and mid ciricsocnum, swa mon sunnandeg don scel, weorþian
mid eallan weorþmendum minne restandæig, þonne ontyne ic iow heofenas þeo-
185 dan, and ic selle iow menigfealde wæstmas sylle and mine bletsunge an iowrum
husum to nytte a oþ ænde eowres lifes, and ge þonne bioþ gehwærfede to me
and to minan halgan, and þonne swa hwæs swa ge biddaþ an minan naman,
eal ic iow sille^m. And ic blissige an iow and ge on me; and ge bioþ halige,
forþon ic eam eowar drihten, and nis ænig oþer butan me anum.[53] Soþ is, þæt
190 ic iow sæcge, þæt ic swerige þurh minne miht and þurh mine þa halgan ænglas,
cherubin and særaphin, þa send cleopiende beorhtum stefnum and þus cweþaþ:
sanctus, sanctus, sanctus, dominus deus sabaothⁿ, pleni sunt celi et terra.

    Þa cwæþ ure [86v] drihten: þurh hiora mihte ic swerige, gef ge ne healdaþ
þane haligan sunnandeg mid rihte, þonne cymeþ micel reng and snaw and micele
195 hagolstanas ofer iow, and micel fer biþ anberned ymb þa monþas utan, þe^o synt
hatene September and October.[54] And ic þanne wille forbærnan ealle eower god
and ealle, þa þe an unrihtum tidum yfel wyrcaþ, oþþe he an þæm dege oþerne
swinggæþ^p, oððe he hus feormaþ oþþe hlafes bakeþ oþþe swereþ oþþe cnytt,
oþþe he hine baþaþ, oþþe he hine efeseþ, oþþe he hine scirþ, oþþe he unalefedlice
200 an þam dege gegeð, þæt he werig biþ, oþþe he ænige unrihtnesse an þan dæge
gefremeþ[55]; þa þe hit doþ, witan hie þanne, þæt hio bioþ ealle awergde fram me in
þa æcan wita and hiora bearn ealle butan æghwilcum ænde.

m wille	o þ < w
n sabaoht	p swing gæþ

Amen, amen, dico vobis. Truly, truly I say to you, if you keep Sunday properly, then I will open the gate of the kingdom of the heavens for you, and I will give you the manifold fruits of my blessings as a benefit in your houses until the end of your life. And if you are converted to me and to my saints, whatsoever you ask in my name, I will give it all to you. And I will rejoice in you and you in me; and you will be holy, because I am your Lord, and there is none other except me. And I swear by my might and by my angels, Cherubim and Seraphim, who cry out with very bright voices and speak thus: *Sanctus, sanctus, sanctus, dominus deus Sabaoth.*

Then the Lord God said: By their might I swear, if you do not keep Sunday properly, then rain and hailstones will come upon you, and a great fire will be ignited over you. And then I will burn up all the sinful who previously worked wrongly: whether [he] bakes bread for himself on that day, or bathes himself, or cuts his hair or shaves himself, or on that day flogs another, or cleans his house, or travels unlawfully on that day, so that he may be weary, or would do any wrong on that day. Those who do it, then they and their children will be accursed by me into eternal torments without end.

Truly I say to you, if you keep holy Sunday properly, with alms-giving and with church attendance, as one should do on Sunday, to celebrate with all honours my rest-day, then I will open for you the channels of heaven, and I will give you manifold fruits and my blessings as a benefit in your houses for ever until the end of your life, and you will then be converted to me and to my saints and then whatever you ask in my name, I will give [it] all to you. And I will rejoice in you and you in me, and you will be holy, because I am your Lord, and there is none other except me alone. Truly I say to you that I swear by my might and by my holy angels, Cherubim and Seraphim, who are crying out with bright voices and speak thus: *Sanctus, sanctus, sanctus, dominus deus sabaoth, pleni sunt celi et terra . . .*

Then our Lord said: By their might I swear, if you do not keep holy Sunday properly, then a great rain and snow and great hailstones will come upon you, and a great fire will be ignited around the end of these months which are called September and October. And I will then burn up all your goods and all those who at unlawful times work evil: whether on that day he flogs another or cleans his house, or bakes bread, or swears, or binds [someone] or bathes, or cuts his hair, or shaves, or travels unlawfully on that day, so that he is weary, or he does any wrong on that day; those who do it, they should know then that they will all and all their children be accursed by me into eternal torments without any end.

167

E 170   Men þa leofestan, syn we þonne gemyndige ure sawle þearfe ægðer ge his rædes ge his mildheortnesse. And iu geara ure yldran ne woldan sunnandæges bebodu healdan; þa wearð drihten hym swyðe eorre[l], swa swa hit be us awriten is, and he ða sende of heofonum beornende[m] ren and swælende leg, and he acwealde mid þy brogan mycelne dæl þisses [p. 66] mennisces cynnes. And þa

175   he geseh manna forwyrd, þæt heo[n] wæron cwelende[o] in[p] þam fyre, þa gereaw him eft, þæt his handgeweorc swylc sar þrowian sceolde. Þa anam he þæt fyr fram manna bearnum. And eft ymbe lytel ongan mancyn eft abeligan God for sunnandæges weorcum, and þa ongan drihten writan[q] þæt gewrit bufan þam seofoðan heofone be sunnandæges weorcum, swa hit herbeforan sægð. And

180   nu doð men þam gelicost syððan, swylce hit wære idel spell and unsoð. Nu he [p. 67] þonne gyt hine to ðam geeadmedde, þæt he Nial þone diacon of deaðe awehte, to ðam þæt he mihte cyðan Godes folce þæt towearde yrre. And þa ðe nu get ne gelefað þisses, þonne bið heom, swa swa þam bocerum bið, þa ðe nellað heora boccræftas Godes folce wel nytte gedon. Forðon þæt Godes folc sceal

185   becuman to lifes wege þurh þa godspellican lare.

l y *above* eo   o cwellende
m y *above* eo   p o *above line*
n i *above line*   q writen

Dearest people, may we then be mindful of the need of our soul, both for his wisdom and for his mercy. And long ago our ancestors would not keep the commands of Sunday. Then the Lord became very angry with them, just as it is written about us, and he then sent from the heavens a burning rain and a burning fire, and he killed with that terror a great part of mankind. And when he saw the destruction of men, that they were dying in that fire, then it again grieved him that his handiwork had to suffer such pain. Then he removed that fire from the children of men. And again after a short time, mankind began again to provoke God to anger on account of their Sunday labours, and then the Lord began to write that letter above the seventh heaven about the labours of Sunday, as it here before says. And now men act just as if it were an empty tale and untrue. Now then he has yet humbled himself to that extent that he awakened Niall the deacon from death, in order that he might make known to God's people the coming wrath. And those who now still do not believe this, then it will be for them just as it will be for those teachers who do not want to make their book-learning very useful for the people of God. Because God's people must come to the way of life through the evangelical teaching.

And æghwylcum men is beboden þurh God sylfne on Cristes naman and on
þære halgan þrynnesse naman [p. 68] and on þære soðan annesse naman and on
drihtnes rode naman, þe he sylf on þrowade, ðæt swa hwylc man, swa þis godspell hæbbe on his gewealde, þæt he hit cyðe Godes folce swyðe genehhe swa
190 þurh hyne[r] sylfne, swa þurh oðerne gelæredne man, swa he þonne eðest mæge.
And gif he þonne gemeleas læt licgan þis gewrit unnyt Gode and Godes folce,
þonne cweð se hælend and að sweræð, þæt he sy awerged[s] fram him and fram his
halgum.[56]

Men þa leofestan, hwæt, Florentius se papa[57] and Petrus se [p. 69] biscop
195 wæron on ða tid on Rome, þa þis gewrit becom on Sanctus Petrus weofod, and
heo[t] wæron þa selestan and þa gecorenestan witan [u]ægðer ge[u] Gode ge mannum.
Soðlice heo[v] wæron gewitan, þæt þis halige gewrit of heofonum com, and heo[w]
ða forðan þus cwædon and micclum cyddon[58]: wit sweriað þurh ðone micclan
anweald mihtiges drihtnes and þurh þa halgan rode, þe Crist for manna hælo on
200 þrowade, þæt hit is soð, þæt wit secgað, ðæt fram nænigum eorðlicum handgewe-
orce næs seo boc awriten, ac on [p. 70] Sanctus Petrus hehaltare hit wæs funden
þus awriten mid gyldenum stafum. Hwylc man is þonne æfre, butan his heorte sy

r y < i *by a later hand*
s y *above first* e
t i *above line*

u–u `ægðer ge´ *by main hand*
v i *above line*
w i *above line*

[q]Ond eghwilcan[q] men is beboden þurh God selfne in Cristes noman and in þaræ
halgan þrinnesse naman and in þare halgan anesse naman and in þare halgan rode
205 naman, þe drihten self an þrowade, se þe hebbe þis gospel an his gewealde, þæt
he hit bodige and cyþe swiþe gelomlice Godes folce swa þurh hine selfne, gef he
gelæred sie, swa þurh oþerne gelæredne mon, þonne he him to cume.[57] And gef
he þonne þæt agemeleaseþ, þæt he lætaþ licgan þis godspyl unnet Godes folce,
þæt hit ne nan mynstermon na sægþ, þonne cweþ drihten and þus aþ swor, þæt
210 he wære awyrged fram him and fram eallum his halgum in þa æcan witu. And þis
bioþ þa monþas September and October, þæt þys fyr an becymþ, þe se diacon ær
bi segde, þæt drihten us to sendan wolde.

Florentius se papa[57] and Petrus se bescup wæron on þa tid on Rome, þa þis
gewrit becom anufan Sancte Petres wiofode, and hie wæran [r]þa salestan[r] witan
215 and þa betstan gecorenestan[s] egþer ge Gode ge mannum. Soþlice hie þæs wæran
gewitan, þæt þis halige gewrit of heofonum com, and hio hit fundan anufan Sancte[t]
Petres altare. And hie þa forþan þus cwædan and miclum cyþdan[58]: wit swerigaþ
þurh þane micelan anwald ures dryhtenes and þurh þa halgan Cristes rode, þe he
for manna helo aþrowade, þæt hit is eal soþ, þæt wit sæcgaþ, þæt fram nanum
220 eorþlicum men þios dryhtnes ærendboc awriten ne wæs, ne mid bocblece,[59] ne mid

q–q *on* deghwilcan
r–r þas alestan

s gorenestan
t Sce, *abbreviation mark omitted*

And to each man is commanded through God himself in Christ's name and in the name of the holy Trinity and in the name of the true Unity and in the name of the Lord's cross, on which he himself suffered, that whichever man who may have this gospel in his power, that he make it known to the people of God very frequently, either through himself, or through another learned man, as he may then most easily [do it]. And if, negligent, he then lets this letter lie useless to God and to God's people, then the Saviour says and swears an oath that he be accursed by him and by his saints.

Dearest people, alas, Florentius the pope and Peter the bishop were at that time in Rome, when this letter came onto the altar of St Peter, and they were the best and choicest wise men both to God and to men. Truly they were witnesses that this holy letter came from the heavens, and they therefore spoke thus and greatly made it known: We two swear through the great power of the mighty Lord and through the holy cross on which Christ suffered for the salvation of men, that it is true what we two say, that that book was not written by any earthly handiwork, but it was found written thus with golden letters on St Peter's high altar. What man is there, unless his heart be utterly pierced with the arrows of the devil, that

And to each man is commanded through God himself in Christ's name and in the name of the holy Trinity and in the name of the holy Unity and in the name of the holy cross, on which the Lord himself suffered, he who has this gospel in his power, that he preach it and make it known very often to God's people, either through himself, if he be learned, or through another learned man, should he come to him. And if he then neglects that, so that he lets this gospel lie useless to God's people, so that no churchman tells it, then the Lord said and thus swore an oath that he be accursed by him and by all his saints into eternal torments. And this will be during the months of September and October that this fire will come which the deacon spoke about before, that the Lord would send it to us.

Florentius the pope and Peter the bishop were at that time in Rome when this letter came upon St Peter's altar, and they were the best wise men and the best and choicest both to God and to men. Truly, they were witnesses of this, that this holy letter came from the heavens, and they found it above St Peter's altar. And they then moreover thus spoke and greatly made known: We two swear by the great power of our Lord and by the holy cross of Christ, on which he suffered for the salvation of men, that it is all true, what we say, that this message of the Lord was written by no earthly man, nor with ink, nor with any earthly substance, but was

eall mid deofles strælum awrecen, þæt he wene, þæt se halga papa and se biscop
dorston swerian mænne að þurh swa miclan mægenþrymme?

205 And hit gebyrede on ða tid, þe þis gewrit becom on Sanctus Petrus weofod,
þæt eall seo stow wearð onrered, and heo abifode eall, and seo byrgen wæs open
geworden and unhlidod, þær Sanctus Petrus lichama inne læg. And gif ge nellað
ge[p. 71]lefan^x, men þa leofestan, þæs ærendgewrites, þonne ne^y geþencað^z ge na,
hu þæt^a deofol þam ancre sæde, hwylc hit in helle wære to wunianne.

210 Ðæt gelamp iu þæt an halig ancer genam ænne deofol and began hine ðreatigan,
þæt he him sæde, hwylc hit on helle wære.[63] And þa cwæð se deofol to ðam ancre:
ne mæg nænig man wordum asecgan fram þam susle þe in^b þære helle is. Ða
cwæð se deofol to þam ancre: þeah ðe seofan men sittan on middanearde, and heo
mihton sprecan on æghwylcere [p. 72] þeode (þe betwux heofonum and eorðan
215 wære þara is twa and hundseofontig^c) and þara manna æghwylc a to life gesceapen
wære, and þara æghwylc hæfde seofon heafda, and þara heafda gehwylc seofon

x y *above second* e   a `se´, þæt *underlined*
y *added at end of line*   b o *above line*
z geþenceð   c `gereorda´, *by a later hand*

nenigum eorþlicum andweorce^u, ac hit wæs^v on Sancte Petres heahaltare funden
þis gewrit þus awriten mid geldnum stafum. Men þa leofestan, hwilc man is þonne
efre, butan his heorte se eal mid deofles strealum awrecan, þæt he wæne, þæt se
halga papa and se biscup dorstan swerigan [87r] menne aþ þurh^w micel megen?

225 And hit gelamp an þa tid, þe þis gewrit becom anufan Sancte Petres wefode^x,
þæt se stow^y wearþ eal onhrered, and hio abiofode eal, and sio bergen wearþ open
geworden and unhlidod, þe Sancte Petres lichama an leg under þam weofode. And
gef eorþlice men nu agemeleasiaþ þisæs gewrites bebodes, þonne ne geþæncaþ
hio na, hu strang hit biþ an helle to bionne.

230 Þonne ^zmanaþ us^z þis halige gewrit, þæt we simle sion gemynegode^a to ure
saule þearfe and þæs ytmestan deges ures lifes and þæs gedales lichoman and
saule.[60] And þonne we sculon ælces unnyttes ^briht ageldan^b an þene bifigendan
domes dege for eallum þam weorcum, þe we nu wiþ Godes willan wercaþ from
nontide þæs sæternesdæges oð ðes monandeges lihtinge. And eac we sculan þær
235 riht ageldan for ures lifes dede, þe we siþ oþþe ær efre gefremedan fram ures
lifes fruman. Ne megan wy þanne ure misdeda behedan ne bedigligan, ac hio
bioþ þanne ealle opene and unwrigene beforan us, butan hio ær geanddette^c bion

u ᛣweorce   z–z mana þus
v `wæs´   a geynegode
w þus   b–b rihta geldan
x w < a   c geᛣdette
y stod

would believe that the holy pope and the bishop dared to swear a false oath by such great might?

And it happened at that time, when this letter came onto St Peter's altar, that all that place became disturbed and it shook entirely, and the tomb was opened and became uncovered where the body of St Peter lay within. And if you will not believe this letter, dearest people, then you are not considering how that devil spoke to the anchorite, what it would be to dwell in hell.

It once happened that a certain holy anchorite took a certain devil and began to threaten him so that he would tell him what it would be [to dwell] in hell. And then the devil said to that anchorite: No man may tell with words about that torment which there is in hell. Then the devil said to that anchorite. Though seven men sit on the earth, and they may speak in each language (of which between the heavens and earth there are seventy-two) and each of those men were ever created for life [i.e. created to live for ever], and each of them had seven heads and each

found on St Peter's high altar, this letter thus written with golden letters. Dearest people, what man is there, unless his heart be entirely pierced with the devil's arrows, that he would believe that the holy pope and the bishop dared to swear a false oath [by] such great might.

And it happened at that time, when this letter came upon St Peter's altar, that that place became all disturbed, and it shook entirely, and the tomb was opened and became uncovered, in which St Peter's body lay under the altar. And if earthly men now neglect the commandment of this letter, then they are not considering how severe it will be to be in hell.

Then this holy letter admonishes us that we be always mindful of our soul's need and of the last day of our life and the separation of body and soul. And then we must render an account for each unprofitable thing on that terrible day of judgement for all those works which we now do against God's will from the ninth hour of Saturday until the dawn of Monday. And likewise we must render an account for the deeds of our life, which we ever did from the beginning of our life. Nor may we then conceal nor hide our misdeeds, but they will then be all open and unconcealed before us, unless they were previously confessed and atoned for. And

tungan, and þara tungena gehwylc isene stemne, ne magon heo^d ariman ealle þa
wita, þe on helle syndon.[64] Men ða leofestan, gemunan we nu forðan þone halgan
sunnandæg, forðan þe he is ealra daga fyrmest, and he wæs se æresta, and he
220 bið eft se nexta. Forðan, men, biddan we urne drihten [p. 73] ælmihtigne, þæt he
us forgife ure gyltas and ure synna, ða þe we æfre geworhtan on urum life, þæt
we magan and motan becuman to ðam ecan life þæs heofoncundlican rices, ðær
we motan a orsorhlice libban and rixian mid urum hælende and mid eallum his
halgum, mid fæder and mid suna and mid þam halgan gaste a in^e ealra worulda
225 woruld a butan ende.[65] Amen.

d i *above line*   e o *above line*

———————

and gebette. And us mon þanne nenigre deda grimlicor ne mengaþ þanne þæs
seternesdeges weorces, siþþan hit non biþ, oþ þæs monandeges lihtinge, buton
240 manslihte and ciricbryca and hlafordswicunga. Gef we þonne, men,[61] willaþ
gewercan Godes willan and þone sunnandeg gehealdan, þonne magon æghweþer
ge us heofona rices eadignesse^d geearnian, ge we megan gesæliglice befleon þa
deorcan and þa dimman stowe helletintrego, þe deofol an wunaþ mid his wea-
gesiþum and mid þam awergdum saulum, þa þanne noldan healdan þises gewrites
245 bebod, þe dryhten ^{e}self awrat^e, ac hlestan deofles larum and noldan to Gode
gecyrran þurh soþe anddetnesse^f and þurh soþe bote. Wa la wa biþ þam mannum,
þe mid deoflum scealan habban heora eardungstowe,[62] þær biþ sar butan frofre,
and ærmþo butan are, and wæana ma þonne hit eniges mannes gemet sie þæt hit
asecgan mege. Dryhten, se an heofonum rixaþ, gescylde us wiþ hellewitu, wiþ
250 þa ecan clammas þurh his wuldar and þurh his weorþment a butan^g ende. Amen.

d n < a   f ꝼdetnesse
e–e selfa wrat   g but::

———————

174

of their heads seven tongues, and each of those tongues an iron voice, they [still] could not enumerate all those torments which are in hell. Dearest people, let us therefore remember now holy Sunday, because it is of all days the foremost and it was the first, and it will be the last. Therefore, people, let us ask our almighty Lord that he forgive our offences and our sins, those which we have ever performed in our life, so that we can and may attain that eternal life of that heavenly kingdom, where we may always live without anxiety and rule with our Saviour and with all his saints, with Father and with Son and with the Holy Spirit for ever and ever without end. Amen.

for no deed will one admonish us more severely than for the work of Saturday after the ninth hour, until the dawn of Monday, except for manslaughter, breaking into a church and betrayal of one's lord. If we then, men, want to do God's will and keep Sunday, then we may both earn for ourselves the blessedness of the kingdom of the heavens, and we may blessedly flee the dark and gloomy place of hell's torments in which the devil dwells with his companions in woe and with the accursed souls, who then would not keep the commandment of this letter, which the Lord himself wrote, but listened to the teachings of the devil and did not want to turn to God through true confession and true atonement. Woe to those men who must have their dwelling-place among devils, where there will be pain without comfort, and miseries without mercy and more woes than it may be any man's ability to tell them. The Lord, who reigns in the heavens, protect us from the torments of hell, from those eternal fetters, by his glory and by his honour, for ever without end. Amen.

Commentary

Letter A

1, *Mẹn þa leofestan, halie, soðlice*: these words are added above the line in the same hand, but do not correspond to anything in the Latin source. Perhaps they were added to improve the introduction, making it sound more like the beginning of a sermon.

2. BN lat. 12,270 (printed in Appendix I) states that the city was Armenia. BN lat. 12,270 and Letter A shorten the travels of the Sunday Letter considerably; compare the list at the beginning of Letter B.

3. Whereas the Latin suggests that those present asked to understand the reasons for the letter's appearance, the Old English suggests that the letter itself states these reasons. In addition, the Old English translator does not connect its arrival on a Sunday with its message of Sunday observance as the Latin does.

4. *On sunnandæg . . . ofer eow*: the list of restrictions generally follows BN lat. 12,270 but omits trade (*mercatum non facientes*, Appendix I, line 12) which, in any case, seems superfluous with the following mention of buying and selling. The Old English also contains an item not in the Latin: the baking of bread. This prohibition is not a regular feature of Recension I, occurring only in the fifteenth-century copy in Graz 248. It is, however, common in Recension II, as in Munich 9550 *panem coxerit* (Delehaye, 'Note', p. 179); cf. C99 *bread bace*, D60 *hlafas bace*, E165 *hlaf baceð*, F198 *hlafes bakeþ*). The Penitential of Theodore also forbids the baking of bread (see Chapter 2, p. 29). For *ofer eow* (BN lat. 12,270 *super nos*) see the Tarragona manuscript: *super vos* (Priebsch, *Letter from Heaven*, p. 35).

5. Cf. Exodus XX.11.

6. No other copies of Recension I have this comment. If the translator's Latin source had the sinful and righteous spending 5220 years in hell as does BN lat. 12,270, he is probably responsible for changing it to 5228. Ultimately, the 5228 figure goes back to discussions of the ages of the world found in various patristic and later medieval sources, including several Old English texts; Eusebius, for instance, assigns this number to the period from creation to Christ's preaching of the Sermon on the Mount; see H. Tristram, *Sex aetates mundi: Die Weltzeitalter bei den Angelsachsen und den Iren: Untersuchungen u. Texte* (Heidelberg, 1985), p. 22. Of interest here is the frequency of this number in the table of Anglo-Saxon and Irish sources provided by Tristram (pp. 36–49), especially the occurrence in BL Cotton Caligula A.xv, 139b: *Adam wæs on helle æfter his forðsiðe ꝺ ealle þa gewitenan sawla mid him oð þone dæg þe ure drihten crist þrowode þæt is þonne*

177

.v. þusend geare ⁊ cc. geara ⁊ xxviii geara Adam hæfde (ed. A. Napier, 'Alteng-lische Kleinigkeiten', *Anglia* 11 (1889), 1–10 at 7). The figure may have also been familiar to our translator from one of the multiple copies of Vercelli XIX.45–8 which states: *Nigon hund wintra ⁊ þritig wintra Adam lifde on þysse worulde on geswince ⁊ on yrmþe, ⁊ syððan to helle for, ⁊ þær grimme witu þolode fíf þusend wintra ⁊ twa hund wintra ⁊ eahta ⁊ .xx. wintra.* The Latin source of this passage appears to be a sermon from a St Père-type homiliary as seen in Pembroke 25, item 34 (Scragg, *Vercelli Homilies*, pp. 310–14). A similar statement, perhaps derived from this homily, appears in the prose *Solomon and Saturn* (*The Prose Solomon and Saturn and Adrian and Ritheus*, ed. J. E. Cross and T. D. Hill (Toronto, 1982), p. 27, with the number repeated in another context, p. 28), and, independently, in another twelfth-century manuscript (Bodl. Hatton 115, 155r). The version in the Caligula manuscript (cited above) may have Irish connections; see M. Förster, 'Die Weltzeitalter bei den Angelsachsen', in *Neusprachliche Studien. Festgabe Karl Luick zu seinem sechzigsten Geburtstage* (Marburg a.d. Lahn, 1925), pp. 183–203 at 191.

7. BN lat. 12,270 *formam hominis*; the change in the Old English (or its source) was perhaps prompted by Philipians II.7: *sed semet ipsum exinanivit formam servi accipiens, in similitudinem hominum factus.*

8. *settað rode tacn geond eower hus*: Not in BN lat. 12,270, but see Vienna 1355 (Appendix IIa, lines 23–4), *cruces per omnes domos aras ponite*, and, even closer, BL Add. 19,725 (Appendix IIb, line 22), *crucem per omnes dom[os] ponite*. Letter B's source was perhaps corrupt at this point for it has *and mid þære halgan rode he us gesenað* (lines 32–3). The act of placing crosses or making the sign of the cross throughout one's property is not mentioned in other Old English homiletic literature, but may be found as part of the ritual in a charm for unfruitful land ('For Unfruitful Land', lines 17–21; *Anglo-Saxon Minor Poems*, ed. Dobbie, pp. 116–17).

9. *mid þreora daga fæstene ealswa Niniuete dydon*: not in BN lat. 12,270, but the three-day fast of the Ninevites appears in Vienna 1355 and BL Add. 19,725 (Appendix IIb, lines 21–2): *triduanas sicut nineuite fecerunt agite.*

10. Cf. Matthew XXV. 34: *possidete paratum vobis regnum a constitutione mundi.*

11. *of eallon þam þe eow drihten alæned hafað*: not in BN lat. 12,270 and perhaps added in Letter A.

12. Many of the punishments listed here are probably derived from the ten plagues preceding the Exodus; similarly the blessing of fruitfulness of the land is specifi-cally promised to those who obey the law in the Pentateuch (see Chapter 3, p. 58).

    ic asendæ ceaferas . . . and gærshoppan: not in BN lat. 12,270, but see Vienna 1355 (Appendix IIa, lines 53–4): *mitto super vos locustas et brucos qui comedunt fructus vestros et mitto super vos lupos rapaces.*

13. *ic asende hearde stanas . . . to amyrrenne*: this section differs in certain respects from BN lat. 12,270. Although Letter A's *hearde stanas* translates *lapi-des grandes*, it then summarizes the Latin details with the general *fela freced-nessa*, and then seems to provide a similar, but not identical, list of punishments in lines 44–7. Of most interest here is the reference to the *hæðen folc þæt forni-*

mað eow and eowre bearn, which appears only in the Old English members of Recension I of the Sunday Letter, not in their Latin sources; see discussion in Chapter 4, p. 75.

wyrrestan gnættas and þa geættrode: Cf. BN lat. 12,270: *bestiolas quas vocant scyniphes venenatas pessimas*; these stinging insects (cf. Lewis and Short s.v. *cinifes*) are likely an allusion to the third plague in Exodus (VIII.16–19); see also the definition offered by Isidore: *sciniphes muscae minutissimae sunt, aculeis permolestae; qua tertia plaga superbus Aegyptiorum populus caesus est; Etymologiae* 12.8.14, ed. W. M. Lindsay, vol. 2 (Oxford, 1911).

14. God's oath invoking the Cherubim and Seraphim is not found in BN lat. 12,270 or in any other surviving copy of Recension I, though Graz 248 (Recension I) names them in the following sentence as one of the parties who intercede for mankind. Letters E and F also include this oath (E159–60, F190–1).

15. For an analogue to the intercession of Mary, Michael, Peter and the twelve apostles, see Chapter 3, pp. 60–1.

16. Cf. BL Add. 19,725, Appendix IIb, line 31: *aperiam uobis cataractas celi*.

17. *þurhwunige mid eow*: an awkward phrase perhaps rendering a corruption of BN lat. 12,270 *permaneat in vobis gloria mea* or simply due to the translator's omission of the last two words.

18. BN lat. 12,270 also adds *et de manibus meis scripta*; the claim is repeated (and there translated by A) in line 85.

19. The manuscript reads *horwum synnum*, which is probably an error; cf. BN lat. 12,270 *emundate corda vestra a sordibus peccatorum*.

20. BN lat. 12,270's *et declarate animas vestras* uses *declarare* in the sense 'to clear of a charge' (cf. R. E. Latham and D. R. Howlett, *Dictionary of Medieval Latin from British Sources* (Oxford, 1975–), s.v. *declarare* sense 2), whereas *geglengan* usually has the sense 'to adorn' or, rarely, the sense 'to set in order, arrange' (cf. *DOE* s.v. *geglengan* senses 1 and 2); perhaps the translator associated *declarare* with *claro* 'to make bright'.

21. *untrywleaste* is not otherwise attested; if it is retained, 'faith' should be supplied in the next clause in order to make sense of the negative particle *ne*. However, it could also be corruption of *treowfæstnes (cf. *treowleasnes, treowfæst*), or, less likely, *untreow* or *un(ge)treownes*, perhaps reading the prefix *un-* as an intensifier here (cf. *Beowulf* 357, *unhar*). The scribe may have been influenced by *untimlican* in the preceding parallel phrase.

22. J. H. Lynch (*Christianizing Kinship*, pp. 124–8) would draw a connection to the co-parenthood of St John which is a feature in other versions of the Sunday Letter, but here it is more likely that spiritual sponsors in general are meant. Cf. Letter B, note to lines 38–9.

23. Cf. Psalm LXVIII.29: *deleantur de libro viventium* and Apocalypse III.5 *et non delebo nomen eius de libro vitae*.

24. Cf. Vienna 1355: *ad ecclesias meas conueniatis et ad sacerdotes meos confessionem faciatis* (Appendix IIa, lines 47–8). BN lat. 12,270 has a passage on making oaths upon the cross here.

25.The 'hanging' (*pendentes*) serpents which suck on the breasts are unique to

BN lat. 12,270 and may be a corruption of the winged (*pennatas*) serpents who mutilate (*lacerant*, perhaps at some stage read as *lacterent*) the breasts, as found in other members of Recension I (See Tarragona (Priebsch, *Letter from Heaven*, p. 37), Basel B VII 7 (Appendix IIc, line 22), Graz 248 (133va), Vienna 1355, and the *nædran gefiðrede, þe etað eowre breost* of B122). The phrase *to slitenne heora flæsc*, which is not represented in BN lat. 12,270 suggests that A's source included something like the Tarragona manuscript's *mittam super vos serpentes pinnatas qui comedant et percutiant mamillas vestras* (Priebsch, *Letter from Heaven*, p. 37) or Vienna 1355's *qui lacerant mamillas* (Appendix IIa, line 75; also Basel B VII 7 and Graz 248). Copies of Recension III containing this image substitute a beast which devours, but does not hang on breasts. This remarkably lurid image is, as far as I know, unique to the Sunday Letter; however, there are similarities with passages in certain apocryphal texts such as in the Apocalypse of Peter, where the mothers of aborted children produce milk which turns into snakes which devour them; M. R. James, *The Apocryphal New Testament* (Oxford, 1924), p. 506. Similarly, in an Irish version of the *Transitus Mariae* ignorant priests are said to be punished by little infants which suck at them as they hang from their sides; S. J. D. Seymor, 'Irish Versions of the *Transitus Mariae*', *Journal of Theological Studies* os 23 (1921), 36–43 at 38; see also Silverstein, *Visio sancti Pauli*, p. 84.

26. Caesarius of Arles mentions children – born lepers, epileptics or demoniacs – who were conceived on the eve of Sundays and feast days (see Chapter 1, p. 11 n. 49); here the children are also punished if women slander others or take overmuch pride in their clothes. This unique occurrence of the compound *freolsnihtum* is an addition to the Latin, but see line 79 for the inclusion of other feast days in the restriction.

27. Letter A omits a lengthy denunciation of women's love of clothing and jewellery, a subject unrelated to Sunday observance.

28. Where BN lat. 12,270 only urges a cessation from work and then promotes good deeds on Sunday, Letter A has a list of specific restrictions which parallels Vienna 1355 *Et rogo uos, ut in sancto die dominico caput non lauetis neque comas tondatis* (Appendix IIa, lines 58–9); cf. B81–2 *Ic hate and ic halsige, þæt ge on sunnandæge eowre heafdu ne þwean ne eower fex ne efesian*. The anathema that follows in Letters A and B comes after the mention of the previous letters in BN lat. 12,270.

29. References to Rome and St Peter's tomb are missing in BN lat. 12,270.

30. The Old English (or its source) replaces the ending with a biblical quotation (cf. Matthew X.41: *qui recipit prophetam in nomine prophetae mercedem prophetae accipit, et qui recipit iustum in nomine iusti mercedem iusti recipit*); a similar process occurs in line 23.

Letter B

1. Vienna 1355: *ad sepulcrum sancti Petri et Pauli*; it is likely that Letter B's source referred to an altar. See Chapter 3, p. 49 n. 88, and note to line 131.

2. *mid gyldenum stafum*: not in the Latin, see discussion, Chapter 4, p. 77.

3. *swa heo þær gewearð*: 'as they there agreed'. On this use of *geweorþan*, see F. Klaeber, 'Concerning the Functions of Old English "geweorðan" and the Origin of German "gewähren lassen"', *Journal of English and Germanic Philology* 18 (1919), 250–71 at 257.

4. This transitional sentence leading into the list of prohibitions is not in the Latin.

5. *and þeh hwam gebyrige, þæt his fyr ut gewite, nis þæt alyfed to begetenne*: this particular restriction is found only in BL Add. 19,725: *focos inluminantes* (Appendix IIb, line 14). Cf. Exodus XXXV.3: *non succendetis ignem in omnibus habitaculis vestris per diem sabbati*. Napier suggests that *begetenne* may be an error for *gebetenne* 'to amend, restore' (cf. *DOE gebetan*, sense A.1.b 'of lamplight: to mend, trim').

6. See Tarragona: *Pecora in eodem die non mulgentes, sed pauperibus uestris aut comparibus non habentes distribuere* (Priebsch, *Letter from Heaven*, p. 35).

7. See J. Bosworth and T. N. Toller, ed., *An Anglo-Saxon Dictionary* (Oxford, 1898; supplement, Oxford, 1921), s.v. *yrnan*, sense II (6): 'of things (machinery): to run a mill'. See Vienna 1355: *molas tornantes* (see BL Add. 19,725: *molas tornantes*, Appendix IIb, line 14).

8. *Adam þone ærestan man*: see BN lat. 12,270: *et postea primum hominem Adam plasmauit* (Appendix I, lines 16–17).

9. See Graz 248: *in die septimo, in die dominico*; cf. Exodus XX.11: *et requievit in die septimo*.

10. *restendæg*: a convenient term which equates the Jewish sabbath and Christian Sunday.

11. In a late Old English sermon entitled *In diebus dominicis*, which is based on the *Visio Pauli*, angels are also said to rest on Sunday *mare þenn on sum oðer dei* ('more than on any other day'); *Old English Homilies and Homiletic Treatises*, ed. Morris, pp. 46–7.

12. *and mid synna . . . weorldgestreona*: this segment, which includes the elements of a confessor and tithing, was probably added by the translator.

13. *And mid þære halgan rode he us gesenað*: this renders Vienna 1355: *cruces per omnes domos aras ponite*, perhaps not a practice known to or undertaken by the translator; see also Tarragona: *crucem Christi in omnibus uenerare* (Priebsch, *Letter from Heaven*, p. 35). He also leaves out the next phrase, *caput cum cinere spargite*.

14. The time reference is not given in any of the Latin versions at this point.

15. This renders the Latin *compatratam de sancto Johanne custodiendo* in Vienna 1355, one of five such references; the others are, however, omitted in Letter B. The *compaternitas sancti Johannis*, 'co-parenthood of St John', was a form of spiritual kinship instituted in the ninth or tenth century on the Continent, but it most probably had little currency in Anglo-Saxon England, except for its appearance here. Letter A mentions *godsibbas* (66), rendering Latin *conpatres*, but does not specify St John. For the practice of the co-parenthood of St John and the meaning of *godsibb* and *godsibbræden*, see Lynch, *Christianizing Kinship*, pp. 124–8 and 148–50.

181

16. The weight is not given in Vienna 1355, but in BL Add. 19,725: *lapides pensantes pondera quinque* (Appendix IIb, lines 27–8), and also in Graz 248: *lapides librantes ponda quinque* (133rb).

17. For an analogue to this intercession by Mary, Michael, Peter and Paul, see Chapter 3, pp. 60–1.

18. *and ele*: cf. Graz 248: *dabo uobis frumentum, uinum et oleum* (133rb).

19. The manuscript reads *bearnum* (see *DOE* s.v *bere-ern* sense 1 'barn-granary'). Retaining the manuscript reading results in the less satisfactory but possible translation 'give prosperity to your offspring'. Vienna 1355: *dabo uobis frumentum, uindemiam et ligna pomifera et amplificabo uitam uestram et uiuetis in pace in seculum*.

20. *gemanigfealde*: the manuscript has *gemanigfealdum*; the verb was perhaps rendering an expected *multiplicabo*; cf. Psalm IV.8: *a fructu frumenti et uini et olei sui multiplicati sunt*; but see Toulouse 208, a Recension III Sunday Letter: *et implebo domos uestras omnibus boni* ('La lettre du Christ tombée du ciel', ed. Rivière, p. 603).

and ic eow sylle heofona rices wuldor aa on ecnesse soðlice is the translator's summary of Vienna 1355: *et amplificabo uitam uestram et uiuetis in pace in seculum*.

21. The last clause is not in the Latin versions; perhaps it echoes scripture (Matthew V.9, cf. I John V.5, III.2); cf. BN lat. 12,270 *ut mereamini habere consortium omnium sanctorum* (Appendix I, line 45).

22. *Beþœnce se fœder þone sunu . . . and þœt nœfre wel ne geendiað*: the Old English is only loosely based on the Latin here. See an elaboration of this theme in Tarragona: *Filii parentes non maledicant, neque parentes filios, quia maledictio patris et matris eradicat fundamenta domos filiorum* (Priebsch, *Letter from Heaven*, p. 36). Family members turning against one another is a sign of the end times in Mark XIII.12.

23. *gað to minum cyricum . . . and healdað þone halgan sunnandœg*: Priebsch (*Letter from Heaven*, p. 8) noticed points of similarity between this passage and one in the *Capitula* of Theodulf of Orléans (c. 24), which states: *Conveniendum est sabbato die cum luminaribus cuilibet Christiano ad ecclesiam, conveniendum est ad vigilias sive ad matutinum officium. Concurrendum est etiam cum oblationibus ad missarum solemnia* (PL 105, col. 198D).

druncennesse and unrihthœmed: see Graz 248: *sobrietatem et castitatem amate* (133rb).

24. Where the Latin merely asks the audience not to neglect the decree, the translator sees a reference to Judgement Day. Cf. BL Add. 19,725: *Haec diffinicio ante oculos uestros non sit dimittenda* (Appendix IIb, lines 40–1).

25. Vienna 1355 has *transmisi ad uos ordinationes quae apud me sunt dictae* [BL Add. 19,725 *condita*] *et non credidistis*; the translator has misunderstood *ordinationes*, 'commands', to mean those in orders. The last clause may be a corruption of original *and ge ne hym willað gelefan*, rendering Vienna 1355's *et non credidistis*.

26. See BL Add. 19,725 *per Iordanem fluuium* (Appendix IIb, line 42).

27. Like the co-parenthood of St John (see note to lines 38–9) this reference to the baptism (apart from the Sunday Lists) is found only in this version. It anachronistically includes the use of the chrism.

28. Vienna 1355's *celum invocavit* only suggests the voice from heaven (*vox de caelo*). The Gospel accounts of the baptism of Christ mention a dove representing the Holy Spirit but no angel as in Letter B; see Matthew III.17, Mark I.11 and Luke III.22. The Old English adds a phrase (*ipsum audite*) from the transfiguration in which a similar statement is made by a voice speaking from a cloud (see Matthew XVII.5, Mark IX.6).

29. *and þær ge eower geswinc sellað*: Vienna 1355 *et ad sacerdotes meos confessionem faciatis*: confession has been replaced with tithing.

30. This appears to render a sentence which appears slightly later in Vienna 1355: *mitto super uos locustas et brucos qui comedunt fructus uestros*. Flying or winged serpents occur again later in the text (line 122) and are a regular feature of the Sunday Letter.

31. This reference to God's mercy for the faithful appears to be the translator's rendering of Vienna 1355's *sed reuertimini ad me, recordamini, populi mei, ut animas declaratas accipiat regnum dei*.

32. *gecerrað to me, and ic to eow*: an interesting parallel may be found in a Recension III version of the Sunday Letter in Munich, Bayerische Staatsbibliothek, clm 21,518: *conuertimini ad me et ego conuertam faciem meam ad uos*; *Diu vrône botschaft*, ed. Priebsch, pp. 40–71 at 66.

33. The clause is not found in Latin versions.

34. Vienna 1355 *die tertio*; cf. Graz 248 *die dominico* (133va).

35. *se sunnandæg is se restendæg . . .* : a Sunday List has been inserted in the text; see discussion in Chapter 4, pp. 93–8. For a parallel to the introductory sentences, see a thirteenth-century sermon based on a Sunday List, which states: *þis dei is þet halie dei þet blescede dei þe blisfulle dei þe murie dei; þe dei seouensiþe brictere þene þe sunne* (*Old English Homilies and Homiletic Treatises*, ed. Morris, p. 139).

36. See Genesis VIII.4: *requievitque arca . . . super montes Armeniae*, referring to a country, not a mountain, but this appears to have been a common error (cf. *Genesis* 1421: *ða on dunum gesæt . . . earc Noes, þe Armenia hatene syndon*; *The Junius Manuscript*, ed. G. P. Krapp, Anglo-Saxon Poetic Records 1 (New York, 1931)).

37. See Latham and Howlett, *Dictionary*, s.v. *architriclinus*, 'governor of the feast' (cf. John II.8–9).

38. References to the Harrowing of Hell are common in England, but are not necessarily a reference to the Gospel of Nicodemus; see Hall, 'The *Evangelium Nichodemi* and *Vindicta Salvatoris* in Anglo-Saxon England', p. 55. Cf. Psalm XXIII.9, CXVII.19, Isaiah XXVI.2.

39. *cyriclicum larum*: *cyriclicum* could be an error for *cyricum*, translating *ecclesias* or haplography for *ic bebeode eallum minum cyricum on cyriclum larum* ('I command to all my churches in ecclesiastical teachings') which would be close to Vienna 1355's *ego ipse mandaui super omnes ecclesias meas per scripturas et libros*. It is also possible that *larum* is an error for *lareowum*.

40. The translator seems to be substituting fast days for the reference to the co-parenthood of John. Cf. Tarragona: *die dominico et festiuitates meas fideliter custodiant* (Priebsch, *Letter from Heaven*, p. 37) .

41. *fuhlas wedende*: raging birds are not found in any Latin Sunday Letter, but see Graz 248: *mitto super vos grandinem, brucus et vermes*; the *bruchus*, a kind of locust, may have been interpreted as a bird. Vienna 1355 places them at an earlier spot in the sermon: *mitto super vos locustas et brucos qui comedunt fructus uestros*, for which Letter B has only the flying serpents (*fleogende nædran*) at that point (B69). Cf. A40–1: *ic asendæ ceaferas on eowre wudas and gærshoppan on eowerne hwæte þæt fornimað eowerne bileofan*.

42. *and heo beoð eow æteowode*: this awkward phrase appears to be an attempt to make sense of '*vermes qui comedunt fruges vestras, et monstrabitur et non dabitur* in Vienna 1355. Some idea of the original may be suggested by Tarragona's *et ad alios demonstrabo et vobis non dabo*, though the object still remains unclear (Priebsch, *Letter from Heaven*, p. 37). An entry for 839 in the Annals of St Bertin (see Chapter 3, p. 42 n. 40) may also be of some help here. It reports on the vision of an English priest, possibly in reference to the Sunday Letter, who declares that for the neglect of Sunday and other, unspecified, sins *anno praesenti fruges non solum in terra, uerum etiam in arboribus et uitibus habundanter ostensa sunt, sed propter peccata hominum maxima pars illarum periit, quae ad usum atque utilitatem humanam non peruenit* ('this very year, fruit came forth in abundance on the land on the trees and on the vines too, but because of the sins of men most of this fruit perished and never came to be consumed or used by anyone'); *Annales Bertiniani*, ed. G. Waitz, MGH, SS rer. Germ. 6 (Hannover, 1883), 19; trans. by J. L. Nelson, *The Annals of St-Bertin*, Ninth-Century Histories 1 (Manchester, 1991), p. 43.

43. Not in the Latin, see the discussion in Chapter 4, p. 75.

44. See note to A70. Cf. Tarragona: *mittam super uos serpentes pinnatas qui comedant et percutiant mamillas uestras* (Priebsch, *Letter from Heaven*, p. 37). *in lehtune*: Cf. Graz 248 *in orto* (133va).

45. Cf. Graz 248 (133va), Basel B VII 7 (Appendix IIc, line 24): *in domibus uestris*.

46. The Old English alludes to earlier warnings, whereas the Latin seems to point to previous letters: *quia praeter hanc non est ulla*.

47. Vienna 1355 omits the reference to Rome at this point, but Basel B VII 7 has *et ad sanctum Petrum ad Romam* (Appendix IIc, lines 28–30). Though *sanctum Petrum* could have been taken as St Peter's tomb, given the occurrence of *sepulcrum* at the beginning of the sermon as well as in Letters E and F, it is more likely that the common ancestor showed this Latin word instead (see Chapter 3, p. 49, n. 88).

48. This section appears to be related to the oath of Bishop Peter in Recension II versions. Letters E and F, however, have a shortened form in which only the power of the Lord and the holy cross are listed.

Letters C and D

1. *Leofan men, us bisceopum . . . þonne hit Gode licwyrðe wære*: See discussion of this new introduction in Chapter 4, pp. 80–1.

2. For the location of Bishop Peter at Antioch, see Chapter 3, p. 51.

3. While the Apostle Paul, not Peter, preached at Antioch (Acts XI.19 ff.), the latter was traditionally seen as the founder of the church there; cf. Ælfric's sermon on St Peter's Chair: *se halga Petrus wæs ahafen on þam dæge on his bisceopstol on þære byrig Antiochian; þone stol he gesæt seofon gear fullice* (*LS* X.220.5–7).

4. That an angel, rather than Christ, writes the letter appears to be a change unique to VK. Munich 9550 says: *est scripta digito Dei et Domini nostri Iesu Christi* (Delehaye, 'Note', p. 180). In Recension III an angel holds the letter in his hands; see Toulouse, Bibliothèque Publique, 208 *angelus autem Domini eam tenebat in manibus* ('La lettre du Christ tombée du ciel', ed. Rivière, p. 600).

5. Cf. Proverbs IX.10 (added in Letter C).

6. Letter C echoes Wulfstan in the addition of *Ic beode*; cf. VK *et custodiant*.

7. For an overview of the Sunday List tradition, see Chapter 3, p. 59 and Chapter 4, pp. 93–8. The translator of Letter C changes the order of the items and adds others from another list known to him (see details in Chapter 3, p. 97). That Sunday was the first day on which God began to create all things is added in Letter C; cf. McNally III *primus dies fuit* (p. 185).

8. The division of the Red Sea into twelve parts or paths is corrected in Letter C. Tom Hall ('The Twelvefold Division of the Red Sea in Two Old English Prose Texts', *Medium ævum* 58 (1989), 298–304) has traced the concept to Jewish legend as well as early commentaries on the Psalms, notably those by Origen, Jerome and Cassiodorus, expanding Psalm CXXXV.13 which states that God *diuisit mare Rubrum in diuisiones*. It may be of importance with respect to the origin of this Sunday List, that, according to Hall, the idea also appears in two Psalter glosses which have Irish connections. The idea was also inserted by the Anglo-Saxon translator in the Old English *Orosius*; see *The Old English Orosius*, ed. J. Bately, EETS ss 6 (Oxford, 1980), p. 26 and Bately's commentary on p. 216.

9. VK's *ab omni placito* which may refer to anything from assemblies to legal proceedings, does not appear in D, but Letter C notes that it is forbidden *ælc gemot ænig mann to fremmanne*.

10. See the four judgements listed in Jeremiah XV.2–4 (death, sword, hunger, captivity); cf. M. Townend, *Language and History*, p. 178. Jeremiah is used for other passages in VK; see note to C91–4 (D47–9) below.

11. While it is difficult to determine how the biblical story of Dathan and Abiram, which has nothing to do with a violation of the sabbath, entered VK, a reasonable speculation might be that it was originally added as a parallel example to Sodom and Gomorrah, mentioned to show how the disobedient will be swallowed up by the earth (D45–6 and C84–6). The households of Dathan and Abiram, we are told, met a similar fate for blaspheming the Lord's name and his priests, which is accurate enough (Numbers XVI.1–40). The story reappears in Letters E and F but is elaborated there; see commentary to lines E122–4, F74–6.

12. The threat of foreign invasion has been expanded from the earlier recension (Munich 9550: *Et uenit gens pagana quae alios occidit, et alios in captiuitatem ducit pro eo quod non obseruatis diem dominicum*; 'Note', ed. Delehaye, p. 179) using passages in Jeremiah, especially V.15 (*ecce ego adducam super uos gentem ... gentem cuius ignorabis linguam nec intelleges quid loquatur*) and VI.22–4 (*ecce populus uenit de terra aquilonis et gens magna consurget a finibus terrae; saggitam et scutum arripiet crudelis est et non miserebitur; uox eius quasi mare sonabit ... audiuimus famam eius dissolutae sunt manus nostrae; tribulatio adprehendit nos dolores ut parturientem*); see Townend, *Language and History*, p. 175. The suggestion that an enemy from the north speaking a different language could have been taken to refer to Viking invasions is considered unlikely by Ian McDougall ('Foreigners and Foreign Languages in Medieval Iceland', *Saga-Book of the Viking Society* 22 (1987–8), 181–233 at 223 n. 5). McDougall notes that similar pagan enemies appear in Latin Sunday Letters, and it is now possible to confirm that these were certainly already present in VK when the Anglo-Saxon translator encountered the text. It remains an open question, however, whether the person who wrote this recension meant to draw on contemporary experiences with pagan invaders (Townend, *Language and History*, pp. 178–9) and found the passages in Jeremiah suitable to his subject. Townend makes much of the paganism of the Vikings, but while it is to be noted that, in the preceding section, VK's *in manus alienorum* was rendered *on hæðenra hand* in C83, the Latin was almost certainly already in the source of VK; see BL Royal 8 F.vi: *trado uobis in manum alienorum* ('John Audelay', ed. Priebsch, p. 401). Cf. D45 *to ælþeodigra handa*. Furthermore, in the passage under question, neither C nor D mention that the invaders are pagans and the reviser of C shortens the passage considerably, omitting the fact that they are to come from the north.

13. See VK *dolor ut parturientem* (Appendix III, line 40); cf. Luke XXI.23. The sentence is omitted in C.

14. The story of the destruction of Jerusalem by Titus and Vespasian – an addition in the VK version of the Sunday Letter – seems to have been well-known to Anglo-Saxon authors. References to it appear in the Anglo-Saxon Chronicle, the Old English translation of Orosius, a homily by Ælfric (*CH* I, XXVIII), his letter to Sigeweard, Blickling Homily VI and in the Old English translation of the *Vindicta salvatoris*. For the latter as well as a discussion of sources, see Hall 'The *Euangelium Nichodemi* and *Vindicta saluatoris* in Anglo-Saxon England', pp. 36–81, especially 59–60 and 71–81. The figures of 1,100,000 people taken capitive and 100,000 dead appear also in Blickling VI (p. 79) and in a homily by Haymo of Auxerre (CXXII, PL 118, col. 657C), but in both of these the groups are reversed, referring to dead and captive, respectively. A comparison to other accounts is provided by M. R. Godden, *Ælfric's Catholic Homilies: Introduction, Commentary and Glossary*, EETS ss 18 (London, 2000), p. 232. Letter D supplies the names, Titus and Vespasian, where there appears to have been a lacuna in VK.

15. *ungemetlice*: *intemporaneas*, 'unseasonable', may have been mistaken here for *intemperans*, 'excessive, immoderate'.

16. The idea that those who would not pay the tithe would be deprived of the other nine tenths by means of drought, frost or pests had some currency at the time. See a comment by Ælfric in Pope XXX.85–7: *Eft is awriten, gif þu æthæfst Gode þa teoþunge, þæt his rihtwisnes benæmð þe þara nigon dæla, and læt þe habban þone teoðan dæl.* The text is based on a homily by Cæsarius of Arles who (quoting Malachi III.10) makes the consequences on crops more explicit (*Sermo* XXXIII.2, ed. Morin, CCSL 103, pp. 144–5). See also Blickling IV, a sermon on tithing likewise based on Caesarius which uses a formulation close to Letter C in *forþon symle æt þæm ytmestan dæge eal hit him wyrþ to teonan þæm þe his Gode wyrneþ* (ed. Morris, p. 51); another copy of this homily similarly states *swa hwilc man swa nyle drihten lufian and his æhta for his naman dælan ðane teoðan dæl, þonne genimeð drihten hie mid teonan* (Bodl. Junius 86, 59v; R. Willard, 'The Blickling-Junius Tithing Homily and Caesarius of Arles', in *Philologica: The Malone Anniversary Studies*, ed. T. Kirby (Baltimore, 1949), pp. 65–78 at 77). These explications are no doubt what the author of Letter C had in mind when he goes on to describe the dramatic devastation of livelihood in the following sentences. The idea, as Pope notes, is also found in the laws; see I Æthelstan 3 (*Councils and Synods*, ed. Whitelock *et al.*, pp. 45–6); Wormald notes that the source of this section (a tract called *De decimis*) is also cited in the Irish Canon Collection (*The Making of English Law*, p. 306).

17. VK has *mana*, probably a corruption of *manci*, 'maimed', or perhaps *muti*, 'mute', as in BN lat. 12,270 (Appendix I, lines 63–4): *Nati uestri nascentur sine oculis et sine manibus et sine pedibus, in opprobrium et spectaculum omnium muti et surdi, et ceci et claudi.* VK adds *leprosi*, which is not found in other Latin Sunday Letters, but see a sermon by Caesarius which also mentions such children, who will be born *leprosi aut epileptici aut forte etiam daemoniosi* ('lepers, or epileptics or perhaps demoniacs'); *Sermo* XLIV.7; ed. Morin, CCSL 103, p. 199. Letter C omits this sentence as well as the following one.

18. Cf. John VIII.47: *qui est ex deo, verba dei audit, propterea vos non auditis quia ex deo non estis* ('And he that is of God heareth the words of God; therefore you hear them not, because you are not of God'). This harsh biblical statement is replaced in Letter C with one exhibiting typically Anglo-Saxon understatement and substituting concrete evil deeds of the listeners for the more abstract notion of being not 'of God'.

19. Cf. Isaiah V.20 and 22: *vae qui dicitis malum bonum et bonum malum, ponentes tenebras lucem et lucem tenebras, ponentes amarum in dulce et dulce in amarum . . . vae qui potentes estis ad bibendum vinum et viri fortes ad miscendam ebrietatem.* This passage from Isaiah was also translated by Wulfstan; see Bethurum XI.140–60.

20. This sentence has suffered some corruption in Letter D. The manuscript has *mid missenlicra gliwa oferfiligað and*, and at least one or two words may be missing here; *mid missenlicra gliwa* is a summary of the musical instruments listed in the Latin, but *mid* is lacking a dative object. The emendation *oferfylle* is a frequent rendering of *crapula*, particularly in the collocation *crapula et ebrietas*. However, the verb *filigað* may also have been in the exemplar along with its, here inadvertently omitted, object. Cf. C137–8: *eall for druncennysse and oferfylle, and swa ge eowerne beorscipe brucað on unriht*.

21. Cf. Ezekiel III.18. VK's ending is omitted in Letter C.

22. Cf. the Welsh *Ebostol y sul* 'I am Peter the Bishop of Antioch, who swear by the power of God, who created the heaven and the earth, and that which is therein, and created man in his own image and form; and by Jesus Christ, the Son of the living God, who was crucified for us, (and) who will come to judge the quick and the dead; and by the Holy Ghost; and by the Trinity (in) Unity inseparable; and by the four evangelists; and by the twenty-four prophets; and by the twelve apostles; and by the bodies of the saints, no man composed this epistle' (ed. Powel, p. 169).

23. *Þæt syndon Godes wiðersacan . . . and riht to wrange*: this list of sinners was most likely taken from a Wulfstan text; see Chapter 4, p. 81.

24. The closest source for this portion of Letter C is a piece found in Munich, Bayerische Staatsbibliothek, clm 14,364, fol. 37 (printed in Wright, *The Irish Tradition*, pp. 82–3): *Tribus modis diabolus securitatem in mente hominis mittit. Primum suggerit homini ut non det confessionem, quia iuuenis es tu. Secundo dicit, quia alii grauius peccauerunt quam tu es diu regnauerunt [var. uixerunt]. Tercium, tu pecca quia magna clementia et misericordia dei indulget tibi peccata tua; et per hanc securitatem ducit e[u]m ad infernum. Tria sunt que deducant hominem ad profundum inferni, id est, cogitatio inmunda, uerbum alienum, opus prauum. Tria sunt que deducunt hominem ad regna celestia, id est, cogitatio sancta et uerbum bonum, opus perfectum. Trea sunt que non remittuntur hic [nec] in futurum, id est, qui plasphemat deum et qui desperat de misericordia dei et qui non credit resurrectionem.* Wright (p. 84), notes that a similar passage occurs in another Old English homily published by A. M. Luiselli Fadda in *Nuove omelie anglosassoni della rinascenza benedettina*, Filologia germanica, Testi e studi 1 (Florence, 1977), 139–57 at p. 145. That homily's source, according to Wright, is a Pseudo-Augustinian homily (*Ad fratres in eremo* LXVIII, PL 40: 1355).

25. A better reading (*uixerunt*) is provided by Einsiedeln, Stiftsbibliothek, 281; see previous note and Wright, *The Irish Tradition*, p. 82 n. 159.

26. *Uton nu forþyg . . . þæt heo wyle*: an almost exact copy of this segment is included in the composite homily that follows Letter C in Lambeth 489 (Ker's article 5). Both of these were likely drawn from a third source; see Chapter 4, p. 81.

Letters E and F

1. Fire only occurs once in Munich 9550: *mittam super uos grandinem, ignem, fulgura coruscationes, tempestates ut pereant labores uestri* (Delehaye, 'Note', p. 180); cf. Tarragona: *Quod si non custodieritis, mittam super uos lapides calidos, ignem et flammam producentes cum magno pondere, qui consumant uos*, and later *Vermis, focus et flamma, quatenus alios comedat uermis et alios cremet ignis* (Priebsch, *Letter from Heaven*, pp. 35–7). The closely related extract in Vat. Reg.

Lat 49 (ed. McNally) has *Comburet uos ignis caelestis*. For the association of Noah's Flood with an apocalyptic fire, see Anlezark, *Water and Fire*, pp. 120–1.

2. For the use of this term in the dating of the translation, see Chapter 4, p. 86.

3. The formula for the period of time during which Sunday was to be observed occurs with much greater frequency in Letters E and F than in other Sunday Letters. This instance is omitted in F.

4. Two or more words have been omitted due to homoeoteleuton; cf. E10–11: *and næs ænig word, þæt ænig man on hine funde, butan hit wære eall soð*.

5. *Forþon hiom sænd God . . . his mæran mildse*: this passage is not in E nor in other Sunday Letters; the level of detail may suggests that it is an expansion in F.

6. Noah preached for a hundred years (120 in E19, *hundtwelftigum wintrum*). Noah's preaching is not related in the Genesis account, but passages such as I Peter X.11 and III.18–20 were interpreted as indicating that Christ's spirit preached through Noah. In deviating from the norm of 120 years, perhaps our author was merely subtracting the age of Noah when he is mentioned in Genesis V.32 from his age of 600 years when the Flood begins in Genesis VII.6. See Anlezark, *Water and Fire*, p. 36.

7. The floodwaters rising from the earth probably refer to Genesis VII.11 *rupti sunt omnes fontes abyssi magnae*.

8. The Genesis account (VII.20) states that the water was fifteen cubits higher than the highest mountain; no other Old English text makes this particular error, though some change the number to forty; Anlezark, *Water and Fire*, p. 165, n. 12. Letter E omits this detail *oððæt þæt wæter wæs heahre, þonne ænig munt æfre wære*.

9. Cf. Munich 9550: *Ista epistola non formata est manu hominis neque scripta, sed est scripta digito Dei et Domini nostri Iesu Christi, et est transmissa de septimo caelo et de throno Dei in terram, qualiter diem sanctum dominicum obseruare debeatis* (Delehaye, 'Note', p. 180–1). *sæternes* for *sæternesdæg* occurs four times in Letter F, but does not appear elsewhere in Old English except in Ælfric's *CH* II, XIV.333 in the following phrase: *on ðam seofoðan dæge ðe ge sæternes hatað*; there this formulation caused sufficient discomfort for seven of the eight variant manuscripts to correct to *sæternesdæg*.

10. This may be a reference to what is called the Sunday respite, here in a negative formulation which states that devils and 'heathen souls' never receive rest. It is possible to trace this notion to statements in early versions of the Sunday Letter (Recension I) that the angels rest in heaven (cf. Vienna 1355: *Quia in die sancto dominico requieuit, et nunc sic debent peccatores et iusti, sicut angeli requiescunt in coelo* (Appendix IIa, lines 21–2)), or perhaps the statement in Tarragona that there is no rest in hell (*deducantur a diabulo in gehenna ignis, ubi nulla erit requies, nisi fletus et ululatus*; Priebsch, *Letter from Heaven*, p. 35). The Sunday respite also occurs in the Sunday List portion of Letters E and F (E102–42, F47–107); cf. *Epistil Ísu* §9, 'For not even folk in hell are punished on that day', O'Keeffe, 'Cáin Domnaig', p. 195.

11. The golden letters mentioned here are never found in the Latin versions, nor do they occur in the related *Epistil Ísu*. They were, however, part of Pehtred's

189

version, since Ecgred mentions this item in his letter (*litterae manu Dei auro*; *Councils and Ecclesiastical Documents*, ed. Haddan and Stubbs, I.615). Golden letters were usually associated with scripture, particularly the Gospels. Byrhtferth in his *Enchiridion* notes that Abbot Pacomius received from an angel verses written with golden letters (*mid gyldenum stafum awritene*) which disclosed the method of calculating Easter (*Byrhtferth's Enchiridion*, ed. Baker and Lapidge, p. 138). Similarly, a composite homily put together mainly from Wulfstan's work states in one passage (not by Wulfstan) that each step taken on the way to church is recorded in heaven with golden letters (Napier LVIII, 302.25–8). Golden letters appear regularly in later Sunday Letters and Sunday Lists; for example, in the Old Norse poem *Leiðarvísan*, preserved in a fourteenth-century manuscript but probably written in the twelfth; see *Den norsk-islandske skjaldedigtning*, ed. Finnur Jónsson, vol. 1 (Copenhagen, 1912–15), AI, 618–26, BI, 622–33. Letter B's inclusion of golden letters is best explained by the influence of Letter E, which precedes it in the manuscript; see Chapter 4, p. 77.

12. Cf. Exodus XXXI.12–14: *et locutus est Dominus ad Mosen discens: loquere filiis Israhel et dices ad eos, videte ut sabbatum meum custodiatis quia signum est inter me et vos in generationibus vestris ut sciatis quia ego Dominus qui sanctifico vos. Custodite sabbatum sanctum est enim vobis qui polluerit illud morte morietur qui fecerit in eo opus peribit anima illius de medio populi sui.* The passage has been cut by E, though the next verse has been retained (E114–21). Letter F explains the last clause as referring to torment in hell in separation from the 'holy company'.

13. Turning water into wine: this item from the Sunday List appears to have been copied into the middle of the scriptural quotation by mistake, perhaps from a marginal note in the exemplar.

14. For a discussion of this element, see Chapter 4, p. 75. Cf. F181.

15. Cf. Munich 9550: *et mittam in uos et domos uestras plagam et conturbationem pessimam* (Delehaye, 'Note', p. 179).

16. Cf. Munich 9550: *Iterum dico uobis, si non custodieritis sanctum diem dominicum, mittam super uos grandinem, ignem, fulgura coruscationes, tempestates ut pereant labores uestri* (Delehaye, 'Note', p. 180)

17. This passage was taken from a source which was copied again later in the same manuscript; see discussion in Chapter 4, pp. 91–3. The law code that corresponds most closely to E is I Cnut 8–18b (with some omissions and differences in order; *Gesetze*, ed. Liebermann, pp. 290–9), but this uses earlier codes which occasionally correspond more closely to Letter E. (These are in II Edgar 1.1–5.1, V Æthelred 11–19, VI Æthelred 16–25.1, and VIII Æthelred 7–17 and are edited in Liebermann, *Gesetze*, pp. 196–9, 240–3, 252–3, 264–5, respectively). My translation of this section is heavily dependent on Dorothy Whitelock's translation of Cnut's code (*Councils and Synods*, pp. 475–81). On the collection of church dues in late Anglo-Saxon England, see F. Tinti, 'The "Costs" of Pastoral Care: Church Dues in Late Anglo-Saxon England', in *Pastoral Care in Late Anglo-Saxon England*, ed. F. Tinti, Anglo-Saxon Studies 6 (Woodbridge, 2005), pp. 27–51.

18. I Cnut 8–8.1: *And gelæste mann Godes gerihta æghwylce geare rihtlice* *georne: Þæt is, sulhælmæsse XV niht ofer Eastran and geoguþe teoðunge be Pentecosten* (cf. II Edgar 3; V Æthelred 11–11.1, VI Æthelred 16–17; VIII Æthelred 7, 9, 12).

19. II Edgar 4: *And sy ælc heorðpæning agyfen be Petres mæssedæg*; cf. I Cnut 9 *And Romfeoh be Petres mæssan* (cf. V Æthelred 11.1, VI Æthelred 18 and VIII Æthelred 10 also have *Romfeoh*).

20. VIII Æthelred 9.1: *And eorðwæstma be emnihte oððe huru be ealra halgena mæssan* (cf. II Edgar 3; I Cnut 8.1 and VI Æthelred 17 leave out *be emnihte*; see *Councils and Synods*, ed. Whitelock *et al.*, p. 99 n. 1). *Cornteoðung*, 'tithe of grain', appears only in E; all others, including Napier XXIII, have *eorðwæstma*, 'produce of the earth'.

21. I Cnut 8.2: *Þæt is se teoða æcer, ealswa seo sulh hit gega* (cf. II Edgar 1.1, VIII Æthelred 7).

22. I Cnut 10 *And cyricsceat to Martines mæssan* (cf. II Edgar 3, VI Æthelred 18.1, VIII Æthelred 11); cf. BTS s.v. *cyricsceat* and *Oxford English Dictionary* s.v. *church-scot*: 'a custom of corn collected on St Martin's day; extended to other contributions in kind and money made for the support of the clergy, or demanded as a traditional ecclesiastical due'.

23. I Cnut 12: *And leohtgesceot þriwa on geare: ærest on Easteræfen healfpenigwurð wexes æt ælcere hide and eft on ealra halgena mæssan eallswa mycel*; see also 'The So-Called "Canons of Edgar"' 54: *and leohtgesceotu þriwa on geare: ærest on Easteræfen, and oðre siðe on Candelmæsseæfen, þriddan siðe on ealra halgena mæsseæfen* (*Councils and Synods*, ed. Whitelock *et al.*, p. 332) (cf. VI Æthelred 19 (no time periods listed), VIII Æthelred 12.1 (has Candlemas only)). The omission of Candlemas in Cnut is an error; see ibid. p. 477 n. 1. See BTS *leohtgesceot* and *Oxford English Dictionary*, *light-shot* s.v. *light*, n., 'a due levied for furnishing the church with lights'.

24. I Cnut 14.2: *And healde man ælces Sunnandæges freolsunge fram Sæternesdæges none oð Monandæges lihtingce and ælcne oðerne mæssedæg swa he beboden beo* (cf. II Edgar 5, V Æthelred 13, VI Æthelred 22.1).

25. I Cnut 15: *And Sunnandaga cypingce we forbeodað eac eornostlice and ælc folcgemot, butan hit for micelre neodþearfe sig* (cf. V Æthelred 13.1, VI Æthelred 22.1, VIII Æthelred 17).

26. I Cnut 16: *And þæt man ælc beboden fæsten healde, si hit ymbrenfæsten, si hit lengctenfæsten, si hit elles oðer fæstæn, mid ealre geornfulnesse* (cf. II Edgar 5.1).

27. I Cnut 16a: *And to sancta Marian mæssan ælcere and to ælces apostoles mæssan fæste man, butan to Philippi and Iacobi mæssan we ne beodað nan fæsten, for þam easterlican freolse, and ælces Frigedæges fæsten, butan hit freols sig* (cf. V Æthelred 14–14.1, VI Æthelred 22.2–22.3).

28. I Cnut 17: *And we forbeodað ordal and aðas freoldsdagum and ymbrendagum and lengctendagum and rihtfæstendagum and fram Aduentum Domini oð se eahtaþa dæg agan sig ofer Twelftan mæssedæge and fram Septuagessima oð XV nihton ofer Eastron* (cf. V Æthelred 18, VI Æthelred 23[K], 25). The marginal addition of *and wifunga* in Letter E appears in the body of the text in Napier

XXIII (but only the CCCC 419 copy, the earliest of the three); this shows that it was either inadvertently omitted in E or, less likely, was not in their common source text and was added to Napier XXIII with a correction to E. The only law code where this particular proscription occurs is in the copy of VI Æthelred in BL Cotton Claudius A.iii (36v) where it is also in the main text (*Gesetze*, ed. Liebermann, pp. 252–3). In I Cnut 17, however, it is omitted. The word *wifung* is otherwise found in contexts which suggest that it could be translated as either 'wedding' or 'sexual relations'. See A. Fischer, *Engagement, Wedding, and Marriage in Old English* (Heidelberg, 1986), pp. 59–62. The inclusion of this item in a list which includes oaths and ordeals, could therefore conceivably point to the public transaction of a wedding rather than sexual relations. Cf. Wormald (*The Making of English Law*, p. 343, n. 370) translates *wifunga* as 'weddings', and Liebermann (*Gesetze* I, 253) as 'Hochzeiten'. But while sexual relations on the eve of Sunday are commonly prohibited in the penitentials and in other texts (see pp. 11 n. 49 and 30), weddings are, prior to this, mentioned in only one doubtful instance in a continental legal text, the Council of Aachen (836), c. 58: *Ieiunium diebus dominicis tenere et canonica interdicit auctoritas et resurrectionis dominice tanta solemnitas. Et ideo placita illis diebus neque nubtias pro reverentia tantae solemnitatis non celebrari visum est* (*Concilia aevi Karolini*, ed. Werminghoff, Conc. 2/1, 722). This lone example may be a scribal error, copying *nubtias*, 'weddings', for *nundinas*, 'markets'; see A.-J. Binterim, *Pragmatische Geschichte der deutschen Concilien vom vierten Jahrhundert bis zum Concilium von Trient* (Mainz, 1812), II, 492.

29. I Cnut 13: *And sawlsceat is rihtast þæt man symle gelæste a æt openum græfe* (cf. VI Æthelred 20, VIII Æthelred 13). The clause on peace and unity on holy occasions which occurs in Napier XXIII (but is omitted in E) is also found in V Æthelred 19, VI Æthelred 25.1, and I Cnut 17.2.

30. I Cnut 18–18b: *And we biddað for Godes lufan, þæt ælc Cristen mann understande georne his agene þearfe. Forþam ealle we sceolon ænne timan gebidan, þonne us wære leofre þonne eall þæt on middanearde is, þær we a worhtan þa hwile, þe we mihton, georne Godes willan. Ac þonne we sceolan habban anfeald lean ðæs þe we on life ær geworhtan; wa þam þonne þe ær geearnode hellewite!* Letter E changes the legal *we* to a more personal *ic*.

31. Similar ideas are expressed frequently in Wulfstan's work. One parallel occurs later in a homiletic appendage to VI Æthelred (46–8) following another brief mention of tithing and Sunday observance: *And þæt hy Godes þearfan frefrian and fedan. And þæt hy wydewan and steopcild to oft ne ahwænan, ac georne hy gladian. And þæt hy ælþeodige men and feorran cumene ne tyrian ne ne tynan* (*Gesetze*, ed. Liebermann, pp. 258–9). A distant echo may be Letter F153–6 and it is possible something in the source suggested the inclusion of this passage; cf. D33–9 and C65–72. See *DOE* s.v. *cystian* 'to lay (a corpse) into a coffin, encase'; this word occurs only here and in Napier XXIII.

32. Cf. Munich 9550: *Quia nescitis illum custodire, propter hoc uenit ira Dei super uos, et flagella in laboribus et in pecudibus uestris quae possidetis* (Delehaye, 'Note', p. 179); and also VK: *mittam in domos illorum infirmitates et pestes* *innumerabiles tam super illos quam filios eorum et super familiam et super peccora eorum que habent in domibus* (Appendix III, lines 48–50).

33. The beginning of the Sunday List, see Chapter 4, pp. 93–8. Letter E's introductory sentence resembles one in VK: *maxime uero custodiendus est dies dominicus, quia dies domini prima est omnium dierum et ultima* (Appendix III, lines 31–2).

34. Cf. Exodus XXXI.15: *sex diebus facietis opus in die septimo sabbatum est requies sancta Domino omnis qui fecerit opus in hac die morietur. Custodiant filii Israhel sabbatum et celebrent illud in generationibus suis pactum est sempiternum inter me et filios Israhel signumque perpetuum sex enim diebus fecit Dominus caelum et terram et in septimo ab opere cessavit.* Again Letter F offers an editorial comment on the scriptural text, claiming that it establishes the need to observe Sunday.

35. This is the story of Korah's rebellion, taken from Numbers XVI.1–40. Korah, Dathan and Abiram apparently resisted the leadership of Moses and Aaron, but E/F say they were punished for not honouring Sunday; Letter E also adds nonpayment of the tithe to their offences, which is neither in F nor in scripture. Perhaps this reflects an interest in the subject of tithing, as is also shown in a long passage excerpted from the Anglo-Saxon laws, which includes several clauses on tithing (E56–98). Though the story of Korah, Dathan and Abiram does not appear often in surviving Old English literature, it does appear in Ælfric's homilies twice: once in Pope XX.217–60, where it is narrated at length as part of a longer piece on the people of Israel, and a much shorter allusion in *CH* II, XXVII.130–5, where it is used as an example of what happens to those who do not believe in a sermon preached by the Apostle James. See also *LS* XIII.221–9. The spelling *Choreb* is possibly due to a confusion with Mount Horeb (Mount Sinai); cf. Psalm CV.17–19, where these names occur together.

36. The number 14,000 is probably taken from the following episode, Numbers XVI.49.

37. Reduced to a sentence and a half and moved in E (lines 183–5). Similar passages are also found in two other Old English texts: Vercelli X.3–8 *þeah man anum men godspel secge, þonne bio ic þæronmiddan. And þam bioð synna forgifene þe ðæt godspel segð and gecwið, and synna þam bioð forgifene þe hit for Godes naman lustlice gehyreð, and þam bið wa æfre geworht þe secgan can and nele, for ðam men sculon þurh ða godcundan lare becuman to life*; Cf. Vercelli IX (L).99–102: *Eala, wa þæm þe cunnon godspel secgean and Godes fold læran and ne willaþ for heora gemelæste. Þæm bið wa æfre geborenum þe hit ne wille mid inneweardre heortan geheran and healdan.* While the former is closer, Vercelli IX has *for heora gemelæste*, and another word, *geborenum*, in common with F. See Matthew XVIII.20: *ubi enim sunt duo vel tres congregati in nomine meo ibi sum in medio eorum.*

38. The belief that the Jordan River stood still during Christ's baptism has been examined by Hall ('The Reversal of the Jordan'). Hall notes that it originated with Psalm CXIII.3, which states in reference to the events recorded in Joshua III that *Iordanis conversus est retrorsum*, 'the Jordan was turned back'; this was later transferred to Christ's baptism in biblical commentaries and in the liturgy for the Epiphany. The evidence for this comes primarily from Eastern sources, the West offering only a few analogues in the period of our text, most notably two Hiberno-Latin commentaries, the *Catechesis Celtica* (ninth century) and Pseudo-Jerome (seventh century) (Hall, pp. 58–61). Charms for the staunching of blood dating from as early as the sixth century also mention the cessation of the Jordan's flow (Hall, pp. 62–3). The clearest example in Old English is that in Vercelli XVI.61–9, which emphasizes the river's fear of the divine. Passages in two poetic texts, *The Descent into Hell* (lines 90–106) and *Exodus* (lines 299–304a), offer further allusions to the reversal motif. In his discussion of its manifestation in Sunday Letters E and F, Hall notes that the miracle is extended into a recurring event in honour of Sunday (p. 73).

39. The connection of Pentecost with the seventy-two languages of the world is commented upon by Whitelock ('Bishop Ecgred', pp. 62–3); for other occurrences of the 72 languages of the world, see H. Sauer, 'Die 72 Völker und Sprachen der Welt: Ein mittelalterlicher Topos in der englischen Literatur', *Anglia* 101 (1983), 29–48. The topos occurs again in Letter E in another context (see E215).

40. Letters E and F offer a slightly different formulation of the Sunday respite, granting respite to all those in hell, if they had been baptized (F), or only to those in 'a place of punishment' rather than hell itself (E). Similarly, Priebsch noted that two Middle High German sermons which are based on Sunday Lists mention the Sunday respite ('Chief Sources', p. 145, n. 2); see Kelle, *Speculum ecclesiae*, pp. 176–8, and Strauch, 'Altdeutsche Predigten', pp. 148–50. The former has all souls in hell resting (Kelle, p. 176), whereas the latter notes that all souls which are not meant to suffer eternally in hell, but are being punished there, receive the respite (Strauch, p. 150, lines 61–3). M. Tveitane notes several connections between these sermons and early Hiberno-Latin materials in a discussion of an Old Norse Christmas homily which also features a respite for those in hell who were Christians ('Irish Apocrypha in Norse Tradition? On the Sources of Some Medieval Homilies', *Arv: Tidskrift för nordisk folkminnesforskning* 22 (1966), 113–16 and 125–31). For other instances of a respite in Old English and its connection to the *Visio Pauli*, see Healey, *The Old English Vision of St. Paul*, pp. 48–50.

41. The story of a man who gathered wood on the sabbath and was put to death, taken from Numbers XV.32–6. For the notion that one may take what another has produced on a Sunday with impunity, see the laws of Wihtræd (Chapter 2, p. 20).

42. According to Wilcox ('Compilation', pp. 23 and 26) the expunction of *me* here and in line 157 belong to the earliest corrections; they appear to be motivated by stylistic considerations.

43. For other versions in which the letter falls on an altar, see Chapter 3, n. 88.

44. This is a possible adjectival formation from *abelgan* (cf. F. Kluge, *Nominal Stammbildungslehre der altgermanischen Dialekte*, 3rd ed., Halle, 1926, §192, p. 95), but given the corrupt state of this text and that this is the only occurrence of this word, a scribal error for *abolgen*, past participle of *abelgan*, is perhaps more likely (cf. E144 *abolgen*; see also *DOE* s.v. *ābolgol*).

45. The locusts and beetles which appear in Letter F are not usually a feature of

Recension II Sunday Letters. One exception is that in the Homiliary of Toledo: *Amen dico uobis, quia misi super populum brucos et locustas, et non cognouerunt me* (BL Add. 30,853 in Grégoire, *Les homéliaires du moyen âge*, p. 226). The destruction of crops (by severe weather) is threatened in Munich 9550: *Iterum dico uobis, si non custodieritis sanctum diem dominicum, mittam super uos grandinem, ignem, fulgura coruscationes, tempestates ut pereant labores uestri; et delebo uineas uestras, et non dabo uobis pluuiam, et auferam a uobis fructus uestros* (Delehaye, 'Note', p. 180).

46. The similarity of these punishments to the ten plagues of Egypt apparently occasioned this editorial comment.

47. For the idea of God's patience expressed here, see Munich 9550. *Ego sum patiens super vos* (Delehaye, 'Note', p. 179), and BL Add. 30,853: *non scitis quia multum patiens sum et misericors ego super ęlectos meos?* (Grégoire, *Les homéliaires du moyen âge*, p. 226). These lines may be echoing the lists of good deeds in other Sunday Letters, for example VK: *Et infirmos debetis visitare, mortuos humilime sepelire, pauperes pascere, nudos uestire, sicientes potare, aduenas adiuuare, captiuos reddimere, peregrinos benigne suscipere, egenis uiduisque solatium prebere, discordantes christianos pacificare* (Appendix III, lines 27–31).

48. Cf. the Tarragona manuscript: *Cruxifixus fui propter uos et resurrexi die Dominico, ascendi ad dexteram Dei, et requiem dedi omnibus die Dominico* (Priebsch, *Letter from Heaven*, p. 37), and BL Add. 30,853: *Surrexi in diem dominicum et omnes requiescere debent in eo die. In cęlis ascendi ad dexteram patris mei, [requieui] ab omnibus operibus meis* (ed. Grégoire, *Les homéliaires du moyen âge*, p. 226).

49. Cf. Munich 9550: *Amen dico uobis, si non custodieritis sanctum diem dominicum de hora nona sabbati usque ad horam primam secundae feriae, anathematizabo uos cum patre meo, et non habetis partem mecum neque cum angelis meis in saecula saeculorum* (Delehaye, 'Note', p. 180).

50. This may be a fanciful rendering of the Tarragona manuscript's proscription against using oxen: *Boues tuos in eodem die non mittas laborare* (Priebsch, *Letter from Heaven*, p. 35).

51. Cf. Munich 9550: *Iterum dico vobis, si non custodieritis sanctum diem dominicum, mittam super uos grandinem, ignem, fulgura coruscationes, tempestates ut pereant labores uestri* (Delehaye, 'Note', p. 180). The flying or winged serpents are not usually found in Recension II. See, however, BL Add. 30,853 *serpentes pinnatas* (Grégoire, *Les homéliaires du moyen âge*, p. 226); cf. Vienna 1355 *serpentes pinnatos* (Appendix IIa, line 75).

52. For the threat of foreign invasion, see Chapter 4, p. 75.

53. Vat. Reg. Lat 49 is the closest analogue to these lines: *et quid quaeritis, dabo uobis; et letabitur propter uos, et scietis quia ego sum Dominus. Iuro uobis per patientiam Dei, et per angelos meos, si non conuerseritis ad sanctam diem dominicam, inducam super uos uindictam magnam, et sustinentiam bonam uestram faciam, uos miseri* (ed. McNally, p. 186). Cf. Tarragona: *et quaecunque petieritis dabo uobis* (Priebsch, *Letter from Heaven*, p. 37).

54. Other Recension II texts do not suggest a date for the destruction while Recension I often has November; see Vienna 1355 (Appendix IIa, line 84). Letter E seems to deliberately omit this detail. The *Epistil Ísu* changes the time to St John's day.

55. Cf. Munich 9550: *Si quis negotium fecerit aliquod in die sancto dominico, exterminabo eum, aut si aliquid in domo sua operatur aut capillos tonserit, aut uestimenta lauerit aut panem coxerit, aut aliud quid inliciti operis in die dominico, exterminabo eum et non inuenient benedictionem neque hic neque in futuro, sed maledictionem. Inmittam in domos eius diuersas infirmitates super ipsos et super filios eorum. Si quis proximum causauerit in die sancto dominico, aut detractionem, aut contentionem, aut inlicitum risum commiserit, inmittam in eum omne malum ut deficiat et dispergetur* (Delehaye, 'Note', p. 179). Cf. Vat. Reg. Lat 49: *Qui faciunt opera in die dominico, et qui tundunt caput in die dominico, et qui purgunt domum in die dominico, hi sunt qui ieciat Deus in tenebras exteriores* (ed. McNally, p. 186).

56. Cf. Munich 9550: *Praecipio vobis sacerdotibus meis ut unusquisque istam epistolam ostendat populo suo, et affirmate illis a me transmissam* (Delehaye, 'Note', p. 180). For the use of the word *godspell* to refer to the Sunday Letter, see Chapter 4, p. 64 n. 6.

57. *Florentius se papa*: this figure, unique to E/F (Y²), was clearly intended to add even more heft to the final oath by Bishop Peter. One may speculate that the name Florentius presented itself due to a reverence for one or more of the following Irish religious of that name: St Florentius, a seventh-century abbot of Bangor; St Florentius II of Strasbourg (d. 693), or perhaps the monk Blathmac, whose Latinized name was Florentius and who was martyred at Iona in 835.

58. The oath is much less elaborate than other such oaths in Recension II; see Munich 9550: *Petrus episcopus indignus, iuro per Maiestatem Dei qui fecit caelum et terram, mare et omnia quae in eis sunt, per Iesum Christum et per sanctam genetricem Mariam, per omnes angelos Dei, per omnes patriarchas, prophetas, apostolos, martyres, confessores, uirgines, per reliquias omnium sanctorum atque electorum Dei, qui ista epistola non formata est manu hominis neque scripta, sed est scripta digito Dei et Domini nostri Iesu Christi, et est transmissa de septimo caelo et de throno Dei in terram, qualiter diem sanctum dominicum obseruare debeatis* (Delehaye, 'Note', pp. 180–1).

59. The phrase *ne mid bocblece* does not occur in E or in other related Sunday Letters.

60. Cf. Vercelli IX.1–8: *Men ða leofestan, manað us and myngaþ þeos halige boc þæt we sien gemyndige ymb ure sawle þearfe, and eac swa ures þæs nehstan dæges and þære tosceadednesse ure sawle þonne hio of ðam lichoman lædde bion. And læten we us singallice bion on gemyndum and on geþancum þæs egesfullican dæges tocyme, on ðam we sculon Gode riht agifan for ealles ures lifes dædum þe we sið oððe ær gefremedon fram fruman ures lifes oð ende; for ðan þe we nu magon behydan and behelian ura dæda, ac hie bioð þonne opena and unwrigena.* For a discussion of this and the followowing additions from other vernacular sermons, particularly those related to those in the Vercelli Book, see Chapter 4, pp. 88–91.

and þæs gedales lichoman and saule: Scragg points to the L version of Vercelli IX which later in the sermon has *ðonne bið oðer deaþ þæs lichoman and þære saule gedal* (lines 35–6). The expression is common enough, and since the rest of the passage parallels the beginning of Vercelli IX, which has *myngaþ þeos halige boc þæt we sien gemyndige . . . þære tosceadednesse ure sawle þonne hio of ðam lichoman lædde bion* (lines 1–3), it is likely that the former was the expression found in the source used by F.

61. Cf. Vercelli IX.18–24: *Gif þæt þonne bið þæt we willað wyrcean his willan and on his lufe þurhwunian, þonne magon we ægðer ge us heofonrice geearnian ge ðonne eac þæt we magon gesæliglice befleon þa stowe and þa dimman tintregan þær helle dioflu on syndon mid eallum hyra weugesiðum, and mid þam sawlum þe hyra larum hlystað and be hyra larum lybbað and to Gode gecyrran nellað þurh soðe andetnesse mæssepreosta and þurh soðe bote.*

62. Vercelli IX(L).29–31: *Wa, la, þam mannum þe mid deoflum sculon habban hyra eardungstowe, þær bið sar butan frofre and ermþa butan are and weana ma þonne æniges monnes gemet sy þæt hit asecgean mæge.* Another, greatly expanded, version of this sentence is in the 'Devil's Account of the Next World', which follows Letter F in the manuscript (see Robinson, lines 17–25). The Vercelli IX version from Hatton 115 (L) is closer, however.

63. Cf. BL Cotton Tiberius A.iii, 87rv: *hit gelamp hwylan æt suman cyrre þæt an ancra gefing ænne deofol þurh Godes mihte. . . . Þa se ancra angan þreatian swyþe þone deofol, þæt he him asæde eal hellewites brogan* (Robinson, 'The Devil's Account of the Next World', lines 1–4).

64. Vercelli IX.108–13: *and þeah .vii. men sien, and þara hæbbe æghwylc twa and hundsiofontig gereorda, swa feala swa ealles þysses middangeardes gereorda syndon, and þonne sy þara seofon manna æghwylc to alife gesceapen, and hyra hæbbe æghwylc siofon [homoeoteleuton in Vercelli IX] tungan, and þara tungena ælc hæbbe isene stemne, and þonne hwæðre ne magon þa ealle ariman helle witu.* E217: the 'men with tongues of iron' motif can be traced back to Virgil's *Aeneid* and was also used, in modified form, by the *Visio sancti Pauli*; see Wright, *Irish Tradition*, pp. 145–56 and 223.

65. Cf. Vercelli IX.8–15: *For þan we habbað micle nydþearfe, þa hwile þe we her syndon on þys lænan life and on þyssum gewitendlicum, þæt we þonne on þære toweardan worulde mægen and moton becuman to life þæs heofoncundan rices and to þam wuldre þære ecean eadignesse, þær we moton siððan orsorglice lybban and rixian butan ælcre onwendednesse mid him, emne swa ure dryhten hælende Crist, and mid eallum his halgum, gif we hit gearnian willað mid urum godum dædum.*

Appendix I

Paris, Bibliothèque nationale de France,
lat. 12,270 (s. xii, Corbie), 31v–32v

This version is that closest to Old English Letter A and is reprinted here (with minor changes) from the edition by H. Delehaye in 'Note sur la légende de la lettre du Christ tombée du ciel', *Bulletin de l'Académie royale belgique, Classe des lettres* 1 (1899), 171–213 at 181–4.

Incipit epistola que de celo uenit in Ierusalem et cecidit ante portam Effrem ibique inuenta est per manus sacerdotis nomine Achor, et ipse transmisit eam ad Armeniam ciuitatem ad alium sacerdotem nomine Ioram, qui transmisit eam in Bethania ciuitate ad alium sacerdotem nomine Machabeum, et ipse transmisit eam
5 ad montem Garganum, ubi est ecclesia sancti Michaelis archangeli. Ipsa autem epistola per uoluntatem Dei Romam peruenit ad sepulchrum sancti Petri et omnes qui erant in ciuitate ubi epistola uenit fecerunt triduanum ieiunium et orationes et elemosinas, ut pius Dominus daret eis auxilium et aperiret sensum in cordibus hominum ad cognoscendam misericordiam domini nostri Iesu Christi, pro qua
10 causa epistola uenisset. Et recognita quod in die sancto dominico aduenisset, preceperunt ipsum diem dominicum magno studio celebrari pacita non custodientes, non iudicantes, non iurantes, mercatum non facientes, nec molentes, non uendentes, non ementes, non herbas in horto colligentes, alios non detrahentes, uenationes non facientes, quia per istas causas mundus erit periturus et propter
15 hoc ueniet iudicium Dei super nos. Cur nescitis, miseri, quia sex diebus Deus fecit celum et terram, mare et omnia que in eis sunt, et postea primum hominem Adam plasmauit per eius preuaricationem per V milia ducentos XX annos, iustos et iniustos in infernum premisit, sed Christus pro uobis formam hominis accipiens in mundum uenit et pro uobis multa sustinuit, et post resurrectionem
20 suam iustos ad gaudia reuocauit. Rogo uos et ammoneo, expergiscimini, dum tempus est, in orationibus uestris, in ieiuniis, in uigiliis, in elemosinis, in multis afflictionibus, ad ecclesiam frequentius pergite, et precipio sequi Deum in cinere et cilicio cum ieiuniis et elemosinis ne pereatis, quia mors cotidiana ante oculus uestros est parata. Castigate uos, miseri, et emite regnum Dei. Notum sit uobis
25 per epistolam istam, si non emendaueritis et diem dominicum non custodieritis et festiuitates sanctorum, et decimas fideliter de omnibus que possidetis non solum de laboribus sed etiam de artibus et de cunctis negotiis uestris siue de carnibus siue per abstinentiam corporis non dederitis, magnam penam sustinebitis in inferno, dicit Dominus. Ego ueritatem dico uobis de his rebus supra dictis quas
30 mihi non soluistis. Agite penitentiam in hoc seculo, et si non uultis emendare,

uel non obseruaueritis sanctum diem dominicum et non credideritis in me et in
mea precepta, transmittam super uos lapides grandes et famem ualidam et tem-
pestatem et ignem et tribulationem, et mittam in os uestrum siue in oculos uel in
aures bestiolas quas uocant scyniphes uenenatas pessimas ad deuorandum uos.

35 Ego sum ueritas et ueritatem denuntio uobis, quia in primo tempore ueniet super
uos ira mea, et sunt contra uos multa pericula parata, ut sic pereatis sicut due
ciuitates Sodoma et Gomorra. Mortui itaque fuissetis in peccatis uestris, si non
interuenisset pro uobis sancta Maria et precatio sancti Michaelis et sancti Petri
ceterorumque apostolorum et omnium sanctorum Dei. Per ueritatem dico uobis,

40 si uos emendaueritis, aperiam uobis ianuam celi et dabo uobis ad tempus fructus
terre et omnem habundantiam, et uitam uestram faciam longeuam super terram,
et eritis uiuentes in secula seculorum. Dico uobis, fidelissimi mei, permaneat in
uobis gloria mea, quomodo uigilando, orando, elemosynam dando, actus malos
derelinquendo, adulteria omnia fugiendo, homicidia declinando. Omnia precepta

45 mea custodite, ut mereamini habere consortium omnium sanctorum. Reuertimini
ad me et ego reuertar ad uos, et credite michi quod epistola hec de mea uirtute et
de manibus meis scripta et de septimo throno sit transmissa. O miseri, emundate
corda uestra a sordibus peccatorum et declarate animas uestras, ut possitis pos-
sidere uitam eternam. Et scitote quia propter decimas uestras quas fraudastis et

50 propter labores importunos quos fecistis in dominicis diebus et propter fidem
quam non obseruastis inter amicos et uicinos uestros et conpatres et omnes fideles Christi, propterea delebo nomina uestra de libro uite si per penitentiam non
emendaueritis et confessionem non receperitis. Ve uobis miseri qui per crucem
estis redempti, per crucem eciam estis dampnati. Ve uobis qui iuratis per crucem,

55 qui iuratis Christi Passionem et obprobria, sputa scilicet et alapas, colaphos[a]
flagella<que>, que omnia pro uobis sustinuit paciens mortem. Ve uobis qui iura-
mentum mendax diligitis. Nonne intelligitis quod dixerim non iurare omnino, sed
sit sermo uester est, est, non, non. Quod autem his habundantius est, a malo est.
Pro iuramento crucis peccatores peribunt, et descendent ad inferos, ubi uermis

60 eorum non moritur et ignis non extinguitur. Mulieres autem non colentes diem
dominicum et festiuitates sanctorum, transmittam super uos serpentes pendentes
ad mamillas, sucgentes quasi filius, et puniemini propter castitatem quam non
habuistis. Nati uestri nascentur sine oculis et sine manibus et sine pedibus, in
opprobrium et spectaculum omnibus muti et surdi, et ceci et claudi, quia non

65 custoditis noctem sanctam dominicam et non refrenastis linguas uestras mal-
edicendo et in iuramentis mendacibus peccando et in uestris uestibus preciosis
superbiendo. Cur tam ornamenta preciosa et purpuram et sericum et omnia que
contra preceptum Domini sunt, diligitis sicut uos pro illorum desiderio perdatis?
Cur diligitis ea que odit Dominus, quamdiu Dominus factor et conditor omnium

70 creaturarum que in mundo sunt non aurum neque gemmas neque uestes preciosas
concupiuit? Rogo uos per epistolam istam, precipio uobis ut in die dominico non
faciatis opera uestra nec in aliis festiuitatibus sanctorum nisi ut uisitetis infirmos
et sepeliatis mortuos et eatis ad oratoria sanctorum. Epistola autem ista cecidit

a colaphosque

in Ierusalem de manu Domini scripta et ad sepulcrum sanctum peruenit per uol-
75 untatem Dei et due antea, et ista tertia est, et post illam nulla ueniet amplius. Qui
audierit hoc breue et non crediderit, anathematus erit. Vos episcopi et sacerdotes,
annuntiate istam epistolam frequenter omni populo et transmittite per prouincias,
ut diligenter suscipiant et credant non ab homine inuentam sed a summi saluatoris
manibus scriptam, et hi qui eam habuerint et uobis annuntiauerint, mercedem
80 recipient in uitam eternam; et uos custodite eam cum omni diligentia et gaudio
propter amorem Christi, ut recipiatis mercedem in uitam aeternam. Amen.

Appendix IIa

Vienna, Österreichische Nationalbibliothek, 1355 (s. xiv/xv), 89r–90v

This version is that closest to Old English Letter B and is reprinted here (with minor
changes) from the edition by R. Priebsch in 'The Chief Sources of Some Anglo-Saxon
Homilies', *Otia Merseiana* 1 (1899), 129–47 at 130–4.

Incipit epistola in nomine trinitatis saluatoris domini Iesu Christi quae de celo in
Ierusalem cecidit per Michahelem archangelum. Ista epistola est inuenta ad portam Effrem per magnum sacerdotem cui nomen Ichor. Ipsa epistola fuit relicta ibi
et ipsam exemplauit et transmisit ad Ermiam ciuitatem ad alium sacerdotem nom-
5 ine Talasium. Ipse Talasius transmisit eam de Ebrea ciuitate ad alium sacerdotem
cui nomen Lebonius et ipse Lebonius transmisit eam ad Capadociam ciuitatem
ad alium sacerdotem nomine Iuram, et ipse Iuras transmisit eam ad Bethaniam
ciuitatem ad alium sacerdotem nomine Marchabeus et ipse Marchabeus sacerdos
transmisit illam epistolam ad montem sancti Michahelis archangeli et ipsa epistola
10 per uoluntatem domini nostri Iesu Christi peruenit ad Romam ciuitatem ad locum
praedestinatum ad sepulcrum sancti Petri et Pauli. Qui erant in ciuitate triduanas[a]
fecerunt in uigiliis et ieiuniis <et> in orationibus, ut pius deus perdonasset eis
auxilium et sensum in corda eorum, pro quali iam ista epistola in Ierusalem et in
alias ciuitates uenisset et per ordinationem domini nostri Iesu Christi inuenerunt,
15 quia propter diem sanctum dominicum aduenisset. Quia in die sancto dominico
sedentes causas indicantes, iurantes, periurantes, olera in orto colligentes, pecudes
mulgentes, molas tornantes,[b] uenationes facientes: propter hoc perit mundus et
propter hoc uenit iudicium dei super populum cunctum praesentem. Cognoscite,
miserae animae, quia in sex diebus fecit deus coelum et terram, solem et lunam,
20 quattuor euangelistas,[c] mare et omnia quae in eis sunt, praeterea hominem Adam

a driduanas
b t::nentes
c ewangelistas

201

plasmauit de terra. Quia in die sancto dominico requieuit, et nunc sic debent peccatores et iusti, sicut angeli requiescunt in coelo. Et rogo uos, expurgate uos in
uigiliis et ieiuniis, in orationibus ad ecclesias meas ambulate, cruces per omnes
domos aras ponite, caput cum cinere spargite, triduanam facite, sicut liberabit
25 uos dominus. Miseri populi, arguite uos, dirigite et emite uobis regnum dei, quia
cottidie mors ante oculos uestros est. Suspiciosa non sit epistola ista. Si bene
feceritis, de manu inimica liberati eritis. Et mando uobis per epistolam istam: si
non emendaueritis et si poenitentiam non egeritis et sanctum diem dominicum et
compatratam de sancto Iohanne non obseruaueritis et decimas non redditeritis,
30 transmitto super uos lapides pendentes ponderibus et aquas calidas usque ad mortem. Ego uero dico uobis, quia in isto mense Nouembri^d proximo uenturo^e quia
fuit sic, perire debuistis, si deprecatio non esset sanctae Mariae uirginis meae et
sancti archangeli Michahelis et sancti Petri apostoli mei et sancti Pauli: per eorum
orationes liberati fuistis. Et dico uobis: si emendaueritis et si poenitentiam egeri-
35 tis, dabo uobis frumentum, uindemiam et ligna pomifera et amplificabo uitam
uestram et uiuetis in pace in seculum. Dico uobis, populi mei, fides acceptabilis
permaneat in uobis et gratiam dei orando, uigilando, elemosinam dando, actus
malos relinquendo, homicidium relaxando, uiduis et orphanis adiuuando. Filius,
pater et mater inter se maledictionem tradent, ad penam sunt reuersi cum igne
40 ardenti et exterminantur. Et dico uobis ad ecclesias meas cum oblacione et luminaribus ambulate et ibi lectiones diuinas audiendo manete, ebrietatem fugiendo,
maliciam <et> auariciam dimittendo, diem sanctum dominicum et compatratam
de sancto Iohanne custodiendo et decimas reddendo. Haec diffinitio ante oculos
uestros ut non sit dimmittenda. Transmisi ad uos ordinationes quae apud me sunt
45 dictae et non credidistis. Coniuro uos, populi mei, per Iordanem, ubi mihi sanctus
Iohannes baptismum tradidit, cum oleo et crismate unxit me, celum inuocauit; per
ista sacramenta uos coniuro, scripturam quam transmitto, ut credatis et ad ecclesias meas conueniatis et ad sacerdotes meos confessionem faciatis. Tendo arcum
meum et aperiam ^{f}sagittam meam^f, ut non pereant peccatores sed peccata dimit-
50 tantur. Sed reuertimini ad me, recordamini, populi mei, ut animas uestras declaratas accipiat regnum dei. Credite uero, quia istam epistolam dominus noster Iesus
Christus de uertice celi misit propter diem dominicum et compatrandam de sancto
Iohanne et propter decimam non redditis. Amen, dico uobis, mitto super uos
locustas et brucos qui comedunt fructus uestros et mitto super uos lupos rapaces et
55 canes malignos qui uos comedunt, et dico uobis, conuertam faciem meam a uobis
et mittam in tabernaculis uestris omnem maliciam et amaritudinem ualidissimam,
et si <non> fueritis ad ecclesias, ego indurabo et non adiuuabo uos et trado uos in
malignantium manus, quia non seruatis diem sanctum dominicum. Et rogo uos,
ut in sancto die dominico caput non lauetis neque comas tondatis; si non cus-
60 todieritis, anathemati eritis; inmitto in domibus uestris famem et tribulationem.
O increduli, quia istam epistolam misi ad uos et noluistis credere, anathemata

d Nouembre
e uentuoso
f–f sagitta mea

erit anima uestra, quia mandaui uobis per duas epistolas meas anteriores, ista est
tertia. Si non obseruatis diem dominicum, mittam super uos pustulas in faciem,
in oculos, in os, in aures, in nares, et in omnia membra, quae uos comedunt usque
65 ad mortem. Amen, dico uobis, propter uos crucifixus fui et resurrexi die tertio.
Cognoscite, gentes insipientes, ego ipse mandaui super omnes ecclesias meas
per scripturas et libros, ut seruetis diem dominicum et compatratam de sancto
Iohanne et decimas reddatis, quia Christiani estis, quia pagani non reddunt decimas et me colere nesciunt, quia non sunt similes uobis. Amen, dico uobis. Neces-
70 sarium est, ut custodiatis diem dominicum et compatratam de sancto Iohanne et
decimas reddatis et in die sabbati de hora nona usque lucescente die lune feriatis:
si non custodieritis, mitto super uos grandinem et uermes qui comedunt fruges
uestras, et monstrabitur et non dabitur quia decimam non reddetis ad ecclesias.
Amen dico uobis. <Si> colligent mulieres holera in die dominico, mittam super
75 eas serpentes pinnatos qui lacerant mamillas usque in finem. Dico uobis, si non
custodieritis diem dominicum, erunt infantes nati qui non audiunt neque uident
neque ambulant et sic pereunt. Ecce iam prophetaui uobis, quia praeter hanc non
est ulla. Et si mandata mea custodieritis, omnia bona habueritis et si reuertimini
ad me. Et si sacerdotes aut diaconi aut monachi aut clerici istam epistolam
80 habuerint et non annunciauerint omni populo, anathema erit anima eorum. Et qui
audierint et non crediderint anathemati erunt. Epistola ista in Ierusalem cecidit et
ad sanctum Petrum peruenit et non apud hominem ullum est scripta sed uerbo dei
dicta et septimo trono transmissa. Et certe credatis: si emendare uos nolueritis,
parati estis ad mortem. Et sciatis, quia in isto mense Nouembri[g] proximo uenturo[h]
85 iram grandissimam uolo uobis manifestare, malitiam et amaritudinem transmitto
super uos, flammam ignis ardentis et uermes uolantes. Et certe credatis, quia totus
mundus in ruina est positus. Et praeter istam epistolam aliam uobis non mittam, et
frequentius annuncietis super populum ut omnipotens deus adiuuet illis.

g Nouembre
h uentuoso

Appendix IIb

London, British Library, Add. 19,725 (s. x/xi), 87v–88r

BL Add. 19,725, a late tenth-century manuscript from around Rheims, contains penitential texts, among other things.[1] A slightly later hand has added material in the margins and empty spaces, including a Sunday Letter on 87v and the bottom margin of 88r. The ink has been rubbed away in places and the margins have been trimmed, resulting in a loss of text. This copy of the Sunday Letter was noted by Priebsch (*Letter from Heaven*, p. 5 n. 2), who noticed the significant lacuna towards the end of the text and suggested that the missing portion had been written on a piece of parchment inserted in this spot but now lost. Letters and words in angled brackets have been supplied from the much later but more readable version in Vienna, Österreichische Nationalbibliothek, 1355 (Appendix IIa) and from Paris, BN 12,270 (Appendix I).

Incipit epistola in nomine trinitatis domini nostri Iesu Christi que[a] de celo in Hierusalem per Michaelem cecidit archangelum et inuenta est ad portas Effraim per manus sacerdotis Achor. Et ipse Achor exemplare[b] misit eam ad Armeniam ciuitatem ad sacerdotem nomine Talasium. Talasius uero misit eam ad Aebream
5 ciuitatem ad sacerdotem nomine Libonium. Libonius misit eam ad Capadociam ciuitat[em] ad sacerdotem nomine Iuoram. Et Iuoras misit eam ad Bethaniam ciuitatem ad sacerdotem nomine Machabeum. Machabeus misit eam ad montem sancti archangeli Michaelis. Et exinde per uoluntatem domini nostri Iesu Christi peruenit ad Romam ciuitatem ad locum predistinatum ad sepulcrum sancti Petri.
10 Qui autem erant in ciuitatem Rome triduanis fe[cerunt] in uigiliis in hieiuniis in oracionibus ut dominus noster donaret auxilium et sensum in corda eorum. Pro[c] quali iam hec epistola in Hierusalem et in aliis ciuitatibus aduenisset, quia in sanctum diem dominicum sedentes et causas iudicantes et periurantes, oler[a in orto] colligentes, focos inluminantes, peccuniam mouentes, molas tornantes,
15 uenaciones facientes et alias eorum similes[d] agentes: propter hoc perit mundus et iudicium domini super cunctum uenerit populum presentem. Cognoscite, miseri anime, quia in sex diebus fecit deus celum et terram sole[m] et lunam et quatuor euangelista, mare et omnia que in eis sunt. Postea hominem plasmauit de terra et in diem <dominicum> ab uniuerso opere requieuit et nunc sic debent facere
20 peccatores et iusti sicut angeli requiescunt in celo. Rogo uos, expergiscimini in oracionibus, in uigiliis, [e]in ieiuniis; in oracionibus[e] ad ecclesias meas ambulate; crucem per omnes dom[os] ponite; super capita [f]uestra cinerem[f] spargite.

a qui	d similias
b ʽexʼemplare	e–e in oracionib- in ieiuniis
c O	f–f uestra ponite cinerem

[1] See R. Haggenmüller, *Die Überlieferung der Beda und Egbert zugeschriebenen Bußbücher* (Frankfurt am Main, 1991), p.70.

Triduanas sicut Nineuite fecerunt agite, sicut[g] liberauit uos dominus. Miseri
populi, arguite uos <et> emite uobis regnum dei, quia cotidiana mors ante oculos
25 uestros est. Et suscipite epistolam istam.[h] Et si non emendauer[itis] et penitentiam
non egeritis et diem dominicum et compatrato de sancto Iohanne non custodieritis et decimas non dederetis,[i] <transmitto> super uos lapides pensantes pondera
quinque. Ego uero dico uobis, quia mense iste Nouembri[j] proximo qui fuit, perire
debuistis, si deprecacio fuisset sancte Marie uirginis et beati archangeli Michaelis
30 necnon et beatorum apostolorum Petri et Pauli et per oracionem eorum liberi
fuistis. Dico autem uobis, si emendaueritis aperiam uobis cataractas celi et dabo
<uobis frumentum> uindemiam, <et> pomam arborum et amplificabo uitam
eternam et uluetis in seculum. Dico uobis populis meis, fides acceptabilis permaneat in uobis et gracia dei, orando, uigilando, elemosinis[k] dando, actos malos
35 derelinquendo, homicidia[l] relaxando, uiduas et orfanos adiuuandos ut mereatis
habere[m] consorcia <omnium sanctorum>. Pater et filius siue mater inter[n] se mal-
ediccionem[o] [t]radentes, ad penas transituri cum <igne> ardenti[p] exterminabun-
tur. Dico uobis; ad ecclesias meas cum oblacionibus[q] [et] luminariis[r] ambulate et
ibi lecciones diuinas audiendo manete,[s] ebrietatem fugiendo et diem dominicum
40 compatrate de sancto Iohanne custodiendo. Haec diffinicio ante oculos uestros
non sit dimittenda.[t] Transmisi ad uos ordinaciones que apud me sunt condita et
non credidistis.[u] Coniuro uos, [v]populi mei,[v] per Iordanem fluuium ubi me sanctus
Iohanne[s] bap[tismum tra]didit, cum oleo et crismate[w] me unxit, celum [x]inu-
ocauit[x]; per ista sacramenta uos coniuro ut hanc †† [scriptur]am credatis <et>
45 ad ecclesias <meas conueniatis et ad sacerdotes meos> confessiones faciatis.
Tendo arcum meum et aperiam sagitt[am ut non pereant] peccatores sed peccata
dimittantur[y] et reuertantur[z] ad me. Recordate miseri [88r] *** et septimo throno
transmissa. Et certe sciatis: si emendare nolueritis, parati estis usque ad mortem.[a]
Et sciatis quia in isto mense Nouembri[b] proximo uenturo [c]iram dei grandissimam[c]
50 uol[o] <uobis manifestare>, maliciam et amaritudinem super uos transmitto et
flamma ignis ardentis et uermes [uolantes]. Et <certe> cre[datis] quia totus mundus in ruina positus est. Et post istam epistolam aliam non mitto, et frequentius
adnun[cietis] ab [uni]uerso omni populi ut deus omnipotens adiuet illis. Amen.

g scio	s manendo
h ista	t dimittendo
i de `de´retis	u credidi`ti´s
j Nouembrio	v–v populis meis
k ele `mo´sinis	w crisma
l omicidias	x–x mihi uocauit
m abere	y dimittuntur
n in	z reuermini
o malediccio:::	a morte
p ardentes	b nouenbrio
q oblaciones	c–c ira dei grandissima
r lum::aria	

Appendix IIc

Basel, Universitätsbibliothek, B VII 7 (s. x, Basel), 1r

Basel B VII 7 is a manuscript of the tenth century containing Augustine's *De consensu evangelistarum* (1v–176v).[1] On 1r an abbreviated version of the Sunday Letter has been copied in another hand. The text is difficult to read in places due to considerable wear and possible water damage. Though it is clear that it represents the final third of Recension I, it is in places quite corrupt. Readings in square brackets indicate an unreadable portion resulting from damage to the manuscript; angled brackets indicate conjectured readings supplied from other copies of that recension. Daggers indicate damaged or corrupt segments for which a conjectured reading is not possible.

Rogo uos fratres ut in diem sanctum dominicum nullum opus autem faciatis: capita uestra non lauetis, ††,[a] nec <comas>[b] uestras tondatis[c] nec aliquod opus faciatis. Nis[i] custodieritis diem sanctum dominicum, anatema er[it] anima uestra, et mittam in uobis famem et tribulacionem incredulam. Epistola ista,
5   quam autem misi ad uos, si hanc[d] credere non uult[is], <anatema erit> anima uestra. Quia mandaui uobis per duas epistolas (et ista est tercia) ut obseruetis diem sanctum dominicum. Et si non obseruaueritis, mittam super uos bestias in facies in oculos,[e] in os[f] i[n] aures et omnia membra[g] uestra, quae comedant[h] uos usque ad mortem. Et si uos non custodieritis, erit ††.[i] Amen dico uobis. Prop-
10 ter uos ueni autem in mundum, propter uos fl[age]llatus, propter uos spineam coronam ac[cepi] et suspensus in ligno et resurrexi diem sanctum [dominicum]. Cognos[cite], gentes <insipientes>, ego <mandaui> super omniam ecclesiam <per> hanc scripturam <ut seruetis> [diem sanctum] dominicum et conpatratum de sancto Ioanne <et> decimas[j] <reddatis> <ad> meos[k] sacerdotes qui ministrent,
15 <quia> [Christiani] estis ††.[l] Pagani non reddant decimas et <me colere nesciunt, quia non sunt similes uobis>. Amen dico uobis. Necessarium est [ut] <custodatis diem dominicum et conpatratum de sancto Ioanne> et decimas uestras †† red-datis †† <et in die sabbati de hora nona usque> in die l[u]nis lucisc[ente] <fer-iatis>. †† Et si non custodieritis, mittam su[per] uos gran[d]inem [et uermes] <qui

a nec pagemini	h conmedant
b manus	i :arrius et sabarrius et belzeb ::::::: permaneatis,
c tondeatis	*there is nothing similar in any related version*
d anc	j de crism:
e oculis	k mei
f hos	l – ueritis, *visible*
g menbra	

---

[1]   G. Meyer and M. Burckhardt, *Die mittelalterlichen Handschriften der Universitätsbibliothek Basel, beschreibendes Verzeichnis*, 3 vols. (Basel, 1960), I, 674–6. I wish to thank Dominik Hunger in reproductions and the curator for supplying me with a photograph of the folio and the university library for granting me access to the manuscript.

20 comedant> fruges uestras. Monstrabo et non dabo uobis si decimas uestras non
<reddatis> ††.[m] Amen dico uobis. Mu[li]eres si coll[i]gerent olera diem sanctum
dominicum mittam super illas serpentes pennatas[n] qui lacer[a]nt mamillas eorum
usque ad mortem. Verumtamen dico uobis, si non custodieri[t]is diem sanctum
dominicum, erunt[o] infantes in domibus uestris <qui> non †† uidere nec audire et
25 sic peribunt. Apostolos meos et prophetas meas <misi> ad uos et non credidisti.
Et autem si[p] quis sacerdos aut[q] pontifex <epistolam> habuerint[r] et [s]sanctae ecclesiae[s] populo non adnunciauerint, anatema erit de <omni> populo anima eius. ††
Epistola ista in Hierusalem cecidit ad portas Effraim †† et ad sanctum Petrum ad
Romam peruenit, et non est a[p]ud hominem[t] facta [est] <sed> [uer]bo dei [di]
30 cta et digito dei scripta et de septimo non[o] transmissa est. Et certe credatis:
et si non audire uoluerint,[u] parati estis ad mortem. Et sciatis quia in isto menso
Nouembri,[v] ira[w] †† grandissima uos expectat; malicias, amaritudines transmitto
<et> ignem et flammam[x] autem ardentem et ue[rmes] uolantes qui uos percutient
si non emendaueritis. Et certe credatis, <quia> tot[u]s mundus in ruina positus est.
35 Frequen[tius] adnunciante <eam populo> meo ut deus omnipotens adiuuet, nos
protegat et defendat usque in secula seculorum.

m reuertimini, *visible*	s sancta ecclesia
n pena/sas	t ominum
o erant	u noluerint
p n[i]si	v NOVbR, *rustic capitals*
q au	w iram
r abuerint	x flamma

Appendix III

Vienna, Dominikanerkloster 133 (102) (s. xv, ? Vienna), 134vb–135vb

Kassel, Murhardsche Bibliothek der Stadt Kassel und Landesbibliothek,
theol. 39 (s. xiv, Michelbach/Marburg), 158r

This Latin version of the Sunday Letter is the source of Old English Letters C and
D. Vienna 133 (V) has been used as the base text since Kassel, theol. 39 (K) contains
only the first portion of the text; minor spelling variants in K have not been recorded.[1]

---

[1] See the description in K. Wiedemann, *Manuscripta theologica: Handschriften in Folio*. Die
Handschriften der Gesamthochschulbibliothek Kassel, Landesbibliothek und Murhardsche Bibliothek
der Stadt Kassel 1.1, ed. H.-J. Kahlfuss (Wiesbaden, 1994), pp. 47–50. The Vienna manuscript
contains a collection of theological works; see F. Unterkircher, *Die datierten Handschriften in Wien
ausserhalb der Österreichischen Nationalbibliothek bis zum Jahre 1600. 1. Teil: Text*. Katalog der
datierten Handschriften in lateinischer Schrift in Österreich 5 (Wien, 1981), p. 58.

Incipit epistola domini nostri [a]Iesu Christi[a] saluatoris mundi de interdictione[b] omnium malorum et de obseruatione omnium bonorum quam angelus[c] suo digito scripsit et in manus[d] Petri episcopi Antiocensis[e] ecclesie tradidit, mandans[f] et adiurans per nomen dei[g] uiui ut diuulgaret Petrus episcopus hec uerba domini
5   et non sua[h] omnibus[i] regibus et[j] episcopis necnon[k] et omni populo christiano.[l] Ego angelus[m] et nuntius dei saluatoris[n] mando et remando[o] imperatoribus ac regibus omnibusque potestatibus[p] ut diligant iustitiam in omnibus causis, seruiant[q] domino nostro Iesu Christo in omni timore, et custodiant maxime diem dominicum in [r]qua multa mirabilia fecit dominus.[r] [s]Primo fecit[s] angelos, archangelos[t]
10   cum omnibus ordinibus celestibus et uniformem[u] materiam. Die dominico fecit quattuor elementa [v]et omnia[v] qua uidentur adque constant [w]sunt facta.[w] Die dominica creauit omnium animas.[x] Die[y] dominica natus est Christus ad redimendum[z] mundum.[a] Die[b] dominica diuisit[c] Mare Rubrum in .xii. diuisiones. [d]Die dominica dominus noster surrexit.[d] [e]Die dominica [135r] misit deus spiritum sanctum
15   super apostolos.[e] Die[f] dominica pluit deus manna super populum Israhelitum per quadraginta annos. Die[g] dominica conuertit[h] aquam in uinum in Chana Galilee. Die[i] dominica benedixit Christus[j] quinque panes et duos pisces et satiauit quinque milia hominum et superfuerunt duodecim cophini de[k] fragmentis. [l]Die dominica recessit sinagoga Iudeorum et nata est ecclesia katholica.[l] Die domi-
20   nica finitus erit[m] mundus. Die[n] dominica iudicabit dominus genus humanum et qui[o] bene uixerunt ibunt in uitam eternam, qui uero mala [p]egerunt cruciabuntur in ignem eternum cum dyabulo et sociis suis.[p] Idcirco[q] precepit dominus deus uobis ut custodiatis diem dominicum a mundano opere scilicet[r] ab[s] inmunditia,[t]

a–a *om.* K
b interitione K
c angelus domini K
d manu K
e Anthiocensis K
f mandans dedit K
g domini dei K
h suis K
i *om.* K
j necnon suis
k *om.* K
l Tale est principium huius epistole K
m angelus domini K
n saluatoris seculi uos K
o remando uobis omnibus in terra K
p peccantibus K
q confornant K
r qua deus mirabilia fecit K
s–s *om.* V
t et archangelos K
u informem K
v–v ex qua uidelicet omnia K
w-w facta sunt K
x creauit animas omnium hominum, *crossed out* K

y Item die K
z redimendi V, remedium K
a–a mundi V, mundum et qui in mundo sunt K
b Item die K
c liberauit filios Israel ab egyptijs et diuisit K
d–d Item die dominico surrexit dominus noster Iesus Christus a morte, *placed following the feeding of the 5000 in* K
e–e *om.* K
f Item die K
g Item die K
h conuertit dominus K
i Item in die K
j *om.* K
k d`e´ V, ex K
l–l *om.* K
m erit finis K
n Item die K
o *om.* K
p–p ibunt in ignem eternum et dyabolo cruciabuntur K
q Nobis idcirco K
r idest K
s de K
t inmunditia carnis K

ab^s fornicatione, ab^s ebrietate, ab^s homicidio, a^s mendacio, a^s rapina, a^s furtu, ab^s
25 adulterio, a^s contentione, ab^s emulatione, ab^s omni nequitia, ab^s omni placito,^{u}
nisi ut uaceret,^{v} orationem dicatis^w in ^{x}ecclesia, ut audiatis^x predicationem a doc-
toribus^y ^{z}seu rectoribus^z ecclesiarum et ut^a uisitetis^b loca sanctorum. Et infirmos
debetis^c uisitare, mortuos^d humilime^e sepelire, pauperes pascere, nudos uestire,
sicientes potare, aduenas adiuuare,^{f} captiuos reddimere, peregrinos benigne
30 suscipere, egenis uiduisque solatium prebere, discordantes christianos pacificare. ^{g}Ecce opera digna coram deo omni tempore, maxime uero custodiendus est^g
dies dominicus, quia ^{h}dies domini^h prima est omnium dierum et ultima. Quod si
aliud feceritis preter quam^i dicta, flagellabo uos durissimis flagellis, idest ponam
quattuor iudicia mea in terram scilicet famem, captiuitatem, gladium, et pesti-
35 lentiam. Et tradam uos in manus alienorum. Exterminabo^j uos et submergere
faciam sicut feci Sodome et Gomorre et sicut feci Dathan, Choreb et Abiran
qui blasphemauerunt nomen meum et meos sacerdotes. Et inducam super uos
gentem deuastandam, cuius linguam nescitis. Scutum et sagittam arripiet contra
uos, et uox illius gentis horribiliter ab aquilone sonabit super uos. Et fama illius^k
40 antequam ueniat terrebit uos, et tribulatio aprehendet uos, dolor ut parturientem.
Si autem^l diem dominicum non custodiuistis et me spretum habuistis, scitote
quidem et memoriter habetote quod ab initio diem dominicum iussi custodiri.
Quicumque negotium seculare in die dominico fecerit uel uestimenta abluerit,
artificium aliquod egerit uel capillos totonderit uel panem coxerit uel aliquam
45 tam illicitam perpetrauerit exterminabo eum et eius fautores suosque adiutores
de regno meo. Et qui talia faciunt non inuenient benedictionem meam. Sed pro
benedictione, quia spreuerunt me et mea uerba, maledictionem meam sine mora
inuenient, et mittam in domos illorum infirmitates et pestes innumerabiles tam
super illos quam filios^m eorum et super familiam et super peccora eorum que
50 habent in domibus. Quare non recordat gens praua et peruersa quod moratur in
ultimo tempore huius mundi quo iussi reges romanorum *** Ierusalimam ciuitatem que mihi pre omnibus ciuitatibus dilectissima fuit quod deduxerunt in die
pasce sancto undecies centum^n milia in captiuitatem et centum milia occisa et
prostrata de illa ciuitate eo quod spreuerunt me et meos doctores et non custodier-
55 unt diem dominicum sicut precepi eis. Si quis contentionem aut detractionem aut
alia turpia opera et inutilia in die dominico fecerit, mittam in eum omne malum

u placito carnis et seculi K

v uacetis V, uaceret idest celebraret in seruitio
  dei K

w diceret K

x–x ecclesia dei et ut audiat K

y predicatoribus K

z–z *om.* K

a *om.* K

b uisitaret K

c *om.* K

d mor-, *end of line* K

e humiliter K

f adiuuarere V

g–g Et no: (*? for* notandum) pre omnibus
  operibus uero dignum est custodiendus
  coram deo omni tempore maxime K

h–h dominica K

i hec K

j et exterminabo uos de hoc seculo ad ignem
  eternum K, *K breaks off at this point*

k illius illius V, *second instance crossed out*

l ut V

m filiorum V

n cetum V

et dispergetur et deficiet a manibus impiorum et quod spreuerunt meum preceptum. Si enim non custodieritis diem dominicum ab omni opere malo tam liberi°
quam serui ab hora nona sabathi usque in secundam feriam, anathematizabo uos
60   coram patre meo qui est in celis et non habebitis partem meam neque cum angelis
meis in secula seculorum. Et si me spreueritis et non obedieritis sacerdotibus et
predicatoribus uestris et doctoribus[p] sapientibus uiam iustam demonstrantibus,[q]
mittam super terram uestram grandinem fulgura coruscationes ignium inex[::]
scanes[r] in ciuitatibus et in uillis tempestates, [135v] intemporaneas siccitates et
65   infertilitates messium arborum, uinearum, omniumque florentium terre. Et si non
fideliter condigneque decimas et primitias de omnibus laboribus siue in agricul-
tura[s] uel in aliquo artificio obtuleritis in nomine dei omnipotentis ecclesiis, tollam
ab uobis nouem partes et insuper faciam ut ceci uel[t] surdi et manci[u] debilesque at
leprosi[v] nascentur in domibus uestris et fames magna aderit uobis in tantum ut nec
70   diues poterit adiuuare inopem. De die dominico satis habetis auditum si ex deo
estis quia qui est ex deo, uerba dei audit, propterea uos non auditis quia ex deo
non estis. Et pro domini nostri Iesu Christi amore ammoneo uos quia finis mundi
est inlumine[w] et uestri anni abbreuiati[x] sunt ut emendetis ea que interdicta erant
uobis a deo tam in ueteri testamento quam in nouo per patres et prophetas, per
75   filium dei, unum deum cum patre et spiritu sancto, et per apostolos et sapientes,
et per mirabilia que ostendit deus in mundo tam in celo quam in stellis et in terra
et in mari et in omnibus creaturis. Nolite ergo facere diem de nocte et noctem de
die. Ve uobis qui uertitis dulce in amarum et amarum in dulce et mane in uespere
et uespere in mane, tympano et lyra et tibia et simphoniis, crapula et ebrietate
80   et nimii[y] in conuiuiis uestris usque ad uentris[z] plenitudinem. Nonne scitis quia
qui deseruit superbie quia <superbia>[a] est suus dominus; qui deseruit auaritie,
auaritia est suus dominus; qui deseruit gule quia gula erit suus dominus et ceteris.[b]
Ergo qui talibus uitiis deseruit uerum deum derelinquit.[c] Idcirco uobis contestor ut hec omnia dimittatis antequam mors subripiat animas uestras in tartarum
85   iehenne. Si quis episcopus uel clericus siue doctor postquam istam epistolam in
manu habuerit eam sibi populo conmisso non recitauerit siue in ciuitate siue in
uilla procul, sine dubio potenter iudicium sustinebit quia quisquis sacerdos non
annunciat[d] peccata eorum saltem in die iudicii eorum exquiretur sanguis[e] ab eo et
reus in presentia dei de peccatis eorum stabit. Si autem annuncciauerit et nequitiis
90   eorum non sit consentaneus et in familiaritate[f] aut in conuiciis non adheserit eis de

o libri V

p docdoribus

q demonstra:ʾtiʹbus V

r *? corruption of* inextinct-, *or* incursiones

s agriculatura V

t ʹuelʹ V

u mana V

v ʹleʹprosi V

w *? for* in limine V

x aberrati V

y *? for* nimium *or* nimietate V

z uentres V

a *om.* V

b ceteriis V

c derelinquunt V

d anucciat V

e saguis V

f familiariete V

peccatis eorum inmunis[g] erit. Ego siquidem Petrus episcopus ecclesie antiocensis per dei potestatem et maiestatem quo creauit celum et terram mare et omnia que in eis sunt, qui formauit hominem ad similitudinem suam, et per Iesum Christum filium eius, dominum nostrum, et per spiritum sanctum procedentem a patre et

95 filio et per sanctam trinitatem et per unitatem inseparabiliter omnia operantem et per quattuor ewangelistas et per prophetas et apostolos et per ordines angelorum et per beatissimam Mariam uirginem et per corpora sanctorum omnium, contestor et coniuro quod uerba que in hac epistola sunt conscripta primitus non fuerunt formata de manu hominis sed de throno dei sunt transmissa et digito angeli con-

100 scripta. Frater mi ualeas tecum[h] cuncta ualeatis, et sic est finis.

g inmunus V   h secum V

Appendix IV

Manuscripts Containing Latin Versions of the Sunday Letter

The following is a list of all Latin versions of the Sunday Letter up to the fifteenth century which have been discovered thus far. Those marked with an asterisk have not been edited nor have I seen a facsimile. Within each recension they are ordered by date. A full accounting of the medieval Latin versions will no doubt find additional copies.

Recension I

[Vatican City, Biblioteca Apostolica Vaticana, Reg. lat. 49 (s. ix/x), 53r, *extract*[1]]
[Vatican City, Biblioteca Apostolica Vaticana, Reg. lat. 852 (s. x), 6v[2]]
Basel, Universitätsbibliothek, B VII 7 (s. x), 1r[3]
London, BL Add. 19,725 (s. x/xi), 87v–88r[4]

---

1   Ed. R. E. McNally in *Scriptores Hiberniae minores*, CCSL 108B (Turnhout, 1973), 186, lines 42–56. These extracts are really too brief to determine to which recension they belong, but there are some elements which are otherwise only to be found in Recension I texts; see discussion on page 49.
2   Only the title (*Incipit epistola Salvatoris Domini nostri*) remains with the rest erased and replaced with another, unrelated text; cf. W. Schmitz, 'Tironische Miscellen', *Neues Archiv* 15 (1890), 602–5 and idem, 'Nochmals ein vom Himmel gefallener Brief und ein Segen gegen Gift', *Neues Archiv* 23 (1898), 762–3.
3   Edited in Appendix IIc.
4   Edited in Appendix IIb.

Tarragona (Spain), Cathedral Library (s. xii?), *transcript of a lost manuscript*[5]
Paris, BN lat. 12,270 (s. xii), 31vb–32vb[6]
Vienna, Österreichische Nationalbibliothek, 1355 (xiv/xv), 89r–90v, *1 of 2 letters*[7]
Graz, Universitätsbibliothek, 248 (s. xv), 133rb–133va, *1 of 2 letters*

Recension II

Paris, BN lat. 8508 (s. x[1]), 57v–63r, *in margin*
Munich, Bayerische Staatsbibliothek, clm 9550 (s. xi), 1r[8]
London, BL Add. 30,853 (s. xi/xii), 231r–232v[9]
Todi, Perugia (s. xii?), *transcript of a lost manuscript*[10]
Vienna, Österreichische Nationalbibliothek, 1878 (s. xii), 35v–36v
Munich, Bayerische Staatsbibliothek, clm 14,673 (s. xii/xiii), 119v–120r, *1 of 2 letters*
Uppsala, Universitätsbibliothek, C212 (s. xiv), 1v–2v
Budapest, University Library, lat. 39 (s. xiv/xv), 86vb–88r
Einsiedeln, Stiftsbibliothek, 726 (s. xiv/xv), 124r
Kremsmünster, Stiftsbibliothek, 283 (s. xiv/xv), 92v–93r
London, BL Royal 11 B.x (s. xiv/xv), 184r
Vienna, Österreichische Nationalbibliothek, 1355 (s. xiv/xv), 91r–92r, *1 of 2 letters*
Bernkastel-Kues, Bibliothek des St. Nikolaus-Hospitals, 128 (s. xv), 129r, *fragment*
*Fritzlar, Dombibliothek, 37 (s. xv), 178v–181v
Hamburg, Bibliothek der Hansestadt, S. Petri-Kirche 30b (s. xv), 35r–36v[11]
Innsbruck, Stiftsbibliothek Wilten (s.n.) (s. xv), 153rb–154ra
London, BL Royal 8 F.vi (s. xv), 24r[12]

---

[5]   Ed. E. Baluze, *Capitularia regum Francorum* II (Paris, 1780), cols. 1396–9; reprinted by Robert Priebsch, *Letter from Heaven*, pp. 35–7. Presumably copied from the manuscript in the twelfth century by Petrus de Marca, archbishop of Paris (ibid., p. 3). Since the manuscript is now lost it is impossible to date this copy; Baluze ascribes it to the Carolingian period, but A. Hauck notes that the conditions described therein could have equally obtained at any time from the seventh to the ninth century (*Kirchengeschichte Deutschlands* (Berlin, 1952), I, p. 516 n. 1). Priebsch considers this the earliest form of the Sunday Letter (ibid., p. 33).

[6]   Ed. H. Delehaye, 'Note sur la légende de la lettre du Christ tombée du ciel', *Bulletin de l'Académie royale belgique, Classe des lettres* 1 (1899), 171–213, at 181–4 (reprinted as Appendix I).

[7]   Ed. R. Priebsch, 'The Chief Sources of Some Anglo-Saxon Homilies', *Otia Merseiana* 1 (1899), 130–4 (reprinted as Appendix IIa).

[8]   Ed. H. Delehaye in 'Note sur la légende', 179–81.

[9]   Ed. R. Grégoire, *Les homéliaires du moyen âge, inventaire et analyse des manuscrits*, Rerum ecclesiasticarum documenta, Series maior, Fontes 6 (Rome, 1966), pp. 226–7. See also H. Delehaye, 'Un exemplaire de la lettre Tombée du ciel', *Recherches de science religieuse* 18 (1928), 164–9.

[10] Ed. J. C. Amaduzzi, *Anecdota litteraria ex mss. codicibus eruta* (Rome, 1773), pp. 69–74. Reprinted by J.-P. Migne, *Dictionnaire des apocryphes, ou collection de tous les livres apocryphes relatifs à l'Ancien et au Nouveau Testament* (Paris, 1856–8), cols. 367–9.

[11] Ed. N. Staphorst in *Die Handschriften der S. Petri-Kirche Hamburg*, ed. T. Brandis (Hamburg, 1967), pp. 345–7; reprinted by R. Röhricht, 'Ein "Brief Christi"', *Zeitschrift für Kirchengeschichte* 11 (1890), 436–42, at 440–2.

[12] Edited by R. Priebsch, 'John Audelay's Poem on the Observance of Sunday', in *An English Miscellany Presented to Dr. Furnivall in Honour of his Seventy-fifth Birthday* (Oxford, 1901), 397–407, at 400–6.

*Mainz, Stadtbibliothek, I 227 (s. xv), 143r–143v
Mattsee, Stiftsbibliothek, 49 (s. xv), 182ra–184rb
Munich, Universitätsbibliothek, 2° 120 (s. xv), 33rb – 34rb
Munich, Bayerische Staatsbibliothek (s. xv), clm 3433, 209vb–210rb
[Munich, Bayerische Staatsbibliothek, clm 12,005 (s. xv), 91r (s. xv), *extract*[13]]
Munich, Bayerische Staatsbibliothek, clm 22,377 (s. xv), 82va–83ra
Rostock, Universitätsbibliothek, theol. 37a (s. xv), 47va–48rb
Uppsala, Universitätsbibliothek, C47 (s. xv), 277rv
Uppsala, Universitätsbibliothek, C133 (s. xv), 145r
Uppsala, Universitätsbibliothek, C226 (s. xv), 52v–53r
Uppsala, Universitätsbibliothek, C364 (s. xv), 183v, 195r
Vienna, Österreichische Nationalbibliothek, 3496 (s. xv), 4r–5r
Wilhering, Stiftsbibliothek, IX 162 (s. xv), 105rb–106va

Recension IIa

Kassel, Murhardsche Bibliothek der Stadt Kassel und Landesbibliothek, theol. 39 (s. xiv), 158r[14]
Vienna, Dominikanerkloster 133 (102) (s. xv), 134vb–135vb[15]

Recension III

Munich, Bayerische Staatsbibliothek, clm 21,518 (s. xii), 1r–1v[16]
Munich, Bayerische Staatsbibliothek, clm 14,673 (s. xii/xiii), 117r–119r, *1 of 2 letters*[17]
Paris, BN lat. 12,315 (s. xii[2]), 37vb–40rb
Vienna, Österreichische Nationalbibliothek, lat. 510 (s. xii), 134r–41v[18]
Munich, Bayerische Staatsbibliothek, clm 2625 (xiii), 39r–47v
Paris, BN lat. 5302 (s. xiii), 52va–53rb
Klosterneuburg, Bibliothek des Chorherrenstifts, 918 (s. xiii), 1ra–3ra
Toulouse, Bibliothèque Publique, 208 (III, 135) (s. xiii), 101r–104r[19]
Klosterneuburg, Bibliothek des Chorherrenstifts, 79 (s. xiii/xiv), 57r
Erlangen, Universitätsbibliothek, 306 (444) (s. xiv), 1r–4r[20]
London, BL Add. 16,587 (s. xiv), 184r–186r

---

13 This is a short fragment found at the end of a copy of the *Visio sancti Pauli*; it is edited in T. Silverstein, *Visio sancti Pauli*, p. 194.
14 The text is written on a smaller leaf bound with this manuscript; it is edited in Appendix III.
15 See Appendix III.
16 Ed. R. Priebsch, *Diu vrône botschaft ze der Christenheit, Untersuchungen und Text*, Grazer Studien zur deutschen Philologie 2 (Graz, 1895), 40–71.
17 Listed in R. Priebsch, *Diu vrône botschaft*, p. 23.
18 Collated with Munich 21,518 as variant text W in Priebsch's *Diu vrône botschaft*.
19 Ed. E. M. Rivière, 'La lettre du Christ tombée du ciel', *Revue des questions historiques* 79 (n.s. 35) (1906), 600–5.
20 Collated with Munich 21,518 as variant text E in Priebsch's *Diu vrône botschaft*.

London, BL Add. 23,930 (s. xiv), 93va–94va
*Venice, Biblioteca Nazionale Marciana, VI, 30 (Z. L. DVII) (s. xiv), 80r–83r
*Dresden, Sächsische Landesbibliothek, App. 2300 (s. xv), 292rb–294vb
*Fulda, Hessische Landesbibliothek, Aa 135 (s. xv), 187rb–188rb
*Leipzig, Universitätsbibliothek, 537 (s. xv), 215r
Mainz, Stadtbibliothek, 1469 (s. xv), 195r–197r
Michaelbeuern, Stiftsbibliothek, 82 (s. xv), 264va–266va
Michaelbeuern, Stiftsbibliothek, 97 (s. xv), 172v–174v

Recension IIIa[21]

[Roger of Hoveden, ed. Stubbs, letter used by Eustace de Flay (s. xiii?)[22]]
Oxford, Bodl. Lat. th. f. 19 (s. xiv), 24r–26r
Oxford, Bodl. Lyell 12 (s. xiv), 263r–264r
*Oxford, Bodl. Douce 54 (s. xv/xvi), 1r–3v
London, BL Add. 6716 (s. xv), 72rb–73vb
*Dublin, Trinity College Library, 516 (s. xv), f. 37r–38v
Graz, Universitätsbibliothek, 248 (s. xv), 133va–134ra, *1 of 2 letters*
*Trier, Stadtbibliothek 530 (s. xv), 121r

---

[21] Three members of this list also contain portions of Recension II: These are Bodl. Lyell 12 and Lat. th. f. 19; and BL Add. 6716.

[22] W. Stubbs, ed., *Chronica magistri Rogeri de Houedene*, 4 vols. (London, 1868–71), IV, 167–9. Reprinted by R. Röhricht, 'Ein "Brief Christi"', *Zeitschrift für Kirchengeschichte* 11 (1890), 436–42 at 438–40. Stubbs lists the following manuscript sources: Bodl. Laud 582 (s. xii); BL Arundel 69 (s. xii); BL Cotton Claudius B 7 (s. xiii); Cambridge, Trinity College Library, O.9.23 (s. xiii); BL Harley 3602 (s. xiii); and BL Arundel 150 (s. xiii).

Glossary

With the exception of the conjunction *and*, the demonstrative and personal pronouns and the verb *beon*, all occurrences have been cited for words with under ten occurrences; if there are more than ten, a representative sample has been provided. Manuscript spellings which may be of interest have been noted in parentheses. Words in square brackets are suggested emendations and are not found in the manuscripts. Negative forms are listed under the positive headword.

Abbreviations

*	hapax legomenon	n.	neuter
acc.	accusative	neg.	negative
adj.	adjective	nom.	nominative
adv.	adverb	num.	numeral
anom.	anomalous	past part.	past participle
art.	article	pers.	person
comp.	comparative	pers.pron.	personal pronoun
conj.	conjunction	pl.	plural
correl.	correlative	poss.adj.	possessive adjective
dat.	dative	prep.	preposition
def.	definite	pres. part.	present participle
dem.	demonstrative	pres.	present
f.	feminine	pret.	preterite
gen.	genitive	pret.pres.	preterite present
imper.	imperative	pron.	pronoun
impers.	impersonal	rel.particle	relative particle
indef.	indefinite	sb.	substantive
inf.	infinitive	sg.	singular
infl.inf.	inflected infinitive	subj.	subjunctive
inst.	instrumental	st.	strong
interj.	interjection	superl.	superlative
interr.pron.	interrogative pronoun	v.	verb
m.	masculine	wk.	weak
marg.	margin		

215

ā adv. *for ever, always, ever* B49 (**aa**), C57, D131, E76, F174 (**aa**), etc.

ābelgan v.st.3 *to (provoke to) anger* E144 (**abolgen**), 177 (**abeligan**), F117 (**abolgel**, see commentary)

ābēodan v.st.2 *to proclaim, announce* B86 (**aboden**)

āberan v.st.4 *to bear, endure* F180 (**abera**, inf.)

ābiddan v.st.5 *to ask* C180

ābifian v.wk.2 *to shake, quake* E206, F226 (**abiofode**)

āblinnan v.st.3 *to desist (from), cease* E120 (**ablan**)

ābyrgan v.wk.1 *to taste, partake of* E12 (**abyrigde**)

ābysgian v.wk.2 *to busy oneself, occupy oneself* A25 (**abysegiað**)

ac conj. *but* A34, B29, C16, D54, E18, F15, 104 (**ah**), etc.

ācennan v.wk.1 *to bear, give birth to*; past part. *born* B124, C42, D16, D24 [gloss], 90

ācennednes f. *birth, incarnation* B100

ācwelan v.st.4 *to die, perish* C80 (**acwolene**)

ācwellan v.wk.1 *to kill, destroy* E174

ācwylmian v.wk.2 *to suffer, be tormented* F104

ācyrran v.wk.1 *to change, transform (some-thing)* E146 (**acerrede**)

ādīligian v.wk.2 *to blot out, erase, destroy* A66 (**adylgie**), B82, 86, 129, F136 (**adilegedan**)

ādl f. *disease, illness* E100

ādrǣdan v.st.7 *to fear, dread* C130

ādrencan v.wk.1 *to drown (someone)* E20, 21, F21

ādrēogan v.st.2 *to do, carry out* C66

ādrincan v.st.3 (intrans.) *to be drowned, drown* B98, E31, 112, F33, 48

āfēdan v.wk.1 *to feed* C38, D23

āfindan v.st.3 *to find, discover* B130

āfyllan v.wk.1 *to cast down* F63 (**afelled**)

āgan v.pret.pres. *to possess, own, have* A36, C8 (**ahton**), 41, 68, 110, 131; *must* A34, C3, 60 (**ah**), etc.

*āgǣgednes f. *transgression* A22

āgen adj. *own* A60, C16, 54, D121, E78, 147, F122

āgēn prep. *against* F75 (**age**), 77

āginnan v.st.3 *to begin* F29 (**agan**)

geāgnian v.wk.2 *to obtain, take possession of* A62 (**geahnian**)

āgyfan v.st.5 *to pay, render* B40, 73, 74, 110

(**ageof-**, all), E59 (**agifen**)

āgyldan v.st.3 *to pay, render* A39, F232 (**ageldan**), 235 (**ageldan**)

āgȳmelēasian v.wk.2 *to neglect* F208 (**agemeleaseþ**), 228 (**agemeleasiaþ**)

āhōn v.st.7 *to hang* F160 (**ahangen**)

āhreddan v.wk.1 *to save, rescue* B34

āht pron. *anything*; as predicate nominative *of any worth* C79

āhwǣnan v.wk.1 *to vex, afflict*; past part. as sb. *one who is afflicted* E85 (**ahwænede**)

ālǣdan v.wk.1 *to lead (out)* D70

ālǣnan v.wk.1 *to lend (referring to God's gifts to his people)* A34

altare m. *altar* F217

ālȳfan v.wk.1 *to permit, allow* B19, 21, E114 (**alefed**), F64 (**alefed**)

ālȳsan v.wk.1 *to deliver, set free* B45, C41 (**alisanna**), 69, D16, 37, E85

āmānsumian v.wk.2 *to excommunicate, curse, separate* A80, C116, D79

āmearcian v.wk.2 *to note down, lay out* D120

āmyrran v.wk.1 *to destroy, kill* A47

ān adj.: emphatic: *one, a single* B41, C43, E39, 52, F86, 97, etc.; unemphatic: *a certain* A3 (2x), C12, 35, E8, 88, F4, 109 (**ænne**), etc.; following a noun, pron.: *alone* A34, D98, E54, F42, 189; pron.: *one (person, thing)* C172, F76; neg. **nān** *no one, no, none* A15, 17, B16, 20, C15, 117 (**nænne**), D120, E70, F92, 209, etc.; pron. A17 (**nanne**)

ancor m. *anchorite, hermit* E209, 210 (**ancer**), 211, 213

and conj. *and* F203 (**ond**), etc. (usually represented by ⁊ in the manuscripts)

anda m.wk. *envy, malice* D31

andetnes f. *confession* A68 (**andettnesse**), B31, F246 (**⁊detnesse**)

(ge)andettan v.wk.1 *to confess* C161, 163, F237 (**ge⁊dette**)

andfenge adj. *acceptable* C73 (**anfenge**)

andgyt n. *meaning, sense* D53

andleofen f. *sustenance, food, provision* D19 (**andlyfene**)

andweardnes f. *presence* D117

andweorc n. *substance (of creation); tool* D13, F221

andwlita m.wk. *face* B89

ānfeald adj. *simple, mere, just* E80, 90

anginn n. *beginning* C19, 25

angrislīce adv. *terribly, in a terrifying man-ner* D49 (**angryslice**)

ānhende adj. *weak, lame* D90

āniman v.st.4 *to remove, take away* D88, E176, F147

ānnes f. *Unity (of the Trinity)* D125 (**annysse**), E45, 187, F204 (**anesse**)

ānrǣdlīce adv. *definitely, decidedly, persistently* C142, D115

ansȳn f. *likeness* B104, E135, F96

antiochisc adj. *of Antioch* D4, 123

anweald m. *power, authority* B138, C41, E199, F218 (**anwald**)

apostol m.wk. *apostle* A52, B44, 104, 138, C14, 51, D99, E69, 135, F95

ār f. *mercy, pity* F248

ārǣfnan v.wk.1 *to suffer, endure* E53

architriclinus m. *governor of the feast* B101 (**architriclines**)

āreccan v.wk.1 *to relate, recount* C154, E97

ārfull adj. *compassionate* F151

ārīman v.wk.1 *to recount, enumerate* E217

ārīsan v.st.1 *to arise* B92, 103, C47, D17, E104, 106, F6, 161, etc.

ārlēas adj. *wicked, impious* C56, D76

āscyrian v.wk.1 *to cut off, banish* F82

āsēcan v.wk.1 *to exact, require* D117

āsecgan v.wk.3 *to tell, relate, express* E212, F37, 249

āsendan v.wk.1 *to send (forth/out)* A4, 40 (**asendæ**), B8, 84, C12, 103, D18, 64, E18, F15 (**asǣnde**), etc.

āsettan v.wk.1 *to place* D43

āspringan v.st.3 *to spring up, rise up* C49, F28

āstīgan v.st.1 *to ascend, arise* C8, F162 (**astah**)

ātēon v.st.2 *to treat, deal with* F112 (**ation**)

āþ m. *oath* A15, B18, 52, E72, 99, 192, 204, F209, 224

āþrōwian v.wk.2 *to suffer* F219

āþswaru f. *oath, oath-swearing* D122

āwæcnian v.wk.2 *to arise (from), be descended* E34, F36 (**awecnigan**)

āweccan v.wk.1 *to awaken* E182 (**awehte**)

āwendan v.wk.1 *to turn, change* C42, 133, 134, 136, F57

āwēstan v.wk.1 *to lay waste, ravage* C92

āwrecan v.st.5 *to pierce (with arrows)* E203 (**awrecen**), F223

āwrītan v.st.1 *to write* B11, 131, C15, D3, 103, E41, 152, F11, 105, etc.

āwyrcan v.wk.1 *to do (something)* E79, 89

āwyrgan v.wk.1 *to curse, condemn (oneself)*; past part. *accursed, damned* B129 (**awerged**), E42 (**awerged**),

46 (**awerged**), 168 (**awergede**), 192, F174 (**awerged**), 201 (**awergde**), 210 (**awyrged**), F244 (**awergdum**)

axe f.wk. *ash, ashes* A28 (**axan**)

āxian v.wk.2 *to ask* F111 (**askede**)

ǣbreca m.wk. *adulterer* C149

ǣcer m. *field, acre* D84, E61

ǣdre f. and wk. *channel, stream* E27 (**ǣddre**), F28 (**edran**)

ǣfen m.n. *evening* D105 (2x)

ǣfest m. *envy, malice* C62

ǣfre adv. *ever* A36, C2, 87, E53, 61, F88, 223 (efre), etc.; neg. **nǣfre** *never* A82, B56, D62, E13, 40, F9 (**nefre**), 42 (**næfre**), 104, 170, 175

æfter prep. (w. dat.) *after* A24, 82, B26, 27, C50, 84, E75, F105, etc.; **æfter þon þe** *after* D113

ǣghwæþer conj. **ǣghwæþer ge . . . ge** *both . . . and* F241 (**ǣghweþer**)

ǣghwylc adj./pron. *each, any, every* E88, 186, 214, 215, 216, F71, 202, 203 (**eghwilcan**)

ǣgþer conj. (pron.) *both*; **ǣgþer ge . . . ge/ and** *both . . . and* C21, 22, D65, 78, E124, 170, F4, 215 (**egþer**), etc.

ǣht f. *possession, property, goods* B32, 120

ǣlc adj./pron. *each, any, every* A57, B28, 41, C54, 59, D33, 109, E33, 57, F3 (**ælc**), 35 (**elces**), etc.

ælmesse f.wk. *almsgiving, alms* A9, 26, 57, B14, 51, 57, F17 (**elmyssan**), 183

ælmihtig adj. *almighty* C6, 8, 28, 131, D87, E220, etc.

ælþēodig adj. *foreign, alien*; sb. *foreigner* C69, D37, 45, E83, F156 (**ælþeoðiodige** for **ælðiodige**)

geǣmtigian v.wk.2 *to free (oneself)* D34 (**geemtigen**)

ǣnig adj./pron. *any* C53, 98, D61, 87, E11, 30, F8, 100, 248 (**eniges**), etc.; neg. **nǣnig** *no, not any* E212, 200, F221 (**nenigum**), 238 (**nenigre**)

ǣr prep. (w. dat.) *before* B87, F92; in phrase as a conj.: **ǣr þon (þe)** *before, until* C30, 109, 157, D50, 111; adv. *soon, previously, beforehand* A49, C41, 112, D56, 121, E7, 53, F17, 97, etc.; comp.: **ǣror** A81; superl.: **ǣrest** *first* C14, 37, 162, E2, 62, 100, 112, F2, 49 (**erest**), 72 (**æryst**); conj.: *before* E20, 25, 26, 101, F21; **ful ǣr** *very soon* F121; **ǣr þonne** *until* F147; **siþ oþþe ǣr** *at all times, ever* F235

217

ǣrendbōc f. *(written) message, letter* F220
ǣrendgewrit n. *(written) message, letter*
B2, 15, C12, D2, 113, E1, 208, F1, 14, etc.
ǣrendraca m.wk. *messenger* D7, 18
ǣrest: see **ǣr, ǣrra**
ǣrist f./m. *resurrection* A24 (**ǣreste**), C50,
172 (**ǣrestes**)
ǣrra adj. *earlier*; superl. **ǣrrest** *first* B26,
D12, 33, E103, 110, 219, F47 (**ǣrysta**)
ǣt prep. (w. dat.) *at, from* B111, C43, 75,
80, 107, 139, 180, D119, E76, 101
ǣtbregdan v.st.3 *to withhold, take away*
A63 (**ǣtbrudon**)
ǣtēow(i)an v.wk.1&2 *to reveal, display,*
show, make known B119, C50, D100
(**ǣtyweð**)
ǣtforan prep. (w. dat.) *before, in the pres-*
ence of C116
geǣttrod past part. of **(ge)ǣttrian** *poi-*
soned, poisonous A47
geǣþan v.wk.1 *to confirm by oath* D122,
123
ǣþele adj. *noble, devout* D40

bacan v.st.6 *to bake* A16, C99, D60, E165,
F198 (**bakeþ**)
baþian v.wk.2 *to bathe, wash* E165, F199
bæftan prep. (w. dat.) *behind* F48
(**beæftan**)
bæþ n. *bath* B111
be prep. (w. dat.) *about, concerning* A38,
C5, 15, D1, 92, E21, 172, F10, 212 (**bi**),
etc.; *by (means of), through* B2, C12,
104, 140; *according to, in accordance*
with C69, 152, D53, F152; *because of, on*
account of C57, D117; *by, no later than*
E58, 59; **bi(g) libban** *to live by (means of)*
B69 (**big**), 118 (**bi**), C127 (**big**)
bearn n. *child* A43, 71, B54, 135, C179,
D65, 90, E2, 24, F13, 67, etc.
bebēodan v.st.2 *to command, bid, enjoin; to*
ordain (a feast/fast) B107, C2, 58, D4, 28,
E65, 123, F77, 203, etc.
bebod n. *command, commandment* A44,
58, B76, 114, C94, 105, E130, 172, F75,
152, etc.
bebyrgan v.wk.1 *to bury* C67 (**bebyrian**),
D36 (**bebyrgeað**), E87 (**bebyrian**)
becuman v.st.4 *to come to, over, upon* B10,
16, C102, 105, E52, 53, F134, 211, etc.; *to*
come to, attain to, enter B50, C175, E185,
222, F89, 104
gebed n. *prayer* A9, 26, B14, 30, 43, 50,
D34

bedīglian v.wk.2 *to conceal* F236
(**bedigligan**)
beflēon v.st.2 *to flee* F242
beforan prep. (w. dat.) *before, in front of*
A2, 31, B35, 59, 60, D40, E55, F237
begān v.anom. *to engage in, do* C97, 99
(**bega**), 101, 145, 154, 155
beginnan v.st.3 *to begin* E210
begytan v.st.5 *to obtain, get* A30, B19, 35
(**begeotað**), 40, C101, 119; *to beget* A73
behātan v.st.7 *to promise, vow* C176
behealdan v.st.7 *to uphold, observe* B108
behindan prep. (w. dat.) *behind* E112
behōfan v.wk.1 *to have need of, require* 124
behrēosan v.st.2 *to fall* E98
behȳdan v.wk.1 *to hide* F236 (**behedan**)
belimpan v.st.3 *to belong to, be the prop-*
erty of E126
belūcan v.st.2 *to shut up (in a place),*
enclose C52 (**belocene**)
bēn f. *prayer, petition* B44
benǣman v.wk.1 *to deprive, take (away)*
C120
bend m. *bond, cord* C81, E93
bendan v.wk.1 *to bend (a bow)* B67
gebendan v.wk.1 *to bind*; past part. *bound,*
in bonds C111
beniman v.st.4 *to take away, deprive* E48
bēodan v.st.2 (w. dat.) *to command, bid,*
enjoin, urge A13 (**budon**), 28, 77, B109,
C21, 26, F51 (**bead, bude**), E70
bēon/wesan v.anom. *to be*; forms: **bēon**
(inf.) F62 (**bion**), etc.; **bēonne** (infl.inf.)
F229 (**bionne**); **eom** (pres.1sg.) – **eam** (B,
E, F); **is** (pres.3sg.); **biþ** (pres.3sg.); **synd**
(pres.pl.) D40 (**sint**), F191 (**send**), 195
(**synt**); **syndon** (pres.pl.) E114 (**syndan**),
F70 (**sindan**); **bēoþ** (pres.pl.) – **bioþ**
(F); **sȳ** (pres.subj.sg.) B140 (**seo**), F103
(**sig**), 116 (**sige**), 207 (**sie**), 223 (**se**); **bēo**
(pres.subj./imp.sg.) F86 (**bio**); **sȳn** (pres.
subj.pl.) – **sion** (F), F118 (**seon**); **wæs**
(pret.1/3sg.) – **wes** (F); **wǣron** (pret.
pl.) F33 (**wǣran**), 74 (**weran**); **wǣre**
(pret.subj.sg.); neg.: **nis** (pres.3sg.); **næs**
(pret.1/3sg.) – **nes** (F); **nǣron** (pret.pl.);
nǣre (pret.subj.sg.)
gebeorg m.n. *protection* E82 (**gebyrge**)
beorht adj. *bright* F191
(ge)bēorscipe m. *carousing, feast* C137,
D106
beran v.st.4 *to carry* C46
geberan v.st.4 *to bear, be born*; past part.
born A74, C40, F88 (**geborenum**)

bereern n. *barn* B47 (**bearnum**)

beren adj. *of barley* C44, D22

besencan v.wk.1 *to cause to sink/plunge (into the earth/hell)* C84, 90, 158, D45, E128, 129, F81 (**besæncte**)

besmītan v.st.1 *to defile* F58

(**ge**)**bētan** v.wk.1 *to repent of, atone for, repent* A40, 67, B37, 83, D97, F238 (**gebette**)

betǣcan v.wk.1 *to enjoin, give, hand over, deliver* C83, D8, E57

betera comp.adj. *better* E95

betst superl.adj. *best* C127, F215

betwēoh prep. (w. dat.) *between* F33, 55 (2x), 68, 69 (**betwioh**, all)

betwux prep. (w. dat.) *between* C35, E31 (**betwyx**), 118, 214

beþencan v.wk.1 *to consider* B54 (**beþænce**), 59 (**beþæncað**), 108

beþurfan v.pret.pres. *to have need (of something)* C125 (**beþorftan**)

bicgan v.wk.1 *to buy* A16

gebīdan v.st.1 *to experience, live to see, endure* E78, 97

(**ge**)**biddan** v.st.5 *to ask, entreat, demand, pray* A25, 57, B111, 113, C64, 174, E77, 157, F19, 187, etc.

bifian v.wk.2 *to tremble, shake*; pres.part. *terrible* B23, 59, F232

bigleofa m.wk. *sustenance, livelihood* A41 (**bileofan**), C38 (**bilyfan**), 45 (**bilyfan**), F4 (**beoleofan**)

gebindan v.st.3 *to bind, fetter* F110 (**gebunde**)

binnan prep. (w. dat.) *within (a time period)* F148

bisceop m. *bishop* A83, C13 (**biscop**), 17 (**biscope**), D8, 113, E194 (**biscop**), 203 (**biscop**), F213 (**bescup**), 224 (**biscup**), etc.

bisceopsetl n. *episcopal seat* C14 (**biscopsetl**)

bisceopstōl m. *episcopal see, bishopric* E59 (**biscopstole**)

bite m. *bite, sting* E93

biter adj. *bitter* D104 (2x)

bitere adv. *bitterly, grievously* C139

biternes f. *misery, hardship* B77

blǣd f. *crops* B47, 69, 118

gebletsian v.wk.2 *to bless* C45, D22

bletsung f. *blessing* B112, C45, 101, D62, 63, E155, F185

blind adj. *blind* D90

bliss f. *bliss, joy* A87, C144

blissian v.wk.2 *to rejoice, exult* E157, F188

blōd n. *blood* D116

blōstma m.wk. *blossom, fruit* D85 (**blosman** for **blosmena**)

bōc f. *book* A67, B83, 86, 130, E201

*****bōcblæc** *ink* F220 (**bocblece**)

bōccræft m. *book-learning* E184

bōcere m. *scholar, learned man* C113, E183, F84

gebod n. *commandment* D76

boda m.wk. *emissary, messenger* C21, D7

(**ge**)**bodian** v.wk.2 *to preach, make known, foretell, announce* D116, 118, 130, E19, F20, 24, 206 (**bodige**)

bodung f. *teaching, preaching* D34

boga m.wk. *bow* B67

bolla m.wk. *cup, bowl* C138

bōt f. *atonement* F246

brēad n. *bread* C99

brecan v.st.4 *to break* F145 (**brecan**)

gebrēgan v.wk.1 *to terrify, frighten* D50

brēost n. *breast, chest, vitals* A70, B69, 122

(**ge**)**bringan** v.st.3 *to bring, lead* C82, 120, 167 (2x), 169, D88

brōga m.wk. *terror, horror* E52, 174, F16

brōþor m. *brother* B53, 74, F75

brūcan v.st.2 (w. gen.) *to partake of, enjoy* C121, 138

bryne m. *fire, burning* D27, E91

gebrytsen f. *fragment* D24

bufan prep. (w. dat.) *above* E178, F31 (**beufan**), 32; adv.: F159 (**beufan**)

bufancweden adj. *above-mentioned* A38

burh f. *town, city* A4 (**byrig**), 5 (**byrig**), 8, 12, B10, C13, 85, 108, 109, 110, D22 (**byrig**), etc.

būtan prep. (w. dat.) *without* A74 (3x), B54, 135, D63 (**buton**), 115 (**buton**), E75, F202, 247; *except* D42, E20, 32, F22, 239 (**buton**); *apart from, in addition to, not counting* B102, E54, 159, F42, 189; *outside* E13, F9; conj. *unless, except* A67 (**buton**), B20, 120, C134 (**buton**), 139, E11, 67, F8, 16, etc.

byrgen f. *burial-place, tomb* A7, 81, E206, F226 (**bergen**)

byrgenstōw f. *burial-place* B131

gebyrian v.wk.1&2 *to behove, be fitting to/for* D88, E56; *to happen, occur* B19; with impers. *hit* E122, 205

byrnan v.st.3 *to burn* A44, B135 (**beornendne**), C87, 123, E173 (**beornende**), F132 (**birnenda**), 141 (**birnende**)

66, E182, 198 (**cyddon**), F165 (**cydde**), 217 (**cyþdan**), etc.

cyþnes f. *testimony*; **eald cyþnes** *Old Testament* D97

gedafenian v.wk.2 *to be fitting, to befit* B28
gedāl n. *separation* F231
dǣd f. *deed* A53, 57, C168, F235 (**dede**), 238 (**deda**)
dǣdbōt f. *penance* A39, 67, B32, 46
dæg m. *day* A9, 21, B13, 17, C15, 71, D16, 42, E28, 104, F164 (**deg**), 200 (**dege, dæge**), etc.
dæghwāmlīce adv. *daily* A31, B35, D99
dǣl m. *part, portion* C120 (2x), D17, 79, E174, F139, 171, etc.; *for (one's) part, for (one's) sake* B39
dēad adj. *dead* C67, 104, D36, E9, F4, 6, 94, 163
dēaf adj. *deaf* D90
dearr v.pret.pres. *to dare* E204 (**dorston**), F224 (**dorstan**)
dēaþ m. *death* A31, B35, 55, C47, 50, D17, 111, E9, 116, F6, 59 (**deaþy**), etc.
delfan v.st.3 *to bury* C104
dēman v.wk.1 *to judge, determine (a sentence)* A15, C54, 151, D25, F93 (**demenne**), 163
dēofol m.n. *devil* C41, 56, D27, 55, E40, 94, F42, 223, etc.
dēope adv. *solemnly, seriously* C2
dēopnes f. *deep place, abyss* E117, 128, 130, F67 (**diopnesse**), 81 (**diopnesse**), 83 (**diopnesse**)
dēor n. *animal, beast* F146
deorc adj. *dark* F243
dīacon m. *deacon* E8, 13, F4 (**diacan**), 10 (**diacan**), 13, etc.
gedīgan v.wk.1 *to survive* F121 (**gedǣgeþ**)
(ge)dihtan v.wk.1 *to dictate, compose* C16, F150
dimm adj. *dim, gloomy* F243
dōm m. *judgement, sentence* A15, B18, 23, D44, 115, F95, 105, etc.
(ge)dōn v.anom. *to do, engage in*; **(ge)dōn** (inf.) B67, 83, C70, 112, E106, 150, F111, 125, etc.; **(ge)dō** (pres.1sg.) D89; **(ge)dēþ** (pres.3sg.) E5, 6, 87 (2x), 102, F3, 60; **dōþ** (pres.pl.) A39, B34, 82, C4, D42, 62, E116, 168, F66, 201, etc.; **dō** (pres.subj./ imp.sg) C165 (2x); **dyde** (pret.1/3sg.) C85, D46, E6, 8, F24; **(ge)dydon** (pret. pl.) A8, 29, 64, B12, E18, 25, 51, F154 (**gededan**); **don on** *to give* B112; **don in**

carcern *to put into prison* F110 (**dede**); **don of life** *to put to death* F113 (**dede**)
drenc m. *drink* E84
drēogan v.st.2 *to engage in, do* C18 (**drugan**), 19 (**dreogað**), 22
drincan v.st.3 *to drink* C136
drūgoþ f. *drought* C124
druncennes f. *drunkenness* B58, C61, 137, 153, D30, 106
drȳge adj. *dry* B97 (**drium**), E111
***drȳgscēod** adj. *dry-shod, with dry feet* C36
dryhten m. *lord, the Lord* A10, 34, B34, 140, C24, 58, D2, 17, E1, 15, Γ14 (**drchtnes**), 20 (**drehtnen**), 218 (**dryhtenes**), etc.
dryhtenlic adj. *of the Lord* C26, 66, 73 (**drihtlican**), 95, D1, 73, F46 (**drehtenlican**)
drync m. *drink* D37
dumb adj. *dumb, mute* A75
dūn f. *hill, mountain* B96
duru f. *gate, door* E154
dyne m. *din, loud noise* E93
dynt m. *blow, stroke* E93

ēa f. *river* B62, E132, F90
ēac adv. *likewise, moreover, also* A11, 34, C17, 29 (ea:), D94, E66, 131, F4, 80, etc.; **eac swylce** *likewise, also* A74, D6
ēacnian v.wk.2 *to bring forth*; pres. part. as adj. *(a woman) in labour* D51 (**eacnigende**)
ēadig adj. *blessed* D126
ēadignes f. *blessedness* F242
ēage n.wk. *eye* A32, 46, 74, B36, 60, 89, E55
eahta num. *eight* A22 (**viii**), E20 (**ehta**), 32 (**ehta**), F22, 34 (**viii**)
ēalā interj. *O, oh* A20, 30, 56, F135
eald adj. *old* C80, D97; comp.sb. **yldran** *forebears, ancestors* D81, E171
ealdormann m. *chief, elder* E123, F74
eall adj. *all* A20, 33 (**eallon**), B42, 86, C15, 22, D6, 15, E79, 97, F184 (**eallan**), 79 (**eallen**), etc.; **mid ealle** *entirely* F142
eall adv. *entirely, utterly* C53, 125, E41, 203, F105, 223, etc.; *universally* E104; **eall for** *entirely on account of* A71, C105, 137
eallswā conj. *just as* A29, 71, C40, 162, E61, F11, 30; adv. *also, likewise* A35, C66, 88
ēalond n. *island* F5
earc f. *ark* B96, E35, F37
eard m. *land, country* D83
eardian v.wk.2 *to live, dwell* C57, 87

221

eardungstōw f. *dwelling-place* F247

ēare n.wk. *ear* A46, B89

earm adj. *poor, miserable, wretched* C142, E82, 83, F18, 101

earming m. *wretch, pauper, beggar* B24, 34 (**ermingas**), C67

earmlic adj. *miserable, wretched* C84 (**earmlycan**), 157 (**earmlica**)

earmlīce adv. *miserably, wretchedly* C80

geearnian v.wk.2 *to earn, merit, bring about* A59, E81, 91, F242

ēaspring m.n. *spring* F30 (**ēasprencguum**)

ēasterǣfen m.n. *Easter-eve* E63

ēasterdæg m. *Easter-day* C112, D70

ēasterlic adj. *(pertaining to) Easter* E71

*****ēastersunnandæg** m. *Easter Sunday* F162 (**eastorsunnandæg**)

ēastre f.wk. *Easter* E58

geēastrod past part. *to have elapsed after Easter Sunday* E74

ēaþe adv. *easily*; superl. E190 (**eðest**)

ēaþelīce adv. *lightly*; **eaþelice lætan ymbe** *to take (a matter) lightly* C160

geēaþmēdan v.wk.1 *to humble, submit* E37 (**geeadmedde**), 181 (**geeadmedde**), F39 (**geeadmette**)

ēaþmōdnes f. *humility* C64 (**eadmodnysse**)

ēce adj. *eternal, ever-lasting* A62, C55, 144, D26, 27 (2x), E91, 118, F68 (**ǣce**), 202 (**ǣcan**), 250 (**ecan**), etc.

ece m. *ache, pain, grief* E92

ecg f. *edge* C78

ēcnes f. *eternity* B49, 80, 141, D131

geedstaþelod past part. of **(ge)edstaþolian** *restored* F36

efestan v.wk.1 *to hasten, hurry* B34

efsian v.wk.2 *to cut (the hair of someone)* A79, B82, C98 (**efesige**), D60 (**efsige**), E166, F199

eft adv. *again* B78, C163, E9, 63, F6, 36, etc.

ege m. *fear* C24, 25, D10, E54, F120

egeslic adj. *terrifying, frightening* F94, 164; superl. C125

egeslīce adv. *terribly* C122

ele m. *oil* B47, 63

elles adv. *else*; **elles . . . butan** *anything other than* D42, E50; **elles oþer** *another* E68

emne adv. *even, just*; **emne swa** *just as* E14

emnniht f. *(autumnal) equinox* E60

ende m. *end* B135, 141, C57, 75, D95, 131, E98, 155, F186 (**ænde**), 202 (**ænde**), etc.

endebyrdnes f. *rank, order (of angels)* C32, D13, 126

endedæg m. *last day* C139

endemes adv. *completely*; **endemes ealle** *all together* C157

endenȳhst adj. *last* C75

geendian v.wk.2 *to end* B56, C53, D25

endleofan num. *eleven* C111 (**xi**), D70 (**xi**)

geendung f. *end, death* C84

engel m. *angel* A49, B29, 64, C13, 16 (**ængel**), 117, D3, 80, E159, F176 (**ænglum**), F190 (**ænglas**), etc.

eorl m. *nobleman* C21

eornostlīce adv. *strictly, solemnly* B30, E66, 74; *therefore, accordingly* D110 (**geornostlice**)

eorþe f.wk. *earth, soil* A20, 54, B25, 94, C31, D12, 43, E27, 29, F30, 79 (**iorþe**), etc.

eorþlic adj. *earthly, worldly* B23, C15, D120, E12, 146, F9, 118, etc.

eorþwæstm m. *crop* F139

ēow: see **þū**

ēower poss.adj. *your* A27, 63, B66, 82, C92, 139, D35, 111, E49, 118, F64 (**iower**), 181 (**iowra**), 189 (**eowar**), etc.

eower 2nd pers.pron.: see **þū**

etan v.st.5 *to eat, devour* B76, 122

ēþel m. *homeland, land* C82, E48

faran v.st.6 *to go, travel, advance* C35, 38, 55, 108 (**foran**), D68, E4, 5, 148, F3, 108, etc.

fatian v.wk.2 *to fetch* B18 (**fatige**)

fæder m. *father* B54 (2x), C116, D79, E224, F163

fæderlēas adj. *fatherless* B52

fæmne f.wk. *virgin* B139, C178, D126

færlīce adv. *suddenly* C102

færunga adv. *unexpectedly, suddenly* C126

fæst adj. *secured, fastened* B106

fæstan v.wk.1 *to fast* B13, 33, 34

fæsten n. *fast, fasting* A9, 26, B14, 33, E67, 68, etc.

fæstendæg m. *fast-day* B109

fæstlīce adv. *firmly, steadfastly* A77; comp. B133

fæþm m. *cubit* F31 (**fædman**)

(ge)feallan v.st.7 *to fall, drop* A2, 80, B2, E2 (**gefealð**), 127, F2 (**gefeallaþ**), 79 (**fillon**)

fēawa adj. *few* F148

feax n. *hair of the head* A79, B82, D60, E165 (**fex**, all)

fēdan v.wk.1 *to satisfy, feed* B99, C68, D20, 36, E113 (**sendan** for **fedan**), F49

fela quasi-sb. *much, many* A41, 45, 50, C29, 153, D109, E10, F7, 160 (**feola**)
feld m. *field* C124
gefeoht n. *battle, war, fighting* C79, D44
fēond m. *enemy* B98, E111, F48
feormian v.wk.2 *to clean* E166, F198
fēower num. *four* C78, D44
fēowertig num. *forty* B99, C38 (xl), D20, E28 (2x), F29 (xl) (2x)
fēorwertȳne num. *fourteen* F80
gefēran v.wk.1 *to go, travel* F123 (**gefereþ**)
gefērræden f. *fellowship* A59 (**geterræddene**)
fīf num. *five* A22, B41, 102, C43, D22 (**v**), 23 (**v**), E9, 143, F6 (**v**), 116 (**v**), etc.
fīftig num. *fifty* F87
fīftȳne num. *fifteen* E58 (xv), 74 (**fiftene**)
findan v.st.3 *to find* A3, B3, 10, E11, 201, F216 (**fundan**), 221
finger m. *finger* D4, 121, 129
firenfull adj. *sinful, wicked* E3, 164
fisc m. *fish* B25 (**fixas**), 102 (**fixum**), C44 (**fixum**), D22 (**fixas**)
fiþerfēte adj. *four-footed* F177
gefiþerian v.wk.2 *to provide with wings*; past part. *winged* B122
flān fm. *arrow, dart* B68, D49
flǣsc n. *flesh* A36, 70
flēogan v.st.2 *to fly* B69, F180 (**fleogende**)
flēon v.st.2 *to flee* C79
geflit n. *discord, (legal) dispute* C62, D31, 74, F77
flōd m.n. *flood* B96, E19, 52, F20, 23, etc.
folc n. *folk, people* A13, 83, B23, 49, C33, 37, D1, 7, E47, 182, F26, 61, etc.
folcgemōt n. *public meeting* E66
fōn v.st.7 *to engage in, undertake* B46
for prep. (w. dat.) *for, for the sake of, on account of* A21, 63, B20, 39, C41, 90, D63, 93, E38, 54, F40, 85, etc.; (w. acc.) *for, as (equivalent to)* D108, F167; conj. *for, because* C7; **for hwilcum þingum** *for what reason* A11; **for hwon** *why* C106
foran adv. *previously* E164
forbærnan v.wk.1 *to burn up, consume by fire* C86, 127, E3, 7, 15, 49, 164, F3, 12 (**forbernan**), 196
forbēodan v.st.2 *to forbid, prohibit* C62, D32, 97, E66, 72, 141, F106
forbūgan v.st.2 *to refrain from, avoid* A58
forbyrnan vb.st.3 *to burn up completely, be consumed by fire* E37 (**forbeornað**), 107
fordōn v.anom. *to destroy, be brought to ruin* B55, 118, 135, C122, D45

forebod n. *prohibition, interdict* D2
foresecgan v.wk.3. *to foretell, predict* E50
foresprecan v.st.5 *to mention before*; past part. *aforesaid* D42 (**forespræcenan**)
forflēon v.st.2 *to flee, abstain from* A58
forgān v.anom. *to abstain from, forgo* C60
forglendrian v.wk.2 *to consume (by burning), destroy* C123
forgrīpan v.st.1 *to seize, grasp, carry off* C157
forgyfan v.st.5 *to give, forgive* C166, 171, E221, F87 (**forgefen**), 178 (**forgefan**)
forgyldan v.st.3 *to pay, repay* C139
forgyltan v.wk.1 *to incur guilt* F44 (**forgelte**)
forgȳman v.wk.1 *to disregard, neglect* C10
forhæfednes f. *self-restraint, abstinence* A27, 36
forhealdan v.st.7 *to withhold, keep improperly* B75, E125
forhogian v.wk.2 *to despise, scorn* D63, 72, 76, 82 [gloss]
forhwȳ adv. *why* D67
forhycgan v.wk.3 *to scorn, despise* D81
forlǣtan v.st.7 *to forsake, abandon* A23, 57, B51, 58, 70, C149, D110, 111
forlēosan v.st.2 *to condemn (to death)* B55
forliger n. *adultery, fornication* C61, D29
forma adj. *first* A21, C28, 74, D41; superl. **fyrmest** *foremost* E219
forniman v.st.4 *to seize, destroy, deprive* A41, 42, D61, F181
forsēon v.st.5 *to despise, hold in contempt, scorn, refuse* C94, 112, 155, 159, D47
forsewennes f. *contempt* C102, 105
forþ adv. *forth, further* E99, F150, 171
forþǣm/forþon/forþȳ [þe] conj. *because, for the reason that, on account of* A18, 75, B35, 71, C87, 163, D11, 52, E43, 102, F44, 123, etc.; adv. *therefore, for that reason* B15, 73, C58, 166 (**forþi**), 173 (**forþyg**), E8, 31, F16, 56, etc.
forþfēran v.wk.1: *to die* past part. *dead* E8, 86
forþsīþ m. *death* C175, E75
forweorþan v.st.3 *to perish, destroy* A18, 29, B22, 42, 68, 125, E126 (**forwurdon**), F39 (**forwyrþaþ**), 78 (**forwurdon**), 142, 148
forwyrd n. *death, destruction* E175, F142
fōt m. *foot* A74, B97, E111
fram prep. (w. dat.) *from* A1, 30, B37, 75, C6, 59, D10, 28, E14, 44, F46 (**from**), 71, 210, etc.

223

frēabeorht adj. *very clear* E160
(freabrihtum)
frēcednes f. *peril, injury, danger* A42, 50
frēcennes f. *danger* F121 (frecynysse)
frēfrian v.wk.2 *to console, comfort* E85
(ge)fremman v.wk.1 *to do* E168, F201, 235;
    gemot fremman *to hold a meeting* C63
frēo/frīg adj. *free* C115 (freoh), D78
frēols m. *holy day, feast, festival* C11, 93,
    128, E71 (2x)
frēols adj. *free* C6
frēolsdæg m. *feast-day* A64, 69, 78, E72
*frēolsniht f. *vigil (of a feast)* A73
frēolsung f. *holy day, festival* E64
frēond m. *friend* A65 (frynd)
fretan v.st.5 *devour, consume* B69, F139
frīgedæg m. *Friday* E71
frignan v.st.3 *to ask* F111 (freni for frein)
frōfor f. *comfort, consolation* D38, F247
frōforlīce adv. *so as to bring consolation*
    C70 (froferlice)
fruma m.wk. *beginning* D7, F236; æt/on
    fruman *at first* D120, 128
frumsceatt m. *first-fruits* D86
frymþ f. *beginning* A31, C95, D57
fugel m. *bird* B117 (fuhlas)
fūl adj. *impure, foul* C149
full adj. *full, satiated* C46, D23
full adv. *very* C139; full ær *very soon* F121
fullfremed adj. *perfect* C170
fūllic adj. *wicked, disgraceful* D74
fullīce adv. *fully, entirely* B139
gefullod past part. of gefullian *baptized*
    B23, C43, E132, F91 (gefulwad)
fulluht m. *baptism* B63, 110, 111, E139
fūlnes f. *foulness, impurity* C60
fultum m. *aid, help* A9
fylg(i)an v.wk.1&2 *to follow, pursue* A28,
    60, C142 (fylian), D107 (filigð), 110
    (filigð)
gefyllan v.wk.1 *to fill* B102, E26, F28
fyllnes f. *fullness* D106
gefylsta m.wk. *helper, assistant* D61
fylstan v.wk.1 *to help, aid, give aid* B52,
    C70, 100
fȳr n. *fire* B19, 104, C86, 126, D27, 83, E1,
    16, F195 (fer), 211, etc.
gefyrn adv. *long ago* A50
fyrst m. *(period of) time, a while* A25, 50

gaderian v.wk.2 *to gather* A17
galileisc adj. *Galilean, of Galilee* D20
(ge)gān v.anom. *to go, walk*; gān (inf.) B107;
    gegæþ (pres.3sg.) E167, F200 (gegeð);

gegā (pres.subj.sg.) E61; gāþ (pres.pl.)
    B124; gāþ (imp.pl.) A27, B56, 78
gangan v.st.7 *to go, walk* B66
gegangan v.st.7 (impers.) *to happen, befall*
    E36, 129, F38 (gegongeþ), 82 (gegangeþ)
gāst m. *spirit, ghost*; halig gast *the Holy
    Spirit* B104, C51, D18, E135, 224, F96
gærshoppa nm.wk. *grasshopper,
    locust* A40, F130 (gershoppan), 138
    (gershoppan)
ge conj. *and*; correl. ge . . . ge *both . . . and*
    B51, 140; ægþer ge . . . ge *both . . . and*
    C21, 22, D65, 78, E124, 170, F215, 242,
    etc.; ægþer ge . . . and eac *both . . . and
    also* F4
gē 2nd pers.pron.: see þū
gēar n. *year* A22, 69, C10, D96, E60, 62,
    F5, 149 (gerum)
gēara adv. *long ago* E18, 171
(ge)gearwian v.wk.2 *to prepare, make
    ready, provide* A30, 31, 50, D38
geat n. *gate* A2, B3, 46, 106
geoguþ f. *the young, youth* C81; (of ani-
    mals) E57, 58
gēomorlīce adv. *sadly* C81
geond prep. *throughout* A28, 84, E7
geong adj. *young* C163 (iung)
georne adv. *eagerly, earnestly, well* B13,
    112, C3, 24 (eorne), D94, E56, 77, etc.
geornfulnes f. *eagerness, diligence, devo-
    tion* A87, E69
geornlīce adv. *eagerly, earnestly* A84
gif conj. *if* A32, 37, B34, 36, C4, 75, D42,
    81 (gyf), E50, 85, F83 (gef), 103 (gif), etc.
gifu f. *gift, grace* B140 (geofena), F102
gegladian v.wk.2 *to appease, please* F101
geglengan v.wk.1 *to adorn, to set in order*
    A62
glīw n. *pleasure, (musical) amusement*
    D105
gnæt m. *gnat* A46
god m. *God* A19, 48, B13, 20, C4, 16, D5,
    11, E77, 89, F17, 78, etc.; *a god* D107
    (2x)
gōd adj. *good* C55, 65, 170, F119; (n.noun)
    goods, good things B48, 127, F196; *good
    deed, good* C70, D3, F156
godsibb m. *fellow sponsor, coparent* A66
*godsibbrǣden f. *coparenthood, sponsorial
    obligations* B39
godspell n. *gospel* E188, F84, 86 (godspyl),
    87, 205 (gospel), 208 (godspyl)
godspellic adj. *evangelical, of the gospel*
    E185, F89

224

grama m.wk. *anger, wrath* C102
grānung f. *groaning, lamentation* B78, E94
grēat adj. *large, great* C122
gremian v.wk.2 *to provoke, vex* C88, 131, E3, F78 (**gremedan**)
grimlīce adv. *severely* C131; comp. F238
grīmme adv. *grimly, cruelly* E91
grindan v.st.3 *to grind* A16
gegrīpan v.st.1 *to grasp, seize, take up* D48, 51
gripe m. *grip, clutch* E94
grund m. *ground, bottom* C36
gryre m. *horror, terror* E92
gȳfernes f. *gluttony* D108
gylden adj. *golden* B11, 132 (**gylgenum**), E41, 152, 202, F43 (**geldenum**), 127 (**geldenum**), 222 (**geldnum**)
gylt m. *sin, offence* C41, E221
gȳman v.wk.1 *to take heed, regard* C130
gȳmelēas adj. *careless, negligent* E191 (**gemeleas**), F120 (**gemerlease**)
gȳmeleast f. *carelessness, neglect* F85 (**gemeleaste**)
gyrd f. *staff, rod* C35
gȳt adv. *yet, still* C19, 114, 125, E99 (**get**), 181 (**gyt**), F124 (**get**), 179 (**gyt**), etc.
gȳtsung f. *greed* D107

habban v.wk.3 *to have* A25, 34, B28, 84, C25, 66, D57, 114, E42, 80, F119 (**hefþ**), 205 (**hebbe**), etc.; neg.: A18 (**nabbon**), D80 (**nabbað**); **habban . . . for** *to count as* F167 (**hefdan**)
hādbreca m.wk. *one who injures one in holy orders* C148
(ge)hādian v.wk.2; past part. *ordained, in holy orders* B60, C22
hagol m.n. *hail* C122
hagolstān m. *hailstone* B41 (2x), E163, F180, 195
hālga m.wk. *saint* A59, C177, D127, E43, 60, F45, 107, etc.
(ge)hālgian v.wk.2 *to hallow, consecrate, sanctify* C6, E39, 141, F41, 56, 73, 106 (**gehalgod**)
hālgung f. *hallowing, consecration* E133, 138, F91, 99
hālig adj. *holy* A1 (**halie**), 13, B44, 65, C12, 51, D18, 125, E45, 187, F131, 162, etc.
hāligdōm m. *holy place* C63
hālignes f. *holiness, sanctity* C5, 15
hālsian v.wk.2 *to entreat, adjure* B29, 62, 65, 81, C156, D5, 94, 111
hām m. *home* C80

hand f. *hand* A3, 74 (**handon**), 85, C20, 83, D45, 114, 120, 128, E125
handgeweorc n. *handiwork* E176, 200, F148
handgewrit n. *document written in a person's own hand* E147, F122
hangian v.wk.2 *to hang* A70
hāt adj. *hot* C87
hātan v.st.7 *to name, call* B4 (2x), C13, 39, E13, F10, 76, etc.; *to command, bid* B30, 66, 81, C21, 140 (**hæt**), D68, 70, E24, F109, 113
gehātan v.st.7 *to promise, vow* B111, 127, F53 (**gehet**)
gehæft m. *captive* E85
gehæft adj. *captive, fettered* C68, 81
hæftnung f. *captivity* C78
hæftnȳd f. *captivity* D44 (**hæftned**), 71 (**hæftned**)
hæftnȳdling m. *captive* D37 (**hæftnedlingas**)
hǣl m. *health, salvation* C48, E199 (**hǣlo**), F219 (**helo**)
hǣlend m. *saviour* A11, 85, B98, 129, C21, 24, D2, 94, E192, 223, F111, etc.
hǣre f. *sackcloth of hair* A29
hærfest m. *autumn, harvest* E2, F2
hǣte f. *heat* D84
hǣþen adj. *heathen, pagan* A42, B113, 119, C83, E40, 47, F42, 181
hē 3rd pers.pron. *he, etc.* forms: **hē** (nom. sg.m.); **hine** (acc.sg.m.) – **hyne** (E), **his** (gen.sg.m.n.); **him** (dat.sg.) – **hym** (B); **hit** (nom.acc.sg.n.) – **hyt** (D); **hēo** (nom. acc.sg.f.) – **hio** (F); **hire** (gen.dat.sg.f.) – **hyre** (C, D); **hī** (nom.acc.pl./acc.sg.f.) – **hy** (B, E, F) heo (B, E), hie (F), hig (C, F), hio (F); **heora** (gen.pl.) – hiora (F), F80 (hioræ); **him** (dat.pl.) – **hym** (B, E), **heom** (A, C, E, F), **hiom** (F)
hēafod n. *head* A79, B81, E216 (2x)
hēah adj. *high, exalted* comp. E30 (**heahre**), F31 (**hegre**), 32 (**hegre**); superl. A85 (**hehstan**), F32 (**hegestan**)
hēahaltare m. *high altar* E148, 201 (**hehaltare**), F123, 221
hēahengel m. *archangel* A6, B3, 10, 43, 137, C31
hēahfæder m. *patriarch* B138, D98, E19; *high father (God)* B105
(ge)healdan v.st.7 *to hold, keep, observe; guard (against something)* A15, 65, B37, 109, C78, 144 (**hylt**), D32, 52, 93 (**gehylt**), E64, 150 (**haldan**), F45

(**heoldan**, *inf.*), 67, etc.; *to possess, own* D102

healf f. *side, half* B105, C10, F163

healfpenigwurþ n. *a halfpenny-worth* E62

hēanlīce adv. *abjectly* C81

hēap m. *company* F61, 63 (**hepe**)

hēapmǣlum adv. *in heaps* C80

heard adj. *hard, severe, strong* A41, C81; superl. D43

hearde adv. *severely, terribly* B90

hefiglīce adv. *grievously*; comp. C164

hell f. *hell* A23, 37, C56, 85, D112, E117, 128, F67, 81, etc.

hellefȳr n. *hell-fire* F62

hellegrund m. *abyss of hell* C87, 90, 168

helletintrega m.wk. *torments of hell* F243

hellewīte n. *torment of hell* E47, 91, F249

hellware m. *inhabitant of hell* E138

(**ge**)**helpan** v.st.3 *to help* D38, 91, E82

hēo: see **hē**

hēof m. *grief, sorrow* E93

heofon mf. *heaven, firmament* A1, 20 (**heafenas**), B3, 24 (**heofonas**), 29 (**heofonnm**), C9, 37 (**heofnan**), D12, 19, E26, 31, F69 (**heofan**), 184 (**heofenas**), etc.

heofoncund adj. *heavenly, celestial* E113

heofoncundlic adj. *heavenly, celestial* C45, E222

heofonlic adj. *heavenly, celestial* B99, C32, 37, 86, D13, E27, 29, F28 (**heofenlican**), 30 (**heofelican**), 50 (**heofenlican**)

heora: see **hē**

heorte f.wk. *heart* A10, E202, F223

heorþpening m. *hearth-penny (Peter's pence)* E59

hēr adv. *here* A1, B1, C3, 86, D1, 25, E1, F1, 103, etc.

hērbeforan adv. *before* D56, 121, E179

here m. *army* C83 (**heries**), 108

heretoga m.wk. *chieftain* C33

hergian v.wk.2 *to harry, ravage* C92, D48

hī, him, hine, hire: see **hē**

hīred m. *household, family* D66

his, hit: see **hē**

hīw n. *form, appearance* A23

gehīwian v.wk.2 *to form* D128

hīwrǣden f. *household* D64

hlāf m. *bread, loaf* A16, B102, C44, D22, 60, E165, F198

hlāford m. *lord* A7, 9, C140, 141, 154, D109

hlāfording m. *master, lord* C143

hlāfordswica m.wk. *traitor, betrayer of one's lord* C147

hlāfordswīcung f. *betrayal of one's lord* F240

hlēowan v.wk.1 *to make warm, shelter* E83 (**hlywan**)

hlīsa m.wk. *repute* D50

hlyhhan v.st.6 *to laugh (at)* E22 (**hlogen**), F25 (**hlogan**)

(**ge**)**hlystan** v.wk.1 *to listen to, attend to* C64, D93 (**gehlyst**); (w. gen.) C129; (w. dat.) F245 (**hlestan**)

hold adj. *faithful, devout* B49

horu m. *impurity, filth* A61

hraþe adv. *quickly, soon* E52

hrægl n. *garment, clothing* D59

hrēofl adj. *leprous* D90

hrēohnes f. *storm, tempest* A44, D84 (**hreognysse**)

gehrēowan v.st.2 *to grieve, rue* E175 (**gereaw**), F142 (**gehreaw**)

hrēowsung f. *repentance, penitence, sorrow* B31

hū adv. *how* C3, 104, D68, E35, 141, F37, 72, etc.

hund num. *hundred* A22, C111 (2x)

hund m. *dog, hound* B76

hundred num. *hundred* D71 (2x), F87 (c)

hundseofontig num. *seventy* E137, 215, F98

hundtēontig num. *hundred* F21

hundtwelftig num. *120* E19

hungor m. *hunger, famine* A44, C78, 80, D44, 91, E49, 100, F16, 121

huntoð m. *hunting, hunt* B21

huntung f. *the hunt, hunting* A17

hūru adv. *at least* E19, F21

hūruþinga adv. *surely, especially* D116

hūs n. *house* A28, B48, 77, C52, D89, E48, 155, F154, 198, etc.

hwā indef.pron. *someone, anyone* B18 (**hwam**); interr.pron. *who, what* C64, 68; **swa hwa swa** *whoever* C97, 129, D59; **hwæs** (gen.) **swa hwæs swa** *whatever* E156, F187; **hwon** (instr.) **be hwon** *by what means, how* C104 (**hwan**); **for hwon** *why* C106 (**hwan**)

hwǣr adv. *where* F109

hwæt interj. *what!, alas* E37, 194, F39 (**hwet**), 113 (**hwæt**), 135, 164

hwǣte m. *wheat, corn* A40, B47, F130

hwīl f. *time, while* C165, F145 (wile); conj. **þa hwile (þe)** *while* A25, E56, 79, 89

hwīlon adv. *once* C85, E147 [gloss]

hwōn adv. *little* E17, F14

hwylc adj. *what, what sort of* A11 (**hwilcon**),

E49, 202, F61, 222; indef.pron. *any* D113 (2x); pron. *what (sort of thing)* C71, E209, 211; adj./pron. **swa hwylc . . . swa** *whichever, whatever* B127, C119, D115, E188, F58, 60

gehwylc pron. *each, every* D75, E75

gehwyrfan v.wk.1 *to turn, convert* E156 (**gehwyrfde**), F186 (**gehwærfede**)

hyge m. *thought, mind* C129

gehyngran v.wk1. *to be hungry*; past part. E84 (**gehingredum**)

(ge)hȳran v.wk.1 *to hear, listen to, obey* A79, B57 (**geherað**), 124 (**gehȳrað**), C24, 140, D34, 54, F88 (**gehereþ**), 177 (**gehære**), etc.

hȳrsumian v.wk.2 (w. dat.) *to obey* B133 (**hersumiað**)

hyrtan v.wk.1 *to hearten, encourage* E85

ic 1st pers.pron. *I, etc.*; forms: **ic** (nom. sg.); **mē** (acc.dat.sg.); **wit** (nom.dual); **wē** (nom.pl.) F236 (**wy**); **ūs** (acc.dat.pl.); **ūre** (gen.pl.)

īdel adj. *empty, vain, frivolous* C168, E180

in prep. (w. dat./acc.) *in, on, into* B3, 80, D130, E35, 46, F7, 37, etc.

inne adv. *inside, within* C52, 64, E207

innoþ m. *womb* C44

intinga m.wk. *cause, purpose* B15

intō prep. (w. dat.) *into* A2, 80, C55

īsen adj. *of iron* E217

iū adv. *formerly, of old, once* E15, 25, 51, 147, 210, F119, 135; **iu geara** E18, 171

iudeisc adj. *Jewish* C48

lā interj. *O, lo* A62, D67, E56, F246

lāf f. *remnant, remainder, spoil* C83, D23, E35, F37

lagu f. *law* C10, 65

lām n. *clay, mud, earth* B27

lama adj. *lame, disabled* D90

land n. *land* C34, 36, 92, 121, D87, E3, F2, 144

lang adj. *long* C153, 164, E34, 140, F36, 105

lār f. *teaching, exhortation* B108 (see commentary), 133, C159, D1, E185, F16, 89, 245

lārēow m. *teacher* C65, D35, 72, 82

late adv. *late*; superl. E60

lāþ adj. *hateful, hostile* C60

gelaþung f. *church, congregation* C49

(ge)lǣdan v.wk.1 *to lead, bring* B97, C33, 34, 81, 111, D47

lǣfan v.wk.1 *to leave (behind)* C46, E89

lǣnan v.wk.1 *to grant, lend* C118

lǣran v.wk.1 *to teach, urge, instruct* C162, 163, E74; past part. *learned* D113, E190, F207 (2x)

lǣs adv. *less* C130

gelǣstan v.wk.1 *to pay a due or debt* E76, F18; *to accomplish, fulfil* B127

(ge)lǣtan v.st.7 *to let, allow, permit, cause* B98, C135, D18, E191, F143, 181 (lete), 208; *to cease* F70; **læt him eaþlice ymbe þæt** *to take (a matter) lightly* C160

lǣwede adj. *lay, not learned* C3, 22

lēactūn m. *(kitchen-)garden* B18 (**lehtune**), 122 (**lehtune**)

gelēafa m.wk. *belief, faith* A14, C49, 174, F17

gelēaffull adj. *faithful, believing* A66, D24 [gloss]

gelēaflēasnes f. *unbelief* C48

leahter m. *sin, vice* D109, 110

lēan n. *reward, recompense* E80, 90

lēap m. *basket* C46

lēasung f. *deceit, falsehood* C61, D30

lenctendæg m. *day of Lent* E72

lenctenfæsten n. *fast of Lent* E68

gelengan v.wk.1 *to prolong, lengthen* A54

lēof adj. *beloved, dear* A51, B50, 64, C1, 179, D72, E56, 76; comp. E79, 88; superl. A1, 59, B1, C109, D1, 92, E8, 170, F222, etc.

lēogan v.st.2 *to lie, deceive* E22 (**luge**), 23 (**leoge**), F27 (**luge**)

lēoht n. *a light* B57

lēoht adj. *bright, light* C136

lēohtgesceot n. *payment for providing lights in church, light-scot* E62

lēsan v.st.5 *to gather, collect* B121

libban v.wk.3 *to live* A55, B70, 118, C4, 104 (**lifian**), 127, 164 (**leofedon**), D26 (2x), E223; pres.part. as adj. C39, 156, D5, 124; pres.part. as sb. *the living* B83, 86, 129, C103 (**lybbendan**)

gelīce adj. (w. dat.) *like, as if*; superl., **þam gelicost . . . swylce** *just like that, just the same* E180

licgan v.st.5 *to lie, be at rest* C80, E76, 191, 207 (**læg**), F208, 227 (**leg**)

līchama m.wk. *body* A27, 36, B77, C90, D127 (**lichoman**), E128, 207, F81, 105, 227, 231 (**lichoman**)

(ge)līcian v.wk.2 (w. dat.) *to please, be pleasing to* B64 (**gecleopode** for **gelicode**), E90

līcwyrþe adj. *pleasing, acceptable* C11

līf n. *life* A54, 62, B120, C3, 145, D26, 130, E48, 81, F61, 90 (**liues**), etc.

līflic adj. *living, of life* A67

līg m (n.) *fire, flame, lightning* A45, B132 (**leg**), E173 (**leg**), F132 (**læg**), 141 (**leg**), 180 (**leg**)

līget m.n. *(flash of) lightning* E54 (**ligette**)

līgræsc m. *lightning, flash of lightning* C123, D83

līhting f. *lighting, dawn* B38, 116, C27, 115, E44, 65, F46, 93, etc.

līhtnes f. *lightness, brightness* B93

lim n. *limb* B89

gelimpan v.st.3 *to happen, occur* C88, E210, F108, 135, 148, 225

lōca interj. *look*; **loca hwa** *whoever* C68; **loca hwæt** *whatever* C64; **loca hwylc** *whichever* C71

lof n. *praise* B141

gelōmlīce adv. *frequently, often* A27, 83, F206; comp. A67

lufian v.wk.2 *to love* B114, C23, 153, 176, D9

lufu f. (wk.) *love* A87 (2x), B21, 121, D82 [gloss], 94, E77

lustlīce adv. *willingly, gladly* F88

gelȳfan v.wk.1 *to believe*; A37, 80, B133, 134 (**gelefan**), F102; w. acc. and **on** A43, 60, B114, F15; w. dat. B61 (**gelefan**), 72 (**gelefað**), D56, 129, E24 (**gelefan**), 25 (**gelefan**), etc.; w. gen. A84, C173, E183, F14 (**gelefdon**), 38 (**geleafan**)

lȳt adv. *little* E51

lȳtel adj. *little, small* A50, F120 (**litelne**), 139 (**letlan**), 145 (**letle**); sb. *a short time* E177

lȳþre adj. *base, sordid, vile* C135

mā indecl.sb. *more* A82, C150, F111 (**me**); w. gen. C143, F248; adj. used as conj. **þe ma þe** *any more than* E24

macian v.wk.2 *to make, create* F77

magan v.pret.pres. *to be able, may, can*; **mæg** (pres.1/3sg) C180, D91, E212; **magon** (pres.pl.) A62, E56, 217, 222, F241; **mæge** (pres.subj.sg.) C160 (**mage**), E97, E190, F249 (**mege**); **mægen** (pres. subj.pl.) F180, 236, 242 (**megan**, all); **mihte** (pret.1/3sg.) E34, 182, F8, 35, 147; **mihton** (pret.pl.) E80, 89, 214

mān n. *wickedness, evil deed* D32, 118

gemāna m.wk. *fellowship* C117

mancwealm m. *pestilence, slaughter* C103

māndǣd f. *evil deed, crime* C62

mānfullīce adv. *wickedly, evilly* C88

manian v.wk.2 *to admonish* F230

manig adj. *many* D11 (**manega**) E23, F15 (**menige**)

man(n) m. *man, person* A1, 15, B16, 102, C16, 62, D1, 113, E11, 110, F8 (**mon**), 72 (**mæn**), etc.; as indef. pron. *one* C25, 46, E67, 76, F110 (**mon**), 113 (**me**), etc.

manna n.wk. *manna* B98, C39, E112, F50

manncynn n. *mankind, men* C47, 54, E7 (**mancyn**), 177 (**mancyn**), F4, 44 (**mankynne**)

mannslaga m.wk. *man-slayer* C148

mansliht m.wk. *manslaughter* A58, B52, C61, D30, F240

mānswara m.wk. *perjurer* C147

martyr (Lat.) *martyr* B138

gemæcca mf.wk. *mate, one of a pair* E33 (**gemacan**), F35 (**gemeccan**)

mǣgen n. *might* F224 (**megen**)

mǣgenþrymm m. *might, power* E204

mǣgslaga m.wk. *kin-slayer* C148

mǣl n. *meal, occasion* C43

mǣnan v.wk.1 *to mean, signify* E50, F61 (**mende**), 94 (**mende**), 164 (**mende**)

mǣne adj. *false, wicked* B52, E204, F224 (**menne**)

mǣre adj. *great, excellent* F20

mǣrsian v.wk.2 *to celebrate, honour* A13, E117, F68

mæsse f.wk. *mass* E60, 62, 63, 69, 70

mæssedæg m. *mass-day, holy day, festival* E59, 65

mæsseprēost m. *mass-priest* A83, B4, 5, 7, 8, 128, C2

mǣst superl.adj. *most, greatest* C22, E28, 148, F29, 62 (**mestan**), 123

mǣst adv. *in the greatest degree* C160

mē: see **ic**

mēd f. *reward* A88, 89

mēdsceatt m. *bribe* C135

(ge)mengan v.wk.1 *to mix, mingle*; past part. *disturbed* E92 (**gemencged**)

(ge)menigfeald adj. *manifold, numerous* E155 (**manigfealde**), F52, 185

(ge)menigfealdan v.wk.1 *to multiply, increase* B48 (**gemanigfealdum** for **gemanigfealde**)

mennisc adj. *human* D25, E19, 41, 174, F20, 53

menniscnes f. *human nature* C30

meolc f. *milk* B20

meolcian v.wk.2 *to milk* B20

228

gemet n. *ability* F248
gemētan v.wk.1 *to meet with, find* D63, 64
mete m. *food* B99, C37, 39, E12, 84, 113, F9, 50
mettrumnes f. *illness, infirmity* B88 (**mettrunesse**)
micclum, micel adv. *greatly, much* A24, E102, 198, F217
micel adj. *great, large, much* A14, 27, B96, C138 (**mycclan**), 153, D91, 96, E87, 198 (**micclan**), F4, 134, etc.
mid prep. (w. dat.) *with* A13, 29, B11, 30, C35, 57, D3, 76, E3, 26, F12, 28, etc.
middan(g)eard m. *earth, world* A18, 23, C20, 40, D2, 25 (**middanerd**), E53, 79, F32, etc.
middel n. *middle, midst* F87
miht f. *might, power* A61, B137, C32, 68, E159, 162, F6, 190, 193
mihtig adj. *mighty, powerful* E199
milde adj. *merciful* A9, C87, F151
mildheortlīce adv. *mercifully, compassionately* E86
mildheortnes f. *mercy, compassion* A11, B78, C165, 173, 175, E149, 171, F124 (**mildheornesse**), 155
milts f. *mercy* C102, F20 (**mildse**), 143
miltsian v.wk.2 *to have or show mercy (on), be merciful* B71, 79, 80
mīn poss.adj. *my* A44, 56, B49, 62, C78, 94, D44, 66, E115, 155, F55, 61, etc.
misdǣd f. *misdeed, transgression* B77, F236 (**misdeda**)
***misgelimp** n. *mishap, misfortune* E145
mislic adj. *various, diverse* E101
missenlic adj. *various* D105
***mistīd** f. *evil time* D84
gemōdigan v.wk.1 *to grow proud, be filled with pride* A76
mōdor f. *mother* A51, C178
mōdorlēas adj. *motherless* B53
mōna m.wk. *moon* B25
mōnandæg m. *Monday* B38, 116, C27, 115, D79, E44, 65, F46 (**monandeges**), 102, etc.
mōnanniht f. *Monday eve, evening of Sunday* E109, 131, 151, F126, 134
mōnaþ m. *month* B42, F195, 211
morgen m. *morning* D79, 105 (2x)
morþwyrhta m.wk. *murderer* C147
gemōt n. *assembly* A15, C62
mōtan v.pret.pres. *may, must*; **mōt** (pres.1/3sg.) C68, 141; **mōton** (pres.pl.) B53 (**motan**), C175, E222 (**motan**), 223

(**motan**), F64 (**motan**)
gemunan v.pret.pres. *to consider, remember* C95, D67, 102, E218
munt m. *mountain, hill* E30, F31, 32 (**munde**)
mūþ nm. *mouth* A45
mylen mf. *mill* B21
gemynd fn. *mind* D57
(ge)myndgian/(ge)myn(e)gian v.wk.2 *to remind, admonish, exhort* A25 (**mynegie**), B126 (**gemyngad**), C2, D94 (**myngie**), E108, F238 (**mengaþ**); *to remember, be mindful of* E170 (**gcmyndigc**), F230 (**geynegode** for **gemynegode**)
mynster n. *minster, church* B110, E76
mynstermann m. *churchman, monk* F209 (**mynstermon**)
myrhþ f. *mirth, bliss* C55

nā adv. *not* A34, B114, C101, 142, E208, F209, 229
nacod adj. *naked* D36, E84
nama m.wk. *name* A3, 66, B29, 129, D5, 47, E13, 157, F5, 203 (**noman**), etc.
næddre f.wk. *serpent, snake* A70, B69, 122, F180 (**neddran**)
(ge)næglian v.wk.2 *to nail* B91
ne particle *not* A29, 33, B20, 56, C4, 15, D48, 51, E25, 41, F10, 42, etc.; conj. *nor* D114, 118, E12, F9; correlative *neither . . . nor* A15, 16, B18, 124, C93, 101, D62, F175, 220, etc.
nēah adj. *near* C132, D96; superl. *last, latest* E220 (**nexta**)
nēah adv. *nearly* F141 (**nioh**)
nēahgebūr m. *neighbour* A66 (**neheboras**)
geneahhe adv. *frequently, sufficiently* E189 (**genehhe**)
nēalǣcan v.wk.1 *to draw near, approach* B134
(ge)nemnan v.wk.1 *to name, call* A4, 5, C89, E104
(ge)nēosian v.wk.2 *to visit* C67, D35, 106, E86
generian v.wk.1 *to save, preserve* E35, F37
nēxt adj. *latest, last* E103 (**nexta**)
nigon num. *nine* C120 (**ix**), D89
nigoþa num. *ninth* D78
niht f. *night* A75, C133 (2x), 136 (3x), D103, 104, E28, 58, 74, F29
genihtsumnes f. *abundance, plenty* A54, F152 (**genihtsumes**)
(ge)niman v.st.4 *to take (away)* B78, C150, E101, 210, F114, 142

niþemest superl.adj. *lowest* E46
(neoðemestan)
nīwe adj. *new* D98
genōh adj. *enough* D92
nōn fn. *the ninth hour, 3 p.m.* C27, 115, E64,
F115, 166, 239
nōntīd f.wk. *the ninth hour, 3 p.m.* B37,
116, E44, 133, F46, 92, etc.
norþdǣl m. *the North* D49
nosu f. *nose* A46
nouembris (Lat.) *November* B42
nū adv. *now* B87, C5, 19, D67, E3, 51, F5,
24, etc.
nȳdþearf f. *necessity, need* D96 (neadþearf), E67 (neodþearfe)
nȳten n. *cattle, beast* D66, F177
nytt f. *use, benefit* E155, F186
nytt adj. *useful, beneficial* E184
nyþer adv. *down, downwards* E127 (nyðer)

octabas num. (Lat.) *eighth (day)* E73
october (Lat.) *October* F196, 211
of prep. (w. dat.) *of, from, by (means of)*
A33, 60, B2, 26, C12, 37, D17, 53, E9,
34, F6, 18, etc.
ofcalan v.st.6 *to make cold, chill* E83
ofer prep. (w. acc.) *over, upon, above* A19,
42, B23, 40, C34, 51, D18, 65, E2, 16, F3,
13, etc.; (w. dat.) F143
ofercuman v.st.4 *to overcome* F122
oferdruncennes f. *drunkenness* D108
oferfaran v.st.6 *to cross* E111, F48
(oferferde)
oferfylgan v.wk.1 *to attack, pursue* D105
(oferfiligað) (but see next word and
commentary)
oferfyll f. *excess, surfeit, gluttony* C137,
[D105] (see commentary)
ofergān v.anom. *to overrun, go over* F119
oferhogian v.wk.2 *to scorn, despise* D90,
F149 (oferhogodan)
oferhygd fn. *pride, arrogance* C90
ofermōdignes f. *pride, arrogance* D107
ofernōn fn. *afternoon (after 3 p.m.)* E4, 39,
F41, 84, etc.
oferyrnan v.st.3 *to flow (over)* E133, F92
ofniman v.st.4 *to take from* B119
ofslēan v.st.6 *to slay* C79, 110, D71
oft adv. *often, frequently* B126, C131, E39,
141 (2x), F51, 105, 106, 154
ofþyrstan v.wk.1. *to thirst, be thirsty* E85
on prep. (w. dat./acc.) *on, in, into, upon* A8,
17, B11, 16, C3, 14, 105 (an), D4, 17, E1,
14, F5 (an), 16, etc.; *in respect to* B52

(2x); on ... geniman *to take from* F114
onǣlan v.wk.1 *to set fire to, ignite* E164
onbǣrnan v.wk.1 *to ignite, burn* F195
(anberned)
onbyrgan v.wk.1 (w. gen.) *to partake of,*
taste F9 (anbergde)
oncnāwan v.st.7 *to know, perceive* A10
oncyrran v.wk.1 *to change, transform* F118
(ancerrede)
ondrǣdan v.st.7 *to fear, dread* D102, F129
(andredan)
onfindan v.st.3 *to find, discover* F8
(anfindan)
onfōn v.st.7 *to receive, accept, partake*
of B71, 110, D38, 62, E41, 139 (onfoð,
onfangen), F43, 100, 170
ongēan prep. *against* A65, C161, D48, E27,
29, F28 (angen), 30 (angen), 75 (ongen)
onginnan v.st.3 *to begin* A1, B1, 56, D1,
E27, 112, 177, 178, F49 (angan), 150
(angan)
ongytan v.st.5 *to consider, perceive, under-*
stand B24 (ongeotað), 107 (ongeotað),
133 (ongeotað), F137 (anget), 139
(andged)
onhagian v.wk.2 *to be within a person's*
power or means C68, E86
onhrēran v.wk.1 *to agitate, disturb* E206
(onrered), F226 (onhrered)
onmang prep. *among* C9, 49
onscunian v.wk.2 *to reject, abhor* D52
onsendan v.wk.1 *to send* D75, 82, 128, 43
(ansǣnde), 95 (ansende)
onspringan v.st.3 *to spring, burst forth, rise*
E27
onstellan v.wk.1 *to establish* F72
(anstealde)
ontȳnan v.wk.1 *to open* E154, F84
onufan prep. (w. dat.) *after* E58; *upon* F130,
214, 216, 225 (anufan, all)
onwacan v.st.6 *to awake* E9
onwendan v.wk.1 *to transgress, pervert,*
change F170 (anwændaþ)
open adj. *open* B46, E76, 206, F226, 237
(ge)openian v.wk.2 *to open* A10, 53, B106
openlīce adv. *openly, publicly* F113, 165
ordāl m.n. *ordeal* E72
orf n. *cattle* F18
orfcwealm m. *pestilence (among cattle)*
C103
ormǣtlic adj. *immense* E55
ormōd adj. *despairing, hopeless* E85
orsorhlīce adv. *without anxiety, safely* E223
ortruwian v.wk.2 *to despair* C173

oþ prep. (w. acc.) *until* B38, 89, C27, 115, D78, 105, E44, 64, F102, 169, etc.; conj. *until* C36

ōþer adj. *other, another* A4, 5, C97, 99, D69, E10, 65, F7, 207, etc.; pron. B136, C141, 150, 164, 172, E159, 166, F189, 197

oþþæt conj. *until* E29, F27, 31, 110

oþþe conj. *or* C97, 142, D74, E60, F235, etc.; correl. **oþþe . . . oþþe** *either . . . or* D59, 86, E165, F197, etc.

oþstandan v.st.6 *to remain* E35 (**oðstodon**)

pāpa m.wk. *pope* E194, 203, F213, 224
pentecosten m. *Pentecost* E58
prēost m. *priest* A3, 4, 5, B74
pund n. *pound* B41
pytt m. *pit, grave* E76

ræd m. *wisdom* E171
rædan v.wk.1 *to read, expound* D114, E14, F11 (**redaþ**)
rēad adj. *red* B97, C34, D17, E111, F48
rēafere m. *robber, plunderer* C149
rēaflāc nm. *robbery, theft* C61, D30
rēcan v.wk.1 *to be concerned for* C159
reccan v.wk.1. *to recount* C155 (**rehte**)
gerēfa m.wk. *reeve* C21
regn/ren m. *rain* A44, B135, C124 (2x), E28 (**hrene**), 163, 173, F29, 132, 141, 194 (**reng**)
rēnscūr m. *rain-shower* A53
gereord fn. *language* D48, E136, 137 (2x), 215 [gloss], F96 (**gehriorde**), 97 (**gehriorde**, 2x)
gereordian v.wk.2 *to feed* C43
rest f. *rest* B29, E40 (2x), F42 (2x), 100, etc.
(ge)restan v.wk.1 *to rest* B27, 96, E120 [marg.], F71
reste(n)dæg m. *a day of rest, sabbath day* A77 (**restedæg**), B28, 93, E115, 117, F55 (**rystedæg**), 65 (**restedæg**), 173 (**restandæg**), 184 (**restandæig**), etc.
rīce n. *kingdom* A24, 30, B35, 48, C9, 145, D62, E154, 222, F176, 242, etc.
rīce adj. *rich, powerful* C132
rīcsian v.wk.2 *to rule, govern, reign* E223 (**rixian**), F249 (**rixaþ**)
rīdan v.st.1 *to ride* B21
riht n. *right, justice* C135 (2x), 152 (2x); **mid/on/to rihte** *justly, properly, lawfully* A43, B37, 40, C71, 113, D88, E43, 46, F18, 173, etc.; **riht agyldan** *to render an account* F232, 235

riht adj. *right, true* C49
***rihtæþelcwēn** f. *legitimate wife* C150
rihtfæstendæg m. *appointed fast-day* E73
gerihtlǣcan v.wk.1 *to put right, amend* A32
rihtlīce adv. *rightly* C4, D26, 86, 102, E57
rihtwīs adj. *righteous* A22, 24, 88 (3x), C55
rihtwīsnes f. *righteousness, justice* C23, D9
gerīm n. *number* D96
rīnan v.st.1 *to rain* B98, D19, E27 (**hrinan**), F29, 30
rōd f. *cross, rood* B30, 91, C47, E188, 199, F160, 204, 218
rodetācn n. *sign of the cross* A28
rȳpere m. *robber, plunderer* C149

sācerd m. *priest* C91, D47, 81, 115
sācerdbana m.wk. *priest-slayer* C148
gesamnung f. *assembly* D24
sang m. *song* B57
sār n. *pain, suffering* D51, E176, F247
sārgung f. *lamentation, grief* E92
sāwol f. *soul* A62, B82, 129 (**sawel**), C3, 33, D15, 76, E40, 128, F61 (**saule**), 100 (**sauwla**), 244 (**saulum**), etc.
sāwolsceatt m. *dues paid for a deceased person (lit. payment for the soul)* E75, 76
sǣ f. *sea* A20, B25, 97, C34, D17, 100, E7, 107, F3, 49 (se), etc.
gesǣlig adj. *blessed, happy* C169
gesǣliglīce adv. *blessedly* F242
sæternesdæg m. *Saturday* B38, 116, C27, 115, D78, E4, 39, F41 (**seternes**), 46 (**sæternesdeges**), 102 (**seternesdæges**), 126 (**sæternes**), etc.
gesceaft f. *creature, creation* B94, D101, 125, E40, 103, 107, 120, F70 (**gescæfta**)
sceatt m. *bribe* C152
scīr f. *district* A84
sciran v.st.4 *to shave (hair)* A79 (**sceran**), E166 (**scerð**), F199 (**scirþ**)
scrift m. *confessor* B31
scrūd n. *dress, garment* A77
scrȳdan v.wk.1 *to clothe* C68, D36
sculan v.pret.pres. *must, shall*; **sceal** (pres.1/3sg.) C81, E95, 97, 184; **scel** C100, 140, 144, 146, F183; **sceolon** (pres. pl.) C177, D36; **sceolan** A74, F170; **scealan** F247; **sculon** A37, C2, 79, 116, 120, F232; **sculan** C80, F89, 234; **scylon** B70, E90; **scylan** B118, E78, 80; **sceolde** (pret.1/3sg.) C17, E126, 176; **scolde** F62, 111, 112, 148; **sceoldon** (pret.pl.) C127; **sceoldan** E150; **scoldan** B42, F72, 125, 141

scyld m. *shield* D49

gescyldan v.wk.1 *to shield, protect* F125, 249

scyldig adj. *guilty* C4, D117, F66 (**sceldige**)

gescyppan v.st.6 *to create, form* B26, 94 (**gescop**), C29, 33, D15, 124, E110, 215, F47 (**gescapen**), etc.

scyppend m. *creator* C28, 179 (2x)

(ge)scyrtan v.wk.1 *to shorten* D96

scyttels m. *bar, bolt* B106 (**scytelsas**)

sē dem.pron./def.art. *that (one), the*; forms: sē (nom.sg.m.); **þone** (acc.sg.m.) – **þane** (F), F70 (**þæne**), F232 (**þene**); **þæs** (gen. sg.m.n.) – **þes/ðes** (F); **þām/þæm/þan** (dat.sg.m.n./dat.pl.); **þ̄/þon/þan** (inst. sg.m.n.); **sēo** (nom.sg.f.) – **sio** (F); **þā** (acc.sg.f./nom.acc.pl.); **þære** (dat.gen. sg.f.) – **þare** (F), F203 (**þaræ**); **þæt** (nom. acc.sg.n.); **þāra/þ̄ra** (gen.pl.); **þy þe** *because* E16; **ær þon** (**þe**): see **ǣr**; **æfter þon þe**: see **æfter**; **to þam**: see **tō**

sēcan v.wk.1 *to seek (out)* A68, B13, C63, D35

secgan v.wk.3 *to say* A11, 38, B42 (**sæcge**), 91, C5, 128 (**gesæd**), D56, 121 (**sæde**), E34 (**sæcganne**), 149 (**sæcgan**), F1 (**sagaþ**), 7 (**sede**), 8 (**sægde**), 212 (**segde**) etc.

gesegnian v.wk.2 *to bless, consecrate* B33 (**gesenað**)

sēl adj. *good*; superl. *best* E196 (**selestan**), F214 (**salestan**)

sendan v.wk.1 *to send* A3,83, B4, 72 (**sænde**), C51, 77, E47, 100, F16 (**sænd**), 122, etc.

sēo: see sē

sēoc adj. *sick, ill* C67, E86

sēocnes f. *sickness, illness, disease* E101

seofon num. *seven* E213, 216 (2x)

seofoþa adj. *seventh* B2, 27, 132, E38, 115, 120, 179, F40, 65, 70 (**vii**)

gesēon v.st.5 *to see* B124, D14 (**gesewene**), E10 (**geseah**), 55, 175 (**geseh**), F7, 109 (**gesawan**), F148 (**geseah**)

september (Lat.) *September* F196, 211

settan v.wk.1 *to set* A27

gesettan v.wk.1 *to set, establish* C14

gesibsumian v.wk.2 *to reconcile* C72, D39

singal adj. *everlasting, perpetual* E93

(ge)sittan v.st.5 *to sit, be seated* B18, 105, C135, E213, F162; **on sittan** *to oppress* E25 (**sitt**)

sīþ m. *time, occasion* C111, 165, D70, E63, F53

gesīþ m. *companion* D27

sīþ adv. *late*; **sīþ oþþe ǣr** *ever, at all times* F235

six num. *six* A21, B24, 27, E114, 119, F64 (**vi**), 69

sixtȳne num. *sixteen* F31

slēan v.st.6 *to strike* C34 (**sloh**)

slītan v.st.1 *to slit, bite, tear* A70

slite m. *slit, tear, bite* E93

*smeart adj. *painful* C76

snāw m. *snow* F194

sōna adv. *immediately* E126, F78

sorgung f. *sorrowing, grieving* E92

sōþ n. *truth* A48

sōþ adj. *true* A48, C28, 40 (2x), D110, E11, 45, F8, 246, etc.; **sōþ is** translating *amen*: B91, 115, E153, F128, 131, etc.

sōþlīce adv. *truly, certainly, indeed* A2, 6, B6, 7, D77, E119, 197, F58, 69, etc.

spell n. *sermon, message, tale* E1, 14, 180, F11

sprǣc/spǣc f. *speech, language* C19, 52, 93, 170 (**spæc**)

sprecan v.st.5 *to speak* C91, E9 (**sprǣc**), 136, 214, F6 (**sprec**), 53 (**sprecende**), 54 (**sprec**), 97, 171

stalu f. *theft* C61, D31

stān m. *stone* A41

standan v.st.6 *to stand, remain, continue* C15, D74, 117 (**stent**), F109 (**stod**)

stapa m.wk. *locust* F138 (? for **gærsstapa**)

stæf m. *a written character, letter* B11, 132, E41, 152, 202, F43, 127, 222

stæpe m. *a step* E133, F92 (**stepe**)

stemn/stefn f. *voice* D49 (**stefen**), E160, 217, F191

stēopcild n. *an orphan* C70, E82

steorra m.wk. *star* D100

stod m. *place* F226 (? error for **stōw** or **stōl**)

storm m. *storm* F179

stōw f. *place* B9, D35, E206, [F226 see stod], F243

strang adj. *arduous, severe* F229; comp. E53 (**strengra**)

stranglīce adv. *severely* E42, F44, 117 (**stranlice**), F135

strǣl fm. *arrow* E203, F223 (**strealum**)

gestrēon n. *gain, property* F19 (**gestrionum**)

sūcan v.st.2 *to suck* A70

sulh f. *plough* E61

sulhælmesse f.wk. *plough-alms* E57

sum pron./adj. *some, one, a certain*; pron. E2; adj. E18, 122, F1, 53

sunnandæg m. *Sunday* A13, 64, B16, 37, C5, 58, D1, 10, E4, 46, F11 (**sunnandeges**), 167 (**sunnændæg**), etc.

sunnanniht f. *Saturday night* A73

sunne f.wk. *sun* B25

sunu m. *son* B54 (2x), 64, 74, C8, 39, D98, 124, E32, 224, F22, 34, 159

sūsl nf. *torment* C85, E212

sūþ adv. *south(wards)* E6, F3

swā adv. *so, as, thus* A81, B26, 34, C4, 82, D91, E22, 29, F38, 103, etc.; conj. B12, 111, D46, 121, E7, 14, F23, 77, etc.; **swa hwa swa** *whoever* C97, 129, D59, **swa hwæs swa** *whatsoever* E156, F187; **swa hwylc(um)** . . . **swa** *whichever* B127, C118, D115, E188, F58, 59; **swa swa** *just as* C16, 85, 113, 128, 175, E123, 172, 183, F84; **swa** . . . **swa** *so/as* . . . *as* C52, 165, D109, F119; **swa** . . . **swa** *either* . . . *or* F206; **swa þæt** *so that* C34, 77, 116

swāþēah adv. *nevertheless* F152 (**sweþeah**)

swǣlan v.wk.1 *to burn*; pres.part. as adj. E173

sweflen adj. *sulphurous* A45, B135, F132, 141

*__sweflic__ adj. *sulphurous* F180 (**swelic**)

swēgan v.wk.1 *to rush, sound, crash* D50

sweltan v.st.3 *to die, perish* E54, 116, F59

geswencan v.wk.1 *to afflict, oppress* D51

sweord n. *sword* C78

(ge)swerian v.st.6 *to swear, make an oath* A16, 48, B18, D122, 124, E45, 99, F198, 224, etc.

swēte adj. *sweet* D104 (2x)

geswīcan v.st.1 *to abstain from, cease from, forsake, desist* A39, C134; w. gen. A53, C18, 132, D55, E100, F138, 146, etc.

geswinc n. *labour, hardship, affliction* A34, 64, B66, 88, D86

geswinclic adj. *laborious* C59

swingan v.st.3 *to scourge, flog, beat* C76, D43, E166, F198 (**swinggæþ**)

swingel f. *affliction, scourge* D43 (**swinglan**)

swipu f. *scourge, whip* C77

swīþe adv. *very, greatly, strongly, vehemently* B17, 90, C2, 4, D95, E29, 38, F25, 30, etc.; comp. *more* C10 (**swyðor**), F62 (**swiþor**); superl. *especially, above all, exceedingly* C59, 73, D41, E144, 145

swīþra comp.adj. *stronger, right* B105, F162

(ge)swutelian v.wk.2 *to reveal, show* A12 (**gesutelod**), D82 (**swuteliað**)

swutole adv. *openly* D122 (**swutele**)

swylc adj. *such, as* C101, D110, E176; pron. **swylce** . . . **swylce** *such* . . . *as* C155 (2x)

swylce conj. *as if, like* E147, 180; adv. **eac swylce**: see **ēac**

sylen f. *grant, gift, giving* B51

sylf pron./adj. *himself, myself, themselves* A48, B137, C16, 50, D56, E15, 17, F11 (**self**), 42 (**sylfe**), etc.; *own* D3, E17, 51, F14, 24, 120

(ge)syllan v.wk.1 *to give, sell* A16 (**syllon**), 53, B20, 67 (**sellað**), C20, D45 (**gesylle**), 130 (**sylþ**), E84, 157 (**selle**), F185 (**selle, sylle**), 188 (**wille** for **sille**), etc.

symle adv. *always, ever* B59 (**simle**), 60 (**simble**), 140 (**simle**), F230

synfull adj. *sinful* A23, B24, 68, 70, E15, 21, F12, 25

(ge)syngian v.wk.2 *to sin* C160, 164

synlēas adj. *sinless* F114 (**senleas**)

synn f. *sin* A61, B31, C161, 163, D111, 119, E221, F87 (**synny**), etc.

syþþan adv. *afterwards* A21, C29, 30, 82, 84, E12, 87, F2, 9, etc.; conj. *after* C8, 9, 42, 44, 47, F166, 239

tācn n. *sign* F55

getācnian v.wk.2 *to indicate, signify, show* E132, F91, 113 (**getanad**)

tāl n. *derision, scorn* C172

tǣcan v.wk.1 *to show, teach, instruct* C52, 65

tǣlan v.wk.1 *to charge, accuse, speak ill of* A17

getellan v.wk.1 *to count, consider* D109 (**getealde**)

teolung f. *cultivation* D87

tēon v.st.2. *to drag, draw* D112

tēona m.wk. *reproach, injury* C121, F154 (**tynan**)

tēonlīce adv. *shamefully, with reproach* C82

getēorian v.wk.2 *to waste away* D76

tēoþan adj. *tenth* C120, E61

tēoþian v.wk.2 *to tithe, pay a tithe* A35, C118

tēoþung f. *tithe* A33, 63, B32, 40, 73, 110, 120, D86, E57, 58, 125, F17 (**tioþunge**)

tīd f. *time, hour, age* C73, D32, 40, 68, 78, E122, 195, 205, F197, 213, 225

tilian v.wk.2 *to labour, toil* C98 (**tylige**)

tīma m.wk. *hour, (period of) time* E78, 88

tō prep. (w. dat.) *to, for, as, in, into*; w.noun/pron. A3, 4, B5, 17, C3, 9, D21, 23, E9, 36, F7, 27, etc.; w.infl.inf. A10, 13, B19,

21, C4, 40, D16, 40, E34, 53, F37, 56, etc.; adv. **þær** . . . **to** *to where* A8, F123; **to þam/þon** *to that extent* E37, 85, 181, F39; **to þam** *for that purpose* E182

tō adv. *too* B17, C19, E17, F14, 105, 120 (2x)

tōberstan v.st.3 *to burst asunder* E126 (**tobærst**), F79 (**tobærst**)

tōbrecan v.st.4 *to break, destroy* C109, 110

tōcyme m. *approach, coming, advent* B77, 90, 123, E52

tōdǽlan v.wk.1 *to divide* D16, E136, F96

tōdrīfan v.st.1 *to scatter, disperse* D75

tōgān v.anom. *to divide, separate* C35 (**toeode**)

togēanes prep. *towards, against* A50

tōslūpan v.st.2 *to dissolve, slip apart* D24 (**tosleap**)

tōsomne adv. *together* E28, F29

tōweard adj. *future, coming, approaching* B45, 134, C107, 172, E182

trēow n. *tree* D85

trēowa m.wk. *covenant* E118

getrēowe adj. *true, faithful* B62, 71; superl. A56 (**getrywestan**)

getrēowlīce adv. *faithfully* A33 (**getrywlice**), C119 (**getrywelice**), D85

trēowþ f. *covenant* F68 (**triowþ**)

trum adj. *firm, fixed* C174

tūn m. *village, town* C126, D83

tunge f.wk. *tongue* A76, E217 (2x)

tuwa adv. *twice* B86

twēgen/twā num. *two* A22, 81, B87, 102, C35, 89, D22 (ii), E6, 33, F35, 97, etc.

twelf num. *twelve* A52 (**xii**), C46, D17, 23 (**xii**)

twēntig num. *twenty* A22

twȳ m.wk. *doubt* C154 (**tweon**), D115 (**twyon**)

tyhtan v.wk.1 *to exhort, urge* C3

þā adv. *then, at that time* B27, 34, C12, E9, 27, F6, 29, etc.; conj. *when* E19, 195, F147, 164, 213; **þa** (. . .) **þa** *then . . . when* C19, 29, 33, E182, F137, 139, etc.

þā dem.pron./def.art.: see **sē**

geþafian v.wk.2 *to permit, suffer, endure* C101, 107, 125

þām/þǽm/þan: see **sē**

þanc m. *thanks* B140

geþanc n. *thought, mind* C162, 168, 170

þanon adv. *thence, from there* B10, 130 (**þanan**), C111

þāra/þǽra: see **sē**

þās: see **þēs**

geþæf adj. *agreeing, content* D118

þǽge pron. (m.n.pl.) *those* A46

þǽr adv. *there* A2, 68, B10, 12, C46, 56, D23, E3, 5, F3, 104 (**þar**), etc.; conj. *where* A6, 8, B62, E79, 89, 148, 207, 222, F123, 247; **þær þær** *there where* C14, 51

þǽre: see **sē**

þǽrinne adv. *therein* D71

þǽron adv. *therein, in* A21, B107

þǽrtoēacan adv. *in addition to that* D89

þæs adv. *accordingly, according as* C154, F7, F121; conj. **þæs þe** *after which* F8

þæs dem.pron./def.art.: see **sē**

þæt conj. *that* B12, 24, C2, 7, D9, 33, E1, 8, F11, 24, etc.; *(so) that, in order that* A9, 29, B53, 84, E36, 167, F35, 182, etc.; *because* F119; **swa þæt**: see **swa**

þæt dem.pron./def.art.: see **sē**

þe rel.particle *who, which, that* A1, 4, B2, 12, C21, 167, D14, E3, F19, 31, etc.

þē 2nd pers.pron.: see **þū**

þēah conj. *though* B18 (**þeh**), E213, F86

þēahhwæþere adv. *nevertheless* B70, C164, D40

þearf f. *need, benefit* B115, 131, C3, 8, 10, 130, D82 [gloss], E78, 87, 170, F231

þearfa adj. *destitute, needy* D36, E86, F154

þearle adv. *greatly* F78

(ge)þencan v.wk.1 *to think of, consider* B126, C106, 132, 161, E8, 208, F228 (**geþæncaþ**)

þēod f. *people, nation* C92, 106, D48, 49, 67, E6, F74 (**þiode**); *language* E214

geþēodan v.wk.1 *to apply oneself to* B17

þēodland n. *the continent, country* E7, F3

þēof m. *thief* C149

þēos: see **þēs**

þēote f.wk. *channel* E26, F27 (**þiotan**), 184 (**þeodan**)

þēow m. *servant, slave* D109; **þēowa** (m.wk.) A23

þēow adj. *servile, bond, not free* C115, D78

þēowian v.wk.2 *to serve* D9, 108 (2x)

þēowtlic adj. *servile* C7, 26

þēs adj./dem.pron. *this, etc.*; forms: **þēs** (nom.sg.m.); **þisses** (gen.sg.m.n.) – **þyses** (EF), F228 (**þisæs**); **þissum** (dat.sg.m.n./dat.pl.) – **þisum** (AE), **þysum** (BDEF), **þison** (AC), **þisan** (F), F101 (**þisam**); **þisne** (acc.sg.m.); **þēos** (nom.f.sg.) – F220 (**þios**); **þissere** (gen.dat.f.sg.); **þās** (acc. sg.f./nom.acc.pl.); **þis** (nom.acc.sg.n.); **þissa** (gen.pl.) – C130 (**þyssera**)

þillic (= þyslic), adj. *such* D7
þīn poss.adj. *your* C166
þing n. *thing, reason, cause, circumstance*
A11, 36, B23, C23, 29, D9, 14, E57, 125,
F100, 118, etc.
geþingian v.wk.2 *to intercede* C178
þingung f. *intercession* A51
þis/þisne/þissa/þissere/þisses/þissum: see
þēs
þolian v.wk.2 *to suffer, endure* A24, 37,
D115
þon/þone: see sē
þonne adv./conj. *then, when* B34, 64, C4,
31, D7, 67, E6, 181, F3, 60 (þanne), etc.;
conj. w.comp. *than* C150, 164, F31
þrēagan v.wk.2 *to chastise, correct* A30
þrēatian v.wk.2 *to threaten, urge, force*
E210 (ðreatigan)
þridda adj. *third* A82, B87, C165, 173, E63
geþring n. *press, tumult* E95
þrittig num. *thirty* C9 (xxx)
þriwa adv. *three times* E62 (þreowa)
(ge)þrōwian v.wk.2 *to suffer* B92, C47,
E176, 188, 200, F160, 161, 205
þrȳ/þrēo num. *three* A8, 29, B13, C9, 167,
169, 171, E32, 33, 123, F22, 23, 34 (2x),
74 (iii)
þrymsetl n. *throne, seat of majesty* A61,
D129
þrynnes f. *Trinity* B2, C16, D125, E45, 187,
F204 (þrinnesse)
þū 2nd pers.pron. *you, etc.*; forms: þū (nom.
sg.); þē (acc.dat.sg); gē (nom.pl.); ēower
(gen.pl.) – F58 (iowar): ēow (acc. dat.
pl.) – iow (F)
geþungen adj. *noble, distinguished* D9
þunor m. *thunder, thunderclap* C122, E54
þurh prep. (w. acc.) *through, by, by means
of* A3, 7, B3, 44, C156, 166, D5, 98, E45,
124, F6, 79, etc.
*þurhsmyrwan v.wk.1 *to anoint thoroughly*
B63
þurhtēon v.st.2 *to perform, carry out* D61
(þurhtihþ)
þurhwunian v.wk.2 *to remain, abide with*
A56
þurstig adj. *thirsty* D37
þus adv. *thus* A12, 48, B11, 131, D123, E87,
152, F20, 53, etc.
þūsend num. *thousand* A22, B102, C44,
111, D23, 71 (2x), E106, F80
þwēan v.st.6 *to wash* B81
þwȳr adj. *perverse, depraved, evil* D54
(þwyran), D67 (þweore)

þȳ adv. *therefore* D28 (þi), 110 (þi)
þȳ dem.pron./def.art.: see sē
geþyldig adj. *patient* F153

ufan adv. *from above* C12, 37
unālȳfed adj. *illicit, unlawful* D61
unālȳfedlic adj. *unlawful* B22
unālȳfedlīce adv. *unlawfully* E167, F114
(unalefedlice), F199 (unalefedlice)
unārīmedlic adj. *countless, innumerable*
D64
unasecgendlic adj. *indescribable, unspeak-
able* C122
unclǣne adj. *unclean, impure* C168
unclǣnnes f. *uncleanness, impurity* A71,
D29
uncūþ adj. *unknown, not understood*; comp.
C7
uncyst f. *vice* D111
under prep. (w. dat.) *under* E126, F227
underfōn v.st.7 *to accept, receive* A68, 84
(underfoo), 86, 87, 88, 89 (2x), B5, 36,
C30, 69
underneoþan prep. (w. dat.) *underneath*
F79 (undernioþan)
understandan v.st.6 *to understand* D95,
E75, 77
underþēodan *to be subject to, submit
(something to someone)* D109, 114
ungecyndelic adj. *unnatural* C126
ungehīwodlic adj. *unformed, without form*
D13
ungelēaffulnes f. *unbelief, incredulity*
E146, F118 (ungeleaffulnysse)
ungelīefed adj. *illicit, not allowed* C99
ungemetlic adj. *immense* D84
ungesǣlig adj. *accursed, unfortunate* C167
*ungeseht adj. *at odds, at variance* D39
ungesibsum adj. *quarrelsome* C71
unhlidian v.wk.2. *to uncover* E207, F227
unlybwyrhta m.wk. *poison-maker, sorcerer*
C151
unmanig adj. *not many, few* F5
(unmenigum)
(ge)unnan v.pret.pres. *to grant* C174, F19
unnytt adj. *useless, unnecessary* D75,
E191, F208 (unnet), 232
unnyttnes f. *that which is unprofitable* B17
unriht n. *wrong, wickedness* C18, 22, 100,
153, 156, E168; *on/to unriht wrongly,
wickedly* C138, E165
unriht adj. *wrong, unlawful* F197
unrihtdǣd f. *evil-doing* C7

unrihtdēma m.wk. *unjust judge* C151
unrihthǣmed n. *adultery, fornication* A58,
  B58, C61, D31
unrihthǣmere m. *fornicator, adulterer*
  C149
unrihtnes f. *wrong* F200
unrihtwīs adj. *unrighteous* C106
geunrōtsian v.wk.2 *to grieve* F25
unscyldig adj. *guiltless, innocent* D119
unsōþ adj. *untrue, false* E180
untīdweorc n. *work done at an improper*
  time E100, F138, 146
untīma m.wk. *misfortune* C121
*untimlic adj. *untimely* A63
*untīmnes f. *misfortune* E49
untrēowleast f. *? faithlessness* A65
  (untrywleaste) (see commentary)
untrum adj. *sick, weak* D35
untrumnes f. *disease, illness* C105, D65
unþēaw m. *evil practice* C133
unwær adj. *unwary, heedless* C161
  (unwara)
unwærnes f. *heedlessness, imprudence*
  C166
unwæstmbǣrnes f. *barrenness, unproduc-*
  tiveness D84
unwrigen adj. *open, unconcealed* F237
ūp adv. *up, away* C8, 36, 46, F146
ūplic adj. *celestial, sublime* C176
ūre poss.adj. *our* A7, 9, B1, 32, C174, 179,
  D2, 17, E57, 58, F111, 113, etc.
ūre 1st pers.pron.: see ic
ūs: see ic
ūt adv. *out* B19, D70
ūtan adv. *about*; ymb . . . utan *during* F195
ūtancumen adj. *foreign* C70, E83
ūtlah m. *outlaw* C100 (utlaga)
uton hortatory auxiliary *let us* C173, E56,
  82, 83, 85

wā interj. *Woe!* C184, D103, 104, E91, 95,
  F88, 246 (2x)
wacian v.wk.2 *to watch, stay awake* A56
wamb f. *stomach* D106
wānung f. *wailing, lamentation* B77, E94
warnian v.wk.2 *to take warning* E56
wascan v.st.6 *to wash* A78 (wahson), C98
  (waxe), D60 (wæsceð)
wæcce f.wk. *vigil, watch* A26, B14, 30, 51
wædl f. *want, poverty* E94
wædla adj. *poor, needy* D38, 91
wæfan v.wk.1 *to clothe* E84
wælcyrie f.wk. *witch, sorceress* C151
wæstm m. *produce, fruit, increase* C122,

123, 125, E155, F185
wæstmbǣrnes f. *fruitfulness* A54
wæter n. *water* B101, C36, 42, D21, E26,
  29, F28, 31, 58
wē: see ic
wēa m.wk. *misery, woe, grief* F52 (wæan),
  248 (wæana)
wēagesīþ m. *companions in woe* F243
geweald n. *power, control, keeping* C41,
  109, E189, F205
weallan v.st.7 *to rage, well up* E29 (weoll)
weax n. *wax* E62 (wexes)
wēdan v.wk.1 *to rage* B76 (2x), 118
wedd n. *pledge, promise* B85
weder n. *(fair) weather* C125
weg m. *way, road* D82, E185, F90 (wige)
wegan v.st.5 *to weigh* B41
wel adv. *well* B56, 64, 65, C95, D93, E184,
  F131
wela m.wk. *wealth, abundance* E49
welig adj. *rich, wealthy* D91 (welega), 102
welwillendlīce adv. *benevolently, kindly*
  C69
wēnan v.wk.1 *to believe, imagine* E23, 203,
  F223 (wæne)
wendan v.wk.1 *to turn* B75, C152, D104
wēofode n. *altar* B11, E195, 205, F214
  (wiofode), 225 (wefode), 227
weorc n. *work, deed, labour* B22, 28, C23
  (worcum), 65 (weorc), C145 (worc),
  D11, 33, E4, 38, F66 (wæorc), 71
  (weorce), etc.
weorpan v.st.3 *to cast out* F60 (weorþaþ
  for weorpaþ)
(ge)weorþan v.st.3 *to become, be* C53
  (wyrð), 86 (wurdan), 134, D76, 89, E8,
  96 (gewurde), 124, F37 (wurdan), 84
  (weorþ), etc.; *to befall, happen* F84, 144
  (geworden); *to make, create* B26; *to*
  agree B12 (gewearð)
wērig adj. *weary, tired* E167, F200
wērignes f. *weariness* B55
werod n. *host, multitude* E111, 127, F48
  (weorude), 80 (weorude), 109
wēsten nm. *desert, wilderness* B100, C38,
  F50
wicca m.wk. *sorcerer, wizard* C151
wīd adj. *wide, far* C53
gewīdmǣrsian v.wk.2 *to spread abroad,*
  publish D5
wīf n. *woman, wife* A69, B20, 102, D51,
  E32, 33, F22, 23, etc.
wīfung f. *sexual relations; (taking a wife,*
  marriage) E72 [marg.] (see commentary)

236

wiht fn. *creature, being* E31, F31, 35
wilde adj. *wild* D83
willa m.wk. *will, desire* A7, C161, E80, F233, 241
willan v.anom. *to desire, wish, want to; shall, will*; forms: **willan** (inf.); **wille** (pres.1/3 pers.sg.) – **wile** (CF); **wyle** (C); **willaþ** (pres.pl.); **wolde** (pret. 3sg.); **woldon** (pret.pl.) – **woldan** (EF); neg.: **nelle** (pres.1/3 pers.sg.) – **nele** (C); D114 (**næle**); **nellaþ** (pres.pl.) B85 (**nyllað**); F177 (**nillaþ**); **noldon** (pret.pl.) – **noldan** (F)
wilsumlīce adv. *willingly, voluntarily* D38
wīn n. *wine* B47, 101, C42, D21, F58
wīngeard m. *vinyard* D85
winter m. *winter, year* B99, C9, 38, D20, E20, F21
wīs adj. *wise* D82
wīsdōm m. *wisdom* C24
wīse f. *way, manner* C78
gewislīce adv. *for certain, truly* B50, C94, D57
gewiss n. *surety, certainty* C138
wist f. *abundance, plenty* D102
wit: see **ic**
wita m.wk. *wise man, leader* E196, F214
gewita m.wk. *witness* E197, F216
witan v.pret.pres. *to know*; **to witanne** (infl. inf.) F56; **wite** (imp./subj.sg.) C94, 138, D56; **witaþ** (imp.pl.) A62 (**witað**); **wāt** (pres.1/3sg.) C7, 140; **witon** (pres.pl.) F120 (**witan**); **witen** (pres.subj.pl.) F54 (**witan**), 201 (**witan**); neg.: **nāt** (pres.3sg.) C104; **nyton** (pres.pl.) C104; **nyte** (imp. pl.) A20, C139, D107
gewītan v.st.1 *to go, depart* B19, C48, D26 (2x), F175 (**gewit**)
wīte n. *punishment, torment, penalty* A37, B45, C77, E95, 97, 169, 218, F114, 202 (**wita**), 210
wītega m.wk. *prophet* A89 (3x), B138, D98, 99, 103, F20
wītnian v.wk.2 *to torment, afflict* A71, C77
wītnungstōw f. *place of torment* F100 (**witincgstowan**)
gewitt n. *understanding* A10
witudlīce adv. *truly, certainly* D14
wiþ prep. (w. acc.) *from, against* C100, D33, E150 (2x), F125 (2x), 233, 249 (2x); *in relation to, in the eyes of, before* C4, E42 (2x), F44, 45
wiþæftan prep. *behind* E89
wiþersaca m.wk. *enemy* C147

wiþerweard adj. *rebellious, perverse, hostile* C106, D67
wiþerwinna m.wk. *adversary, opponent* E125
wiþsacan v.st.6 *to deny, reject* D47, E18, F15, 175 (**wiþsacæ**)
wiþstandan v.st.6 (w. dat.) *to withstand* F147
wiþtēon v.st.2 *to refrain from* A76 (**wiðtuga**)
wō(h) *wrong, error* B83 (**wo**), C135 (**woge**, **woh**), D26 (**woh**)
wolcn n. *cloud, sky* E26, F27
word n. *word, statement* A79, B72, 85, C23, 130, D6, 53, E11, 22, F24, 26, etc.
woruld f. *world* A39, C75, 107, E10, 34, F7 (**weorulde**), 35 (**weoruld**), 97 (**weoruld**); **worulda woruld** *for ever* A55 (**worulda world**), D131, E224, F174 (**weorulde weoruld**); **æfre to worulde** *for ever* C117 (**worolde**), E98; **a to worulde** *for ever* C146
*****woruldgalnes** f. *worldly lust* F85 (**weoruldgalnesse**)
woruldgestrēon n. *worldly riches* B32
woruldlic adj. *worldly* D10, 29, 59
wrang n. *wrong* C152 (2x)
wræcca m.wk. *outcast, wretch, exile* C69 (**wreccan**), D38 (**wreccan**)
gewrit n. *writing, letter, message* A1, 6, B15, 65, C15, 20, D119, 130, E15, 37, F40, 228, etc.
(ge)wrītan v.st.1 *to write* A85, E15, 37, 141, 178, F127, 159
wuce f.wk. *week* E9, 143, F6, 116
wudian v.wk.2 *to cut wood* F109 (**wudede**), 112 (**wudade**)
wudu m.. *wood, forest* A40, C123, F108
wudubearu m. *grove* F136 (**wudebeorwas**)
wuduwe f.wk. *widow* B52 (**widewum**), C70, D38, E82
wuldor n. *glory* B35, 48, 50, 72, 141, F171, 250 (**wuldar**)
wuldorlic adj. *glorious* B93
wulf m. *wolf* B76
wundor n. *wonder, miracle* C29, D11, 99, E10, F7
wundorlic adj. *wondrous, glorious* D19, E34, F36 (**wundarlic**), 138 (**wunderlice**)
wunian v.wk.2 *to dwell, endure, exist* C9, 146, 177, D15, 67, E95, 209, F243
wurþian v.wk.2 *to honour, celebrate* A69 (**wurðiað**), E123, F76 (**weorþian**), 183 (**weorþian**)

wurþmynt m. *honour* F184 (**weorþmen-dum**), 250 (**weorþment**)

wurþung f. *honouring, celebration* E138 (**weorðunge**), F91 (**weorþunge**), 99 (**weorþunge**)

(ge)wyrcan v.wk.1 *to work, do, make, create* A20, 85, B22, 24, C30, D60 (**wyricð**), 103, E119, 142 (**worhte**), 165, F114 (**wer-ceþ**), 233 (**wercaþ**), 241 (**gewercan**) etc.

wyrgnes f. *cursing, a curse* D64 (**wirignysse**)

gewyrht fn. *deed* C55

gewyrhta m.wk. *fellow worker, accomplice* D61

wyrm m. *serpent, worm* B117, E93

wyrs adv. *worse* C11

wyrsa comp.adj. *worse* E98 (**wyrse**); superl. *worst* A46, C77 (**wyrstan**), D44

wyrt f. *plant, vegetable, produce* A17, B18, 122

wyrtūn m. *garden* A17

yfel adj. *evil* A53, 57, B22, 56, C131, 162, D3, 54, F3, 52, 158, 197, etc.

yfele adv. *evilly* C165

yfelnes f. *evil, wickedness* F59

ylca adj. *same* A6, 13, C37, 45, D53, E5, 6, 50

ylding f. *delay* D64

yldran: see **eald**

ymb/ymbe prep. (w. acc.) *about, concerning, around* B1, C160, F195; *after* E177

ymbegang m. *a going about, performance (of something)* D3 (**embegange**)

ymbrendæg m. *Ember-day* E72

ymbrenfæsten n. *Ember-fast* E68

yrfe n. *cattle* B20, E100 [*gloss*]

yrlic adj. *angry* E38 (**eorlicum**), F40 (**eorlicum**)

yrming m. *wretch* A20, 30, 63

yrmþ f. *misery, distress* C107, E94, 97, F248 (**ærmþo**)

yrnan v.st.3 *to run (a mill)* B21 (**eornenne**)

yrre n. *anger, wrath* A19, 49, B54, 58 (**eorre**), 84 (**eorre**), C78, E150, 182, F125, 134 (**erre**)

yrre adj. *angry* E172 (**eorre**)

ȳst f. *storm* D83

ȳtemest superl.adj. *last, uttermost* D41 (**yte-mysta**), 68 (**ytemestan**), F231 (**ytmestan**)

Names

Aaron *Aaron*, brother of Moses F75

Abiron *Abiram*, a biblical figure C90, D46, E122, F76

Achor *Achorius*, a priest A3, B4 (**Achorius**)

Adam *Adam* A21, B26, C41, E110, F47

Angelcynn *the English people, England* E5 (**Angelcyn**), F2 (**Angelcing**)

Antiochia *Antioch* (city) C13

Armenia *Armenia*, here a mountain B96 (see commentary)

Bethania *Bethany* (town) A4

Brytwealas (m.pl.) *the Britons of Wales* E5

Cappadocia *Cappadocia* B8

Cham *Ham*, son of Noah E33

Chana *Cana*, town in Galilee D21

Cherubim *the Cherubim*, an order of angels A49, E159, F191

Chore *Korah*, a biblical figure E122 (**Choreb**), F76 (**Choreb**) (see commentary)

Crīst *Christ* A7, 23, B100, 139, C8, 39, D8, 15, E37, 186, F6, 90, etc.

Dathan *Dathan*, a biblical figure C89, D46,

E122, F76 (**Dathon**)

Effrem *Ephrem* (town) A2, B4, 6 (**Ebream**)

Egypte (pl.) *Egyptians* B97, C34, F144

Florentius *Florentius*, a fictitious pope E194, F213

Garganus *Mt Garganus*, mountain in Italy where St Michael appeared A6

Gomorra *Gomorrah* (city) C85, D46

Hierusalem *Jerusalem* A2, 12, 81, B130, C108, D69, 72

Iacobus *St James the Apostle* E70

Iafeth *Japheth*, son of Noah E33

(St) Iohannes *St John the Baptist* B39, 62

Ioram *Ioram*, a priest A4 (**Ioram**), B5 (**Ieremiam**)

Iordan/Iordanis *Jordan* (river) B62, E131, F90

Israhela (gen.pl.) *of the Israelites* D19, E112, 117, 118, F49, 54, 67, 69, 74, 75

Iudei (pl.) *the Jews* D24

Lebonum *Lebonum*, a priest B7 (2x)

Machabeus *Machabeus*, a priest A5, B8 (**Machabium**), 9 (**Machabium**)

(St) Maria *(the Virgin) Mary* A51, B43, C40, 178, D126, E69

(St) Martinus *St Martin of Tours* E61

(St) Michael *Michael* (archangel) A6, 51, B3, 9, 44

Moyses *Moses* C33, 88, E111, 124, F48, 53, etc.

Nial *Niall*, an Irish deacon E13, 143, 181, F5, 10, 116

Ninivete (pl.) *the Ninevites* A29, B33

Noe *Noah* B96, E21, 24, 25, 32, 35, F20, 22, 23, 26, 34, 37

(St) Paulus *St Paul the Apostle* B44

(St) Petrus *St Peter the Apostle* A7, 52, B11, 13, C14, 50, E18, 148, F14 **(Petrys)**, 122, etc.

Petrus *Peter*, a bishop C13, D4, 121, 123, E194, F213

Philippus *Philip the Apostle* E70

Romane (pl.) *the Romans* D68

Rōme *Rome* A7, 81, B10, 130, C108, E195, F213

Scotland *Ireland* E9 **(Sceotlande)**

Scottas (m.pl.) *Scots* (of Ireland) E2 **(Sce-otta)**, F2 **(Scotta)**, 5 **(Scotta)**

Sem *Shem*, son of Noah E32

Seraphin *Seraphim* A49, E160, F191 **(særaphin)**

Sodoma *Sodom* (city) C85, D46

Talasius *Talasius*, a priest B6 **(Talasius, Tala)**

Titus *Titus*, a Roman emperor C110

Vespasian *Vespasian*, a Roman emperor C110

Bibliography

Algra, N. E., 'Grundzüge des friesischen Rechts im Mittelalter', in *Handbuch des Friesischen*, ed. H. H. Munske (Tübingen, 2001), pp. 555–70

Anlezark, D., *Water and Fire: The Myth of the Flood in Anglo-Saxon England* (Manchester, 2006)

Assmann, B., ed., *Angelsächsische Homilien und Heiligenleben* (Kassel, 1889)

Bacchiocchi, S., *From Sabbath to Sunday: A Historical Investigation of the Rise of Sunday Observance in Early Christianity* (Rome, 1977)

Baker, P. S., and M. Lapidge, ed., *Byrhtferth's Enchiridion*, EETS ss 15 (Oxford, 1995)

Barlow, C. W., ed., *Martini episcopi Bracarensis opera omnia* (New Haven, 1950)

Bately, J., ed., *The Old English Orosius*, EETS ss 6 (Oxford, 1980)

— 'Old English Prose before and during the Reign of Alfred', *Anglo-Saxon England* 17 (1988), 93–138

Baukham, R. J., 'Sabbath and Sunday in the Medieval Church in the West', in *From Sabbath to Lord's Day: A Biblical, Historical, and Theological Investigation*, ed. D. A. Carson (Grand Rapids, 1982), pp. 300–9

Belfour, A. O., ed., *Twelfth-Century Homilies in MS Bodley 343*, EETS os 137 (London, 1962)

Bethurum, D., ed., *The Homilies of Wulfstan* (Oxford, 1957)

Biblia sacra iuxta vulgatam versionem, ed. R. Weber, 3rd ed. (Stuttgart, 1975)

Binchy, D. A., ed., *Corpus iuris Hibernici ad fidem codicum manuscriptorum*, 6 vols. (Dublin, 1978)

Binterim, A.-J., *Pragmatische Geschichte der deutschen Concilien vom vierten Jahrhundert bis zum Concilium von Trient*, 7 vols. (Mainz, 1812)

Bischoff, B., 'Wendepunkte in der Geschichte der lateinischen Exegese im Frühmittelalter', in his *Mittelalterliche Studien* I (Stuttgart, 1966), pp. 205–73

Bishop, T. A. M., 'Notes on Cambridge Manuscripts; Part III: MSS Connected with Exeter', *Transactions of the Cambridge Bibliographical Society* 2 (1954–8), 192–9

Bittner, M., ed., *Der vom Himmel gefallene Brief Christi in seinen morgenländischen Versionen und Rezensionen*, Denkschriften der Kaiserlichen Akademie der Wissenschaften, Phil.-hist. Klasse 51 (Vienna, 1906), 1–240

Boretius, A., ed., *Capitularia regum Francorum I*, MGH, Capit. 2 (Hanover, 1883)

Borsje, J., 'The *Bruch* in the Irish Version of the Sunday Letter', *Ériu* 45 (1994), 83–98

Bosworth, J., and T. N. Toller, ed., *An Anglo-Saxon Dictionary* (Oxford, 1898; supplement, Oxford, 1921)

Breatnach, L., *A Companion to the Corpus iuris Hibernici*, Early Irish Law Series 5 (Dublin, 2005)

Brotanek, R., ed., *Texte und Untersuchungen zur altenglischen Literatur und Kirchengeschichte* (Halle, 1913)

Brunel, C., 'Versions espagnole, provençale et française de la lettre du Christ tombée du ciel', *Analecta Bollandiana* 68 (1950), 383–96

241

Brunner, K., *Altenglische Grammatik nach der angelsächsischen Grammatik von Eduard Sievers*, 3rd ed. (Tübingen, 1965)

Budny, M., *Insular, Anglo-Saxon, and Early Anglo-Norman Manuscript Art at Corpus Christi College, Cambridge: An Illustrated Catalogue*, 2 vols. (Kalamazoo, MI, 1997)

Campbell, A., 'An Old English Will', *Journal of English and Germanic Philology* 37 (1938), 133–52

— *Old English Grammar* (Oxford, 1959)

Cate, J. L., 'The English Mission of Eustace of Flay (1200–1201)', in *Études d'histoire dédiées à la mémoire de Henri Pirenne* (Brussels, 1937), pp. 67–89

Charles-Edwards, T., 'The Penitential of Theodore and the *Iudicia Theodori*', in *Archbishop Theodore: Commemorative Studies on his Life and Influence*, ed. M. Lapidge, Cambridge Studies in Anglo-Saxon England 11 (Cambridge, 1995), 141–74

Clayton, M., 'Delivering the Damned: a Motif in OE Homiletic Prose', *Medium ævum* 55 (1986), 92–102

— and H. Magennis, *The Old English Lives of St Margaret*, Cambridge Studies in Anglo-Saxon England 9 (Cambridge, 1994)

Clemoes, P. A. M., ed., *Ælfric's Catholic Homilies: The First Series*, EETS ss 17 (Oxford, 1997)

Cockayne, O., ed., *Leechdoms, Wordcunning and Starcraft of Early England*, Rolls Series, 3 vols. (London, 1864–6)

Colgrave, B., and R. A. B. Mynors, ed. and trans., *Bede's Ecclesiastical History of the English People* (Oxford, 1969)

Collins, R., *Visigothic Spain, 409–711* (Malden, MA, 2004)

Cross, J. E., '*De ordine creaturarum liber* in Old English Prose', *Anglia* 90 (1972), 132–40

— ed., *Cambridge Pembroke MS 25: A Carolingian Sermonary used by Anglo-Saxon Preachers* (London, 1987)

— and A. Hamer, ed., *Wulfstan's Canon Law Collection*, Anglo-Saxon Texts 1 (Cambridge, 1999)

— and T. D. Hill, ed., *The Prose Solomon and Saturn and Adrian and Ritheus* (Toronto, 1982)

Cubitt, C., *Anglo-Saxon Church Councils, c. 650–850* (London, 1995)

Delehaye, H., 'Note sur la légende de la lettre du Christ tombée du ciel', *Bulletin de l'Académie royale belgique, Classe des lettres* 1 (1899), 171–213

— Review of Carl Schmidt, 'Fragment einer Schrift des Märtyrer-Bischofs Petrus von Alexandrien', *Texte und Untersuchungen zur Geschichte der altchristlichen Literatur* 20.4b (1901), 1–50, in *Analecta Bollandiana* 20 (1901), 101–3

— 'Un exemplaire de la lettre Tombée du ciel', *Recherches de science religieuse* 18 (1928), 164–9

Deletant, D., 'The Sunday Legend', *Revue des études sud-est européenes* 15 (1977), 431–51

Dictionary of Medieval Latin from British Sources, ed. R. E. Latham, D. R. Howlett *et al.* (London, 1975–)

Dictionary of Old English: A to G on CD-ROM, ed. A. diP. Healey *et al.* (Toronto, 2008)

Dobbie, E. V. K., ed., *The Anglo-Saxon Minor Poems*, The Anglo-Saxon Poetic Records 6 (New York, 1942)

Bibliography

Drew, K. F., *The Law of the Salian Franks* (Philadelphia, 1991)

Dumaine, H., 'Dimanche', *Dictionnaire d'archéologie chrétienne et de liturgie*, ed. F. Cabrol and H. Leclercq, 15 vols. (Paris, 1907–53), IV, cols. 859–994

Fadda, A. M. L., ed., *Nuove omelie anglosassoni della rinascenza benedettina* (Florence, 1977)

Fehr, B., ed., *Die Hirtenbriefe Ælfrics in altenglischer und lateinischer Fassung*, Bibliothek der angelsächsischen Prosa 9 (1914; reprinted with a supplement to the introduction by P. A. M. Clemoes; Darmstadt, 1966)

Fischer, A.. *Engagement, Wedding, and Marriage in Old English* (Heidelberg, 1986)

Follett, W. F. *Céli Dé in Ireland: Monastic Writing and Identity in the Early Middle Ages* (Woodbridge, 2006)

Förster, M., 'Beiträge zur mittelalterlichen Volkskunde', *Archiv für das Studium der neueren Sprachen und Literaturen* 121 (1908), 31–46

— 'Die Weltzeitalter bei den Angelsachsen', in *Neusprachliche Studien. Festgabe Karl Luick zu seinem sechzigsten Geburtstage* (Marburg a.d. Lahn, 1925), pp. 183–203

— 'Zur Liturgik der angelsächsischen Kirche', *Anglia* 66 (1942), 1–51

— 'Vom Fortleben antiker Sammellunare im Englischen und in anderen Volkssprachen', *Anglia* 67–8 (1944), 1–171

Frantzen, A., 'The Tradition of Penitentials in Anglo-Saxon England', *Anglo-Saxon England* 11 (1982), 23–56

— *The Literature of Penance in Anglo-Saxon England* (New Brunswick, NJ, 1983)

Garmonsway, G. N., ed., *Ælfric's Colloquy*, 2nd ed. (London, 1947)

Geisel, C., *Die Juden im Frankenreich: Von den Merowingern bis zum Tode Ludwigs des Frommen* (Franfurt/Main, 1998)

Gneuss, H., *Hymnar und Hymnen im englischen Mittelalter*, Buchreihe der Anglia 12 (Tübingen, 1968)

— 'Origin and Provenance of Anglo-Saxon Manuscripts: The Case of Cotton Tiberius A.iii', in *Of the Making of Books: Medieval Manuscripts, their Scribes and Readers. Essays Presented to M. B. Parkes*, ed. P. R. Robinson, and R. Zim (Aldershot, 1997), 13–48

Godden, M. R., ed., *Ælfric's Catholic Homilies: The Second Series*, EETS ss 5 (Oxford, 1979)

— 'Anglo-Saxons on the Mind', *Learning and Literature in Anglo-Saxon England: Studies Presented to Peter Clemoes on the Occasion of his Sixty-Fifth Birthday*, ed. M. Lapidge and H. Gneuss (Cambridge, 1985), pp. 271–98

— *Ælfric's Catholic Homilies: Introduction, Commentary and Glossary*, EETS ss 18 (London, 2000)

Goldenberg, R., 'The Jewish Sabbath in the Roman World up to the Time of Constantine the Great', in *Aufstieg und Niedergang der römischen Welt: Geschichte und Kultur Roms im Spiegel der neueren Forschung*, ed. H. Temporini and W. Haase, ser. II, 19/1 (Berlin, 1972), pp. 414–47

Graus, F., *Volk, Herrscher und Heiliger im Reich der Merowinger, Studien zur Hagiographie der Merowingerzeit* (Prague, 1965)

Grégoire, R., *Les homéliaires du Moyen Âge, inventaire et analyse des manuscrits*, Rerum ecclesiasticarum documenta, Series maior: Fontes 6 (Rome, 1966)

Grosjean, P., 'A propos du manuscrit 49 de la Reine Christine', *Analecta Bollandiana* 54 (1936), 113–16

Gwynn, E. J., and W. J. Purton, ed., 'The Monastery of Tallaght', *Proceedings of the Royal Irish Academy*, 29C (Dublin, 1911), 115–80

Haddan, A. W., and W. Stubbs, ed., *Councils and Ecclesiastical Documents relating to Great Britain and Ireland*, 3 vols. (Oxford, 1869–78)

Hall, T. N., 'The Reversal of the Jordan in Vercelli Homily 16 and in Old English Literature', *Traditio* 45 (1989–90), 53–86

— 'The *Evangelium Nichodemi* and *Vindicta Salvatoris* in Anglo-Saxon England', in *Two Old English Apocrypha and their Manuscript Source: The Gospel of Nichodemus and The Avenging of the Saviour*, ed. J. E. Cross, Cambridge Studies in Anglo-England 19 (Cambridge, 1996), 36–81

— 'The Early Medieval Sermon', in *The Sermon*, ed. B. M. Kienzle (Turnhout, 2000), pp. 203–69

Harmening, D., *Superstitio: Überlieferungs- und theoriegeschichtliche Untersuchung zur kirchlich-theologischen Aberglaubensliteratur des Mittelalters* (Berlin, 1979)

Hartmann, W., *Die Synoden der Karolingerzeit im Frankenreich und in Italien* (Paderborn, 1989)

Healey, A. di P., *The Old English Vision of St. Paul* (Cambridge, MA, 1978)

Hen, Y., 'Introduction: The Bobbio Missal – from Mabillon onwards', in *The Bobbio Missal: Liturgy and Religious Culture in Merovingian Gaul*, ed. Y. Hen and R. Meens (Cambridge, 2004), pp. 1–18

Hennessy, W., ed. and trans., *Chronicum Scotorum. A Chronicle of Irish Affairs, from the Earliest Times to A.D. 1135, with a Supplement Containing the Events from 1141–1150* (London, 1866)

Herbst, L., ed., *Die altenglische Margaretenlegende in der Hs. Cotton Tiberius A.III* (Göttingen, 1975)

Herren, M., and S. A. Brown, *Christ in Celtic Christianity: Britian and Ireland from the Fifth to the Tenth Century* (Woodbridge, 2002)

Hill, J., 'Archbishop Wulfstan: Reformer?', in *Wulfstan, Archbishop of York: the Proceedings of the Second Alcuin Conference*, ed. M. Townend (Turnhout, 2004), pp. 309–24

Hoffmann-Krayer, E., and Hanns Bächtold-Stäubli, H., ed., *Handwörterbuch des deutschen Aberglaubens*, 10 vols. (Berlin, 1927–42)

Hogg, R. M., 'On the Impossibility of Old English Dialectology', in *Luick Revisited: Papers Read at the Luick Symposium at Schloß Lichtenstein*, ed. D. Kastovksy and G. Bauer (Tübingen, 1988), pp. 183–203

— *A Grammar of Old English* (Oxford, 1992)

Hough, C., 'Penitential Literature and Secular Law in Anglo-Saxon England', *Anglo-Saxon Studies in Archaeology and History* 11 (2000), 133–41

Huber, H., *Geist und Buchstabe der Sonntagsruhe* (Salzburg, 1958)

Hughes, K., 'Evidence for Contacts between the Churches of the Irish and English from the Synod of Whitby to the Viking Age', in *England before the Conquest: Studies in Primary Sources Presented to Dorothy Whitelock*, ed. P. Clemoes and K. Hughes (Cambridge, 1971), pp. 49–67

— *The Church in Early Irish Society* (London, 1966)

Hugo von Reutlingen, 'Chronicon', in *Die Lieder und Melodien der Geissler des Jahres 1349 nach der Aufzeichnung Hugo's von Reutlingen. Nebst einer Abhandlung über die italienischen Geisslerlieder von Heinrich Schneegans und einem Beitrage zur Geschichte der deutschen und niederländischen Geissler von Heino Pfannenschmid*, ed. P. Runge (Leipzig, 1900), 23–42

Hull, V., 'Cáin Domnaig', *Ériu* 20 (1966), 151–77

Hunt, D., 'Christianising the Roman Empire: The Evidence of the Code', in *The Theodosian Code: Studies in the Imperial Law of Late Antiquity*, ed. J. Harries and I. Wood (London, 1993), pp. 143–58

Irvine, S., ed., *Old English Homilies from MS Bodley 343*, EETS os 302 (Oxford, 1993)

Johnson, R., *St. Michael the Archangel in Medieval English Legend* (Woodbridge, 2005)

Jones, W. R., 'The Heavenly Letter in Medieval England', *Medievalia et humanistica* 6 (1975), 163–78

Jost, K., ed., *Die 'Institutes of Polity, Civil and Ecclestiastical'* (Bern, 1959)

— *Wulfstanstudien*, Schweizer anglistische Arbeiten 23 (Bern, 1950)

Jungmann, J. A., 'Die Heiligung des Sonntags im Frühchristentum und im Mittelalter', in *Der Tag des Herrn. Die Heiligung des Sonntags im Wandel der Zeit*, ed. H. Peichl (Vienna, 1958), pp. 59–75

Kalbhen, U., ed., *Kentische Glossen und kentischer Dialekt im Altenglischen* (Frankfurt am Main, 2003)

Kelle, J., ed. *Speculum ecclesiae* (Munich, 1858)

Kelly, F., *A Guide to Early Irish Law*, Early Irish Law Series 3 (Dublin, 1988)

Kennedy, A. G., 'Cnut's Law Code of 1018', *Anglo-Saxon England* 11 (1983), 17–81

Kenney, J. F., *The Sources for the Early History of Ireland: Ecclesiastical: An Introduction and Guide* (New York, 1966)

Ker, N. R., *Catalogue of Manuscripts Containing Anglo-Saxon* (Oxford, 1957)

— 'The Handwriting of Archbishop Wulfstan', in *England before the Conquest. Studies in Primary Sources Presented to Dorothy Whitelock*, ed. P. Clemoes and K. Hughes (Cambridge, 1971), pp. 315–31

Klaeber, F., 'Concerning the Functions of Old English "geweorðan" and the origin of German "gewähren lassen"', *Journal of English and Germanic Philology* 18 (1919), 250–71

Klingshirn, W. E., *Caesarius of Arles: The Making of a Christian Community in Late Antique Gaul* (Cambridge, 1994)

Kluge, F., 'Zur Geschichte der Zeichensprache, angelsächsische *Indicia monasterialia*', *Techmers internationale Zeitschrift für allgemeine Sprachwissenschaft* 2 (1885), 116–37

— *Nominale Stammbildungslehre der altgermanischen Dialekte*, 3rd ed. (Halle, 1926)

Kornexl, L., ed., *Die Regularis concordia und ihre altenglische Interlinearversion* (Munich, 1993)

Kottje, R., *Studien zum Einfluss des alten Testaments auf Recht und Liturgie des frühen Mittelalters (6.–8. Jahrhundert)*, Bonner historische Forschungen 23 (Bonn, 1970)

Krusch, B. ed., *Gregorii Turonensis miracula et opera minora*, MGH, Scriptores rerum Merovingicarum 1/2 (Hanover, 1969)

Lapidge, M., '"Precamur Patrem": An Easter Hymn by Columbanus?' in *Columbanus: Studies on the Latin Writings*, ed. M. Lapidge (Woodbridge, 1997), pp. 255–63

— and R. Sharpe, *A Bibliography of Celtic-Latin Literature, 400–1200* (Dublin, 1985)

Latham, R. E., and D. R. Howlett, *Dictionary of Medieval Latin from British Sources* (Oxford, 1975–)

Lees, C., 'The "Sunday Letter" and the "Sunday Lists"', *Anglo-Saxon England* 14 (1985), 129–51

Lees, C., 'Theme and Echo in an Anonymous Old English Homily for Easter', *Traditio* 42 (1986), 115–42

Lendinara, P., 'The Kentish Laws', in *The Anglo-Saxons from the Migration Period to the Eighth Century: An Ethnographic Perspective*, ed. J. Hines (Woodbridge, 1997), pp. 211–43

Liebermann, F., ed., *Die Gesetze der Angelsachsen*, 3 vols. (Halle, 1903–16)

Liuzza, R. M., ed., *The Old English Version of the Gospels*, 2 vols., EETS os 304, 314 (Oxford, 1994)

Logeman, H., ed., *The Rule of S. Benet: Latin and Anglo-Saxon Interlinear Version*, EETS os 90 (London, 1888)

— 'Anglo-Saxonica Minora', *Anglia* 11 (1889), 97–120

Luick, K., *Historische Grammatik der englischen Sprache* (Stuttgart, 1964)

Lutterbach, H., *Sexualität im Mittelalter: Eine Kulturstudie anhand von Bußbüchern des 6. bis 12. Jahrhunderts* (Cologne, 1999)

Lynch, J. H., *Christianizing Kinship: Ritual Sponsorship in Anglo-Saxon England* (Ithaca and London, 1998)

Maassen, F., ed., *Concilia aevi Merovingici*, MGH, Conc. 1 (Hanover, 1893)

Mac Airt, S., ed., *The Annals of Inisfallen: MS Rawlinson B. 503* (Dublin, 1951)

Maclean, D., *The Law of the Lord's Day in the Celtic Church* (Edinburgh, 1929)

Mansi, P., ed., *Sacrorum conciliorum nova, et amplissima collectio*, 31 vols. (Florence and Venice, 1759–98)

McNally, R. E., ed., *Scriptores Hiberniae minores, Pars 1*, CCSL 108B (Turnhout, 1973)

— '"In nomine dei summi": Seven Hiberno-Latin Sermons', *Traditio* 35 (1979), 121–43

McNamara, M., *The Apocrypha in the Irish Church* (Dublin, 1975)

McNeill, J. T., and H. M. Gamer, *Medieval Handbooks of Penance* (New York, 1990)

McReavy, L. L., 'The Sunday Repose from Labor', *Ephemerides theologicae Lovanienses* 12 (1935), 291–333

— '"Servile Work" I. The Evolution of the Present Sunday Law', *The Clergy Review* 9 (1935), 269–84

Meyer, K., 'Göttliche Bestrafung der Sonntagsübertretung', *Zeitschrift für celtische Philologie* 3 (1900), 228.

Meyer-Marthaler, E., 'Die Gesetze des Bischofs Remedius von Chur', *Zeitschrift für schweizerische Kirchengeschichte* 44 (1950), 81–110, 161–87

— ed., *Lex Romana curiensis*, Sammlung schweizerischer Rechtsquellen. 15: Die Rechtsquellen des Kantons Graubünden (Aarau, 1959)

— *Römisches Recht in Rätien im frühen und hohen Mittelalter*, Beihefte der schweizerischen Zeitschrift für Geschichte 13 (Zürich, 1968)

Migne, J.-P., ed., *Patrologia Latina*, 221 vols. (Paris, 1857–66)

— ed., *Dictionnaire des apocryphes, ou collection de tous les livres apocryphes relatifs à l'Ancien et au Nouveau Testament*, 2 vols. (Paris, 1856–8)

Mone, F. J., ed., *Quellen und Forschungen zur Geschichte der teutschen Literatur und Sprache* (Aachen, 1830)

Morin, G., 'A propos du travail du P. Delehaye sur la lettre du Christ tombée du ciel', *Revue bénédictine* 16 (1899), 217

— '*Sermo de dominincae observatione*: Une ancienne adaptation latine d'un sermon attribué a Eusèbe d'Alexandrie', *Revue bénédictine* 24 (1907), 530–4

— ed., *Sancti Caesarii Arelatensis sermones*, 2 vols., CCSL 103–4 (Turnhout, 1953)

Morris, R., ed., *The Blickling Homilies with a Translation and Index of Words together with the Blickling Glosses*, EETS os 58, 63, 73 (London, 1967)

Morris, R., ed., *Old English Homilies and Homiletic Treatises*, EETS os 29 (1867)

Napier, A., ed., *Wulfstan: Sammlung der ihm zugeschriebenen Homilien nebst Untersuchungen über ihre Echtheit* (Berlin, 1883)

— 'Altenglische Kleinigkeiten', *Anglia* 11 (1889), 1–10

— 'Contributions to Old English Literature: 1. An Old English Homily on the Observance of Sunday', in *An English Miscellany Presented to Dr. Furnivall*, ed. W. P. Ker and A. S. Napier (Oxford, 1901), pp. 357–62

Oakley, T. P. *English Penitential Discipline and Anglo-Saxon Law in their Joint Influence* (New York, 1923)

— 'The Cooperation of Mediaeval Penance and Secular Law', *Speculum* 7 (1932), 515–24

O'Donovan, J., ed. and trans., *Annals of the Kingdom of Ireland, by the Four Masters*, 7 vols. (Dublin, 1854)

O'Dwyer, P., *Céli Dé: Spiritual Reform in Ireland 750–900*, 2nd ed. (Dublin, 1981)

O'Keeffe, J. G., 'Cáin Domnaig', *Ériu* 2 (1905), 189–214

— 'Poem on the Observance of Sunday', *Ériu* 3 (1907), 143–7

O'Mara, V. M., *A Study and Edition of Selected Middle English Sermons*, Leeds Texts and Monographs, n.s. 13 (Leeds, 1994)

Otero, A. de Santos, 'Der apokryphe sogenannte Sonntagsbrief', *Studia patristica* 3 (Berlin, 1961), 290–6

Owst, G. R., 'The People's Sunday Amusements in the Preaching of Mediæval England', *Holborn Review*, n.s. 17 (1926), 32–45

Payer, P., 'Early Medieval Regulations concerning Marital Sexual Relations', *Journal of Medieval History* 6 (1980), 353–76

Pfannenschmid, H., 'Die Geißler des Jahres 1349 in Deutschland und den Niederlanden', in *Die Lieder und Melodien der Geissler des Jahres 1349 nach der Aufzeichnung Hugo's von Reutlingen. Nebst einer Abhandlung über die italienischen Geisslerlieder von Heinrich Schneegans und einem Beitrage zur Geschichte der deutschen und niederländischen Geissler von Heino Pfannenschmid*, ed. P. Runge (Leipzig, 1900), 87–218

Pontal, O., *Die Synoden im Merowingerreich* (Paderborn, 1986)

Pope, J. C., ed., *Homilies of Ælfric: A Supplementary Collection*, 2 vols., EETS os 259, 260 (London, 1967–8)

Powel, T., 'Ebostol y sul', *Y cymmrodor* 8 (1887), 162–72

Priebsch, R., *Diu vrône botschaft ze der Christenheit, Untersuchungen und Text*, Grazer Studien zur deutschen Philologie, ed. A. E. Schönbach and B. Seuffert (Graz, 1895)

— 'The Chief Sources of Some Anglo-Saxon Homilies', *Otia Merseiana* 1 (1899), 129–47

— 'John Audelay's Poem on the Observance of Sunday', in *An English Miscellany Presented to Dr. Furnivall in Honour of his Seventy-fifth Birthday* (Oxford, 1901), pp. 397–407

— 'Quelle und Abfassungszeit der Sonntags-Epistel in der irischen "Cain Domnaig"', *Modern Language Review* 2 (1906–7), 138–54

— *Letter from Heaven on the Observance of the Lord's Day* (Oxford, 1936)

Raith, J., *Die altenglische Version des Halitgar'schen Bussbuches* (Hamburg, 1933)

Renoir, E., 'Christ (lettre du) tombée du ciel', in *Dictionnaire d'archéologie chrétienne et de liturgie*, ed. F. Cabrol and H. Leclercq, 15 vols. (Paris, 1907–53), III, cols. 1534–46

Richards, M. P., 'The Manuscript Contexts of the Old English Laws: Tradition and Innovation', in *Studies in Earlier Old English Prose*, ed. P. E. Szarmach (Albany, 1986), 171–92

— *Texts and their Traditions in the Medieval Library of Rochester Cathedral Priory* (Philadelphia, 1988)

— 'Anglo-Saxonism in the Old English Laws', in *Anglo-Saxonism and the Construction of Social Identity*, ed. A. J. Frantzen and J. D. Niles (Gainesville, 1997), pp. 40–59

Rivière, E. M., 'La lettre du Christ tombée du ciel', *Revue des questions historiques* 79 (n.s. 35) (1906), 600–5

Robinson, F. C., 'The Devil's Account of the Next World: An Anecdote from Old English Homiletic Literature', in his *The Editing of Old English* (Oxford, 1994), pp. 196–205

Robinson, P. R., 'Self-Contained Units in Composite Manuscripts of the Anglo-Saxon Period', *Anglo-Saxon England* 7 (1978), 231–8

Röhricht R., 'Ein "Brief Christi"', *Zeitschrift für Kirchengeschichte* 11 (1890), 36–42 and 619

Rordorf, W., *Der Sonntag; Geschichte des Ruhe- und Gottesdiensttages im ältesten Christentum*, Abhandlungen zur Theologie des Alten und Neuen Testaments 43 (Zürich, 1962)

Russell, J. B., 'Saint Boniface and the Eccentrics', *Church History* 33 (1964), 235–47

Sauer, H., ed., *Theodulfi capitula in England. Die altenglischen Übersetzungen, zusammen mit dem lateinischen Text*, Münchener Universitäts-Schriften, Texte und Untersuchungen zur englischen Philologie 8 (Munich, 1978)

— 'Zwei spätaltenglische Beichtermahnungen aus Hs. Cotton Tiberius A. III', *Anglia* 98 (1980), 1–33

— 'Die 72 Völker und Sprachen der Welt: Ein mittelalterlicher Topos in der englischen Literatur', *Anglia* 101 (1983), 29–48

Sawyer, P., 'Early Fairs and Markets in England and Scandinavia', in *Anglo-Saxon History: Basic Readings*, ed. D. A. E. Pelteret (New York, 2000), pp. 323–42

Schabram, H., *Superbia: Studien zum altenglischen Wortschatz* (Munich, 1965)

Schaefer, K., ed., 'An Edition of Five Old English Homilies for Palm Sunday, Holy Saturday, and Easter Sunday' (Ph.D. diss., Columbia University, 1972)

Scheibelreiter, G., 'Sonntagsarbeit und Strafwunder: Beobachtungen zu hagiographischen Quellen der Merowingerzeit', in *Der Tag des Herrn: Kulturgeschichte des Sonntags*, ed. R. Weiler (Vienna, 1998), pp. 175–86

Schmidt, C., 'Fragmente einer Schrift des Märtyrer-Bischofs Petrus von Alexandrien', *Texte und Untersuchungen zur Geschichte der altchristlichen Literatur* 20, 4b (1901), 1–50

Schmitz, G., ed., *Die Kapitulariensammlung des Ansegis*, MGH, Capitula, n.s. 1 (Hanover, 1996)

Schott, C., 'Pactus, Lex und Recht', in *Die Alemannen in der Frühzeit*, ed. W. Hübener (Bühl/Baden, 1974), pp. 135–68

Schreckenberg, H., *Die Christlichen Adversus-Judaeos-Texte und ihr literarisches und historisches Umfeld (1–11. Jh.)*, 3rd ed. (Frankfurt/Main, 1995)

Scragg, D. G., 'The Corpus of Vernacular Homilies and Prose Saints' Lives before Ælfric', *Anglo-Saxon England* 8 (1979), 223–77

— ed., *The Vercelli Homilies and Related Texts*, EETS os 300 (Oxford, 1992)

— 'Cambridge, Corpus Christi College 162', in *Anglo-Saxon Manuscripts and their Heritage*, ed. P. Pulsiano and E. Treharne (Aldershot, 1998), pp. 71–83

Silverstein, T., *Visio sancti Pauli: The History of the Apocalypse in Latin together with Nine Texts* (London, 1935)

Sisam, C., and K. Sisam, ed., *The Salisbury Psalter*, EETS os 242 (London, 1959)

Skeat, W. W., ed., *Ælfric's Lives of Saints*, EETS os 76, 82, 94, 114 (London, 1881–1900)

Spindler, R., ed., *Das altenglische Bussbuch. Ein Beitrag zu den kirchlichen Gesetzen der Angelsachsen* (Leipzig, 1934)

Strauch, P., ed., 'Altdeutsche Predigten', *Zeitschrift für deutsche Philologie* 27 (1895), 148–209

Stubbs, W., ed., *Chronica magistri Rogeri de Houedene*, 4 vols., Rolls Series (London, 1868–71)

— ed., *The Memorials of St. Dunstan*, Rolls Series (London, 1874)

Stübe, R. *Der Himmelsbrief. Ein Beitrag zur allgemeinen Religionsgeschichte* (Tübingen, 1918)

Tangl, M., ed., *Die Briefe des heiligen Bonifatius und Lullus*, MGH, Epp. Sel. 1 (Berlin, 1916)

Tenhaken, H. P., ed., *Das nordhumbrische Priestergesetz: Ein nachwulfstanisches Pönitential des 11. Jahrhunderts* (Düsseldorf, 1979)

Theodosiani libri XVI cum constitutionibus Sirmondianis et leges novellae ad Theodosianum pertinentes, ed. T. Mommsen and P. M. Meyer, 2 vols., 2nd ed. (Berlin, 1954)

Thomas, W., *Der Sonntag im frühen Mittelalter. Mit Berücksichtigung der Entstehungsgeschichte des christlichen Dekalogs dargestellt.* Studia theologiae moralis et pastoralis 4 (Göttingen, 1929)

Tinti, F., 'The "Costs" of Pastoral Care: Church Dues in Late Anglo-Saxon England, in *Pastoral Care in Late Anglo-Saxon England*, ed. F. Tinti, Anglo-Saxon Studies 6 (Woodbridge, 2005), 27–51

Townend, M., *Language and History in Viking Age England: Linguistic Relations between Speakers of Old Norse and Old English*, Studies in the Early Middle Ages 6 (Turnhout, 2002)

Tristram, H., *Sex aetates mundi: Die Weltzeitalter bei den Angelsachsen und den Iren: Untersuchungen und Texte* (Heidelberg, 1985)

Tveitane, M., 'Irish Apocrypha in Norse Tradition? On the Sources of Some Medieval Homilies', *Arv: Tidskrift för nordisk folkminnesforskning* 22 (1966), 111–35.

Van Dam, R., *Leadership and Community in Late Antique Gaul* (Berkeley, 1985)

Van Esbroeck, M., 'La lettre sur le dimanche, descendue du ciel', *Analecta Bollandiana* 107 (1989), 267–84

Wenisch, F., *Spezifisch anglisches Wortgut in den nordhumbrischen Interlinearglossierungen des Lukasevangeliums*, Anglistische Forschungen 132 (Heidelberg, 1979)

Werminghoff, A., ed., *Concilia aevi Karolini*, MGH, Concilia 2 (Hanover, 1906–8)

Whitelock, D., 'Wulfstan and the So-Called Laws of Edward and Guthrum', *The English Historical Review* 221 (1941), 1–21

— *English Historical Documents I: c. 500–1042*, 2nd ed. (London, 1979)

— 'Bishop Ecgred, Pehtred and Niall', in *Ireland in Early Medieval Europe*, ed. D. Whitelock, R. McKitterick, and D. Dumville (Cambridge, 1982), pp. 47–68

—, M. Brett and C. N. L. Brooke, ed. and trans., *Councils and Synods with Other Documents relating to the English Church. I. A.D. 871–1207. Part I. 871–1066* (Oxford, 1981)

Wilcox, J., 'The Compilation of Old English Homilies in MSS Cambridge, Corpus Christi College, 419 and 421' (Ph.D. diss., Cambridge University, 1987)

— 'The Dissemination of Wulfstan's Homilies: The Wulfstan Tradition in Eleventh-Century Vernacular Preaching', in *England in the Eleventh Century: Proceedings of the 1990 Harlaxton Symposium*, ed. C. Hicks (Stamford, 1992), pp. 199–217

— *Wulfstan Texts and Other Homiletic Materials*, Anglo-Saxon Manuscripts in Microfiche Facsimile 8 (Tempe, 2000)

Willard, R., 'The Address of the Soul to the Body', *Publications of the Modern Language Association of America* 50 (1935), 957–83

— *Two Apocrypha in Old English Homilies* (Leipzig, 1935)

— 'The Blickling-Junius Tithing Homily and Caesarius of Arles', in *Philologica: The Malone Anniversary Studies*, ed. T. Kirby (Baltimore, 1949), pp. 65–78

Williams, I. F., 'The Significance of the Symbol ę in the Kentish Glosses', *Otia Merseiana* 4 (1904), 81–3

— 'A Grammatical Investigation of the Old Kentish Glosses', *Beiträge zur Anglistik* 19 (1905), 92–166

Wood, I., 'How Popular was Early Medieval Devotion?', *Essays in Medieval Studies* 14 (1997), online at http://www.illinoismedieval.org/EMS/index.html.

Wormald, P., 'Æthelred the Lawmaker', in *Ethelred the Unready: Papers from the Millenary Conference*, ed. D. Hill (Oxford, 1978), pp. 47–80

— 'Archbishop Wulfstan and the Holiness of Society', in *Legal Culture in the Early Medieval West. Law as Text, Image and Experience* (London and Rio Grande, 1999), pp. 225–51

— '"Inter cetera bona . . . genti suae": Law-making and Peace-keeping in the Earliest English Kingdoms', in *Legal Culture in the Early Medieval West. Law as Text, Image and Experience* (London and Rio Grande, 1999), pp. 179–99

— *The Making of English Law: King Alfred to the Twelfth Century. Volume I: Legislation and its Limits* (Oxford, 1999)

— 'Archbishop Wulfstan: Eleventh-Century State-Builder', in *Wulfstan, Archbishop of York: the Proceedings of the Second Alcuin Conference*, ed. M. Townend, Studies in the Early Middle Ages 10 (Turnhout, 2004), 9–27

Wright, C. D., 'The Irish "Enumerative Style" in Old English Homiletic Literature, Especially Vercelli Homily IX', *Cambridge Medieval Celtic Studies* 18 (1989), 27–74

— 'Catachesis Celtica', 'Dies Dominica', in *Sources of Anglo-Saxon Literary Culture: A Trial Version*, ed. F. M. Biggs, T. D. Hill and P. E. Szarmach, Medieval and Renaissance Texts and Studies 74 (Binghamton, NY, 1990), 93–4 and 117–18

— *The Irish Tradition in Old English Literature*, Cambridge Studies in Anglo-Saxon England 8 (Cambridge, 1993)

— and R. Wright, 'Additions to the Bobbio Missal: *De dies malus* and *Joca monachorum* (6r–8v)', in *The Bobbio Missal: Liturgy and Religious Culture in Merovingian Gaul*, ed. Y. Hen and R. Meens (Cambridge, 2004), pp. 79–139

Zeumer, K., ed., *Lex Visigothorum*, MGH, Leges nationum Germanicarum 1 (Hanover, 1902)

Index

Page references in bold type indicate texts of the Sunday Letter.